Gardening: Plains and Upper Midwest

Gardening: Plains and Upper Midwest

ROGER VICK

Fulcrum Publishing
Golden, Colorado

Originally published in Canada by
Western Producer Prairie Books
Saskatoon, Saskatchewan.

Book Design by Ann E. Green
Cover Illustration by Joyce Kitchell
Chief Interior Illustrations by John R. Maywood

Library of Congress Cataloging-in-Publication Data

Vick, Roger, 1934–
[Gardening on the prairies]
Gardening : plains and upper Midwest / Roger Vick : with introduction by Jan Riggenbach.
p. cm.
Originally published under title: Gardening on the prairies.
Includes bibliographical references and index.
ISBN 1-55591-068-8 (pbk.)
1. Gardening—Great Plains. 2. Gardening—Middle West. I. Title.
SB453.2.G74V53 1990
635'.0978—dc20 90–13812
CIP

Printed in the United States of America

10 9 8 7 6 5 4 3 2

Fulcrum Publishing
350 Indiana Street
Golden, Colorado 80401

To all home gardeners who have ever
contemplated a wilderness,
and envisioned a garden

CONTENTS

ACKNOWLEDGMENTS xiii

FOREWORD BY JAN RIGGENBACH xv

USDA PLANT HARDINESS ZONE MAP xviii

PREFACE xix

CHAPTER I: SOIL 1
- Back to Basics with Soil Texture 1
- Organic Matter Matters 2
- Will That Be Vinegar or Bicarbonate of Soda? 6
- Hold the Salt 7
- Soil by the Truckload 8
- Getting It All Together 8
- Take Your Time 9
- Tips for Improving Your Soil 9

CHAPTER II: FERTILIZERS 11
- Plant Nutrition 11
- The Big Three—Nitrogen, Phosphorus, and Potash 11
- Minor Elements 12
- Selecting Suitable Chemical Fertilizers 13
- Application Rates and Procedures 14
- Organic and Specialty Fertilizers 18

CHAPTER III: LANDSCAPING 21
- Professional Help 21
- The Plan 22
- Three Outdoor Areas 29
- Three Landscape Plans 32
- Construction and Planning 39

CHAPTER IV: LAWN BUILDING 41
- Preparing the Subgrade 41
- Making Your Bed 42
- Choosing the Best Seed for You 45

A Time to Sow 47
Sowing the Seed 47
Mulching, Yes or No? 48
After-care for the Newly Seeded Lawn 48
Sod for Instant Results 50
Upgrading an Existing Lawn 53
Lawn Maintenance 54

CHAPTER V: PLANT SELECTION AND PURCHASING 55
Plant Names 55
Hardiness 57
Availability 59
Quality 60

CHAPTER VI: TREES AND SHRUBS 61
Debits and Credits 61
Planting and Transplanting 62
Survivability 66
Difficult Sites 68
Deciduous Trees 69
Deciduous Shrubs 74
Hedges 85
Vines 88
Tender Roses 91

CHAPTER VII: CONIFERS 95
The Pros and Cons of Coniferous Trees 95
Planting and Transplanting 96
Care of Conifers 100
Selecting a Conifer 102

CHAPTER VIII: FRUIT 107
Strawberries 107
Raspberries 109
Bush Fruits 111
Fruit Trees 114

CHAPTER IX: BULBS AND PLANTS WITH FLESHY ROOTS 123
Spring Bulbs 123
Hardy Lilies 128
Tender Types 130

CHAPTER X: HERBACEOUS PERENNIALS 137
Preparations 137
Special Plant Groups 140
Growing Tips 143
Wintering 144
Selecting Suitable Perennials 144
Herbaceous Perennials for the Plains 145

CHAPTER XI: ANNUALS 161
Versatility 161
Difficult Sites 163
Transplanting or Seeding? 164
Plants for Special Needs 164
Selection 166
Annuals for the Plains 166

CHAPTER XII: MEADOW GARDENING 183
Plants Suited to the Meadow Garden 184
Meadow Making 185
Meadow Maintenance 185

CHAPTER XIII: VEGETABLES 187
"Putting In a Garden" 187
Making the Most of It 188
What to Grow 188
Form a General Strategy 191
Site Preparation 194
Seeds 195
Transplants 198
Tubers and Sets 203
Perennial Vegetables 204
Outdoor Plant Protection 205
Pests and Diseases 207
Thinning and General Maintenance 209
Pickin' and Packin' 210

CHAPTER XIV: THE HOME GREENHOUSE 213
Choosing a Site 213
Selecting a Plan 215
Solar Greenhouses 218
Construction 219
The Interior 224
Heating 225
Ventilation 226
Cooling and Humidity 227
Water 228
Shading and Lighting 228

CHAPTER XV: WEEDS 231
Keeping the Weeds at Bay 231
Herbicides 234
Be Philosophical—Hoe in Hand 239

CHAPTER XVI: INSECT PESTS 241
The Case for Integrated Pest Management 241
Cultural Controls 242
Chemicals 243
Some Pest *Curricula Vitae* 246
A Final Word 268

CHAPTER XVII: PLANT DISEASES 273
What Is a Plant Disease? 273
Disease Control 274
Diagnosing Diseases 276
Selected Disease Problems in Garden Plants 278

CHAPTER XVIII: TOOLS 291
Spades and Forks 291
Hoes and Hoeing 292
Rakes 292
Cutting Tools 294
Mowers 296
Irrigation Sprinklers 298
Miscellaneous Garden Equipment 299
One Last Word on Tools 304

CHAPTER XIX: MONTH-BY-MONTH 305
- January 305
- February 306
- March 307
- April 308
- May 310
- June 312
- July 313
- August 314
- September 315
- October 317
- November 318
- December 318

GLOSSARY 321

BIBLIOGRAPHY 337

SOURCES 341

INDEX 343

ABOUT THE AUTHOR 363

ACKNOWLEDGMENTS

Many people have consciously or unconsciously contributed to this book. My thanks to numerous horticultural colleagues across the prairie provinces and, in particular, to the staff at the University of Alberta Devonian Botanic Garden, who have often fielded an assortment of my horticultural concepts and biases. I also wish to thank the horticultural staff at Olds College for checking the glossary and suggesting additions; my editor for asking a thousand perspicacious questions and for mending an equal number of split infinitives; the artists John R. Maywood and Uwe Jablonowski, who worked under difficult time constraints; and especially Lydia for her patience as the book germinated, grew, was pruned, and grew again.

FOREWORD

by Jan Riggenbach

Above all, gardening should be fun. But, in order for the undertaking to be fun, it must also be successful.

When Roger Vick moved from his native England to the northern prairie, he encountered some unfamiliar challenges—namely, drought, bitter cold, alkaline soil, drying wind, and blistering heat.

Like Vick, every home gardener who lives in the prairie states has a first-hand acquaintance with these threats to the plants in our yards. Some of us learn to master the challenges of our frequently inhospitable climate by trial and error. Other would-be gardeners drop out along the way, frustrated by failures.

Most how-to garden books—written where soils are acid, temperature fluctuations less brutal, and winds more moderate—aren't much help for dealing with our rugged climate, where temperatures soar from well below zero in January to more than 100 degrees in July.

Now, at last, we have a survival manual for our plants and those of us who tend them here on the prairie, written by an expert prairie gardener. Vick began at once to develop his survival secrets when he was "transplanted" from the mild climate of England to the rigorous conditions on the northern prairie. In *Gardening: Plains and Upper Midwest*, he shares both the know-how and the inspiration to make tending your own prairie garden more successful and fun.

Written with down-to-earth instructions unencumbered by a lot of horticultural gobbledygook, Vick intends this volume to be a guide for the average home gardener. Here's help choosing those hardy plants that are most likely to succeed in your yard. After all, if you live in a place where winter lasts six months, it doesn't make sense to grow plants that must be covered all winter long in order to live. Instead, choose from Vick's list of plants that will add color and interest to your landscape in winter, as well as in summer.

Look also to *Gardening: Plains and Upper Midwest* for help with problem soils, such as those with a high concentration of soluble salts, and for suggestions to control the insects and diseases most frequently encountered on the prairie, such as tent caterpillars and leaf spots. Vick even offers a sensible explanation to make botanical names easier to swallow.

Gardening: Plains and Upper Midwest will serve as a resource book for beginners and experienced gardeners alike: the easy-to-use format includes answers to all the most common landscape and garden questions. You don't have to read the book from cover to cover to learn the secrets of Vick's gardening success.

However, once you discover the sense of humor which Vick weaves throughout the text, you'll want to read every word for pure enjoyment. For example:

> "If the compost is too wet, the aroma will be such that passers-by might stop and check the soles of their shoes."
>
> "Avoid the common error of pushing as well as pulling the rake, as this method can result in a surface wavy enough to frighten a good-sized rowboat."
>
> "Stake the dahlias at planting time since stakes driven in later can hurt more than their feelings."

Where else can a prairie gardener turn for help dealing with the warm chinook winds that blow in from the Rockies and take winter temperatures on a roller coaster ride? Who else cautions newcomers to the prairie to forego the usual liming of the soil, since prairie soils are normally quite alkaline, often already too much so for many plants?

Best of all, though, is the inspiration that Gardening on the Plains provides. You don't need any special qualifications to garden successfully on the prairie. Remember, Vick advises, it isn't the color of the thumb that makes a happy gardener, but rather the quality of the soil under the thumbnail. And that quality can be easily changed with Vick's step-by-step directions, producing not only a fertile soil but also a happy gardening experience.

People garden for a lot of reasons: a pretty landscape, fresh vegetables, beautiful flowers. But beneath all those reasons lies a profound enjoyment. A young friend once found Bertrand Russell, the British philosopher, in a state of profound contemplation. The young man asked Russell why he was so meditative.

Bertrand's answer: "Because I've just made an odd discovery. Every time I talk to a sage, I feel quite sure that happiness is no longer a possibility. Yet when I talk with a gardener, I'm convinced of the opposite."

Most of us gardeners don't need a philosopher to tell us that gardening often leads to happiness. And nobody knows better than Roger Vick that satisfaction in the garden goes hand in hand with the success the gardener experiences there. *Gardening: Plains and Upper Midwest* will lead you to a larger measure of both success and satisfaction.

USDA PLANT HARDINESS ZONE MAP

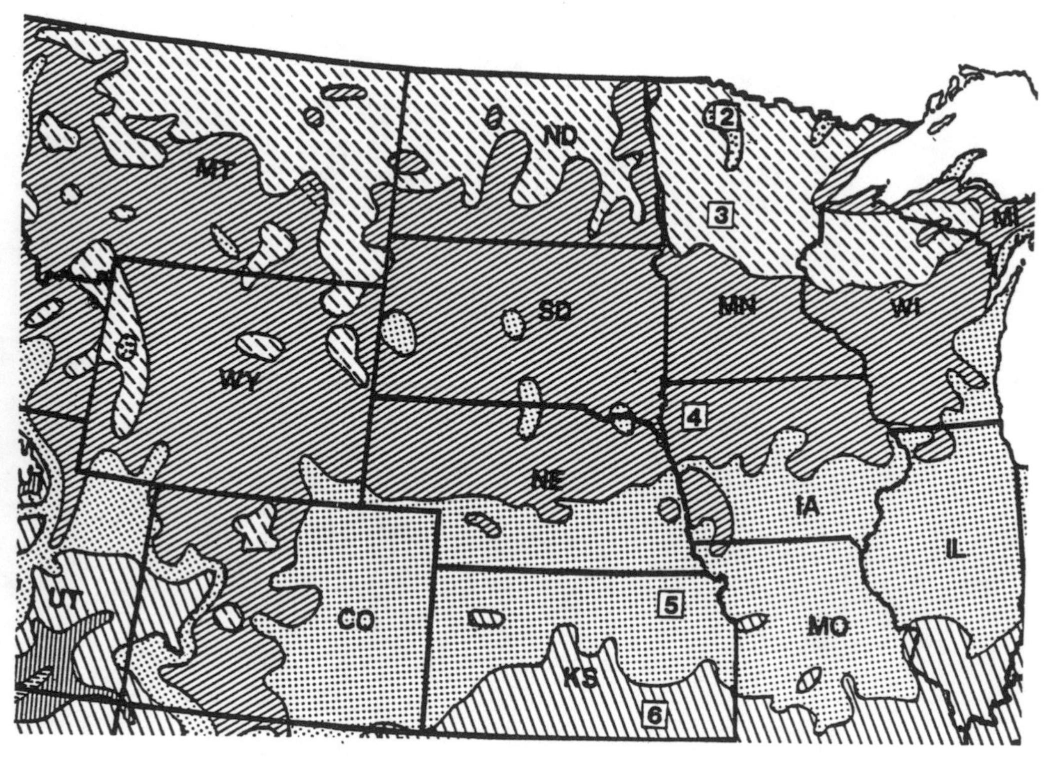

RANGE OF AVERAGE ANNUAL MINIMUM TEMPERATURES FOR EACH ZONE

ZONE 1	BELOW -50°F
ZONE 2	-50° TO -40°
ZONE 3	-40° TO -30°
ZONE 4	-30° TO -20°
ZONE 5	-20° TO -10°
ZONE 6	-10° TO 0°

PREFACE

One of my early childhood memories involves a rather disappointing attempt that I made to transplant a healthy weed into a plant pot because there were no house plants available at the time. My Uncle Jack's expression of utter disbelief was matched only by his emphatic directive to get rid of that "thundering thistle." It was disposed of in return for a tabletop-sized patch of spare land, and, with a few pennies spent on seed, I was able to raise more respectable plants like lettuces, radishes, and marigolds, all mixed with candytuft for good measure.

There are people, I believe, who have never experienced this innate urge to nurture weeds in plant pots. People like you, perhaps, who find themselves with a chunk of land quite incidental to the main acquisition of a home, but land that still demands some kind of attention to complement the building and to maintain property value.

For some time there has been a need for concise and up-to-date gardening information consolidated into one handbook for the average home gardener living in the high plains states. This book is intended to fill that need by cutting through much of the fine detail used by the professional and the dedicated amateur gardener and presenting some clear direction to everyone else.

If you are new to gardening on the plains, you will find here a combination of traditional and current gardening methods and listings of plants that will improve your chances of success no matter how much of a novice you may be.

If you have already tried gardening in this region and have not been entirely satisfied with the results, I encourage you to take a fresh look. You may have been trying to heed advice intended for climates milder than our own or to follow books written with the novice gardener in mind. This guide recognizes a difficult gardening environment, with winter temperatures that may fall to minus forty degrees Fahrenheit, and summer temperatures hot enough to sizzle your zucchini. Add the problems of low annual rainfall and drying winds that tend to desiccate young plants before they become properly established, and you have typical high plains gardening conditions. Quite a challenge indeed. But, by following the guidelines and recommendations gathered here, much can be accomplished.

Satisfaction and ease of maintenance often go hand in hand in the garden, and to these ends I have listed some plants and procedures that have proven most satisfactory in our region. There are other plants and other methods, but by applying the principles outlined here you will acquire a sound foundation for more ambitious plains gardening, should that ever be your desire. There are always specialized texts that deal at length with any one of the topics included here, and they are available to those readers who wish to delve deeper. A brief list of further reading material and addresses of sources of horticultural information for the area in which you live may be found at the back of this book.

I have omitted a number of common "solutions" to problems because I consider them to be of doubtful value. Most gardening principles in use today are based on sound observation and experience, but we should never become so complacent that we can't dispute these methods. The value of earthworms in the garden, the usefulness of staking newly planted trees, the advantages of spraying conifers with antitranspirants, and the use of traditional seed rows in the vegetable garden have all been called into question in recent years. Just listen to gardeners of any horticultural show—finding differences of opinion on almost anything, you will notice, except the general satisfaction that gardening brings. As time goes on, I hope that you too will discover, if you have not already done so, that home gardening on the high plains can be fun.

CHAPTER I

Soil

There's no doubt that soil is the basis of your garden success, and the quickest way to a satisfying garden is through soil maintenance and improvement. Remember, it isn't the color of the thumb that makes a happy gardener, but rather the quality of the soil under the thumbnail. Few home owners admit to having good soil to work with, and it's a sad fact that in many residential areas any good topsoil was stripped and sold before construction of the building; however, poor soil should be no excuse for a poor garden if you have the means to improve it.

Soil conditions vary considerably from place to place; even within one state there may be a number of soil variations caused by past geological and ecological conditions and our subsequent modification of the soil since it was first broken. The advice offered in this chapter should be used in conjunction with recommendations from your local cooperative extension agent.

Because there is little point in thinking about improving or maintaining your soil unless you know what you already have, let's first consider soil texture.

BACK TO BASICS WITH SOIL TEXTURE

Ideal soil consists of about 65 percent mineral particles, about 25 percent air and water, and the remaining 10 percent humus. The composition of your soil is important because plants need a steady supply of moisture to do well. Sufficient moisture on its own is not enough, for once the root system has moisture for its needs, it must also be able to "breathe" in order to make use of this moisture. An example may serve to demonstrate this point.

Someone who wants to make sure that his newly planted crabapple is off to a good start may water the poor thing morning and night for weeks. In this constantly wet soil there is no space for air, and the leaves remain small and start to turn yellow. Now the concerned gardener sees that the tree looks unhealthy, and his first urge is to rush out and give it another drink.

If you can think of soil as containing both water and air at the root level, then you are not likely to fall into this common trap. The composition of your garden soil should allow retention of sufficient moisture for the plants' needs while allowing the excess water to drain away to leave a moist (not saturated) soil.

The mineral particles are normally classified into three soil types: sand, silt, and clay. Any particles larger than 1/8 inch in diameter are considered gravel or stones and not a component of true soil. Clay is composed of minute irregular particles and is sticky and very plastic when moist. (A plastic soil is one that, when moist, can be molded and worked like modelling clay.) Sand by itself is easily recognized. It is gritty, loose, and nonplastic. Silt is the term used for material of a particle size between sand and clay, feeling like flour to the touch when dry, smooth and slippery when moist, only slightly plastic and never actually sticky. Because soils consist of varying percentages of sand, silt, and clay, about a dozen different soil textures are recognized. Loam, a generally desirable soil, consists of about 40 percent sand, 20 percent clay and 40 percent silt.

If your soil is too sandy, it will not retain moisture. Even if well watered, the garden will soon start to react like a desert. Although certain plants are well adapted to survive desiccation, many of these are tough weeds, and those desirable plants that can survive the conditions often flourish only briefly when moisture becomes available. A heavy clay soil is equally undesirable. The fine particles leave little room for air; the soil quickly gets waterlogged, and the plants "suffocate." The ideal soil allows water and roots to penetrate with ease and holds air as well as moisture. Soil of good tilth is not only easy for plants to live in, but also easy for you to work with. If your soil texture is not a loam but falls into the extremely heavy clay or very sandy-textured soils, don't despair; there are solutions.

If your soil is waterlogged because it is a low area with a high water table or because a hardpan of impervious clay lies beneath the topsoil, there are two elementary courses of action to take. One is to raise the level of the land to improve the overall drainage of the site, and the other is to work in lots of coarse sand to make the soil more permeable by water. Coarse or "sharp" sand, with grains measuring from 1/48 to 1/16 inch, is quite suitable for amending soils. Avoid using very fine sand; it may work into existing clay to form soil approaching the texture of concrete. Sandy soil that loses moisture quickly will benefit from the addition of a good clay topsoil. Whatever kind of soil you have—sandy, heavy clay, or loam—it will be improved by that magic ingredient—humus.

ORGANIC MATTER MATTERS

Humus is the almost completely decomposed organic matter of plant and animal residues such as peat, straw, leaves, wood shavings, bark chips, lawn clippings, and manure. When humus isn't absolutely essential to plant

growth, it is highly advantageous because of the minerals it releases during decomposition. Also, there is nothing like it for improving the tilth of the soil. A hard-to-work clay soil will develop a more crumblike structure and can be easily worked, while open sandy soils are improved by the moisture-holding capacity of humus. It furthermore accommodates the important micro-organisms that benefit plant life. I could rave on, but enough to say that humus tops the gardening charts as the most popular additive to soil. There are three main sources of humus available to the home gardener: manure, peat moss, and compost. Nowadays, unless you own livestock or live near a riding stable or feedlot, you may not be able to obtain manure at a reasonable price. The owners of the manure may be only too willing to get rid of it, but the cost of hauling it any distance may be prohibitive. Another problem in the urban community is the incongruous farm aroma that comes with manure. So, if you are fortunate enough to get some in the city, I advise you to turn it under as soon as possible to avoid the withering stares of annoyed neighbors.

If you don't have the delightful problem of manure in your garden, don't despair; you can always obtain bales of clean, wholesome peat moss to build up the organic content of your soil. Processes peat moss has been dried, pulverized, and baled tightly in plastic for the general market. You might be able to find a local supplier who will deliver the product loose by the truckload, but in comparison to the densely packed bales it will seem as if you are accepting delivery of a truckload of feathers. Unless your garden is very large, you will probably find it just as cheap to shop around for bales and arrange your own transportation. Peat moss is very absorbent and has a water-holding capacity of from 100 to 300 percent of its own dry weight.

If it bothers you to buy peat moss and at the same time throw away large quantities of lawn clippings and garden vegetable waste, you might want to consider working a compost heap. Note that the operative word is "working." If you simply save your grass mowings (together with vegetable waste from the kitchen and garden) and pile them all together at the end of the garden, you may be disappointed with the results. There's a little more involved than just throwing the ingredients together. Such a pile usually smells bad for a while as it ferments and subsides, and then just sits around without much evidence of further decomposition.

The secret of working a compost heap is to aim for a rapid breakdown of materials by providing optimum levels of moisture and air. A heap that is either too wet or too dry, or starved for air, is going to take more than one of our prairie seasons to break down to a suitable condition for use.

This being the case, you may be tempted just to dig the fresh green garden waste into the soil without allowing it to first break down into humus. It sounds reasonable, but the results are not nearly as satisfactory from the standpoint of soil improvement. So two things should be considered. First we need to recognize material suitable for composting. Then we need to get it in the right mood to perform.

Good composting candidates include vegetable kitchen wastes, leaves from deciduous trees, and all the discarded greens from the vegetable garden like cabbage leaves, bolted lettuce, and unused Swiss chard. Grass clippings are great, and weed tops are acceptable unless they have gone to flower or seed. If there is the slightest evidence of disease on beans, potatoes, or other garden vegetables, you should pack them away to the garbage rather than risk overwintering a problem and spreading it around. You should also avoid any kind of animal wastes or meat scraps as these will draw flies and other disease bearing insects to the compost heap, bringing on the possibility of diseases, not to mention a vile odor.

Various methods are used to create good compost. An old system calls for layers of soil alternating with the layers of organic material—a system that works quite well if the layers are thin, but which makes for hard work in construction and in turning the pile. An alternative method (one that I

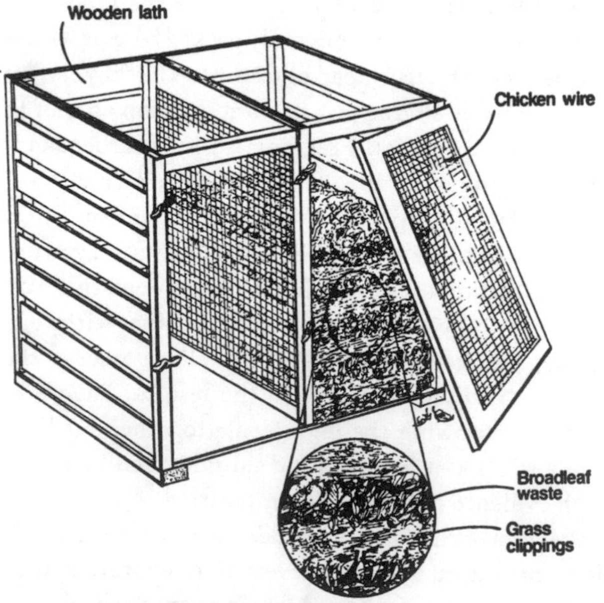

Home-made compost bin. Regular forking of the material from one side of the bin to the other ensures breakdown of garden waste into usable compost.

prefer) involves routine attention once or twice a week, but no great expenditure of patience or energy.

Instead of piling alternate layers of greenstuff and soil, use thin layers of grass mowings, alternating with other plant waste. No commercial compost starter is needed, but you should add a light sprinkling of nitrogen fertilizer to alternate layers to replace the nitrogen used by bacteria in the process of decomposition.

The frame to hold the compost is easily assembled. I made mine from spare two-by-fours and scrap one-inch slats. The dimensions are approximately 3 x 5 x 3 feet high. It is of open lath construction, and open at the front. A lath divider down the center separates the frame into two bins, both accessible from the front. The resulting shape from above looks something like a capital E that has fallen on its face. A front panel made of chicken wire with a wooden frame is held in place with four wing nuts.

The idea is to fill one side bin only. Then once or twice a week move the front panel to the vacant side and fork the compost over to the vacant bin to provide aeration and mixing. You might well find that this regular forking of good earthy stuff (mildly reminiscent of a barnyard chore) satisfies a subconscious yearning for a more rustic era.

Just a few composing tips while we're on the subject. First, don't use your lawn mowings following a treatment with Weed 'n Feed or other herbicides; chemical residues hang around longer than you'd think and adversely affect your garden plants. Second, if you first chop the large leaves of garden waste this way and that with a really sharp square-mouth spade, they will break down more quickly. If material like cabbage stalks do not chop easily, then they are too tough for the pile and should be donated to the trash pickup, together with your contaminated lawn mowings. Make sure that the dry outside parts get a turn in the middle.

Lastly, apart from the regular shifting from one spot to another, the main art of the job is to keep the pile moist without getting it wet. Most recommendations are for sprinkling with water as the layers are built up. This is all right with very dry material such as autumn leaves and dead grass, but most garden wastes are moist enough, and during a wet summer (a rare circumstance in our climate) it even helps to keep a board over the top to prevent the pile from getting too soggy. If it's too dry, compost will not ferment and decompose; if too wet, the aroma will be such that passers-by might stop and check the soles of their shoes. When the pile is sweet enough that you could make your bed in it, you will know that it is ready for use.

It is obvious that organic matter is of great benefit in nearly all situations. Improving the water-retention capacity of your soil by adding humus to the point where it constitutes about 5 or 10 percent of the soil bulk is of prime importance. Work that decomposing organic matter well into the soil, and the battle is more than half won.

WILL THAT BE VINEGAR OR BICARBONATE OF SODA?

Once you have dealt with the general composition of your soil, you can turn your attention to finer points of detail. For instance, the soil may be acid or too alkaline. While I don't advocate adding vinegar or bicarbonate to rectify the condition, there are equivalents that do help bring soil to a neutral pH. You will come across the pH frequently in gardening literature in reference to the acid-alkaline balance of the soil. It is simply a scale from 0 to 14 with 7 indicating a neutral condition; the higher the number, the more alkaline the soil. Few plants enjoy or even tolerate levels of acidity or alkalinity outside the optimum range (for garden soil) of 6.5 to 6.8. Levels of pH much above or below this range will chemically "lock up" certain chemical nutrients that are essential to plant growth.

Newcomers often assume that garden lime should be added to our soils as a matter of course. They often come from places where the substrata and heavier precipitation result in an acid soil; but plains soils are normally quite alkaline enough, and frequently too alkaline, for many plants. Despite this fact, some plains gardeners have been tempted to add lime as it has the incidental benefit of improving the texture of soil by forming slightly larger particles from the very small clay ones; and limed soil discourages certain soil grubs and larvae. Tempting though it is to improve soil structure chemically and at the same time annoy the grubs nibbling at the cabbage roots, I advise against adding lime unless a pH test indicates that it is needed to bring your soil to a more neutral condition.

Your cooperative extension agent will test the pH of your soil for a fee. Bear in mind, though, that if you have more than one test conducted, the test results may differ depending on the testing methods used, and the particular sample submitted—your soil sample is probably less than one one-millionth of the total topsoil in your garden. Alternatively, you can obtain an inexpensive soil reaction tester such as the LaMotte Soil Testing Kit or the one put out by Sudbury Laboratories in Massachusetts. This quick test is achieved with the addition of a few drops of reaction solution that turns color according to the acidity or alkalinity of the soil. By matching the color obtained against a lime-test color chart you can tell, to a close enough degree, if your soil is within the acceptable range. There are also a number of pocket

pH meters that give an instant reading on a dial when the electrobe is inserted into the soil. It seems, however, that they often fail to work properly after a short period of use, and I suggest you leave them on the shelf.

If the tests indicate that lime is needed, it should be applied very sparingly—just enough to dust the soil surface white—and then worked into the soil. Test again after three or four weeks and apply more lime if necessary.

Acidifying the soil is something of a problem. The alkalinity often comes from a virtually unlimited source in the substrata beneath. To add enough sulphur to neutralize this alkalinity, 5 to 10 pounds per 100 square feet, would be expensive. Results of sulphur treatment are very gradual and often of short-lived effectiveness. The best ways to improve alkaline soil are to add humus (which adds acidity to the soil as it decomposes) and to use fertilizers with an acid base.

HOLD THE SALT

A condition of soil salinity is a problem in some prairie soils and is usually due to poor subsoil drainage and high evaporation.

If your soil has a moderately high concentration of soluble salts, your plants may be affected without showing obvious symptoms. The plants do not grow as fast as they normally would, but this isn't likely to be noticed without comparative plants. If soluble salt levels (commonly but mistakenly called "alkali") become quite high, then plants appear to suffer from drying, even when the soil is well watered. The lower leaves wilt first, followed by marginal drying of leaves progressively up the plant. The reason for this situation of "water, water everywhere, and not a drop to drink" is the movement of the fluid in the roots out to the higher chemical concentrations of salts in the soil. In such a situation high fertilizer concentrations only add to the problem. As a general rule, it is always better to avoid heavy applications of inorganic fertilizers. Little and often is the best policy.

Epsom salt (magnesium sulphate) and Glauber salt (sodium sulphate) are the salts most commonly present in our saline soils. Some gardeners actually add Epsom salt to their soil in small quantities. This is usually done in spring when seeding vegetables, as a sprinkle of Epsom salt down the rows discourages root maggots. A little may not upset your plants, but to be on the safe side you should first have your soil tested for soluble salt content.

If soluble salt levels become too high, leach the accumulated salts below the root zone if possible, applying several heavy waterings and allowing the soil to dry normally between treatments. The addition of humus helps by allowing the soil to hold more water, thereby diluting the salt concentration. Unfortunately, there is no chemical treatment that will correct the saline condition, and any treatment will be of limited benefit if salty groundwater is present.

SOIL BY THE TRUCKLOAD

If you have moved into a new area of town where much of the topsoil has been removed or if you wish to start over on an old lot, you may decide to bring in good quality topsoil by the truckload. Shopping for soil can be as uncertain for the layman as shopping for a used car, but you can protect yourself by dealing if possible with a local supplier who has been in the business long enough to establish a good reputation. Find out if others in the neighborhood have purchased soil recently, and if they are satisfied. It also helps to know something about the recent history of the product. If it has been stripped and stockpiled while a housing project was under construction, the soil may have been compacted when wet by machinery and its own weight and it will need some time for aeration. Be aware that the scraper operator removing good soil from cropped farmland may have been tempted to blade down beneath the topsoil layer to include worthless subsoil that will make up a percentage of the load for which you are expected to pay good money. The best way to determine if the soil is of good enough quality is to obtain a sample from the supplier and send it to your district agriculturist for a soil test.

Arrange to be at home when the soil is delivered; check the size of the truck box; 3 x 2 x 1 yard high is 6 cubic yards; and look to see if the load is similar to the original sample. If a dumped load turns out to be very different from the sample provided earlier and if you haven't accepted delivery by signing or paying for it, you have every right to have the supplier load it up again and take it away.

Don't be put off by weeds. Soil that is full of perennial weeds like quack grass, Canada thistle, or nettle will take time and energy to clean up and for a large garden will be more trouble than it's worth, but don't reject soil out of hand because it bristles with a heavy crop of annual weeds. They can be cut off with a sharp hoe before they go to seed, gradually eliminating the problem over several season as the seeds already in the soil germinate. Although the ideal is to obtain rich and weed-free soil, the soil that demonstrates its fertility with weed growth is preferable to weed-free soil of unknown quality.

GETTING IT ALL TOGETHER

If you are having a load of topsoil delivered, you may decide this is the time to bring in other soil additives as well. If you are doing this, it is best

to have one element delivered and spread evenly over the entire area before dumping the next one. For ease of dumping and spreading, start with the heaviest additive and finish with the lightest, for example, sand first, then loam, then peat.

With the additive dumped in piles, you now need to move it by wheelbarrow into evenly spaced smaller piles throughout the area. Use a shovel to spread the wheelbarrow piles, followed by a raking to ensure even spreading over the entire area. If you have a garden tractor with a blade, you can do the job sitting down, and for a large area the task can be accomplished a little faster.

Once the last additive has been evenly spread, you can broadcast a complete fertilizer, rent a rototiller, and work the whole thing down like a cake mix. Work the area several times in more than one direction to ensure a good mix. The machine is fine for initial mixing, but it's best not to pulverize the soil year after year.

TAKE YOUR TIME

If you have had to bring in new soil, try not to be in a great hurry to put it to work. It needs a little while to itself. Even soil of good texture and fertility will benefit from being allowed to lie fallow for the first season. This allows time to get rid of annual weeds germinating from seed and to find the roots of any perennial weeds that sprout during the first few months.

Even if the soil should turn out to be relatively weed free, the fallow period is useful. Because many soils are stockpiled before being sold, they need time for aeration, so turning the soil several times during the season by digging or plowing is of great benefit. This is why growing potatoes is so often recommended on "new" soil for the first season; the regular hilling of the rows, together with the smothering foliage of the potato tops, takes care of most weeds, and the digging of the harvest followed by leveling of the land does wonders for soil aeration.

TIPS FOR IMPROVING YOUR SOIL

Texture is too sandy. Incorporate organic matter in the form of well-matured compost or manure; add a good clay topsoil. These measures will improve the water-holding capacity and nutrient level of your soil.

Texture is too heavy with clay. Incorporate sharp, coarse sand and composted organic matter. Both will improve aeration and water penetration.

Soil dries out too fast. Incorporate manure, compost, peat, or decomposed organic matter. Mix thoroughly.

Soil stays too wet. Either improve subdrainage or raise the level of the land. Incorporating coarse sand will improve percolation of water through the topsoil but will not help if the water table is high.

Soil is too acid. Not yet common in our area, but acid rain from industrial regions could increase soil acidity to the point where the pH will need to be raised. If a soil test signifies its need, hydrated lime should be applied sparingly (a light dusting only, and worked into the topsoil), and the soil tested again in three or four weeks.

Soil is too alkaline. This condition often occurs in conjunction with soil salinity. The highly alkaline soil can be corrected to some extent by adding humus and using fertilizers with an acid base, such as 21-0-0 or any other analysis with sulphur added. (See your local supplier for recommendations.) Sulphur is expensive and at the rate of 5 to 10 pounds per 100 square feet, it is feasible for small areas.

CHAPTER II

Fertilizers

PLANT NUTRITION

It used to be that the scent of fine flowers in a flourishing garden had to compete with the less fragrant aroma of horse donations. There are no longer enough horses to satisfy all the garden soils, and the transportation of cattle manure from feedlots is not always a practical alternative. Not to worry. While organic matter is essential—as stressed in the last section—we can now obtain all the required plant nutrients from relatively clean and odorless chemicals.

Many people tend to view all chemicals with some suspicion—especially when associated with food—but there is no need for concern over the normal use of garden chemicals. Nitrogen is nitrogen, whether it comes from a natural process like the breakdown of organic matter or whether it is in the form of chemical in a paper sack. The same holds true for phosphorus, potassium (found in potash), and all the lesser plant nutrients. The only problem that I have noticed with the use of chemicals is the risk of applying too much in the mistaken belief that if a little is good, then a lot must be better.

THE BIG THREE— NITROGEN, PHOSPHORUS, AND POTASH

Nitrogen, phosphorus, and potash are the three primary elements that serve special functions within the plant. Phosphorus is a general gardening term for fertilizers such as superphosphate and rock phosphate that provide usable phosphoric acid. Potash is the general gardening term for fertilizers (mainly containing potassium carbonate) that supply usable potassium.

Check any bag of fertilizer and you will find three prominent numbers such as 16–20–0. The first number is the percentage of total nitrogen, the second is the percentage of available phosphorus, and the third represents the percentage of soluble potash. The remaining percentage (64 percent in the case of 16–20–0) is inert carrier for the active ingredients. The three figures on the bag or container always appear in the same order—nitrogen-phosphorus-potash.

Nitrogen promotes fast leaf and stem growth, and a healthy green color. This is especially desirable in leafy vegetables, such as lettuce and cabbage, or in lawn grass. A nitrogen deficiency shows up first as pale green or yellow leaves; too much nitrogen creates weak, sappy, and leggy growth at the expense of flowers and fruit. Nitrogen moves readily in moist soils, but if the soil remains flooded or saturated for some time, much of the nitrogen is lost. In a suitably aerated soil, nitrogen will supply food for beneficial soil bacteria, which break down raw organic matter into beneficial humus.

Nitrogen is the element most often needed in our prairie soils. Not only is it used up by plants and bacteria, but much of it is wasted as it washes down beneath the root zone. Ammonium sulphate (21–0–0) is a common nitrogen fertilizer.

Phosphorus increases root growth and hastens maturity, two aspects of plant growth that are particularly important to our plains region. With a short growing season, we need to get our crops off to a fast start in the spring and have them ripen early before hard frosts. Phosphorus also increases winter hardiness, so important with many borderline hardy woody ornamentals, and increases both disease resistance and the nutritional value of edible crops. A phosphorus deficiency may show up as slow growth and late maturation, and the leaves may be thickened and purplish in color. Phosphorus moves very slowly in the soil, so it should be incorporated at the root zone.

Most prairie garden soils will respond well to the addition of phosphorus and it should always be added (along with nitrogen) whenever manure and compost is incorporated into the soil. Ammonium phosphate (11–48–0) is a suitable choice.

Soluble potash in the soil works with the other two primary elements to ensure plant vigor, disease resistance, and an improved winter hardiness. Signs of potash deficiency in plants can be seen as edgeburn on lower leaves, mottled, spotted, streaked or curled leaves, or leaves that drop prematurely.

Potash is usually present in good quantities in prairie soils, but you might want to apply some occasionally just to be on the safe side. It is found in such "complete" fertilizers as 10–30–10.

MINOR ELEMENTS

We are fortunate that our soils are rarely lacking in any of the minor chemical elements needed in minute quantities for healthy plant growth. But if your plants are stunted, or the leaves show signs of light green coloration with even lighter veining, or the leaves are thickened and purplish, it might be a good idea to have your soil tested. The test will also show your soil pH level (degree of acidity/alkalinity), which is often a cause of plant distress. An alkaline soil condition can "lock up" phosphorus so it

is unavailable to the plants. This reduces the availability of important trace elements, and deficiencies become evident. Remedies for soils that are too acid or too alkaline can be found in the preceding chapter on soils.

SELECTING SUITABLE CHEMICAL FERTILIZERS

There are many good granular fertilizers on the market, cleaner to handle and less likely to cake in storage than the earlier powdered kinds. A few examples of common ones locally available are 16–20–0, 21–0–0, 10–30–10, 11–48–0, 0–0–60. Notice that some are heavily weighted to one or another of the three main nutrients, while others supply one element only.

Unless you are working to soil analysis recommendations, it is a good idea to start with a "complete" fertilizer such as 10–30–10 for the entire garden, and then supplement with others depending upon the situation. For lawns, 21–0–0 is a good choice if your soil is not too acid; 27–14–0 is also popular for lawn applications. For soils that have too much acidity, use either 16–0–0 or 15–0–0 to help bring the soil back toward a neutral condition.

For vegetable gardens, shrubs, and flower borders, you could aim for something higher in phosphorus, like 16–20–0 or 11–48–0. Apart from price and convenience, an important consideration is to avoid using the same fertilizer year after year. If you change often, you will avoid the buildup of certain chemical elements and the possible depletion of others.

You may hear about slow-release nitrogen fertilizers in future. Most of those now available were developed for areas with a higher rainfall than ours, and in our shorter drier growing season, the nitrogen is not released at an adequate rate. We will have to wait for formulations developed for our own climate. I believe that the slow-release concept will become popular, allowing us to make one fertilizer dose provide "all season relief."

With all chemical fertilizers your selection of brand name is immaterial, other than for factors of price and packing convenience.

There are some fertilizers that I avoid, namely, liquid fertilizers, tablets or fertilizer sticks, and those claiming to contain micro-nutrients and special additives. These are an expensive way to add nutrients, and you can safely assume that all micro-nutrients or trace elements needed for healthy plant growth are present in adequate amounts in your ordinary soil. I also avoid the very high nitrogen analysis fertilizers like 34–0–0 and 46–0–0. These are best left for farm use, as they are so concentrated that they are difficult to apply evenly, and they often produce patchy results.

Low analysis fertilizers like 5–8–7, 4–8–4, and 4–12–4, commonly sold south of the forty-ninth parallel, have lots of inert carrier and quite low percentages of active ingredients. You are probably paying more for the active ingredient because of the bulk and handling of the product, but otherwise they are quite satisfactory.

Special plant food mixtures in attractive packages marked "Rose Food," "African Violet Food," and so on are at best misleading. There are too many unknown factors related to your particular soil (including existing nutrient levels) for anyone to present a set formulation for a particular kind of plant. For my own garden roses I often use 16–20–0 granular fertilizer that comes in 44-pound bags. It's readily available in my area and good value for money. This formulation encourages good growth and flowering all summer. Then, in late August or early September, I attempt to nudge the rose plants towards dormancy by applying a little potash in the form of 0–0–60. For house plants I use a complete and readily soluble crystalline fertilizer that is dissolved in water. I use it infrequently and at half the manufacturer's recommended dose. In general, there are more problems caused by overfertilizing container plants than by not fertilizing at all. Foliage plants get a formulation higher in nitrogen (for example, 12–6–3), while flowering house plants are given one higher in phosphorus (for example, 15–30–15).

APPLICATION RATES AND PROCEDURES

Once you have decided on a fertilizer, you need to know how best to apply it to different parts of your garden.

Lawns

The following table contains some suggested rates of application for commonly used formulations of lawn fertilizers.

There are many more formulations available. If you have a fertilizer that is not included in the above table, you can divide the nitrogen percentage into 80 to get the number of pounds per 1000 square feet. Chapter four on lawns covers the special needs of a newly seeded lawn.

The recommendations in the table are for single applications to a lawn, presuming you are going to make four such applications in one season. There's a strong temptation to decide how much lawn fertilizer is needed for a full season's growth, and to apply it all at the same time. This "camel" concept is wasteful because much of the nitrogen will be used or dissipated by the end of the season. Shortly after a one-shot application, the grass grows so fast that a lawn mower hardly cools off between mowing sessions, and you understandably lose enthusiasm for the exercise. A better plan is to make lighter applications three or four times each season—early in the months of

May, June, July, and August. There is something to be said for saving the last application until late fall, just before the ground freezes hard for the winter. This fall fertilizer is then ready to go to work as soon as growth commences the following spring.

Before applying fertilizer to the lawn, first mow the grass and remove the clippings so the fertilizer granules will filter down to the soil. Fertilizer can stick to wet grass and cause chemical burns during the growing season, so choose a dry day for applications. Break up any lumps of fertilizer before starting.

The easiest method of application is by using a spreader, applying half of the fertilizer in one direction and the remaining half at right angles to the first. A broadcast spreader that you hang around your neck is handy; if you are using a wheeled drop-spreader, take special care to avoid leaving unfertilized strips or overlapped areas. Further discussion of both kinds of spreaders can be found in the chapter on tools. Avoid filling the spreader on the lawn, and select a smooth surface such as a concrete path or driveway so any spills can be swept up. As soon as the fertilizer is spread, water the lawn thoroughly with a garden sprinkler to dissolve and soak the chemicals into the ground.

LAWN FERTILIZER GUIDE

Fertilizer Percentage			Amount per Application
Total nitrogen	Available phosphorus	Soluble Potash	Pounds per 1,000 square feet
34	0	0	2
27	14	0	3
26	3	3	3
21	0	0	4
16	20	0	5
15	0	0	5
13	16	10	6
12	6	3	7
11	51	0	7
11	48	0	7
10	30	10	8
10	6	4	8
8	12	6	10
7	40	6	11
5	10	5	16

Vegetables and Soft Fruits

In the vegetable garden and soft fruit plantings, the ideal situation is to make three fertilizer applications, one broadcast at seeding and planting time, followed by a row side application once the crops are up and growing, and possibly another row side application three weeks before harvest. A weak solution of phosphorus fertilizer (marketed as a "starter solution") is one planting-time option that is becoming popular. Alternatively, fertilizers high in phosphorus and potash can be incorporated when the garden is dug over in the fall.

The following table gives suggested rates of application for broadcasting fertilizers in the vegetable or soft fruit garden.

VEGETABLE AND SOFT FRUIT FERTILIZER GUIDE FOR BROADCAST APPLICATIONS

Fertilizer Percentage			Amount per Application
Total nitrogen	Available phosphorus	Soluble Potash	Pounds per 1,000 square feet
28	14	0	4
23	23	0	5
21	0	0	6
16	20	0	8
13	16	10	9
11	48	0	11
8	38	15	15
4	8	4	30
0	25	0	14

There are many more formulations available. If you intend to use a fertilizer for broadcasting in the vegetable or soft fruit garden that is not included in the above table, you can divide the nitrogen percentage into 120 to get the number of pounds per 1000 square feet.

Broadcasting fertilizer on row crops is not always the most economical method of application. Instead you can place a narrow strip of fertilizer 2 inches to each side of the row and about 1 inch below the seed depth—without the fertilizer coming into contact with the seed. Later side dressings of fertilizer are spread along the row, cultivated lightly into the ground, and watered in.

For an average row spacing of 2 feet, a suitable quantity of 11–48–0 would be 1 ounce for ever 39 inches of row length. In other words, a full 10 ounce soup can will do an 11-yard row. Here are some more examples of suitable rates when applied as a side dressing to rows of vegetables and soft fruits.

VEGETABLE AND SOFT FRUIT FERTILIZER GUIDE FOR SIDE DRESSING

Fertilizer Percentage			Amount per Application
Total nitrogen	Available phosphorus	Soluble potash	Ounces per yard of row*
28	14	0	.5
23	23	0	.5
16	20	0	.75
13	16	10	1
10	30	10	1
8	38	15	1.5

*Figures rounded off

Woody Ornamental and Tree Fruit Feeding

Established ornamental and fruiting plants can perform well from one moderate fertilizer application (at lawn application rates) in spring, as soon as growth commences. As phosphorus promotes root development, I recommend an analysis that is higher in phosphorus than in nitrogen or potash. Trees and shrubs that are near fertilized lawns will not need additional nutrients, as the far-reaching roots will take up adequate amounts from that source. A handful of fertilizer well worked into the planting hole will get transplanted trees off to a good start.

The standard recommendation for tree feeding has been to drill holes into the ground at about the extent of the tree canopy (drip-line) and to pour measured amounts of granular fertilizer into each hole, followed by a soaking with the water hose. The fertilizer is limited to the vicinity of each hole, with much of the active ingredient being leached down beyond the reach of the root system and wasted. Furthermore, the feeder roots at the location of each hole are likely to be injured by chemical burns from the high concentration. Broadcast fertilizer applications spread evenly around and just below the drip-line, then worked into the surface and watered in, will provide a greater return for your fertilizer dollar.

Herbaceous Perennials and Annuals

Borders of annual and herbaceous ornamentals can be treated to any of the commonly available granular fertilizers in spring; just avoid the use of high nitrogen kinds around plants grown for flowers or fruit.

Fertilizer for annual bedding plant areas and for new herbaceous perennial borders is best broadcast on the soil, and worked under, several days before planting. For old herbaceous perennial borders I like to spread the fertilizer around the plants in spring, about the time they start into growth. I then dig or fork it in, and water.

ORGANIC AND SPECIALTY FERTILIZERS

Another way of applying nitrogen, phosphorus, potash, and other nutrients to our plants is through the use of those long-acclaimed organic materials like dried blood, hoof and horn meal, and steamed bonemeal. The very words are like magical incantations, yet the chemicals they release are the same as those supplied by commercial inorganic fertilizers. These often expensive organic products must undergo some chemical change in the soil before their nutrients are released, so they are slow-acting over a longer period of time than inorganic fertilizers. Here is a list of those you might come across. Note that bone-meal has a basic reaction on soil pH, that is, it increases soil alkalinity and should be used in moderation if your aim is a more acid soil.

Organic Material	Normal Analysis	Normal Application Rates [Pounds per 1,000 sq. ft]	Effect on pH
Activated sludge	5–4–0	40	acid
Animal tankage	7–9–0	30	acid
Blood Meal	12–0–0	15	acid
Hardwood ashes	0–1–5	60	basic
Hoof and horn meal	13–0–0	15	—
Linseed meal	5–1–1	40	acid
Soybean meal	6–0–0	35	—
Steamed bone-meal	3–20–0	60	basic

Another popular organic additive, horse or cattle manure, does not belong in the above table; it is added more for its bulk to improve the condition of the soil. The analysis of manures will vary, but often approximates 5–3–5 when mixed—as they usually are—with some straw bedding. Application rates of 1,000 pounds per 1,000 square feet are beneficial as long as the material is worked well into the soil before planting. If the manure is quite high in straw content, apply nitrogen at the same time to avoid the nitrogen deficiency that accompanies decomposing straw.

Large quantities of organic fertilizers are needed before the nutrient level approaches that of granular fertilizers. Unless you have a cheap source of supply, the use of materials like these is not economically feasible, so look for your local best buy. In my own district this is a mushroom farm that disposes of used horse manure for little more than the price of loading a pickup truck. This product, spread to cover the bare ground in fall and turned under in spring, is a good source of humus, but I supplement the low nutrient value with seasonal applications of chemical fertilizers. There may well be suitable organic fertilizers in your own area. To find them, I suggest that you contact members of your nearest gardening club or horticultural society, enthusiasts who are most likely to have sniffed out any good local organic products.

CHAPTER III

Landscaping

My first opportunity to do some professional landscaping turned out to be a real let-down. I was fresh from college with a new diploma in horticulture and brimming with all the latest ideas, yet my position as foreman of the plant-breeding section at a federal research station hardly allowed full rein for creative horticultural expression in landscape design. Consequently, it was with unbounded enthusiasm that I jumped at an offer to take on a moonlighting contract to landscape the new police headquarters in town.

After viewing the stark building on its naked lot, I drew up plans for the planting of foundation shrubs, lawn, entrance walk, and shade trees. For good measure I planned a herbaceous border and space for annual bedding plants. On presenting these suggestions for consideration, my enthusiasm was dashed when I was told that "landscaping" in the local sense was a euphemism for installing a lawn.

Granted, lawns are an important part of most landscape designs. They are best complemented, however, by at least a few ornamental plants to provide interest and to soften the sharp outline of buildings and other elements of the hard landscape. The term "hard landscape" refers to the parts of the property other than soil and plants; it includes the driveway, patio, pool, arbor, terrace, trellis, fences, and walls. Consider the "soft landscape" as the plants (including lawns) and the general topography of the land.

PROFESSIONAL HELP

You might want to engage a landscape architect to design the outdoor area for you. These professionals may work for an hourly rate or for a percentage of the cost of construction, and may not even be available if busy on lucrative industrial and commercial contracts. If you do obtain the services of a landscape architect, once you have an acceptable plan you must then find a landscape contractor able and willing to do the actual construction as specified, or be prepared to carry out the concept yourself.

Alternatively, you could hire a landscape contractor to draw up a suitable working plan and carry it through to completion. Landscape contractors often supply rough plans for a minimal fee in anticipation of getting the contract. Growers of nursery stock also supply plans on the same basis. The advantage of these low-cost plans may be offset by the enthusiasm of the designer/supplier/contractor to saturate your area with landscape materials. It is understandable that some nurserymen might succumb to the temptation to include a few extra high-priced conifers, for example, adding to their sales of nursery stock. Overplanting (that is, the spacing of plants too close together to allow their mature development) is a common practice, and may be approved by the home owner under certain circumstances. But more on this later.

THE PLAN

There is nothing very difficult in designing your own landscape plan if you take the project step by step. An advantage to the do-it-yourself design is that you will more easily understand why materials are placed where they are and be more likely to feel self-assured when it's time to make necessary modifications.

Whether revising the design of an old garden or designing the grounds of a new home, you will find that a little initial planning will save you time and trouble in the future. Incidentally, the long-term cost and effort involved in maintaining your landscape year after year will certainly exceed your initial expenditure. Bear this in mind so you do not get too carried away with elaborate plans.

First, draw a plan of the property to scale on graph paper, making all property lines, buildings, existing trees, and pathways. In broken lines, accurately indicate any sewer lines, septic tanks, gas pipes, water lines, and overhead wires. On the buildings, mark in all entrances and windows on the main floor.

Contact your town or city hall to get the latest word on such regulations as maximum heights for fences, hedge allowances, and easements, so your design will comply with local bylaws. Then add to your preliminary plan any unsightly objects that should be screened from view and any attractive views that you wish to incorporate into your design. Note the direction of prevailing winds, and don't forget a "north" arrow so you will be reminded of sun and shade situations.

Make several photocopies of your scale drawing and use them for sketching tentative garden arrangements until you find one that seems appropriate. Before inviting the whole family to get involved in this "what if" exercise, let's define the main objective, as well as good design concepts, so we can produce a plan that would have met with the approval of the late William Strunk, Jr.

As far as I know, Strunk was never noted for his landscape designs, but his general principles will help us establish a sound approach to landscaping. A Cornell University professor of English, Strunk strongly advocated developing individual style, while adhering to conventional expression. His battle cry was "brevity" and he declared that a sentence should contain no unnecessary words, a drawing no unnecessary lines, and a machine no unnecessary parts. If the eminent Professor Strunk had ever considered landscape design, it is certain that he would have extolled the virtues of landscape simplicity, eliminating all unnecessary ornaments and plants (including trees). It has been left, however, for others to apply Strunkian principles to landscape design.

- Keep the landscape design simple.
- Use materials and a design in keeping with those of your buildings.
- Keep the design in harmony with those of neighbors and community.
- Make the design functional.

To elaborate a little on each point: The first edict suggests that if you are not satisfied with the plan, then most likely the garden is too cluttered. Try removing something.

Next bear in mind that modern bungalows, split levels, and ranch-style homes call for an informal design. Formal and semiformal landscaping is more appropriately used with homes of the traditional style.

In making sure that your design harmonizes with those nearby, try not to be too distinctive in the public-view area. If yours is one of an avenue of open lawns, then a front yard of brick walls or wrought iron fences would be incongruous and detract from the harmony of the neighborhood. Similarly, formal hedges that extend to the public sidewalk may be controlled by local bylaws. A front area composed entirely of creeping junipers might be a great temptation if you need to display originality and hate mowing lawns, but apart from the note of discontinuity that this would impose on the neighborhood, and a possible contravention of local bylaws, junipers soon become overgrown and need to be thinned out or replaced.

Other interesting variations like crushed rock decorated with a wagon wheel and bison skull, or a scaled-down replica of Stonehenge, would be fascinating to construct, but they are really no substitute for the conventional front yard.

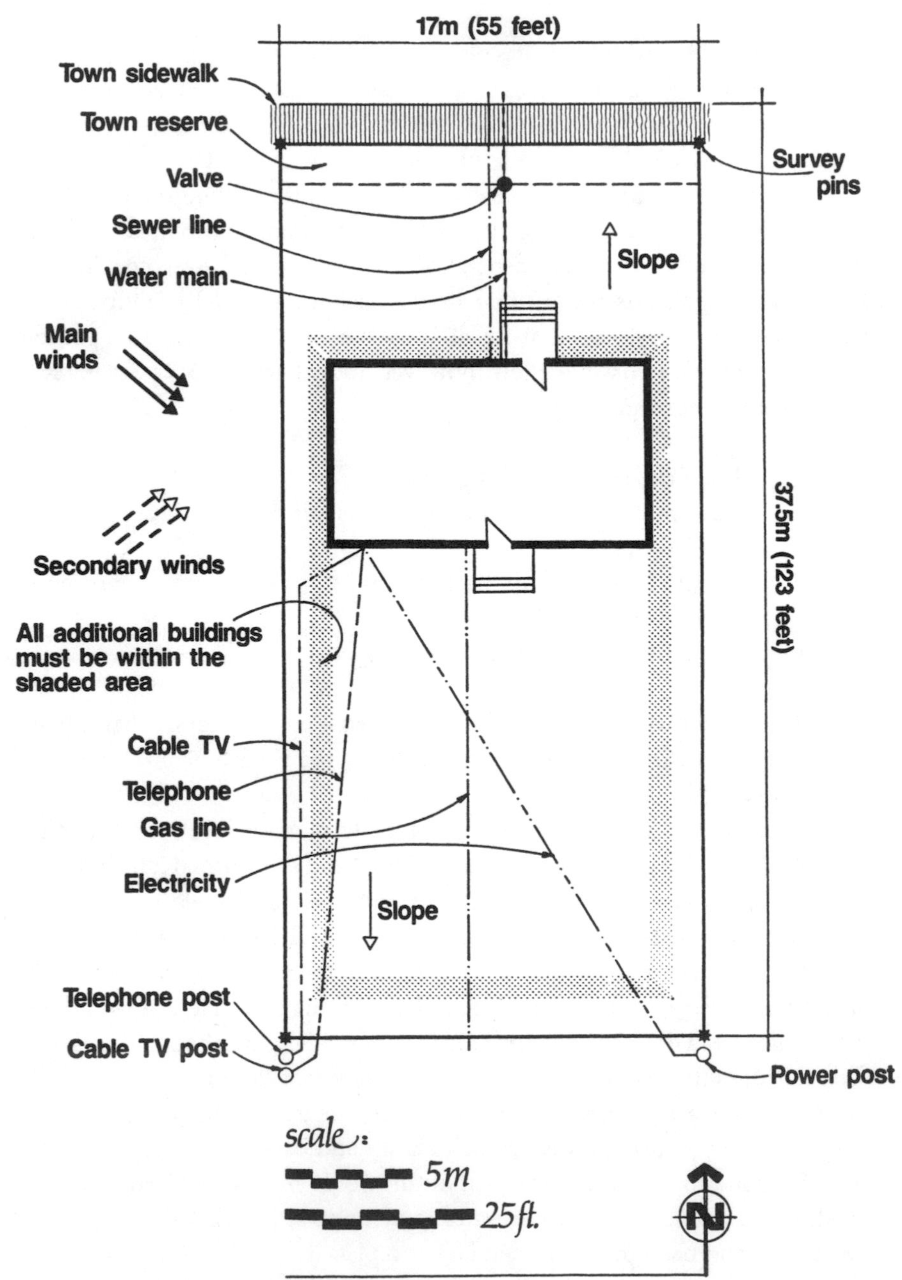

The starting point for your landscape design is a scale drawing of your lot. In this typical plan, the location of utilities, the orientation of the lot, and the direction of the prevailing winds have all been marked. The following three designs all have a similar plan as their starting point.

"What? No sense of originality or adventure?" you say. "What a stuffy attitude."

Not necessarily. We know that some of those who behave and dress in a conventional manner in public are having a wild old time behind closed doors. The same could apply to your garden. Save any unconventional individuality of landscape expression for the areas beyond the public view.

This brings us to the fourth and last general concept, that of a functional design—functional in the sense that not only is each element in a convenient place, but also privacy is provided where needed, maintenance is relatively simple, and plant materials are those that withstand our climate.

The last point is all-important. The main difference between landscaping in our region and landscaping elsewhere lies with the choice of suitable plants for our climate. In addition to consulting the plant listings in this book, I suggest that you take a walk to look at properties similar to your own that are already developed. You will soon get a feel for what appeals to you, and also notice situations that you would like to avoid. In particular, you will see which kinds of trees and shrubs grow happily in your area.

Once you have done a survey of your neighborhood, consider your own individual needs and preferences. Do you want a fast-growing tree or a tall hedge to provide a screen, a spiny shrub to form a barrier, a compact small

Trees suitable for planting in the home garden come in a variety of sizes and forms. Tall, upright trees are useful as focal points in the landscape; wide-spreading ones provide shelter and shade.

hedge to form a property divider, or a climbing vine for an exposed wall or trellis? Do you want upright trees, those that have drooping branches, or just good shade trees? Many shrubs, especially evergreens, come in compact globe forms; other form cushions or mats of low-growing vegetation.

Consider too the colors these plants will contribute to your yard year-round. Many trees and shrubs, most notably fruit trees, have showy spring blossoms. Others have distinctive foliage colors throughout the summer months. Purple-leaf crabapples, silver buffalo-berry, and the golden elder are just a few examples of woody plants that have foliage colors other than green. Some trees and shrubs come into their own with a dazzling array of fall colors. An important consideration in landscape design in our climate is the planting of trees and shrubs that will contribute to the landscape even when the thermometer plummets. Evergreens, and deciduous trees with colorful bark, such as white-barked birches, the copper-barked Amur cherry, and species of red and yellow-green dogwood, all enhance the winter garden.

When considering each plant as a possible candidate for your own garden, judge its size, general appearance, and location (sun or shade). In older districts you will see that while large trees often make majestic and impressive specimens, there is generally a trade-off as a tree comes into conflict with its surroundings. The main things to watch for in this regard are overhead and underground utilities, and plantings that crowd adjacent properties and the foundations of buildings. Because of their demand for soil moisture and nutrients, and their blocking of sunlight, trees and large shrubs also have an adverse effect on lawns, flower beds, and vegetable gardens.

Shrubs can be used to cover unsightly architectural features or to give definition to a special planting area. Low shrubs are useful as ground covers.

Here are more guidelines that will help you select trees and shrubs for a particular effect.

Trees with showy flowers
Malus (flowering crabapples)
Prunus maackii (Amur cherry)
Prunus padus 'Commutata' (mayday)
Prunus virginiana 'Shubert' (Shubert chokecherry)
Sorbus (mountain-ash)

Shrubs with showy flowers
Amelanchier alnifolia (saskatoon)
Caragana (caragana)
Crataegus (hawthorn)
Cytisus (broom)
Daphne cneorum (rose daphne)
Forsythia (forsythia)
Genista tinctoria (dyer's greenweed)
Hydrangea 'Annabelle' (Annabelle hydrangea)
Lonicera (honeysuckle)
Philadelphus (mockorange)
Potentilla fruticosa (shrubby cinquefoil)
Prunus (flower plums and cherries)
Prunus tomentosa (Nanking cherry)
Prunus triloba 'Multiplex' (double-flowering plum)
Ribes alpinum (alpine currant)
Rosa (roses)
Syringa (lilacs)
Viburnum (cranberries)

Trees and shrubs with distinctive foliage color
Cornus (dogwood selections)
Elaeagnus augustifolia (Russian olive)
Hippophae rhamnoides (common sea-buckthorn)
Juniperus (juniper selections)
Malus (crabapples, purple-leaf selections)
Physocarpus opulifolius 'Luteus' (golden ninebark)
Picea pungens glauca (Colorado blue spruce)
Populus alba (white poplar selections)

Prunus virginiana 'Shubert' (Shubert chokecherry)
Sambucus 'Sutherland Golden' (Sutherland golden elder)
Shepherdia argentea (silver buffalo-berry)
Spiraea bumalda 'Goldflame' (Goldflame spirea)

Trees and shrubs with good autumn foliage color
Acer ginnala (Amur maple)
Betula (birch)
Cotoneaster lucidus (hedge cotoneaster)
Euonymus (burning bush)
Fraxinus (ash)
Parthenocissus quinquefolia (Virginia creeper)
Prunus (flowering plums and cherries)
Ribes (currants)
Rosa hybrids (roses)
Sorbus (mountain-ash)
Viburnum (cranberry)

Trees and shrubs with conspicuous winter bark
Betula (birch), several kinds with white bark
Cornus (dogwood), red or yellow-green twigs
Pinus sylvestris (Scotch pine), orange-brown bark
Prunus maackii (Amur cherry), copper bark
Salix alba 'Britzensis' (redstem willow), red twigs
Salix alba 'Vitellina' (golden willow), yellow twigs

Trees with an upright branching habit
Caragana arborescens 'Sutherland' (Sutherland caragana)
Malus baccata 'Columnaris' (pyramid crabapple)
Populus alba 'Pyramidalis' (boleana poplar)
Populus tremula 'Erecta' (Swedish columnar poplar)
Sorbus aucuparia 'Fastigiata' (European mountain-ash selection)
Thuja occidentalis (columnar white-cedar selections)

Trees and shrubs with drooping branch (weeping habit)
Betula pendula 'Gracilis' (cut-leaf weeping birch)
Caragana arborescens 'Pendula' (weeping caragana)
Caragana arborescens 'Walker' (Walker caragana)
Salix alba 'Tristis' (white weeping willow)

Some popular shade trees
Betula papyrifera (paper birch)
Betula pendula 'Gracilis' (cut-leaf weeping birch)
Fraxinus (ash)
Prunus virginiana 'Shubert' (Shubert chokecherry)
Quercus macrocarpa (bur oak)
Tilia cordata (little-leaf linden)

Fast-growing trees for screening
Acer ginnala (Amur maple)
Acer negundo (Manitoba maple)
Populus (poplars)
Prunus virginiana 'Shubert' (Shubert chokecherry)
Salix pentandra (laurel-leaf willow)
Ulmus pumila (Manchurian elm)

Shrubs with globe form
Abies balsamea 'Hudsonia' (dwarf balsam fir)
Caragana frutex 'Globosa' (globe caragana)
Picea abies 'Nidiformis' (nest spruce)
Picea glauca 'Echiniformis' (hedgehog spruce)
Picea pungens 'Globosa' (dwarf blue spruce)
Pinus mugo mugo (mugho pine)
Thuja occidentalis 'Little Gem' (green globe white-cedar)
Thuja occidentalis 'Woodwardii' (Woodward globe white-cedar)

So much for the preliminary theoretical training and your field laboratory studies. Now back to the plan. After reading through the next section, you should be able to divide your plan into three sections and consider each as an almost separate unit.

THREE OUTDOOR AREAS

With your "as is" plan in front of you, first decide how much of the property should be allotted for certain purposes. The front yard comprises the main approach to the house and includes the area visible to the public. This public area usually takes about 25 percent of the available land.

Normally, a similar amount of space is assigned in the back yard for the service area; such things as clothes drying, trash disposal, tool shed, cold frame, and compost pile. The vegetable garden and greenhouse may be relegated to this section too, unless vegetable gardening is a major interest or the greenhouse a special showpiece. The final design will depend on personal priorities.

The remaining half of the garden is available for the particular needs of the family—outdoor recreation or a quiet oasis of lawn with ornamental flowers, shrubs, and trees. Let's call this the private area.

In locating these elements of the design on your plan, consider that you will want a pleasant view from the living room and kitchen; the children's play area should also be easily seen from the house; the service area is best kept out of sight. Remember to include screens (hard barriers or woody plants) to hide unwanted views and to afford some privacy from adjacent buildings.

If there are existing trees, shrubs, or other features worth keeping, try to work them into your plan at an early stage. In general, when sketching in the various garden features in each area, start with the hard structures (walks, decks, walls, pools) and use plants as the furnishings.

The Public Area

Your property will increase in value with the development of a well-designed front yard. As mentioned earlier, the part of the garden visible to the public should blend reasonably well with others nearby, and the hard materials should match or harmonize with those of the house. The path should provide convenient access, with no unnecessary curves.

A broad, uninterrupted lawn makes the property appear wider, so try not to spoil the effect by planting island trees, shrubs, and flower beds. For the same reason try to locate the walkway and drive to one side to avoid unnecessary fragmentation of the lawn. An unbroken stretch of grass also reduces the maintenance time involved in mowing and edging.

Except for shade or as a noise barrier in the front yard, limit the use of large- or medium-sized trees to the rear of the house. Shrubs should be used near the house to hide undesirable architectural features (such as a high foundation line) or to emphasize desirable features such as a fine front entrance.

Fashions in landscaping change slowly, but the old concept of planting shrubs (like mugho pine, juniper, and potentilla) along the front of every home is gradually giving way to alternatives. Just to be different, the architecturally acceptable base of a home may be left open to relieve the monotony. And instead of placing trees and shrubs to create the best impression for a passer-by, plants may be used to create a sense of enclosure and arrival at the entrance area. This last idea would never work for me because my wife would always imagine an escaped convict hiding in the undergrowth. You have to talk these ideas over with the family before trying something different.

Judicious use of upright plants may still be utilized to partially obscure the sharp corners of the house and reduce its hard appearance. Most designers agree that showy flower borders and alpine gardens are best placed in the private area to the rear of the house.

The Private Area

If you felt shackled by convention in the design of your front landscape, you may now express yourself with abandon in your own back yard. If you have one major garden objective (at the time of writing, mine is the growing of tender roses) then more than half the private area can be devoted to your specialty. I know someone who has grown a comprehensive collection of herbs for the past twenty-five years or so; another specializes in lilies and does some hybridizing; another grows fruit trees and grafts several different selections onto each tree. Many people have extensive greenhouses in their back yards. These are all keen gardeners, and the space devoted to their specialty is amply rewarded with the satisfaction their hobbies bring.

For most home owners, however, a quiet retreat is all that is asked. Some must have a patio for barbecues, or a shady arbour screened against insects, a sandbox and a swing play area for little ones, an open space for badminton, a pool for cooling off on a hot summer day—it all depends on the family's needs.

The larger and more diverse the interests of those who will use the garden, the more need for give and take at this planning stage. Why not involve the entire family at the decision-making level and consider the needs of the pets too? When a good variety of ideas have been considered, decide on a compromise and firm up your plan without trying to crowd too much in. Sketch in the full spread of trees and shrubs in appropriate places for shade, screening, or balance, but avoid placing them directly over or under utility services.

As with the front yard, you will probably want to keep any lawn area unbroken for ease of maintenance. Plan for the paths to be on the same level as the lawn to facilitate mowing and edging.

The Service Area

The location of the service area may be dictated by an obvious place for garbage removal, and it should be easy to reach from the house. Preferably the service area should not be overlooked from the living room, and it may be screened from the private and public areas by a hedge, fence, or trellis. A dog run may be located here to keep Fido off the lawn and planted areas.

THREE LANDSCAPE PLANS

A typical small residential lot cannot include everything, but it can be satisfying if designed to fit the priorities of the family. The figures in this section illustrate just three alternatives for the same-sized lot, featuring different lot orientation and different family priorities. Combinations of these and hundreds of other figures (existing or waiting to be drawn by you) provide infinite variety.

If your garden has more or less space than the one illustrated, your plan will vary in the number and variety of plants and the number and size of features. The basic procedure, however, remains the same.

- Using graph paper, take note of what already exists;
- Decide on your own family priorities;
- Draw several alternative plans;
- Decide on one plan;
- Implement the plan, either all at once or over several seasons;
- Be prepared, in time, to modify the design as family priorities change.

Plan A

The priorities of the Anderson family are

- A two-car garage (with the main entrance from the rear lane);
- Fences, side and rear;
- Security gates, side and rear;
- Easy access to garbage pickup area;
- An unobstructed view from the neighbor's window to their rear door for security;
- A raised deck for picnics;
- Flowers and a few favorite vegetables and herbs.

The main public area feature of the Anderson's garden is a clear expanse of well-kept lawn. This melds with those of the neighbors on each side to give an impression of uncluttered space. The two upright conifers (white-cedars) at the northwest corner, together with the small shade tree (mountain-ash)

PLAN A

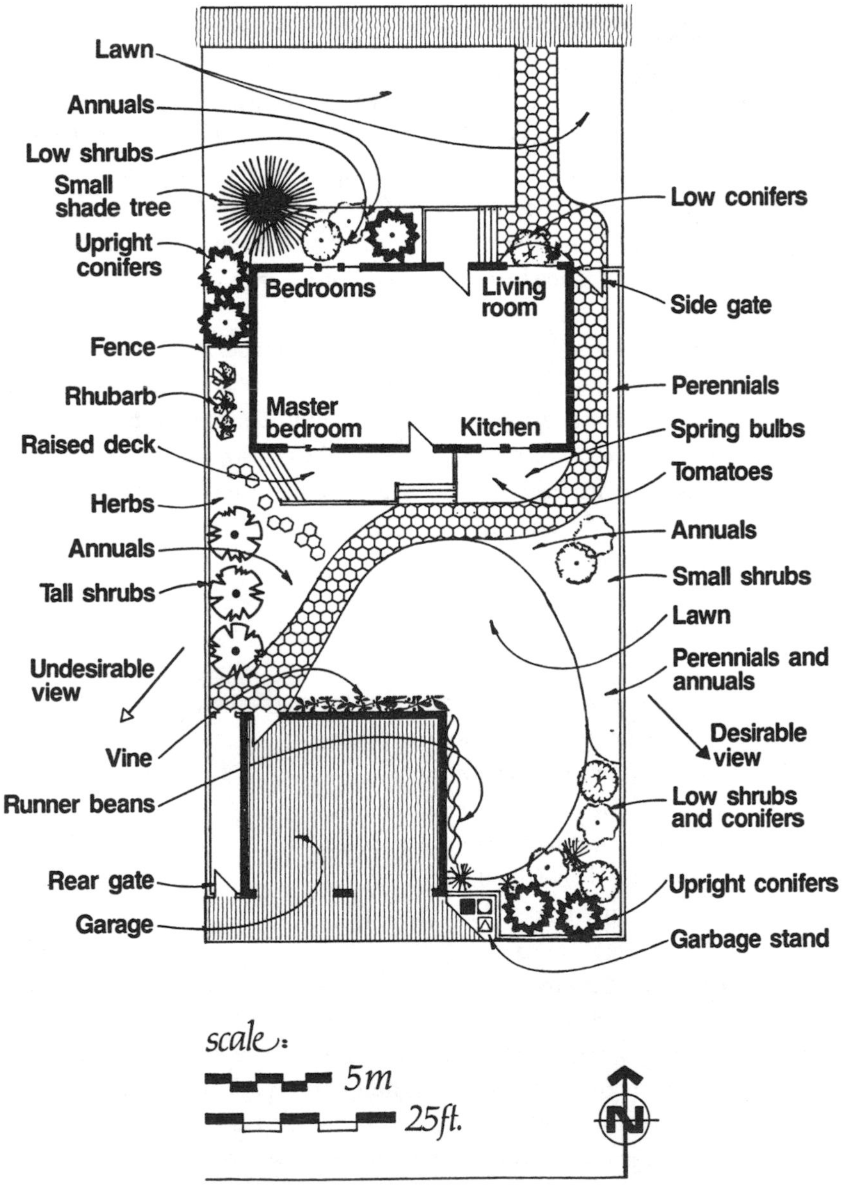

Lawn
Annuals
Low shrubs
Small shade tree
Upright conifers
Fence
Rhubarb
Raised deck
Herbs
Annuals
Tall shrubs
Undesirable view
Vine
Runner beans
Rear gate
Garage
Bedrooms
Living room
Master bedroom
Kitchen
Low conifers
Side gate
Perennials
Spring bulbs
Tomatoes
Annuals
Small shrubs
Lawn
Perennials and annuals
Desirable view
Low shrubs and conifers
Upright conifers
Garbage stand

scale:
5m
25ft.
N

The ornamental plantings in this yard provide splashes of color and soften the contours of the security fence around the property.

not only soften the boxy look of the house corner but also provide some insulation against the prevailing wind. The same upright white-cedar is repeated at the northwest side of the entrance porch. The low shrubs (potentilla) hide a rough foundation line. The conifers (mugho pines) in front of the living room window are kept low to maintain a clear view of the front walk.

The private area also has an open lawn to increase the apparent size of the lot. The public area theme of white-cedar and potentilla is repeated in the far southeast corner, where (except for one upright cedar planted as a focal point) the low, round white-cedars and flowering shrubs help create an illusion of distance. This effect is enhanced by herbaceous perennials and annuals along the east fence by the tapered border with progressively lower plants. The desirable view is left unobstructed.

The garage has a trellis for a vine (Virginia creeper) on the north side. This structure and the tall lilac shrubs by the west fence obscure the undesirable view to the southwest. The sun trap under the kitchen window has flowering bulbs replaced each summer by the tall staking tomatoes. The patch of land at the southwest corner of the house has been used for herbs such as dill and chives and for an ample supply of rhubarb.

Plan B

The priorities of the Baker family are

- A car parking pad off the street (no rear lane);
- Shade for the living room window;
- A children's play area;
- A patio for summer cookouts;
- A good supply of vegetables in season;
- Fruits for dessert and preserves;
- Low maintenance where possible.

A shade tree ('Patmore' green ash) overshadows the living room window of the Baker residence. This helps keep the house cool in summer, allowing filtered sunshine through the rest of the year. Low conifers (creeping junipers) extend alongside the neighbor's parking pad to soften the straight edge; they also provide transition from the street to the green ash to the house. The same blue-green junipers are repeated to the east of the front entrance to visually pull the front view together. The parking pad and all main paths are concrete for ease of maintenance, and there are no steps to hinder the travel of the snow blower and lawn mower.

PLAN B

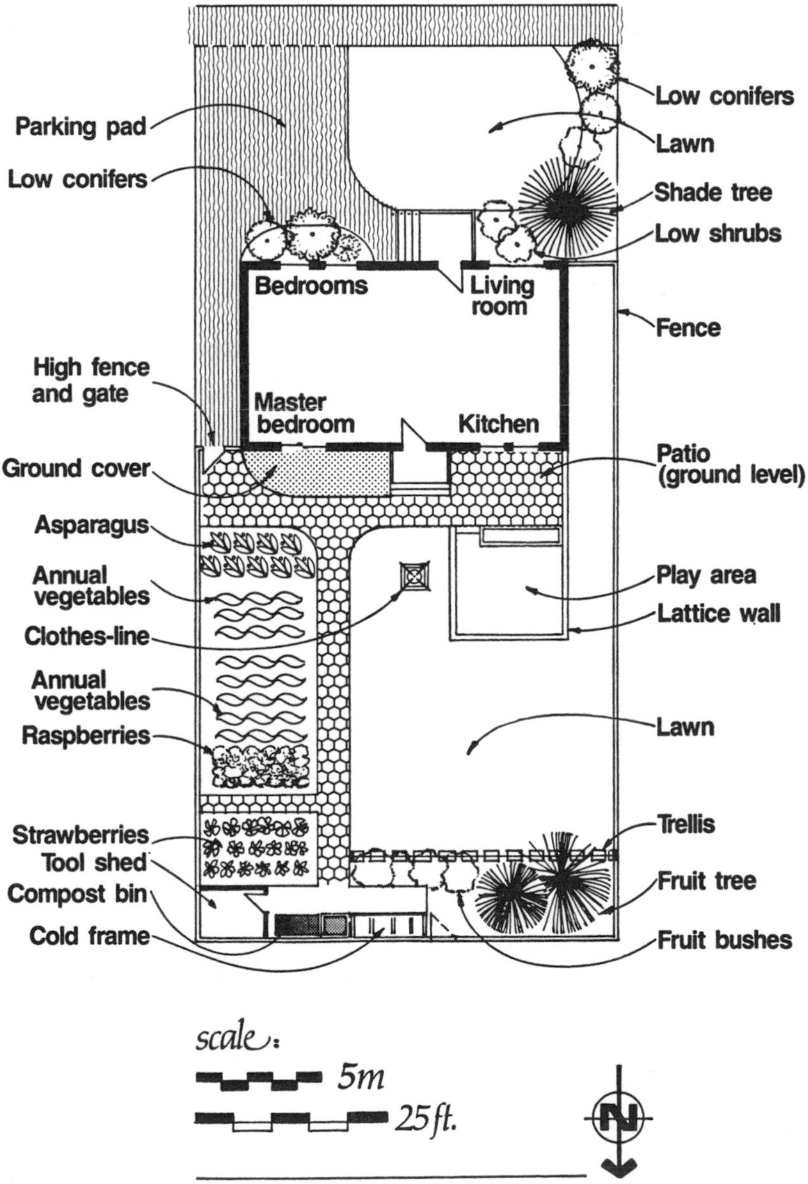

Parking pad
Low conifers
High fence and gate
Ground cover
Asparagus
Annual vegetables
Clothes-line
Annual vegetables
Raspberries
Strawberries
Tool shed
Compost bin
Cold frame
Bedrooms
Living room
Master bedroom
Kitchen
Low conifers
Lawn
Shade tree
Low shrubs
Fence
Patio (ground level)
Play area
Lattice wall
Lawn
Trellis
Fruit tree
Fruit bushes

scale:
5m
25ft.
N

Fresh fruit and vegetables, low maintenance, and a safe place for the children to play are the priorities for this family.

The private and service areas are enclosed by a stained wood fence. The one side entrance has a latch operable from the front but inaccessible to small children from the inside. The patio is paved with colored concrete tiles. A low wall of decorative lattice concrete blocks extends from the house to enclose the children's play area but allows a clear view of the area from the kitchen window. The lawn has a clothes drying stand (easily set aside at lawn-mowing time) but is otherwise left clear for games such as lawn darts and croquet.

An open wooden trellis at the north end of the lawn is used for supporting sweet peas, but this and the variegated goutweed groundcover at the northeast corner of the house are the only strictly ornamental plants in the private area.

The remainder of the garden is devoted to vegetable and fruit. A tool shed, compost bin, and cold frame are located in the northeast corner. The 'Dolgo' crabapple tree in the northwest corner provides springtime blossoms, fruit for canning, and some shelter from the prevailing wind.

Plan C

The priorities of the Chipman family are

- Shelter from a busy street;
- An environment attractive to birds;
- Off-street parking at the front of the house;
- A single-car garage at the rear;
- A small conservatory for year-round plants;
- A secluded garden retreat;
- Flowers.

The Chipman family have time for bird watching, hanging baskets, and tub planters. Living on a street with traffic day and night, a main priority is to use trees as a visual screen and sound barrier. To this end three tall conifers (Colorado blue spruce) have been established at the front of the house. The one closest to the street is offset from center to avoid planting over the sewer line and water main, and to avoid a too symmetrical planting. Smaller plantings at the driveway exit permit a clear view of oncoming traffic. A driveway with carport at the front door permits off-street parking and a safe exit without backing onto the street.

At the rear a single-car garage provides some protection to the garden from the prevailing northwest wind. The sheltered spot immediately south

PLAN C

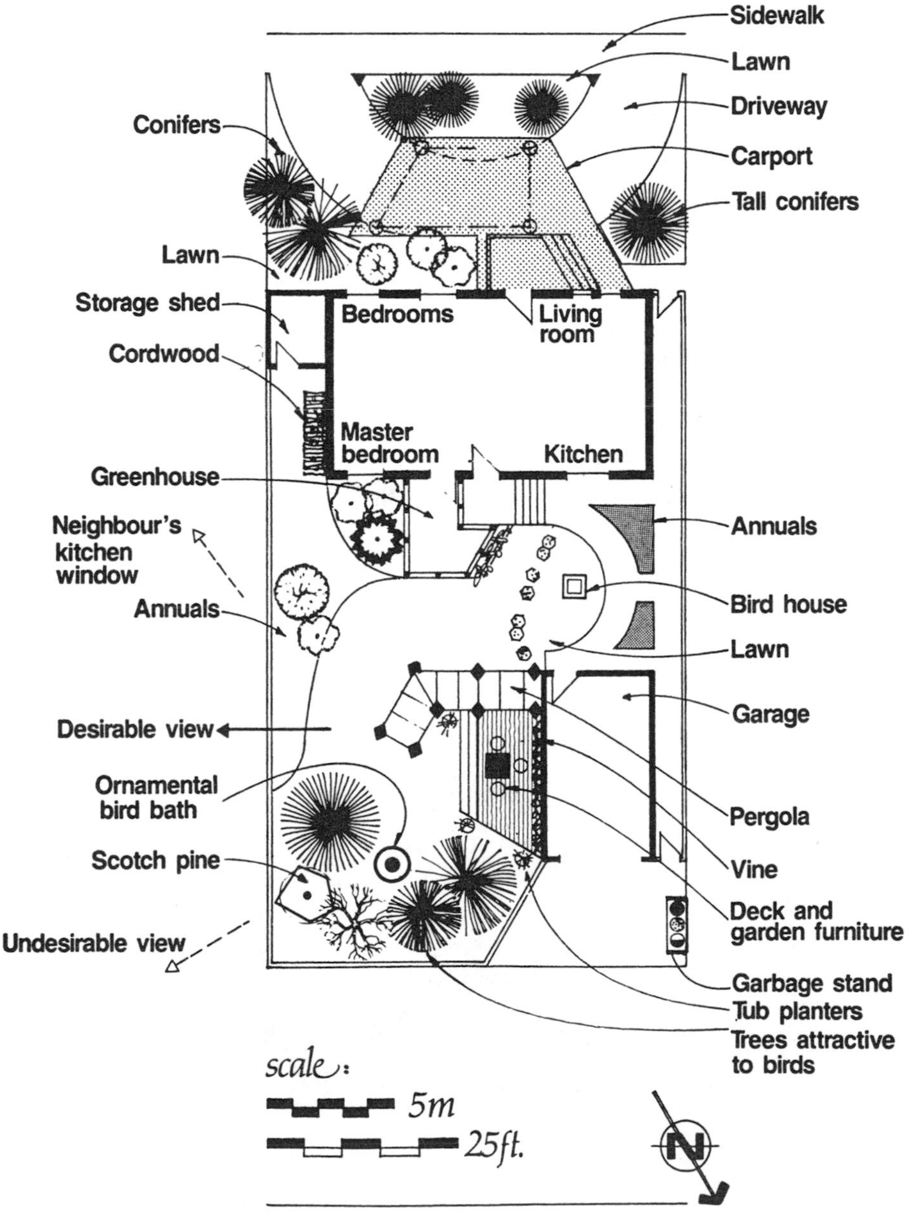

Sidewalk
Lawn
Driveway
Carport
Tall conifers
Conifers
Lawn
Storage shed
Cordwood
Bedrooms
Living room
Master bedroom
Kitchen
Greenhouse
Neighbour's kitchen window
Annuals
Annuals
Bird house
Lawn
Garage
Desirable view
Ornamental bird bath
Pergola
Scotch pine
Vine
Deck and garden furniture
Undesirable view
Garbage stand
Tub planters
Trees attractive to birds

scale:
5m
25ft.

N

This yard has been designed as a quiet retreat from the hustle and bustle of city life.

of the garage has been chosen as the site for the wooden deck. It is furnished with tub planters, garden furniture, and a portable screened enclosure for use when mosquito populations are high. This retreat is also sheltered from the house side by a pergola on which a lath wall has been added. (This screen helps to deaden noise further and provides a shade-house environment for hanging baskets and greenhouse plants on summer vacation.)

From this quiet retreat a pleasant view of the neighbor's garden has been kept open, while an addition to the pergola screens the neighbor's kitchen window. Trees (including a Scotch pine) block the view of utility poles and the garage across the lane, while a focal point (east from the deck) has been added in the form of an ornamental bird bath. Birds are also welcomed with a bird feeder hanging from the pergola, a nesting box viewed from the kitchen window, and by the choice of deciduous trees and shrubs—saskatoon berry, cotonester, green ash, pincherry, red elder, red osier dogwood, and Russian olive.

Annual bedding plants in two contrasting colors are used along the south fence and two island triangles to the north; different colors are used each year to add interest. A golden clematis on a wooden trellis clothes the south side of the garage.

The public, private, and service areas of this well-landscaped yard blend in a design that is both functional and attractive.

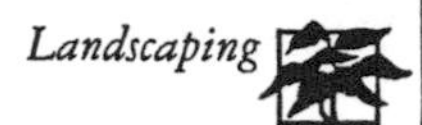

CONSTRUCTION AND PLANNING

When you actually plant the garden, stick to the plan. Start by installing the hard landscape such as fences, paths, and patios. Next, work on the soil, then the soil grade, add ornamental plants, and finally seed or sod the lawn.

A word of caution. It is always tempting to plant two or three trees for every one indicated on the drawing, just to fill up the empty space until they mature. If you can promise yourself that the excess plants will be removed before they begin to crowd each other, well and good. But these additional plant materials rarely get removed in time, and the resulting overlapping and shading spoils the original design.

No landscape remains static, and changes are to be expected as time goes on. The children outgrow the sandbox and swing, and the extra space is used to grow more vegetables for hungry teenagers. The family shrinks, and the vegetable garden is put into lawn and herbaceous perennials. A shade tree becomes too large and is taken down before its removal becomes too much of an expense and liability. In time, the whole outdoor property will grow and mature, and add substantial value to your home.

CHAPTER IV

Lawn Building

PREPARING THE SUBGRADE

It is important to build your lawn on a sound base. The rough grading of land around the home is generally the responsibility of the building contractor, and perhaps there won't be much opportunity to oversee the quality of this basic landscape work. But if you are fortunate enough to be able to control the operation or to provide input at this phase, there are several things to watch for.

Any original topsoil should be stockpiled to one side before building construction starts and should never be mixed with the inferior subsoil. Topsoil is usually distinguished by its darker color and more friable texture. Friable refers to the condition of a soil without hard or wet lumps. Subsoil is usually hard to work and lacks the microorganisms and organic matter needed for good plant growth.

Sewage pipes leading away from the building should be inspected before backfilling commences to ensure a snug, watertight seal at the pipe joints. Any seepage here will later attract tree roots, eventually resulting in pipe blockages.

If you can arrange to have your utilities (electricity, natural gas, and water lines) buried along the same part of the property, it will be easier to plan your landscape design. Scattered utilities limit your plan and make it difficult later to place even a garage in the clear.

See that the French drain around the foundation of the building (if called for) is installed according to specifications on the building plan. If it has to be redone later, your foundation shrubs and other plantings close to the house will be disturbed or ruined.

With the utilities and drainage installations properly in place, ensure that the building rubbish is hauled away. Too often piles of waste lumber, roofing tiles, metal pipes, and cans are buried on the property. The metal corrodes and the piles subside, resulting in valleys where none were intended. On the other hand, concrete and rocks that are well broken up will pose no problem as long as they are well buried beneath the subgrade. When sunk in a pit at the lowest corner of the property, rubble may even serve the useful purpose of assisting water drainage.

Nowadays, homes are generally designed so underground water runs away from the house, but if the subsoil is poorly drained it may be necessary to install French drains. If you have a subdrainage problem, I suggest that you call on professional help for the work and check with your local department of public works concerning requirements and local bylaws.

The subgrade should follow the lines of the final grade and slope gently away from the buildings. In regions of low precipitation such as ours, we must avoid excess runoff and loss of precious rainwater. Under such conditions a slope of 1 in 50 or a 1-inch drop over a distance of about 4 feet would be ideal. Your practiced eye might be able to judge a grade closely enough for your needs; however, the most particular of home owners might call in a professional surveyor to stake and mark the elevation points for a perfect grade.

For ease of maintenance, a slope should not exceed 1 in 16, so if the height of land between the house and the edge of the property is steep, it may mean that a terrace will have to be installed somewhere. Terraces certainly play an important part in landscape design, but they result in more maintenance work later on.

If the property is large, there may be some native trees and shrubs worth keeping. Generally, though, especially on the average city or town lot, native trees are too large to be useful in the home landscape. Frequently they have nuisance traits such as suckering roots or messy seed. Assuming, however, that existing trees or shrubs are to be retained, don't smother the roots by raising the grade around them, and avoid cutting away the surface soil in their vicinity. Allow the trees undisturbed grade for at least twice the radius of the canopy, and bear in mind that their feeder roots are likely to travel just beneath the surface for a distance far greater than the height of the tree or shrub.

After the subgrade is completed by the building contractor, see if you can arrange to loosen up the earth where it has been compacted by trucks and machinery. This subsurface cultivation will do much to assist drainage and help tree-root penetration. Work the entire area over with a heavy-weight rototiller to a depth of about 8 inches, but avoid working on soil that is saturated with moisture. Watch the classified ads for machine operators who rototill, plow, or disk at reasonable rates.

MAKING YOUR BED

With the subgrade completed, building contractors usually dump a few loads of topsoil and spread it a few inches deep over the entire area so it is ready for either seeding to lawn or landscape planting. Sometimes they leave you to find your own topsoil. For a good lawn at least 5 inches but preferably 8 inches or more of good quality topsoil is needed. Chapter one on soil in this book contains some pointers about bringing in this precious commodity.

Once the topsoil is spread evenly over the subgrade to a depth of at least 5 inches, you can improve the texture and moisture-holding capacity of clay or sandy soils with the addition of organic matter such as peat moss in the amount of about 1 inch to every 4 inches of topsoil. Spread the peat evenly over the surface in preparation for mixing in with a rototiller. On heavy clay soils the addition of coarse builder's sand is of great benefit; it can be applied at the same rate as the peat moss.

Adding the Fertilizer

The analysis and quantity of fertilizer applied to the seed bed is not critical. Suggested formulas and rates of application are to be found in Chapter two on fertilizers. At this stage in the life of a lawn, I recommend a formulation low in nitrogen, as nitrogen seems to retard grass seed germination. This element can easily be added once the grass is growing. It is important to spread fertilizer as uniformly as possible to avoid uneven growth. Rather than attempt to push a wheel-type fertilizer spreader over soft ground, I suggest you use the broadcast type that hangs as a bag or hopper around the neck, the spinning blades operated by turning a handle (see chapter on tools).

The thrifty landscaper usually does all the spreading of soil, sand, peat moss and fertilizer before bringing in the rototiller. If you don't own a good rototiller with forward travel gears, it would pay to rent rather than buy, as you will probably have little need for the machine once the basic landscape work is completed.

If you are considering the installation of an underground irrigation system, this is a good time to set it in place. Alternatively, if you proceed with lawn construction now, you could always add a system later. Trenching pipes under an established lawn is commonplace, and the scars heal within a season or so. A discussion of lawn irrigation systems can be found in the chapter on tools.

Be Gentle but Firm

The soft, newly rototilled soil must now be firmed. If the mix is quite dry, water the seed bed gently but thoroughly. Then, in a day or so, after the soil is dry enough that it no longer sticks to your boots, pack it down. I must

A weighted ladder can be used to help smooth the grade before final raking and seeding or sodding of a lawn. This phase of the operation might attract a number of family members willing to lend a land.

admit to a personal prejudice against rollers. There is more weight per square inch under your foot than under the heaviest roller that you can pull, so for a small- to medium-sized lawn area, I suggest you tramp the entire area once all over instead. You may break the monotony by raking a little from time to time. Extensive areas can be firmed with a small garden tractor.

The Rake's Progress

Once the seed bed has been packed down, use an ordinary garden rake to remove small sticks, stones, and other debris. The best way to do this is to start at the highest point of land and, with the handle held as low as can be easily managed, pull the rake head lightly towards you. Lift the rake head, set it down away from you and pull again alongside the previous swath. Avoid the common error of pushing as well as pulling the rake, as this method can result in a surface wavy enough to frighten a good-sized rowboat. With practice, the weight of the rake head is held up a little where hollows exist and pressed down on the humps so a level surface is soon achieved.

The first time over, the main objective is to collect the rubbish so it can be gathered and carried away to another part of the garden that requires fill.

On very large areas it is faster to use a garden tractor and harrow.

Now give the hand rake or harrow a rest while you contend with the larger hills and valleys. The rake can deal nicely with the smaller humps and hollows, but it cannot easily defeat mountain ranges. So turn to an oversized rake in the form of a section of ladder that can be towed around by a rope attached to each end. About this time you should be able to take a break in the shade because enough kids and dogs will be attracted by the operation, willing to serve as both pulling power and (with a wide board lashed to the center as a platform) enough weight, to rub the high land off into the valleys.

A second raking will likely be needed, this time starting from the lowest point of land to avoid shifting too much soil to the low end. Any big lumps of soil remaining can be pounded into submission with the rake head or incarcerated where they will do no harm. Alternate the ladder and the hand rake until you are so proud of the result that it seems a shame to seed to grass.

CHOOSING THE BEST SEED FOR YOU

There are many commercially available combinations of various grass seeds. These mixtures are intended to provide alternative blends for a variety of soils, sites, and pocketbooks. They are offered under such names as Evergreen, Green Carpet, Sun & Shade, Playground, and Economy Mix. In the United States federal laws require that each bag of seed be tagged to indicate the percentage of each grass seed, purity, viability, and date of the test.

For an ordinary grass area you may wish to obtain a ready-made mixture from a local retailer. For high profile lawn areas I suggest that you purchase seed of two or three choice grass cultivars (cultivated varieties) and mix them yourself.

Here are the names of some grass species commonly used in home lawns in our region. Check with your local extension agent. Some municipalities have zoned against certain grass types due to water usage.

Kentucky bluegrass ***(Poa pratensis)*** A valuable lawn grass that matures into a durable turf, Kentucky bluegrass spreads rapidly by creeping roots to fill in bare patches and is winter hardy. It is the best choice for sunny and fertile locations. It requires large quantities of water for optimum growth.

Creeping red fescue ***(Festuca rubra)*** This fescue is used extensively in shady areas where Kentucky bluegrass does not thrive. It does better than most grasses on poor, dry soils and is often mixed with Kentucky bluegrass to improve the durability of the lawn.

Roughstalk bluegrass *(Poa trivialis)* This species is well adapted to moist and shady locations but is not suitable for open, sunny places. It is sometimes added to creeping red rescue for moist and shady areas.

Redtop *(Agrostis alba)* Redtop has been popular in the past for its fast growth after seeding. But with the recent improvement in bluegrass and fescue cultivars and because of redtop's tendency to produce a coarse, open sod, it is currently recommended only for difficult sites where water is scarce.

Cultivars of these species of grasses have been propagated for their superior traits. In lawn grasses, cultivars have been developed for their abilities to remain green for most of the season and to thrive and produce a close turf under adverse conditions such as heavy foot traffic and close mowing, as well as for their winter hardiness and disease resistance. Cultivar names you are likely to encounter when you talk lawn grasses with your supplier include the Kentucky bluegrass cultivars 'Baron,' 'Nugget,' 'Sydsport,' 'Majestic,' and 'Park.' The once popular 'Merion' is no longer highly recommended. 'Dormie' is more resistant than most to snow mold.

Cultivars of creeping red fescue include 'Nova Rubra,' 'Durlawn,' and 'Pennlawn.' When choosing seed for your lawn, it is a good idea to include more than one cultivar of any given species in order to increase the lawn's tolerance of adverse conditions.

When you come to choosing which is the best grass seed mix for you, there are probably as many recommendations as there are horticultural advisors, and exact ratios may vary depending on where you live. But to keep it simple, I would suggest the following.

LAWN SEED MIXTURES		
Sunny Sites where lawns can be watered	**Shady sites where lawns can be watered**	**Sun or shade where water is scarce**
A mixture of 75% Kentucky bluegrass plus 25% creeping red fescue	A mixture of 60% creeping red fescue, 20% Kentucky bluegrass, and 20% roughstalk bluegrass	A mixture of 60% creeping red fescue 20% Kentucky bluegrass, and 20% redtop

Rates of seeding for different mixes of seed in different locations vary slightly. However, considering the time and money invested in establishing your new lawn, the cost of seed is relatively insignificant and there is little point in seeding any lighter than 5 pounds per 1,000 square feet. A reputable seed store should be able to give you assistance with the amount of seed you need for your particular size of lawn.

A TIME TO SOW

The best times to sow grass seed in our part of the world are late summer and early fall. Our spring season is short, and grass seed that germinates early in summer has to face high temperatures and dry, blustery winds. On the other hand, seed sown from mid-August to mid-September will often germinate quickly and start life in the relatively cool conditions in which it thrives.

If you have no choice but to seed your lawn in spring or early summer, pray for miserable weather or be prepared to spend more time on mulching and watering. Everything considered, spring and summer would be best devoted to preparing a good seed bed with time for it to settle and subsequent elimination of sprouting weeds.

All your efforts to this time have been in preparation for the moment of actually seeding the lawn, but before you begin, check off four things on your preparation list:

- Stir your grass seed mix to ensure that it is well blended.
- Remeasure the total lawn site to confirm the area.
- Weigh out the total amount of seed mix required.
- Divide the required seed approximately in half and plan to spread the entire area twice.

SOWING THE SEED

Choose a calm day for sowing the lawn, or the fine seed will drift beyond the boundary. Very small areas can be seeded by hand, but a mechanical applicator assures a more uniform result. A hopper on two wheels (commonly used for fertilizing) can usually be set for grass seed, and the wheel marks over the raked surface serve as a guide for good coverage without unnecessary overlapping. A broadcast seeder of the bag kind that hangs around the neck is excellent for lawn seeding, but straight edges are best applied by hand and with the hopper seeder. Whichever method of seeding is used, even coverage is best obtained by taking half the required seed and applying it in one direction, north-south if you like. Then repeat with the remainder of the seed at a right angle.

After all the seed is on, rake the area once in one direction to work some of the seed down just beneath the surface. The regular garden rake will do, or you can use the broader sweep rake normally used for leaves. Keep a light touch so as not to change the soil grade. Some lawn makers love to pull a roller over the area to firm the seed in, but I believe that you gain little by this operation and I do not recommend doing it.

MULCHING, YES OR NO?

On seeded slopes and on open areas where water is scarce, you might consider spreading a mulch of short and relatively weed-free straw or hay. This helps to prevent washing of the soil and slows evaporation of soil moisture. One 70-lb. bale will be enough to cover 1,000 square feet of lawn area one or two straws deep. Once the grass is well up, most of the straw should be raked off.

Peat moss and sawdust are not satisfactory for mulches on newly seeded lawns because they are too light and will most probably blow away. You can cover small seeded areas with burlap and cheesecloth to keep the soil moist, pegging the material down with short pieces of wire to hold it in place. This will encourage fast germination, and you will have to check daily after the first week and remove the material as soon as the seed starts to sprout.

In special circumstances, then, lawn mulches serve a useful purpose, but any lawn that is reasonably level is better off without a mulch.

AFTER-CARE FOR THE NEWLY SEEDED LAWN

It is of prime importance at this stage to keep the area uniformly moist and to keep people from tramping across the lawn site. A neat "Newly Seeded Lawn" sign would tell those who can read all that they need to know, but a more subtle and effective way is to surround the area with tiny wooden stakes linked by white string. Just make sure that no one is likely to become ensnared in the dark and hold you responsible.

Until the area is soaked, there will be no chance of germination, so you can hope for rain or you can resort to the watering hose and sprinkler. I would certainly recommend that you wait for rain rather than get into the sort of mess that I have seen from time to time with garden hoses being dragged across the seeded area and puddles that float the seeds and wash them down rivulets. Just as sad is the devastation caused by boots compacting the wet soil and collecting mud and seed as the gardener attempts to move a sprinkler to a new position. However, under prairie conditions there is often no choice but to irrigate. If you do have to add water, I suggest that you apply a small-droplet spray from the sidelines and keep the soil uniformly moist but not saturated.

If you have installed an underground irrigation system prior to seeding, be sure to use misting-type nozzles at this stage, as the normal heavy droplet type may cause some soil erosion before the grass appears. Talk to your irrigation equipment supplier about this and see if you can borrow or rent misting nozzles until the lawn is firm enough to take the regular sprinkler pattern. (For sodded lawns the regular nozzles are satisfactory from the start.)

It's hard to wait patiently for the first sight of green, but in two or three weeks (given a few gentle showers or attention with the sprinkler), the grass will be up and may be first sighted by looking across the area with your eye at ground level. If you find such a position difficult to achieve casually, just drop something and glance sideways as you pick it up.

As you wait for the thick green carpet of lawn that you so richly deserve, you might be disappointed to see instead the finest crop of annual and biennial weeds that you have ever seen. Stinkweed, shepherd's purse, pigweed, and the like always know a fertile seed bed when they see one, and move in without invitation. This invasion is not all bad. First, it proves that you have soil that will grow plants; if it won't grow weeds, the grass is not likely to fare any better. Then there is a benefit of the shade that weeds provide for the germinating grass. Successful grass germination depends upon moisture and temperature conditions being right, and there is nothing like the shade of broadleaf annual weeds to get the grass started. Once the grass is tall enough to be mowed, the weeds will be cut off and put out of action, and the grass will soon fill in.

There is a strong urge to make that first cut of a newly seeded lawn. In one dramatic move you can turn your ragged meadow into something that resembles a lawn—even if it does look a little thin in parts and stubbly with severed weeds. But please keep your mower tethered until the grass is 2 inches high in places, and then set the mower to cut the grass back to about 1 1/2 inches high. On dry, windy sites you should allow the grass to grow a little longer before cutting, then cut it back one-third and maintain the length at about 2 inches.

Choose a dull day for this first mowing, and make sure that the soil is dry and firm enough to support the mower without gouging ruts with the wheels when turning. Both rotary and reel-type mowers are suitable, but the blade must be especially sharp this first time over to avoid pulling and damaging the roots. If the mowing is light, the grass clippings can always be left on the lawn as a mulch, but once the clippings and weed tops start to bunch up and threaten to smother the grass, a bagging attachment should be used on the mower.

If perennial weeds such as dandelions, thistles, and creeping lawn grasses continue to thrive on your new lawn, it is a good idea to dig them out without delay before they spread, even if it results in some damaged patches that need reseeding.

SOD FOR INSTANT RESULTS

An alternative to sowing grass seed is to take squares or strips of rooted grass and lay them on a prepared soil surface, much as you would lay floor tiles. The uncut grass area is correctly called turf grass, and the pieces cut from the turf grass, sod.

There are those who claim that sodding is the most reliable means of obtaining a good lawn, while others dismiss the instant lawn as just another sign of our impatient times and denounce it as unnecessarily expensive. In truth, there is a place for both the seeded and the sodded lawn. While sodding does cost more, there are times when the convenience of a sod lawn is an attractive proposition.

A mud lawn may show promise, but there's nothing like a bright patch of green to banish the "under construction" look. Usually the rush to green is dictated by commercial considerations, and in some cases the additional cost of sodding is recompensed by accelerated property sales. Some municipal regulations state that new housing development lots be sodded within a stipulated period after first occupancy.

In the seed versus sod discussions, everyone seems to agree that sod is the answer when attempting to establish grass on a slope. Sodding saves the considerable trouble of trying to mulch a seeded slope and of contending with erosion and watering problems until it becomes established. However, grass on a slope greater than 1 in 16 is not a good idea because of the extra trouble in mowing, the problem of water running off instead of soaking in, and a consequent tendency of sloped lawns to suffer from drought.

Sod used for lawns should be nursery grown for that purpose. Deal only with an established nursery supplier, preferably one who specializes in lawn sod and grows the product locally. Suppliers should be able to tell you what mixture of seed is in their sod and provide a guarantee to that effect. They may also guarantee it to be free of perennial grass weeds like quack grass (*Agropyron repens*) and bromegrass (*Bromus species*).

The nursery sod should be of uniform thickness and not much more than 1/2 inch thick at the roots. It should hold together during lifting, transportation, and laying.

Be sure to avoid using sod cut from ordinary pasture, as it will contain coarse grasses that are not at all suitable for lawns.

A sod lawn does not

- Take the place of good soil and site preparation;
- Guarantee success in shade or in dry sites;
- Succeed any better than grass seeding if the soil is poorly drained or infertile.

Preparation of the lawn site is the same for sodding as for seeding, so there is no difference in cost for the initial stages. However, including the price of sod, delivery, and installation, and sodded lawn can cost up to twenty times as much as one grown from seed.

Laying Sod

The best time for laying sod is in early spring or at the end of summer, as the cooler weather favors fast root penetration to the soil layer beneath. Sod growers rightly point out, however, that it may be laid anytime that the soil isn't frozen. In the heat of summer, of course, you will have to water more often.

Time the ordering and arrival of your sod so you can lay it within a couple of days of delivery. This will reduce the risk of sod deterioration because of heat buildup (like a compost heap) or desiccation.

Laying sod is an alternative to seeding a lawn. Work from a straight edge or from the bottom of a slope up, laying the sod in a brick-wall pattern.

With the soil prepared—levelled as if for seeding and moist but not wet—start laying the squares or strips, commencing at the low end of the site and working up the slope. Another method of laying the sod is to start at the house or sidewalk to ensure one easy straight edge. Stagger the joints brick-wall pattern, and butt them close enough to be friendly without crowding or stretching them.

To avoid messing up the prepared soil area, place a broad board on the first strip of sod you lay, kneel on it, and move it forward over the sodded area as the job progresses. After the sod is laid, walk over your board to tamp down any high lumps, and if necessary lift the corners to build up a little soil underneath the sod.

SODDING	
Benefits	**Disadvantages**
Provides instant effect. Useful on slopes where seeded soil might wash out. Useful for back yards where dogs romp. Gives a good start in hot, dry weather. Longer season in which it can be done.	More expensive. More labor intensive to install. Choice of grass is limited and sometimes uncertain.
SEEDING	
Benefits	**Disadvantages**
Cheaper due to lower cost of seed and application methods. Any seed or mixture of seed can be sown. Seed is easily stored and transported.	Difficult to establish on slopes. A full season needed to establish a lawn. Adverse weather during germination can mean failure and a need for reseeding.

Then top-dress the whole area lightly with a little dry topsoil and work it into the cracks with a straw broom or the back of a garden rake. Finally, water the new lawn thoroughly to soak the topsoil beneath the sod and keep it moist for three or four weeks. By then, the roots should have become well established in the soil beneath.

Your own circumstances will dictate whether or not to start your lawn with sod or with seed, but to help you make up your mind, here are a few points worth consideration.

UPGRADING AN EXISTING LAWN

If your lawn has seen better days, or if you have inherited someone else's disaster, you might be tempted to churn it all up and start from scratch. First, however, evaluate the site to see if renovation might work instead. As long as the soil depth is 5 inches or more, you might well work wonders in one season of intensive special care. Consult the chapters on diseases, and weeds, and take note to deal with any such problem in season.

Sometimes lawns discolor in patches. The discoloration may be caused variously by insects, disease, moss, fertilizer spills, salt burn, or by construction damage. The root of the problem, so to speak, should be determined and corrected. For example, if moss appears, it may be killed by a chemical moss killer, but the moss is a sign of an acid soil, and the soil acidity should be corrected or the moss will soon return.

The discolored lawn areas can be repaired by spot treatments and prompt action should be taken to prevent further deterioration. A patch left bare is a temptation weeds just can't resist. If pet urine or chemical spills have caused the problem, it's a good idea to first flood the damaged site several times to leach away any toxic elements still in the soil. If you are going to reseed a patch, first rake the area vigorously to remove the dead grass and expose the soil. A sprinkling of fine soil or peat moss will improve the site; then reseed the patch as outlined for lawn seeding. If you are going to use sod, first cut a piece to the approximate shape and size of the damaged area using a sharp square-mouthed spade or halfmoon lawn cutter. Set the sod patch into place, leaving it just slightly higher than the surrounding grade, as the new piece may settle a little. Chink around the edge with soil and coarse sand to fill any gaps and water regularly for a couple of weeks to be sure the new sod becomes well rooted.

Reseeding in the early spring or late August is a good plan for tired old lawns. First cut the grass—in stages if necessary—as short as possible without scalping the soil. Then use a dethatching rake pushed and pulled firmly over the lawn to loosen the soil and remove the dead grass. Spread a thin layer (1 inch) of good soil mix over the area and reseed as described earlier. By following regular fertilizing, watering, and mowing practices, the lawn may well surprise you with a rapid recovery.

LAWN MAINTENANCE

Whatever kind of lawn you have installed or inherited, it will require some care and attention on a regular basis to ensure that it always looks its best. To sum up the maintenance procedures for an average home lawn, apply four light applications of fertilizer each season, one early each month from May through August. If the fertilizer is 16-20-0, then each application should be about 5 pounds per 1,000 square feet. See the table on page 15 to determine the rate for different fertilizer analyses. We are warned not to extend the fertilizing of a lawn past mid-August for fear of producing soft growth that will not be hardy enough to endure our prairie winter. It appears more likely, however, that a healthy lawn with adequate fertilizer and water will go into winter in better shape than one that is starved into dormancy.

Methods of fertilizer application are covered on pages 15–18. Remember, fertilizer should be applied to dry grass and watered in without delay to avoid the burn associated with wet grass coming into contact with strong chemicals.

Dethatching the lawn is an annual springtime ritual performed on many home lawns, but do you really need to dethatch every year? If you remove grass clippings every time you mow, the thatch should not have to be raked and removed that often. Just use a rake (or a stiff-bristle broom) to raise the nap if the grass is compressed after a winter of snow and ice, allowing fresh air and sunshine to fight lawn diseases. Excess thatch does serve as a breeding zone for pests and disease and also tends to reduce water penetration to the grass roots; however, clippings from a light mowing left on the lawn will not significantly contribute to thatch buildup and will help conserve moisture and eventually return some nutrients to the soil.

Regular mowing at 2 to 2 1/2 inches is recommended for our region—the higher cut for dry, windy sites. If the lawn grows to twice its "after-cut" length while your back is turned, raise the cutting height of the mower the first time over to avoid stress to the grass, and let the grass recover for a few days before cutting again.

If there is one factor more than any other that determines the success of a lawn, it must be water. For any number of reasons it may not be practical for you to water every time the soil starts to dry out, but if it can be done without contravening a local bylaw or upsetting your budget, always provide a good soak before the lawn shows stress. Occasional deep watering is far better than frequent light sprinkling, as shallow watering encourages shallow and vulnerable root systems.

CHAPTER V

Plant Selection and Purchasing

What should I grow and where should I get it? Suggestions for choosing plants appear in several others chapters (conifers, herbaceous perennials, bulbs), but it might help for me to bring the main points together here. What you should grow depends on which plants are likely to be happy in your local climate—usually referred to as "hardiness." There is little point in discussing plants that you cannot obtain, so an equally important factor is availability. No selection or purchase is complete without a consideration of quality. Interwoven with this trio is the question of plant names—common and botanical. Let's start with plant names.

PLANT NAMES

"Are they trying to baffle me with science? Who needs those long Latin plant names anyway? They just use them to stretch out a short list of hardy plants." I can sympathize with the new gardener who makes such comments, and if you are truly reluctant to tackle those long (or short) botanical names, then they are best left alone. Otherwise, before rejecting them, give them a chance to work for you. They don't have to be memorized, and they can work to your advantage. For example, if you have an order to discuss or a particular plant with your supplier using the common name only, there's a real chance of the two of you talking at cross purposes with entirely different plants in mind. Common names can, and often do, refer to more than one kind of plant.

If you want to be precise in your plant order or your discussion of the plant, write down the full botanical name as well as the common name if it has one. And if you have to pronounce the botanical name—say during a telephone conversation—just enunciate the tongue-twister in clear, short syllables, and you will be understood by any competent horticulturist. You will, incidentally, gain his immediate attention and respect.

Remember, there is no one right or wrong way to pronounce botanical names, any more than there is a correct way to say clematis (CLEM-a-tis, clem-AY-tis or clem-AH-tis). Some pronunciations are more frequent in some parts of the world than in others, but as long as they are clearly spoken, they are internationally acceptable and understood.

You will find that botanical names are essential when dealing with lesser known plants—especially among herbaceous plants.

The first word of a botanical name is the generic name, the *genus*, followed by one specific name, the *species*. A wild plant, or group of plants, that varies in some small but significant way from the originally documented plant has an additional name tagged on. This difference is nearly always added to the genus and species in the form of a *variety* name. To take one example, all roses are of the genus *Rosa*. The pink-flowering Japanese rose in particular is known world-wide by its botanical name, *Rosa rugosa* (genus and species). The occasional white-flowered form of this Japanese rose becomes *Rosa rugosa alba*.

As gardeners we are naturally interested in varieties because they increase plant diversity in the garden. We really sit up and take notice when a plant is selected for an exceptional attribute—something that makes a particular plant stand out above all others of its kind. This something special may be its size or shape, length of blooming season, disease resistance, drought tolerance, or anything else that makes a plant special in the garden. Some such plants are found in the wild and brought under cultivation, but nowadays most are the result of long and detailed programs of plant breeding designed to achieve a predetermined goal. This objective can be anything, from a winter hardy pear or edible-pod peas to a new flower color in a familiar ornamental shrub.

In our example of the white-flowered Japanese rose, a good selection is now sold as *Rosa rugosa* 'Alba.' (Note that the variety *alba* has been replaced by the cultivar form 'Alba.') In this older selection the Latin word has been retained, but all more recent cultivars have fancy names that cannot be confused with other elements of the botanical name; typically, *Rosa* 'Prairie Dawn' and *Rosa* 'Cuthbert Grant.' Notice that the species name has been dropped from the last two examples, which makes good sense when a cultivar has been derived from more than one species.

These special plants are sometimes grown and observed for years before being named and released. Occasionally, they become widely accepted under a trial number (as with the apple 'Heyer #12'). Normally, however, a distinctive name is selected and, ideally, registered. This avoids a name being used for more than one cultivated selection within a genus. These cultivated varieties are known as "cultivars," an important concept in today's gardening world.

In order that all perennial plants of a given cultivar are identical to the original superior plant, cultivars often have to be grown from cuttings or propagated by grafting. Perennial plants grown from seed do not always have exactly the same traits as the parent plant. For this reason, cultivars come with a higher price tag than those plants without a cultivar name, which can be grown in quantity from seed. The extra cost of a cultivar may be worthwhile if, for example, you need a tree that will not outgrow its location in twenty years or so, or if you want to be sure of the foliage color and ultimate shape.

Availability of cultivars varies to some extent from year to year depending on a number of factors, including consumer demand, the foresight of nurserymen in anticipating that demand, and the degree of success achieved by propagators. Your local commercial grower will be a good source of current information, and the mail-order catalogs provide word on new releases.

Virtually all the vegetables and annual flowers grown from seed in the home garden are the result of careful breeding and selection. Vegetables, in particular, have been developed to meet a wide variety of needs. Some of the qualities to be found in different tomato cultivars, for example, include those with fruit very small (such as the 'Sweet 100 Hybrid') and very large (such as the 'Beefeater' selections with fruit weighing over 2 pounds each). Disease resistance has been achieved with some tomato cultivars; fruit set at low temperatures and fast maturity are important in short-season climates; meaty and juicy kinds are available; and some have yellow or pink skins.

Other vegetables, and many flowers, also come in a wide range of cultivar forms "designed" for different purposes. Take time to examine at least one good seed catalog in order to fully appreciate the difference. There is no need to limit the potential of your garden to whatever happens to be available on the supermarket seed stand.

Most home gardens of today are superior to those of our plains pioneers. This is due in part to new skills, improved chemicals, and sophisticated equipment. To a large extent the improvement comes from the steady advance of plant development and selection of the past few decades. Watch for new cultivars. They give you the edge in creating a better home garden.

HARDINESS

The term hardiness relates to such details as the adaptability of the species to the local soil, humidity, precipitation, length of the growing and dormant seasons—as well as summer and winter temperature extremes. The most elementary zone maps are based only on extremes of temperature, while more sophisticated ones take into consideration those other factors—like rain- and snowfall and the length of the growing season—that have a bearing on plant survival.

Chinooks, warm fronts that move in from the Rockies and raise winter temperatures many degrees for several days before receding, can be devastating to your landscape. Each time a chinook passes through, some of the natural winter dormancy of your plants is lost. Even if premature growth is not evident to you, severe winter-kill may become evident the following spring.

Whatever system is being used, plant hardiness zone maps can only serve as a rough guide to what might or might not be satisfactory in your own garden. Whether you live within or outside the shelter of a town or large city makes a difference in the suitability of a borderline hardy tree or shrub. And even within your own garden there are at least two micro-climates—sun and shade. There may also be a wet soil habitat and a dry one. Selecting the most suitable site within the garden obviously has some bearing on whether or not the plant is "hardy" enough for you.

When it comes to the winter survival of plants, most observations are directed towards trees and shrubs because their above-ground parts have to face whatever nature throws at them. Herbaceous perennials are not affected in this way because the tops naturally die down for the winter, and it is only the more protected crown and root sections that must survive to renew full growth the following year. Therefore, a wide selection of herbaceous perennials can be grown on the plains. Likewise, most annual plants can be grown in our area. We just avoid annuals (including vegetables) needing a long season in which to perform—or most likely we cheat by planting those that have been started early in a greenhouse or other controlled environment. For these reasons, only the trees and shrubs discussed in this book have been graded for hardiness. You will find that most herbaceous perennials and annuals grown and sold on the plains will survive and thrive as long as they are provided with their preferred cultural conditions of soil, light, and moisture.

While a harsh climate, therefore, might be considered slightly restricting when selecting herbaceous perennials, and something of an inconvenience when growing annuals, it is in the area of trees and shrubs that a new prairie gardener faces the shocking reality that our winters are too long, too cold, and too unpredictable to allow us to grow the woody fruits and ornamentals that thrive in less severe climates. However, there are compensations. Many gardeners in milder climates would cheerfully sacrifice their magnolia for a Colorado blue spruce, if only the conifer would thrive without its cold dormant season. Once we stop "reaching for the magnolia" and take a close look at what will do very nicely in our area, the picture is much more encouraging.

Beginning gardeners should start with woody plants that have been proven hardy enough for their own location. In addition to consulting the hardiness ratings in this book, take note of what is already growing well in your vicinity and inquire as to which plants the local commercial growers are willing to guarantee for a full year. When you have discovered what will and will not grow in your own climatic region and you have made a start with reliably hardy plants, then you may want to experiment with less hardy subjects such as hybrid tea roses. Such exotics can be grown successfully by providing special care and protection. The chapter on trees and shrubs will give you more information on the relative hardiness of a wide range of woody plants.

AVAILABILITY

Some readers will remember the extensive plant lists printed by nurserymen several decades ago and their offers of unusual as well as common plants. The percentage of avid hobby gardeners willing to pay for rare plants seems not to have increased in recent times, and as the old plantsmen who founded the nurseries give way to their more businesslike successors, the trend is to a limited selection of strictly profitable items.

We may never again see local nurseries carrying, for example, twenty or more different named cultivars of peonies, but there are still some nurseries that specialize, using catalogues and a mail-order service. Such outlets are useful for hobby gardeners who look for a greater variety of, say, lilies, daylilies, irises, fruits, roses, lilacs, or shrubby potentillas than are available locally. Before ordering, send for a current catalog and check their terms of sale and payment, shipping charges, and quantity discounts.

These companies are not to be confused with the other kind of mail-order merchandisers that offers "miraculous" plants or quantities of plants at "amazingly low" prices. These are no bargain, and if a plant offer appears to be too good to be true, it almost certainly is.

For most of us the local nurseryman or garden center is the best place to start looking for needed plants. The advice of a well-established tradesman with practical experience in your area is a great asset. If he doesn't have the plants that you want, discuss the possibility of his ordering them for you from a wholesale supplier.

One of the most obvious sources of plants for your garden is the horticulture section of a department store. A few of these stores may supply good quality and selection but (in my experience) not many. Purchases for large department stores are often made by buyers who have no special knowledge of the horticultural industry, and they buy in bulk for a number of stores in different plant hardiness zones. The sales staff may be on temporary loan from the hardware department, and it is sad but true that much of the advice gratuitously given at these sales outlets is misleading.

QUALITY

With a little practice anyone can recognize quality in dormant plants. First observe the sales or storage environment. Bare-root trees and shrubs should always be in a cool and shady place, the roots covered by a moist medium like wood chips or peat moss. (The pessimist will be aware that this is no guarantee that the roots have not been dried out in transit.) The ends of young twigs should be supple, and a thumb-nail surreptitiously dug into the twig near the tip should reveal a fresh green sap layer just beneath the bark. Buds should be dormant, not sprouting shoots or leaves.

The most suitable size of tree or shrub varies with the kind being purchased, but as a general rule you should avoid the very smallest sizes because they may take several seasons before they make satisfactory growth. The largest sizes should also be avoided (unless moved by tree spade) because the limited root size in relation to the top means that they take longer to become established.

The roots of evergreen conifers must be growing in a moist soil ball (burlap or container). Look the needles over for signs of yellowing, browning, or shedding that tell a tale of stress, and check for fine cobwebbing that reveals spider mite activity.

If possible, you should buy your herbaceous perennials as plants growing in soil. Again, they are best stored for sale in a cool, shady area rather than the hot, dry environment of a typical retail display area.

If they are only available packaged in a carton or plastic bag, reject any that have long pale sprouts and make sure that the roots are moist. Be suspicious of the condition of plants sealed in airtight plastic bags, as the lack of air circulation soon leads to overheating and decay.

Plant selection, be it vegetable, fruit or ornamental, is the gardening activity that most reflects our individuality and is therefore well worth some time and contemplation.

CHAPTER VI

Trees and Shrubs

This chapter will focus on deciduous (leaf-losing) trees and shrubs. Starting with advice on planting and transplanting, it will then examine the mystery of survivability ("hardiness") and move on to a commentary on deciduous trees and shrubs as a guide to selecting those most suited to your garden. The chapter ends with special notes on tender roses, climbing plants, and hedges.

All the suitable trees discussed are found in one section, followed by a separate section on shrubs. Because this arrangement arbitrarily places a woody plant in the tree or the shrub category, the first step is a simple differentiation between the two. A tree may be defined a woody plant with a single trunk and a mature height of at least 8 feet. Shrubs have more than one trunk and are generally, but not always, smaller.

Although the woody plants are grouped this way for ease of reference, remember that some plants defy precise categorization. There are some, such as clump birch, with more than one trunk, but they are trees nevertheless. And there are some shrubby specimens, like hawthorn and elder, that can be turned from a shrub into a tree by pruning to a single trunk.

Trees and shrubs form the basic landscaping framework for the high plains garden. They provide screens, shade, and color interest. When choosing trees and shrubs for your garden, take into consideration the size and shape of the mature plant and the variety of blossoms, foliage, and bark colors available. Foliage with colors other than green can be a real asset in the landscape. Golden-yellow, silver-grey, and red-purple are all attractive in moderation but should not dominate the green. The only color forms that fail are the pale yellow- and partly yellow-foliaged plants that may give the impression of nutrient deficiency. (This is especially noticeable with yellow-tipped evergreen foliage found on some selections of juniper.) Trees with attractive bark can provide color interest in your garden long after the leaves have fallen in the autumn.

DEBITS AND CREDITS

Think carefully about what you want from a tree or shrub. For example, if you experience the benefit of vigorous growth soon after planting, chances are that the tree or shrub won't know when to stop growing and may overwhelm both home and garden. Trees such as flowering crabapples offer the advantage of glorious springtime blossoms, but the tree must still contribute to the landscape during the remaining fifty weeks of the year. Showy fruit, such as that produced by the mountain-ash, may be a strong point in favor of growing the tree, especially if you like to attract waxwings and other birds during the winter. On the other hand, fruit or seed of any kind eventually sheds onto lawns and sidewalks. Thus, a notation such as "bird attraction" would appear in one person's credit column, but in the debit column of someone who considers birds noisy and messy. Bear in mind too that some trees are more susceptible to disease than others. Apple trees often suffer from fireblight, birch trees from leaf miners, and cotoneaster from pear slugs. Be prepared to deal with these conditions if necessary.

PLANTING AND TRANSPLANTING

Planting Options

Spring is the ideal time to plant deciduous trees and shrubs. Because the time between the soil thawing to a workable condition and the start of leafing out is so short, most nurserymen have to dig their deciduous plants in late autumn and store them over winter in order to have them available for spring planting. Bare-root stock should be planted while the plants are still

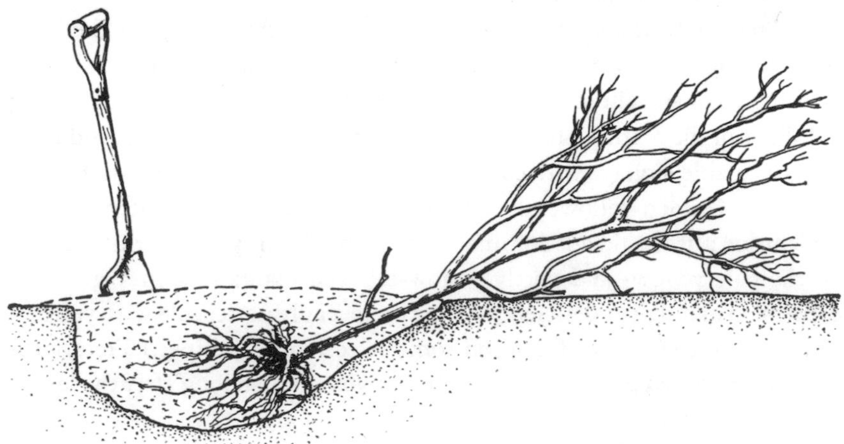

Heeling in can minimize moisture loss in bare-root trees and shrubs waiting to be planted. Dig a hole in a sheltered place, set the tree or shrub at a steep angle, loosely covering the roots and part of the stem with soil. Water well.

dormant, so when you go to buy bareroot stock of woody plants, avoid those coming into leaf. Check for peeling or otherwise damaged bark. The wood beneath the bark should be supple, not brittle. Bare roots dry out very easily, so they should be covered by a moist medium while the plants are on display—we have to hope they have not been left to dry out earlier.

Container-grown plants may be planted at any time during the growing season as long as you take care not to break up the soil ball. Look for plants that are growing with their roots firmly in the soil. Some suppliers cheat by potting up unsold bare-root stock at the end of the spring sales season, and the plants then suffer from having been planted while in leaf.

Ideally, you should try to retain a good covering of soil to protect the delicate root system, but this is not always possible when moving heavy and bulky plants. If soil falls away from the roots, get the tree to its new home as quickly as possible. A root covering of moist burlap will help to retain moisture. Deciduous trees and shrubs can also be transplanted in the fall, as soon as the foliage withers but several weeks before the soil freezes down through the root zone.

Planting Procedures

If you have purchased bare-root stock from a nursery or garden center, it's always a good idea to soak the roots for a few hours (or overnight) in water as soon as you get the plants home. You should be able to take the smaller plants straight from the pail of water to the planting hole.

Remember that bare roots must never be exposed to sun or wind; at hot or windy sites, the fine hairlike roots, composed of delicate moisture-absorbing plant cells, can dry up and become useless in less than a minute. New root hairs may grow, but often too late to save the first flush of budding shoots, and these too die off.

If you have bare-root woody plants on hand before the site is ready, find a sheltered and shady spot and heel them in so the roots and part of the stem are covered. By setting them at a very steep angle—approaching the horizontal—less of the stem is exposed to drying winds and the root is not smothered. Don't forget to water the root area after heeling it in. If you have plants that have not been heeled in, waiting around to go into a hole, keep the bare roots covered with a wet material such as burlap until they are planted and covered with soil.

Dig the final planting hole deep and wide enough to take all the roots of the bare-root stock when spread out. The hole for container-grown plants should be large enough to take the soil ball. The general rule is to plant at the original nursery depth or just an inch lower so a water-holding saucerlike depression is left over the root area once the plant is firmed in. Plants with a swelling or "joint" on the stem a short distance up from the root should normally be planted with this graft union just beneath the soil surface, but not if this would bury the root deep in the anaerobic zone.

The roots of newly planted trees will benefit from both water and a fertilizer high in phosphorus. If the subsoil is very dry, fill the hole with water the day before planting the tree and let it drain away; soil that is too wet cannot be firmed around the newly planted tree. A handful or two of fertilizer may be mixed into the soil that you are going to use to fill the hole, but newly planted specimens are not hungry. I prefer to give a light top dressing of fertilizer the following spring.

The roots of bare-root stock should be spread out in the hole. Container-grown plants present somewhat of a dilemma if they are to be planted when in full leaf. As the plant is actively growing, the root ball should be left

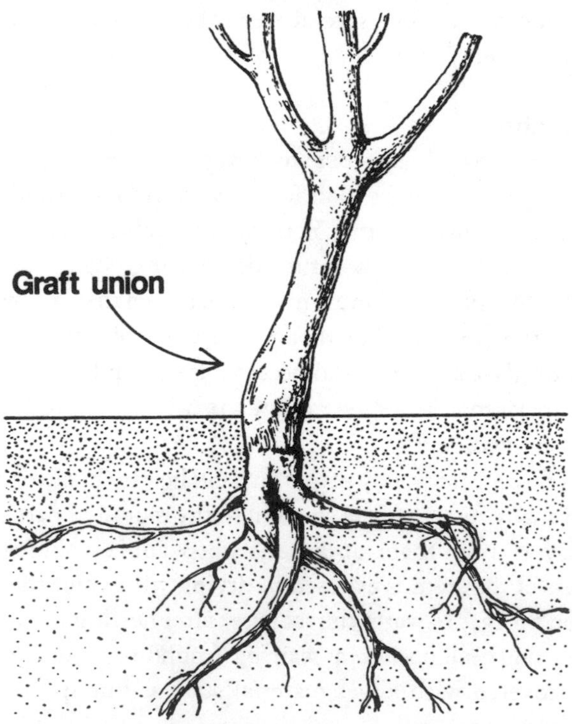

The tree or shrub should be planted at the same depth as it was growing originally, and never any deeper. Thus, while the graft union should preferably be planted just beneath the soil surface, it may have to be set higher, as illustrated.

undisturbed. However, the roots of container-grown stock often grow round in circles in the pot and this condition must be corrected if the plant is to develop a healthy root system later. Remove container-grown stock from the pot and try to gently pry one or two roots out of the soil ball so they can grow out into the surrounding soil. If it is not possible to do this without disturbing the remainder of the root ball, it is better to cut the roots in one or two places with pruning shears. This will encourage the development of new, lateral roots.

Once the plant is in the hole, fill the hole with soil, tamping it down firmly as you go, until you have a saucerlike depression around the stem of the tree. Then water thoroughly to settle the soil. You should water your newly planted tree well for the first few weeks of life in its new quarters, but be sure to let the soil dry out a little between waterings to give the roots a chance to breathe—overwatering can be fatal.

After planting, prune back the plant a little so that the recently disturbed root system does not have to work so hard to nourish the above-

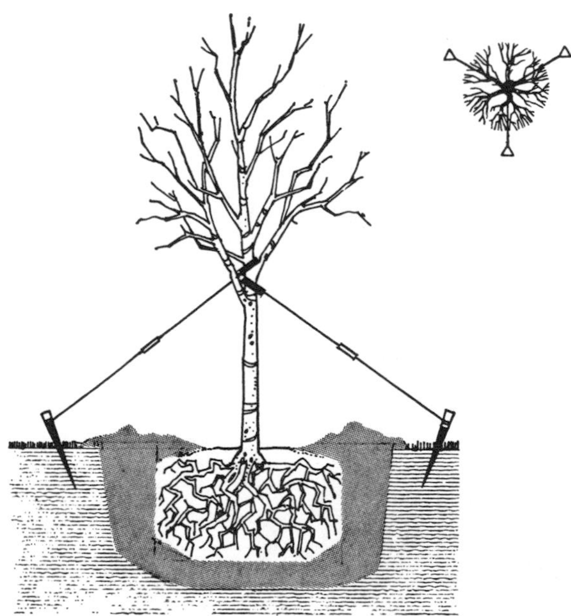

The planting hole for bare-root stock should be large enough for the roots to be spread out. Fill the hole with good topsoil and tread it down firmly, leaving a saucerlike depression around the trunk of the tree to hold water. If you do have to stake newly planted trees, use three ties spaced equidistantly around the tree and cover them with soft rubber tubing or some other material so they don't cut into the bark.

ground parts of the tree. At very windy sites you might have to use a stake or guy ropes to prevent your tree from flying away, but tie only if absolutely necessary. There is some evidence that tied trees fail to develop strong anchor roots and are more subject to windthrow later on. If you have to tie newly planted trees, see that the ties don't rub or bind, and remove them by the end of the first season.

SURVIVABILITY

The limitations of zonation maps have been discussed in chapter five on plant selection. The hardiness ratings used for trees and shrubs in this book sidestep the zonation numbering system and refer instead to a plant hardiness index.

Depending upon their relative "survivability," plants have been indexed to one of the four hardiness groups: A, B, C, or D. The A type are generally considered hardier than plants in the B list; B plants hardier than C, and so on. The division into groups and the use of letters instead of numbers (avoiding confusion with the hardiness zone maps) are my own responsibility. The hardiness ratings have been adapted from zone maps.

Reference Lists for the Plant Hardiness Index

Hardiness A

Betula papyrifera (paper birch)
Caragana arborescens (common caragana)
Lonicera tatarica (Tartarian honeysuckle)
Malus baccata (Siberian crabapple)
Picea pungens (Colorado spruce)
Pinus mugo mugo (mugho pine)
Syringa vulgaria (common or French lilac)
Ulmus americana (American elm)

Hardiness B

Acer negundo (Manitoba maple)
Betula pendula (weeping birch)
Hippophae rhamnoides (common sea-buckthorn)
Juniperus sabina (savin juniper)
Prunus maacki (Amur cherry)
Sambucus racemosa (redberried elder)
Thuja occidentalis (white-cedar or arborvitae)
Tilia cordata (little-leaf linden)

Hardiness C
Acer ginnala (Amur maple)
Elaeagnus augustifolia (Russian olive)
Juniperus chinensis (Chinese juniper)
Pinus cembra (Swiss stone pine)
Populus alba (white poplar)
Prunus cistena (purple-leaf plum)
Rosa 'Blanc Double de Coubert' (shrub rose cultivar)
Viburnum lantana (wayfaring tree)

Hardiness D
Abies concolor (silver fir)
Acer saccharum (sugar maple)
Euonymus alata (winged burning bush)
Hydrangea paniculata grandiflora (pee gee hydrangea)
Populus nigra 'Italica' (lombardy poplar)
Salix alba 'Tritis' (white weeping willow)
Spiraea x vanhouttei (Vanhouttei spirea)
Tamarix ramosissima (tamarisk)

How to Use the Hardiness Index

First look at the names of plants listed under each of the hardiness ratings A, B, C, and D. Those listed under Hardiness A will grow satisfactorily anywhere in the plains region, including your immediate area, and you can assume that any others marked "A" in this book will be of similar hardiness.

Next, take a look at those listed under Hardiness B. If these also grow in your location, you can safely expand your list of possibilities to include not only the A hardiness plants, but also any others included in this book with a B rating. If hardiness B plants are satisfactory in your area, check the C list. By the time you reach the Hardiness D list, you may recognize (unless your garden is in a very favorable district of the plains) that trees and shrubs in this category are of borderline hardiness, worth trying only once the more reliable kinds have been established.

When checking these four lists to determine which group most closely represents the limit of plant hardiness in your own community, view the list as an entire group, rather than making a decision based on one or two plant names. Although there will always be cases where occasional tender or borderline hardy plants will become well established in defiance of any attempt to categorize them, these pleasant surprises should not be allowed to sway your judgment of what is reliably hardy in your own vicinity—at least not until you have established a sound basis of plants for your landscape. Once you have your reliable plants established, you can certainly try something a little different in a favored microclimate.

An alternative means of selecting the hardiness grade for your area is to check the main lists in this book for trees and shrubs that you do know are satisfactory in your own or neighbors' gardens and municipal parks. Note the hardiness ratings given for those plants, and others of the same hardiness ratings should suit your garden just as well.

If you are uncertain of the names of plants growing in your vicinity, check with your local cooperative extension agent, university horticulture department, or experienced garden center staff. They will recognize which hardiness groups are satisfactory for your area.

DIFFICULT SITES

Where the soil is in reasonably good condition and the site is not crowded by buildings or other trees, the selection of suitable woody plants is a matter of hardiness and personal choice. There are some parts of most gardens, however, that have less than ideal growing conditions—perhaps too wet, too dry, or too shady. Here are some suggestions for trees and shrubs that will tolerate such adversity better than most.

Trees and shrubs for dry locations

Acer ginnala (Amur maple)
Acer negundo (Manitoba maple)
Amelanchier alnifolia (saskatoon)
Caragana (caragana)
Elaeagnus augustifolia (Russian olive)
Fraxinus pennsylvanicaa subintegerrima (green ash)
Hippophae rhamnoides (common sea-buckthorn)
Juniperus (junipers)
Prunus besseyi (western sandcherry)
Shepherdia argentea (silver buffalo-berry)
Ulmus pumila (Manchurian elm)

Trees and shrubs for moist and wet* locations

Alnus (alder)*
Betula (birch)
Cornus sericea (red osier dogwood)

Fraxinus nigra (black ash)
Larix laricina (tamarack)
Populus (poplar)
Salix (willow)*
Thuja occidentalis (white-cedar)
Tilia (linden)
Viburnum (cranberry)

Shrubs for shady locations
Amelanchier alnifolia (saskatoon, service berry)
Cornus (dogwood)
Lonicera tatarica (Tartarian honeysuckle)
Paxistima canbyi (pachistima)
Ribes alpinum (alpine currant)
Sorbaria sorbifolia (Ural false spirea)
Viburnum (cranberry)
Viburnum lantana (wayfaring tree)

DECIDUOUS TREES

Apart from choosing trees that will do well in the general area where you live or those that are adapted to any particularly difficult sites within your garden, you will want to have some idea of the size those innocent saplings may reach when they mature. Many factors affect the final dimensions of trees, including climate, soil types, and available space. To give the novice some guidance, however, I have distinguished between small trees (those that normally grow no taller than 30 feet) and tall trees (those which can be expected to exceed this height).

Maples—In the Debits and Credits sections of this chapter, I mentioned that some trees have bad habits. Heading the tree list for this reason, as well as for its alphabetical position, is *Acer negundo*, the tall-growing box elder (B). Once planted in great number as a fast-growing shelterbelt tree and landscape specimen, the box elder has lost favor because of its uneven growth, weak wood, and susceptibility to aphids.

The most delightful of maples suited to our region is *Acer ginnala*, the Amur maple (C), particularly valued for its beautiful autumn foliage colors. Although it may be pruned to a small single stem tree, it is usually seen as a large shrub. The more traditional tree-growing maples of U.S., such as *Acer saccharum*, the sugar maple, and *Acer saccharinum*, the silver maple (both D), are not well suited to plains gardens because of their borderline hardiness.

Alder—The native species *Alnus* or alder (A/B) are largely overlooked by the nursery trade and home gardeners but are useful for planting in wet organic soils. They can be grown as either small trees or large shrubs and have interesting drooping catkins in spring.

Birch—*Betula papyifera* or paper birch (A) is a tall, shallow-rooting native tree valued for its white bark. It is available in both single-stem or clump form. *Betula pendula*, the white or silver birch (B), is another tall, white-barked birch. This one, native to Europe and Asia Minor, provides the popular cut-leaf weeping cultivar 'Gracilis' with its lacelike foliage on fine, drooping branchlets. All birch trees are currently falling out of favor because of repeated infestations by leaf miner and bronzed borer insects. They also need frequent watering in times of drought.

Hawthorns—Many *Crataegus* or hawthorns (A and B) tend to form shrubs, but they can easily be pruned early in life to create a very small single-stem tree of character. The one most likely to be found as a small tree is *Crataegus x mordenensis* 'Snowbird' (C), with white flowers in spring and dark green glossy foliage. A similar cultivar 'Toba' (D) has less vitality.

Russian olive—Grown mainly for its narrow silver foliage, *Elaeagnus angustifolia*, the Russian olive (C), is useful for its distinctive foliage color and fine texture. It may be grown as either a small tree or a large shrub, and it doesn't sucker like its shrubby native cousin *Elaeagnus commutata*, the wolf willow. It does drop a considerable amount of seed and so it should be planted away from patios and decks.

Ash—Ash trees are some of the most important ornamental and shade trees suited to our region. They are more uniform in growth than most trees and subject to few pests and diseases. Ash trees tend to leaf out late and defoliate early, allowing precious sunlight through to the garden and home in spring and fall, yet providing shade during the heat of summer. They do best where water is in good supply.

The most commonly planted ash is *Fraxinus pennsylvanica subintegerrima*, the tall-growing green ash (B), as well as its cultivar 'Patmore,' a seedless kind with shiny olive-green leaves. Similar but slower growing is *Fraxinus nigra*, the black ash, with its recent cultivar 'Fall Gold,' which tends to hold its yellow foliage a little longer at the end of the season. A smaller species of ash is *Fraxinus mandshurica*, the Manchurian ash (C). This slow-growing tree produces a compact, round-headed appearance, and because it is earlier leafing, the new foliage is easily damaged by late spring frosts. A hardy and seedless selection of Manchurian ash called 'Mancana' is another newly tested cultivar. Remember, the ash trees with their "paddle" seeds (samaras) are not to be confused with *Sorbus*, the mountain-ash, a quite different genus with clusters of attractive red "berries" (pomes).

Larch—The larch trees (or tamarack, as our native species is called) are actually conifers. They do bear cones and have needlelike foliage, but because they shed their needles each fall, they are included here with the deciduous trees. This shedding of needles has sometimes led the uninitiated to believe them to be dead spruce in winter, but the trees make up for this cruel deception with an abundance of soft green needles when spring arrives.

The native *Larix laricina* or tamarack (A) is vigorous when young and well suited to poor soils and poorly drained sites. It does not attain the very large size of *Larix decidua*, the European larch, or *Larix sibirica*, the Siberian larch (both A/B), which become much too large for the average home garden.

Flowering crabapple—Very popular among small ornamental trees are the flowering crabapples (A through C). They are valued for their early spring flowers, ornamental fruit, and in some cases their purplish foliage. The grandpa of the group is the white-flowered *Malus baccata,* Siberian crabapple. Its tiny fruit are fit only for the birds, yet it is one of the parents of our hardier crabapples. More ornamental are certain hybrids of the Siberian crab, *Malux x adstringens*. Collectively these hybrids are referred to as the rosybloom flowering crabapples, or simply the rosybloom crabs, and are noted for their wealth of pink blossoms that cover the trees in spring.

Some of the more commonly grown rosybloom cultivars are these: 'Almey' has purplish red leaves that turn green with a bronze cast and red flowers with a white marking at the base of each petal. The tree has a spreading habit and some susceptibility to fireblight. 'Makamik' is similar to 'Almey' but more upright. 'Hopa,' the original pink flowered selection, introduced by Dr. N.E. Hansen of Brookings, South Dakota, in 1920, is sometimes listed as "Hoppi" or "Pink Sunburst." It also shows white in the center of each pink flower. The fruit is rich in pectin, so it has some use in jelly making. 'Royalty' is widely grown but seems to become susceptible to fireblight about seven years after planting. Its pink flowers do not show up well against the dark leaves. 'Thunderchild' is similar to 'Royalty' except that it is fireblight resistant and the dark foliage doesn't intensify until after the pink flowers, affording better contrast. 'Selkirk' (B) and 'Strathmore' (C) are two other popular rosyblooms.

Most of the white-flowered cultivars of flowering crabapple, such as 'Kerr,' are also grown for their fruit, which may be used for canning. The selection 'Columnaris' (sometimes listed as "Pyramidalis") is narrow and upright in habit but susceptible to fireblight. The tiny yellow fruit is ornamental but not edible.

Poplars—Poplars vary in their foliage, growth habits, and hardiness, but all are tall growing. Some, like *Populus x petrowskyana*, the Russian poplar (A), are female and produce annoying cotton fluff in June. The male selection of this same hybrid, *Populus x berolinensis*, the Berlin poplar (A), has the same advantages of hardiness and vigor, yet does not produce the cotton.

Populus 'Northwest,' the Northwest poplar (A), is a commonly planted tree, satisfactory but becoming too large for the average city lot. Many gardeners look for a lombardy poplar type, tall and narrow growing. While the lombardy is not hardy enough for the plains, there are a few substitutes. One of the best of these is *Populus tremula* 'Erecta,' the Swedish columnar poplar (A). 'Tower' (B) is a narrow hybrid that may replace the older 'Griffin,' which is more susceptible to canker disease. *Populus alba* 'Pyramidalis,' the boleana poplar (C), is fairly upright in habit and has unique foliage with maplelike leaves, dark green on the upper surface and white beneath. The *Populus tremuloides*, or Aspen, is a popular tree for the home landscape but tends to send up sucker sprouts from the roots into cultivated soil.

The cherry group—One of the first trees to leaf out and to show elongated clusters of white flowers in spring is *Prunus padus* 'Commutata,' the mayday (A). Its black cherries are inedible and messy when they drop. The true mayday is tall growing and does not sucker at the roots, but many specimens so named are hybridized with the chokecherry and do spread by underground shoots.

More choice and more widely planted is *Prunus virginiana* 'Shubert,' the Shubert chokecherry (A), with deep purple foliage. The new leaves of these small trees are often green, and they contrast in an interesting way with the mature dark leaves. Both the mayday and the Shubert chokecherry are drought resistant once established.

A close relative is *Prunus maackii,* the Amur cherry (B). Again, the flowers are white, and the fruit black and inedible. But this small tree is

 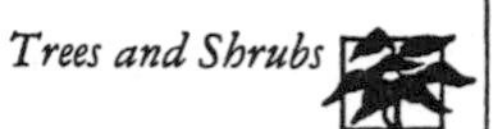

valued for its copper-brown bark, which is exceptionally attractive in the winter landscape.

Oak—*Quercus macrocarpa*, the tall-growing bur oak (A), is the most reliable oak for our region. Because of their deep tap-root, oaks will survive drought quite well. It is this taproot that makes the transplanting of established oaks more difficult than most other deciduous trees.

Willows—All our cultivated willows are tall growing and do best in a moist location, but a willow with a thirst adequately quenched will need more space to grow than most gardeners can spare. Willows will also tolerate locations with a high water table and wet soil. Those most commonly planted include *Selix pentandra*, the laurel-leaf willow (B), with attractive, deep glossy green foliage, and *Salix alba*, the Siberian willow (B). The latter is usually planted in the golden twig form 'Vitellina' or the silver leaf form 'Sericea.'

Travellers who have seen the weeping willow of the west coast and other milder regions may look for something similar for the plains garden. However, the big weeping willow, *Salix babylonica*, is not hardy, and if you are looking for delicate pendulous branches, the weeping birch is the best substitute. The white weeping willow, *Salix alba* 'Tristis,' has heavier pendulous branches, but it is not very hardy and not as graceful as the weeping birch or the true weeping willow.

Mountain-ash—Mountain ash (A) are commonly planted and useful trees for home gardens. White flower clusters in spring are followed in the fall by orange-red berries (pomes) attractive to birds. The autumn foliage color of some is often outstanding. Sunscald and fireblight may pose minor problems, but both conditions can be controlled with some effort. (See Chapter on diseases.)

Sorbus aucuparia, the small to eventually tall-growing European mountain-ash, is most common. Fall foliage color is excellent in many trees, but some years the leaves tend to hang on, dry and brown, all winter. Several forms or hybrids of this species may be found, including 'Fastigiata,' an upright branching form, and 'Rossica,' the Russian mountain-ash. The true 'Rossica' has sour but edible fruit that lack the usual bitterness. Although plants are sold as 'Rossica,' the genuine item seems to be rare on the plains.

Sorbus americana, or American mountain-ash, a smaller, spreading tree, lacks the strong red and orange shades of the European mountain-ash in September, but the yellow leaves do fall cleanly. The showy mountain-ash found wild in northeastern North America, *Sorbus decora*, is also popular because of its bushy growth habit and larger flowers and fruits.

Lilac—While many lilacs are large shrubs, only *Syringa reticulata*, the Japanese tree lilac (A), belongs on the small tree list. It is quite suited to small gardens and produces large clusters of creamy white nonfragrant flowers in early June.

Linden or basswood—Of the two species of linden (basswood) grown on the plains, the more suitable is *Tilia cordata*, the little leaf-linden (B). The tree is small and quite symmetrical, and appropriate for small gardens. *Tilia americana*, the American basswood (C), has larger leaves and therefore displays a more coarse-textured effect, as well as being tall-growing and less compact in habit. A few hybrids between the little-leaf and the American show promise of being superior to both parents as garden specimens. I consider the best of these currently available to be the small tree *Tilia x flavescens* 'Wascana' (B).

Elms—Although dutch elm disease has destroyed elms in milder climates, much of our region can still enjoy the stately, tall-growing *Ulmus americana,* the American elm (A). It is suitable only for large properties, and in some places its sale or transportation is restricted. *Ulmus pumila*, the Manchurian or Siberian elm (B), is less highly esteemed. The branching and leaves are finer in texture, but the small tree will sometimes produce more seed than leaves after winter or other stress, and sudden die back is common. You may well see *Ulmus japonica*, the Japanese elm (A), become available as an acceptable elm for home gardens. The cultivar of this species most likely to be found is 'Jacan.' Testing continues, but this appears to be a smaller tree under cultivation than the American elm and less temperamental than the Manchurian elm.

DECIDUOUS SHRUBS

As with trees, it is useful to know the size to which your carefully chosen shrub is likely to grow. And, once again as with trees, dimensions can vary; however, in the following section, shrubs that tend to grow larger than 10 feet in height are described as large; those that rarely exceed 5 feet are called small; and those in between are described as medium in stature.

Serviceberry—The wild *Amelanchier alnifolia* (A) and its cultivars may be grown as ornamental plants, as well as for fruit. These medium-sized shrubs are suitable for shady places.

Caragana—Caraganas or peashrubs, are some of the most useful and distinctive woody plants suited to our region. Hardy and attractive, with fine-leaved foliage and yellow pea flowers, and tolerant of drought, the caraganas also come in a variety of shapes and sizes. Flooding the root system for several days will spell their doom, but in sun and well-drained soil there is little to equal them for survivability. Their faults lie in a tendency for the larger specimens to split at the base or graft union, and for common caragana to produce unwanted seedlings.

Caragana arborescens is the common caragana or pea shrub (A). This large shrub is successful enough to survive neglect, and it becomes naturalized in abandoned gardens. More choice is the upright form, *Caragana arborescens* 'Sutherland' (A), a nonspreading selection that should be more widely offered in the trade. It can be grown as either a large shrub or a small tree. The finely cut-leaved *Caragana arborescens* 'Lorbergii,' fern-leaf caragana (A), suggests a lacy and exotic look to the garden. The shade cast by the wide spreading branches of this large shrub is not dense, providing just enough shade for herbaceous perennials that do best in dappled sunlight. A similar ferny foliage is found on *Caragana arborscens* 'Walker' (A), a weeping form usually grafted atop a pole of common caragana at the 3- to 5-foot height. On its own roots it sprawls as a woody ground cover. Another small shrub much like 'Walker' but without the finely cut foliage is *Caragana arborescens* 'Pendula,' the weeping caragana (A). Both 'Walker' and 'Pendula' are very formal subjects when grafted as a standard, and must be pruned free of suckers and dead wood, spring and fall, to keep them tidy.

If you find the larger caraganas too rambunctious and the standards too formal, there are two others that are low growing. *Caragana pygmaea,* the pygmy caranga (A), is a nonsuckering but spiny shrub; *Cargana frutex* 'Globosa,' the globe caragana (A), does produce suckers but is not spiny.

Dogwood—Especially valued for their winter bark color, dogwood shrubs are suitable for shady, moist places and will also tolerate sun. They need to be pruned of all old stems on a regular basis to encourage bright new growth with good color. White flowers in spring and white berries later also have some ornamental value. A number of dogwood cultivars are blessed with variegated foliage, but these do not have exceptionally bright twigs and are not as hardy.

The wild *Cornus sericea* (formerly *Cornus stolonifera*), the red osier dogwood (A), is a medium-sized shrub with attractive red twigs that show up well in winter against the snow. A yellow-stem form is *Cornus sericea*

'Flaviramea,' the yellow-twig dogwood (A). Exceptionally bright red twigs are evident on the similar *Cornus alba sibirica*, the Siberian dogwood (A). The small and less hardy variegated-leaved forms are *Cornus alba* 'Argenteo Marginata,' the silver variegated dogwood (C), with silver and green leaves; and *Cornus alba* 'Gouchaultii,' the golden variegated dogwood (C), with leaves heavily marked with yellow, white, and pink. Both are best in the shade.

Cotoneaster—The well-known, medium-sized hedge plant with inedible black fruit is *Cotoneaster lucidus* (often listed as *Cotoneaster acutifolius*), the Peking cotoneaster (A). Other than tempting the pear slug, cotoneaster has few faults and could be used more as an individual specimen shrub. It does take shearing very well, however, and is most often used as a hedge.

Less compact and less amenable to shearing is *Cotoneaster integerrimus*, the European cotoneaster (B), with red berries and a susceptibility to fireblight. Another small cotoneaster, this one spreading close to the ground with stiff branches and small glossy leaves and red berries, is *Cotoneaster horizontalis*, the rock cotoneaster (D). Throughout most of our region this groundcover plant must have shelter and winter protection to survive.

Hawthorn—The names of the various *Crataegus* species, hawthorns (A/B), are somewhat confused in the trade, but any offered locally should be worth growing as a large barrier shrub or specimen plant. The ones available here have clusters of white flowers in spring and attractive red, orange, or black fruit in autumn. Most are thorny.

Often planted in parks, but less frequent in the nursery trade, are *Crataegus sanguinea* (Siberian Hawthorn) and *Crateagus rotundifolia* (the fireberry), which produce ornamental red fruit. The North American *Crateagus douglasii* (Douglas hawthorn) and the Asian species *Crataegus chlorosarca* (Manchurian black hawthorn) are black fruited. Hawthorns occasionally show signs of fireblight (which must be promptly cut out) and may attract pear slugs. The plants look particularly appealing when pruned to a small tree shape, as the zigzag trunk creates an impression similar to a bonsai tree.

The brooms—*Cytisus* and *Genista* are two small shrubs of the pea family well suited to sunny sites and light, well-drained soils. They both produce yellow pea flowers in the summer, and while they may die back to some degree each winter, they produce abundant new stems the following year and flower on new growth.

Several species of *Cytisus* or broom (B) are available from time to time.

Like other members of the pea family, they have a tap-root and do not take kindly to a bare-root move; therefore, plant directly from a container with little soil disturbance. *Genista tinctoria*, dyer's greenweed (B), is similar to *Cytisus* but more upright in growth habit.

Daphne—*Daphne cneorum,* the rose daphne (D), is a small shrub grown in sheltered and moist locations for its very early rose-pink blossoms. It attains only about 8 inches in height, so it will often receive the snow cover it needs for winter protection.

Burning bush—*Euonymus*, the burning bush plants, are grown mainly for their interesting and colorful seed and pods and for autumn leaf color. The hardiest is *Euonymus nana* 'Turkestanica,' the Turkestan burning bush (B), a small shrub with narrow leaves and an upright growth habit. Used as a foundation plant in sun or shade, it is most interesting in the fall when the dull pink seed pods open to reveal bright orange-scarlet seeds.

The medium-sized *Euonymus alata*, winged burning bush (D), also tolerates shady places, and the ornamental red fruits hang on into winter. A small version of the same species, *Euonymus alata* 'Compacta,' the dwarf winged burning bush, is a little hardier (C) but does not have the same bright fall foliage colors seen in milder regions.

Forsythia—Until recently, the only forsythia that could be relied upon to survive plains conditions was *Forsythia ovata*, and even then the stems and flower buds would usually freeze and die above the snow line. Now, with the introduction of the medium-sized *Forsythia* 'Northern Gold' (A/B), stems are likely to remain alive to the tip and produce an abundance of yellow flowers early in spring before the leaves appear. The growth habit of forsythia is too loose and spreading for specimen planting in the open, but they look at home against a wall in sun or shade.

Sea-buckthorn—Not the easiest of plants to establish, *Hippophae rhamnoides*, the common sea-buckthorn (B), is a striking specimen when grown in the right location. For contrast in the garden there is little to beat the narrow silver foliage on spiny golden brown twigs. Suited to sun or shade, this large shrub will sucker widely and stabilize loose sand or gravel soils. The bright orange fruit of the female plant is ignored by birds, leaving it to hang on as decoration throughout the winter. To increase chances of fruit production, obtain both male and female plants.

Hydrangea—Hydrangeas are well known as potted gift plants, with heavy round clusters of greenish white bloom turning pink or blue as they mature, but they are not intended to be used outdoors. The small garden specimen *Hydrangea paniculata grandiflora,* the pee gee hydrangea (D), is also tender here, but it is prized in sheltered sites for its large flowers turning pink in August. I am most impressed with the new *Hydrangea* 'Annabelle' (B), a small shrub valued for its comparative hardiness, large white blossoms, and superior vigor. Use it as a foundation plant in partially shaded locations with good soil moisture.

Butternut—*Juglans cinerea,* the butternut (C), is included here for its distinctive foliage. Each leaf is divided into a number of soft and slightly drooping leaflets. Suitable for the large shrub border or as a small tree in a protected spot, some prairie specimens have reached fruiting size.

Honeysuckle—One of the hardiest flowering shrubs is *Lonicera tatarica,* the Tartarian honeysuckle (A). Satisfactory in shade as well as sun, superior cultivars of this small- or medium-sized species have been selected for such attributes as distinctive flower color and compact habit. The common 'Zabelii' (often mistakenly listed as *Lonicera korolkowii zabelii,* a different plant) has dark green leaves, dark red flowers, and red fruit. 'Beavermor'—from the federal Beaverlodge and Morden research stations—has bright red flowers, each petal edged in contrasting pink, and fruit. I consider the best selection so far to be the compact 'Arnold Red' with dark red flowers and fruit, recommended for its resistance to the recent and devastating annual infestations of honeysuckle aphids.

While the pale yellow flowers of *Lonicera caerulea edulis,* the sweetberry honeysuckle (B), are not showy, it is a symmetrical, compact shrub that can be relied upon to leaf out early. Despite its common name, the dark blue, juicy fruit has a very bitter taste and only the less bitter selections have been used for jam and wine. *Lonicea xylosteoides,* the Clavey's dwarf honeysuckle (C), is a small, compact shrub suitable for foundation plantings and low hedges in sheltered sites.

Pachistima—*Paxistima canbyi,* the low evergreen or cliff green pachistima (C), is often listed in catalogues with herbaceous perennials. Used as a groundcover, the branches of this small shrub will slowly root and spread in sun and shade. The flowers and fruit are inconspicuous.

Mockorange—Noted for its pure white flowers in June or July, *Philadelphus*, the mockorange (C/D), is not suitable for exposed or dry gardens. I have seen robust small- or medium-sized shrubs of mockorange flowering well in the protection of urban surroundings, yet in the less favored parts of our region they either die back to the snow line or may flower only low on the bush where the snow has protected the buds. A few hardier selections are being tested, but those presently available should be considered only for sheltered sites. *Philadelphus lewisii* 'Waterton' is perhaps the most commonly grown, and *Philadelphus x virginalis* 'Minnesota Snowflake,' with its double white fragrant flowers, is one of the more attractive selections.

Ninebark—*Physocarpus opulifolius,* the common ninebark (C), is a useful medium shrub for sun or shade, with fresh spring foliage and decorative crimson seed pods. The flowers are pinkish white and not particularly showy. The most frequently grown selection is *Physocarpus opulifolius* 'Luteus,' the golden ninebark (B). Its leaves are colorful when grown in full sun. A more suitable plant for the small garden is *Physocarpus opulifolius* 'Nanus,' the dwarf ninebark, with dark green leaves and white flowers.

Shrubby Cinquefoil—The better selections of *Potentilla fruticosa,* sometimes called cinquefoil or buttercup bush (A), deserve a place in any garden. They are small and do not spread out of control, and they provide plentiful bloom from spring to early summer until the end of the growing season. The foliage is fine textured, and the shrubs tolerate hard trimming or cutting back. The dry remnants of the flowers are untidy looking and may be sheared off at the end of the season. After several years, the entire plant may need to be rejuvenated by cutting back close to the ground.

There are more than a dozen different small, shrubby potentilla selections being offered in the trade. The white-flowered cultivars are 'Abbotswood' (C) and 'Snowflake' (B). Among the many yellow-flowered ones are 'Parvifolia' (A), with small flowers, grown for its very small, fine-textured leaves; 'Coronation Triumph' (A), with the longest seasonal blooming period of any of our hardy shrubs; 'Dart's Golddigger,' with a low spreading habit, sage green leaves, and large, deep yellow flowers; and 'Maanelys' (A), also called 'Moonlight,' a little taller than most and well suited to shearing as a low hedge. 'Tangerine' and 'Red Ace' (B/C) are not as spectacular in flower as their names suggest.

Plant breeders everywhere are searching for potentillas with double flowers and stronger colors. With progress being made in the orange to red shades, we can look forward to even more variety in this popular flowering shrub.

Flowering plums—*Prunus triloba* 'Multiplex,' the double flowering plum (B/C), has a number of other common names including rose-tree of China and double-flowering almond. The medium-sized shrub will grow with vigor in sheltered sites and produce a mass of double pink blossoms about the last week in May. Smaller and hardier, but with fleeting single flowers, is *Prunus tenella,* the Russian almond or single flowering almond (B). Neither shrub has particularly attractive features when not in bloom. On the other hand, *Prunus cistena,* the purple-leaf plum (C), has small, pale pink, rather inconspicuous flowers, but provides season-long contrast with its deep purple foliage.

Flowering currants—Useful for shady places as well as in sunny locations, *Ribes alpinum,* the alpine curant (A), provides some of the earliest green foliage in spring. This medium-size shrub responds well to the garden shears, so it can also be used as a hedge. Grown for its yellow flowers, *Ribes aureum,* the Missouri or golden flowering currant (B), is small and has a more loose and open growth habit. It also provides fruit suitable for jelly making.

Shrub roses—Many shrub roses are hardy enough for the most difficult of garden sites. They grow and flower best in sunny sites but also serve well in partial shade. Because the tops do not die back significantly, they come into flower earlier than the more tender roses, such as the hybrid teas. Plant hybridizers are fond of developing hardy shrub roses with ever improved flowers, longer blooming period, and superior hardiness. Here, listed by flower color, are the shrub roses that I consider the best available for our region.

High on the list of pink-flowering shrub roses is the medium-sized 'Therese Bugnet' (A). It flowers double, soft pink, blooming intermittently from June to freeze-up. 'Prairie Dawn' (B) is similar but large. In six years mine reached 10 feet in height and spread. 'Morden Centennial' (C) is a small, repeat-blooming cluster rose that has a loose, floppy growth habit in my garden.

Of the magenta- or violet-red-flowered shrub roses, the hardiest cultivar is 'Hansa' (A), a medium shrub that flowers in June. Also with magenta or purple-pink flowers, *Rosa rugosa,* the Japanese rose (A), is small but has quite large single flowers and very healthy looking foliage—wrinkled and glossy above.

A good double white-flowered shrub rose is the small 'Blanc Double de Coubert' (C); its name is often abbreviated in catalogues. Less common nowadays, but well worth growing, is the similar but slightly hardier 'Marie Bugnet' (B). Hardiest of all the whites is the small, single-flowered Japanese *Rosa rugosa* 'Alba' (A). 'Schneezwerg,' sometimes called 'Snowdwarf,' (B) is small and produces semidouble white flowers with yellow centers. It blooms all summer into fall but needs deadheading to keep it tidy.

The earliest of the shrub roses to flower in my own garden is *Rosa spinosissima* 'Altaica,' the Altai rose (A/B). The large single flowers are cream in color and borne on tall spiny canes. This medium shrub produces a few repeat flowers at the end of the season to go with its unusual black rose-hips.

Yellow is less common as a flower color in shrub roses, and a favorite of mine is *Rosa foetida* 'Persiana,' the Persian yellow (C). Its flowers are double, globular, and deep yellow. Kept free of blackspot, this medium shrub will survive many years in a sheltered site, spreading by root suckers. The small *Rosa x harisonii,* the Harison yellow (C), is a spiny hybrid of the Scotch rose and the Persian yellow and has semidouble yellow flowers. Less common is 'Agnes' (D), a small shrub with fragrant, double amber-yellow flowers.

Of the few good red-flowered small hardy shrub roses suitable for the plains, 'Cuthbert Grant' (C) is notable for flowers that may approach hybrid tea form. It was selected as Manitoba's centennial rose. A lighter looking rose is 'Champlain' (C); it produces many clusters of bright red, semidouble flowers all summer until hard frost. 'Morden Cardinette' (C) was named for its cardinal red flowers. These blooms are plentiful all season but tend to ball and fail to open, especially in cool wet weather.

A shrub rose grown for the purplish color of its foliage and stems is *Rosa rubrifolia,* the redleaf rose (D). The smallish pink flowers are rather inconspicuous against the dark foliage.

Willows—Willows in the wild are generally found in moist soils. In the garden they tolerate drier conditions but respond well to irrigation. One of the most satisfactory of the willows for the small home garden is *Salix purpurea* 'Gracilis,' the arctic willow (C). This medium shrub is sometimes called dwarf willow, but the size is very variable. As currently listed in the trade the forms 'Gracilis' and 'Nana' is synonymous.

The large *Salix alba* 'Britzensis' is the redstem willow (D), or 'Chermesina' in the trade. Branches should be cut to near ground level in spring to encourage new, bright red stems. Considering that it is normally cut back in this way, it can be grown in harsher climates than its D hardiness rating would suggest.

A recent introduction, *Salix brachycarpa* 'Blue Fox' (B), is a small shrubby willow with silver-blue foliage.

Elders—Elders are fast-growing shrubs, sometimes appearing uninvited, the fruit distributed by birds. When neglected, elders are untidy shrubs, but when regularly maintained by pruning, they can provide interest and diversity in the garden. They produce balls of white flowers in spring, followed by clusters of red fruit in August. Personally, I like the elder best when pruned to a single-stem, small tree form. The most reliable elder is probably *Sambucus racemosa,* the redberried elder (B), which can be grown as a large shrub or a small tree. Its fruit can be used for jelly or wine making. An old large golden form with deeply cut leaflets is 'Plumosa Aurea,' the golden plume elder (B). *Sambucus* 'Sutherland Golden' is a more recent introduction with yellow leaves all season. Yellow foliage in elders develops best in full sunlight.

Silver buffalo-berry—Native to coulees and river valleys, *Shepherdia argentea* (B) is a thorny, silver-leaved medium shrub. Its flowers are inconspicuous, but its sour orange berries are good for jelly making after frost. Both male and female plants should be planted if you expect fruit production. It tolerates saline soils.

False spirea—*Sorbaria sorbifolia,* Ural false spirea (A), obtains its name from the similarity of its foliage to that of the mountain-ash and of its flower clusters to certain spireas. This is a small, tough, and reliable shade plant, but it flowers best in the open in July. The suckering root system demands increasing space or the removal of exploring roots to keep the clump within bounds.

The spireas—The various *spireas* have won a place in plains gardens with their spring or summer flowers, and there are a few with ornamental foliage. These small shrubs can be grown in a variety of soils and sites. Some are hardier than others, and most need annual thinning of old branches to keep them tidy. Of the early, white-flowered kinds, *Spiraea x arguta,* the garland spirea (C), with flat clusters of white flowers on gracefully arching branches is commonly grown. *Spiraea media,* the oriental spirea, and *Spiraea x pikoviensis* (both A) are similar but hardier than the garland spirea. *Spiraea trilobata,* the three-lobed spirea (B), features lower stems with more foliage than other *spireas* of this type. The well-known *Spiraea x vanhoutei* (D) is less reliable in

our region. More robust than most is *Spiraea trichocarpa,* the Korean spirea (A), at its best in the latter part of June when covered in sprays of white blossoms.

Very different from these early, white-flowered kinds in flower and form is *Spiraea x billiardii,* the billiard spirea (A), which produces upright pokers of pink flowers from mid-July to August. The other pink spireas are generally low-growing plants that tend to die back during the winter, but flower in summer with flat-topped clusters on new growth. Most frequently grown of this type is *Spiraea x bumalda* 'Froebelii' (C). More tender is *Spiraea x bumalda* 'Goldflame' (D), with its golden yellow spring foliage later turning to bronze and scarlet.

Lilacs—Many people in hot climates where lilacs don't do well envy our shrubs with their clusters of colorful, fragrant springtime flowers. The common lilac was frequently planted in the pioneer prairie gardens of the 1880s. Today there are lilacs available with colors ranging from deep purple and pink to lilac and white, some with the individual florets with double petals to give greater substance to the clusters. Of the five or so lilac species grown in plains gardens today, *Syringa vulgaris*, the common or "French" lilac (A), is still the most popular. Of the hundreds of named kinds of common lilac, which range from large to small, the following are the most often available.

Single flowered, white: 'Vestale'
Double flowered, white: 'Mme LeMoine,' 'Edith Cavel,' 'Miss Ellen Willmott,' and 'Mme Casimir Perier'
Single flowered, cream: 'Primrose'
Double flowered, lilac: 'Michel Buchner', 'Vivand-Morel' and 'Alphonse Lavalle'
Double flowered, pink to mauve: 'Belle de Nancy' and 'Montaigne'
Single flowered, wedgewood blue: 'President Lincoln'
Doubled flowered, light blue: 'President Grevy'
Single flowered, purple: 'Andenken an Ludwig Späth' ("Ludwig Spaeth"), 'Volcan,' and 'Congo' (magenta)
Double flowered, purple: 'Charles Joly'

A complaint about the common lilacs is that the suckering roots have to be removed to prevent them spreading out of bounds. Lilacs also need to be rejuvenated every ten to fifteen years by cutting the largest and weakest branches down to the ground.

Flowering a little earlier than the common lilacs and nonsuckering are the small *Syringa x hyacinthiflora* selections (B). These include 'Gertrude Leslie,' with flowers double white and fragrant; 'Sister Justena,' single white; and one that should be more frequently offered, a floriferous pale pink called 'Doctor Chadwick.'

The medium, fast-growing lilacs are best represented by *Syringa x prestoniae*, the Preston lilacs (A/B). These hybrids are nonsuckering and have larger leaves than the common lilacs. Among the most popular of this group are 'Royalty,' flowers dark purple, fading to violet; 'Coral,' bright pink; and 'Hiawatha,' rose pink, fading paler.

Two late-flowering lilac species are grown mainly as fast-maturing, large hedge material rather than for their small rose to lilac flowers. These are *Syringa josikaea*, the Hungarian lilac (B), and *Syringa villosa*, the late or Chinese lilac (A). At the other extreme in size is the dwarf or little leaf lilac. This is *Syringa meyeri* 'Palibin' (A), slow growing with fragrant violet flowers.

Tamarisk—For the milder parts of our region or for very sheltered sites, *Tamarix ramosissima,* the tamarisk (D), has extremely fine-textured foliage reminiscent of asparagus tops. Small pink flowers are occasionally produced in late summer by this small shrub.

The cranberry group—The hardiest of the cranberries are quite tolerant of the hardships imposed on plants by industrial conditions and are also useful in moist to wet soils and in shade. In general, they have attractive, simple opposite leaves, large white flower clusters, interesting fruit, and often delightful fall foliage colors. The best known are the large native *Viburnum trilobum*, highbush cranberry (A), and its close relative the Eurasian *Viburnum opulus,* known as the European cranberry. While the highbush cranberry provides tart but edible fruit for turkey sauce at Thanksgiving, the fruit of the European species is of ornamental value only. The latter is often seen in the cultivar *Viburnum opulus* 'Nanum,' the dwarf cranberry bush (A), growing to about 20 inches tall. It doesn't flower, but it makes a good low hedge.

Another sterile selection is *Viburnum opulus* 'Roseum' (also referred to as *Viburnum opulus sterile*) or snowball (D). This small shrub is noted for its large white "snowball" flower clusters early in the growing season. The highbush cranberry also has its neat and compact version in *Viburnum trilobum* 'Compactum' (A).

Viburnum lentago, the nannyberry (B), is usually a medium-sized shrub on the plains, but it can grow as a small tree. Its flat clusters of white flowers are followed by blue-black berries (drupes). *Viburnum latana*, the wayfaring tree (C), is also a medium shrub, but it differs in its wrinkled and woolly dark green leaves, which turn purplish in the fall. The fruit, which is attractive to birds, is red and turns black. Often both red and black fruit are in a cluster at the same time.

HEDGES

As research stations were established at various locations across the Great Plains, one of the first demonstration plantings was a hedge trial. Close rows of virtually all kinds of woody trees and shrubs, deciduous and evergreen, were planted. Each row was trimmed to determine which ones might serve as hedges. A surprising number of unlikely subjects did conform under the restraint of the hedging shears, and it was found that even a conifer like the white spruce could be kept under control with persistent trimming.

Apart from evaluating the plants for their persistence and density under the shears, a preferred method of shaping and maintaining the hedge emerged. Researchers found that the best results were obtained if the sides were tapered gradually so the top of the hedge was a little narrower than the bottom. Hedges with perpendicular sides and those tapering narrower at the bottom tended to be less dense, as the upper part of the hedge shaded out and defoliated the lower branches.

Some woody plants are suitable as spiny barriers, some as tall screens, and others for low trimming. More information about the hedge plants listed here can be found in the preceding sections on trees and shrubs or in the following chapter on conifers. Before selecting a hedge plant, decide if yours is to be a low demarcation (between sections of the garden, perhaps) or a larger physical barrier or screen.

Spiny shrubs

Caragana pygmaea (pygmy caragana)
Crataegus (hawthorn)
Rosa hybrids (hardy shrub roses)

Hedges (tall)

Acer ginnala (Amur maple)
Caragana arborescens (common caragana)
Cornus sericea (red osier dogwood)
Lonicera tatarica (Tartarian honeysuckle)
Physocarpus opulifolius (common ninebark)

Salix pentandra (laurel-leaf willow)
Syringa josikaea (Hungarian lilac)
Thuja occidentalis (white-cedar selections)

Hedge plants (for low trimming)
Caragana pygmaea (pygmy caragana)
Cotonester lucidus (Peking or hedge cotonester)
Lonicera xylosteoides (Clavey's dwarf honeysuckle)
Potentilla fruticosa (shrubby cinquefoil)
Prunus tomentosa (Nanking cherry)
Ribes alpinum (alpine currant)
Salix purpurea 'Gracilis' (arctic willow)
Viburnum lantana (wayfaring tree)
Viburnum opulus 'Nanum' (dwarf cranberry bush)

In general, shrubs with small leaves and close branching make the best clipped hedges, but almost any other shrub can be used as an informal hedge.

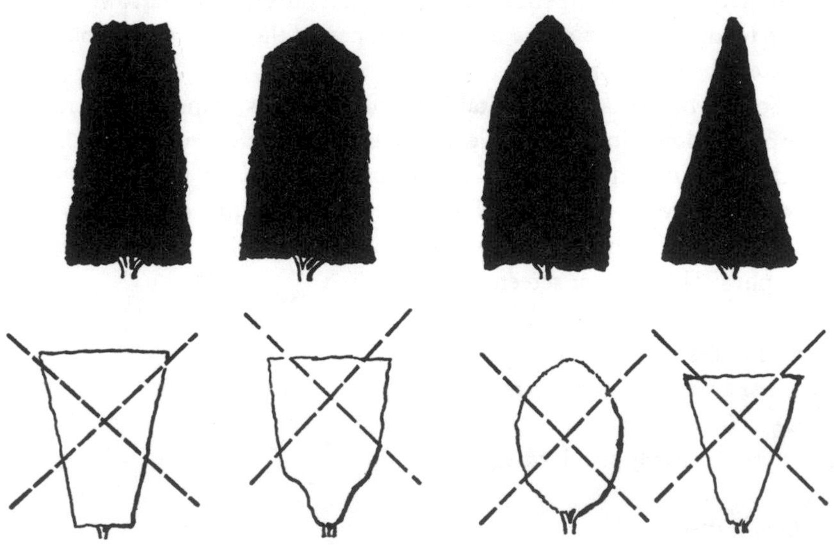

Whatever shape you choose for your hedge, it is better to have the top of the hedge narrower than the bottom. If the top branches overshadow the lower ones, the lower branches tend to lose their leaves. Narrow-topped hedges are also less subject to damage from heavy, wet snow than broad-topped ones.

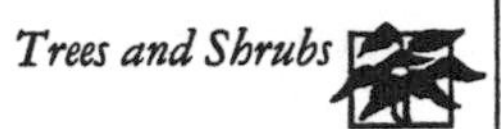

While flowering shrubs such as *Potentilla fruticosa* are attractive as a hedge in bloom, the flowers tend to delay trimming, with the result that the hedge is often ragged and uneven. If a closely trimmed hedge is needed, there is little to beat *Cotonester lucidus*.

Hedge Planting

When planting a hedge, you will find that young plants just a couple of years old are more easily handled and get started at a more uniform rate than older plants. The correct time for the job is in spring while the plants are still dormant.

First, to determine the number of plants required for a given length of hedge, divide the length of the row by the recommended spacing between plants, and add one more for the end of the row. You might also wish to add another 5 percent for insurance. The extras can be planted separately for one year in a holding plot, just in case they are needed to fill gaps or to replace slow starters.

The normal spacing for hedge plants is about 18 inches apart. Large shrubs like lilac can be planted a little farther apart, or alternatively started

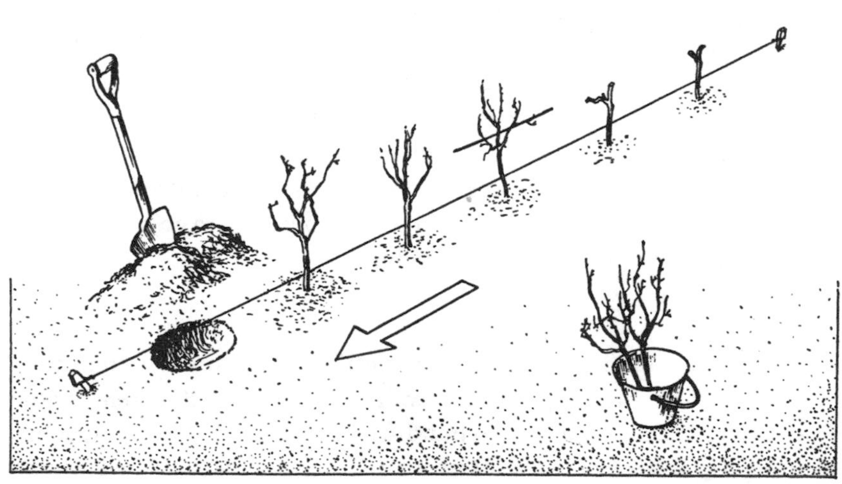

A taut length of string is an invaluable aid when planting a hedge. Keep plants moist while they are waiting to get into the ground and, once planted, prune them back to encourage bushy growth.

at the same close spacing, with the expectation that alternate plants will be dug out as soon as the row starts to grow together. I usually cut a stick to the appropriate spacing to make the job go faster.

Follow the same principles for planting hedges as for specimen plants, ensuring that the plants are kept cool and moist (in a pail of water or under wet burlap perhaps) until the roots are covered by soil. The section on transplanting deciduous trees and shrubs (pages 62–66) will provide more detail.

When planting a hedge, I suggest that you stretch the garden line along the row to be planted and keep it taut until the plants are all in place. By spading one side of the hole close against the garden line, and placing each plant against the line as it is planted, the row will come out straight. Just to be sure that I don't get an unwanted curve in the row, I frequently check that the line is tight. Dig all the holes and be sure that they are aligned before starting to plant. Another advantage to predigging the holes is that the actual planting stage goes faster, with less chance of the roots drying out before they are in place.

Once the hedge is planted, prune the tops back to about half their height to encourage the first basal branching. Water by soaking the root area and mulch lightly with straw or fine dry soil until the plants are growing well. Wait until the following spring to replace any that don't keep in step.

By the end of the first summer, the new hedge can be lightly sheared, and then sheared once or twice every season, allowing some new growth to remain until it reaches the desired height and spread. With age, some hedges become obstinate and refuse to be contained within your idea of a suitable size and shape. When this happens, you can rejuvenate early in spring by cutting the hedge down to leave short stumps from which new growth will appear. Or, if you wish to retain the height of the hedge during the rejuvenation period, cut down half the branches of each plant in two successive years. If the hedge still grows too large or unruly for the location, then there will be no recourse but to grub out the roots and start again with a smaller type of hedge.

VINES

Vines, or climbers as they are often called, can be used in a number of ways. They can dress up a plain wall or screen, modify temperature fluctuations in a poorly insulated building, adorn a garden archway, or hide an unsightly object from view. Many of these vines have elongated stems or branches, but they don't actually climb, twine, or cling to supports and need to be tied to a trellis or other support frame of wood or wire. Only the Virginia creeper, specifically the Engelmann ivy form, actually clings to walls. Before smothering your home in climbers, consider the stress on the building and the likelihood that birds, animals, and insects will use the vine for a home or for recreation.

There's a recent trend to expand on the versatility of vines and permit them to trail and clamber over small trees and shrubs. This casual effect can be temporarily pleasing in an informal garden, but this practice is likely to cause the support plants to grow unevenly or to be strangled or smothered out completely.

The number of woody vines suited to plains conditions are quite limited. Climbing roses, for example, are not satisfactory here, and most other woody climbers die back to the ground each winter and may be considered herbaceous. The perennial vines may be supplemented by such annual alternatives as the scarlet runner bean, the colorful sweet peas, or *Echinocystis lobata*, the wild cucumber. This last produces a fast screen from seed each year and many inedible but ornamental pods.

Another alternative to the woody vines is *Humulus lupulus*, the hop plant—also used commercially for beer making. This is an herbaceous perennial vine for quick screening. It has the disadvantage of suckering roots, and it frequently attracts leaf hopper insects. The other vines, the ones being considered here, are really woody climbers, even though some (like the Jackman clematis) often die back to the ground each year and perform like herbaceous perennials.

A tall vine in the following list is one that attains heights of 10 feet or more under ideal conditions.

Dutchman's pipe—*Aristolochia durior,* the Dutchman's pipe (D), is a tall-growing vine with twining stems and large, kidney-shaped leaves. The common name alludes to the interesting shape of the dull purple-green flowers.

Bittersweet—A tall-growing coarse-textured climber for a sturdy trellis or fence is *Celastrus scandens*, the American bittersweet (B). Suited to well-drained soils, this vine is noted for its attractive orange-red fruit, often used in winter bouquet arrangements. By planting three or more specimens, you increase your chance of having both male and female plants, and therefore of better fruiting.

Clematis—Clematis are tall climbers. A well-grown, large-flowered clematis is an impressive sight when in full flower in late summer, but it is a challenge to establish. You can't rely on the top growth coming through the winter unscathed, so the first rule is to plant only those clematis that flower on new wood. The Jackman group are suitable, but avoid clematis of the Florida and Patens groups, as they flower only on old wood.

Because of its large, rich purple flowers, *Clematis* 'Jackmanii,' the Jackman clematis (B/C), usually heads the list of woody climbers. Similar large-flowered clematis like 'Rosy O'Grady' and the red-flowered 'Ville de Lyon' are more tender (D).

There are several requirements for success with these large-flowered clematis of the Jackman group. Obtain substantial container plants that are at least two years old. Plant them against a building or other shelter where they are exposed to at least six hours of sunlight. Keep the soil cool and moist. (Allowing the roots to travel beneath an adjacent sidewalk or driveway often provides ideal conditions.) To improve your chances of success, provide winter protection by mounding the base of the vine in late fall. (Use the same method of mounding as recommended for tender roses, described on page 93.) Once you have flowered your 'Jackmanii,' you may consider it worthwhile to lower the support trellis and the vine to the ground and cover them with straw to preserve some of the old wood. Should you decide not to go to this additional trouble of lowering the vine for winter, or if the tops die back despite your best effort, chances are that an established root will send up strong shoots to perform a yearly encore.

Hardier than 'Jackmanii' is *Clematis tangutica*, the golden clematis (B), with golden yellow flowers in midsummer, followed by silvery plumed seed heads. New plants can be grown from the seed, and volunteer plants usually appear uninvited.

The toughest of all available clematis is *Clematis ligusticifolia*, the native western white clematis and its kind (A), providing dense cover and small white flowers in July. A popular hybrid with larger, more prolific white flowers and more boisterous growth is *Clematis* 'Prairie Traveller's Joy.'

Honeysuckle—The only climbing honeysuckle satisfactory in this area is *Lonicera x* 'Dropmore Scarlet Trumpet' (C), a small climber. New growth is soft and twining, but the old wood becomes thick and heavy. Once established, some of this old wood needs to be cut out each year to rejuvenate the plant and encourage blooming. Problems are encountered with aphids on the soft young growth and with a viral disease prevalent in some areas causing the leaves to become pale and mottled. Removal of the plant is the only remedy for this condition. When in bloom, however, all is forgiven, as the vine produces scarlet blossoms from early summer until hard frost.

Virginia Creeper—For the sort of height that will cover a two-story building there is *Parthenocissus quinquefolia*, the Virginia creeper (B/C). Flowers are inconspicuous, but the orange-red shades of the fall foliage can be very impressive. Some plants of Virginia creeper are listed as the 'Engelmannii' type, or Engelmann ivy. These have rather small leaves, and the tendrils have "suction pad" disks at the tips that allow the plant to climb walls without a trellis support.

Be aware that any plant that actually clings to the wall surface can be hard on the building. There was a time when ancient monastery and castle ruins of Europe were clothed in ivy, until it was realized that the vines were accelerating the deterioration of the structures.

Individual plants vary in the degree of their climbing ability and fall coloration, so if a friend or neighbor has a plant with the characteristics that you are looking for, you might want to see if you can beg or buy a piece to get started.

Grape—*Vitis vulpina* (also referred to as *Vitis riparia*) is the riverbank or wild grape (C/D) native to much of North America, including the southeastern parts of our region. Once established on a support by a house in a sheltered location, the wild grape will soon reach the eaves with little or no annual winter kill. It eventually forms a substantial screen. The clusters of small grapes are purple-black with a dense bloom. They are sour but sometimes used in jellies.

TENDER ROSES

Shrub roses have been mentioned earlier as being useful and reasonably hardy additions to the landscape. However, the growing of tender roses—the hybrid tea, floribunda, and grandiflora types—requires special gardening techniques for success. Some plains gardeners plant the tender roses for a single season of bloom and hope that a few may survive a season or two longer. But tender roses make expensive "annuals," and unless you obtain suitable plants, even the first season will yield flowers far too little and too late.

If you don't mind giving hybrid tea and other tender roses some extra time and attention, the winter survival rate will jump to about 80 percent, and the satisfaction rate will be even higher. The basics of successful tender rose growing can be summed up as follows.

Obtain quality (number-one grade) plants in dormant condition, avoiding those that are already sprouting and those with greatly reduced roots. If local suppliers have only inferior plants, try a specialist rose nursery—which means ordering by mail. Select a sunny open site for your roses. Plant early (late April or early May in most of our region), as soon as the ground can be worked and the roses become available. Plant them at an angle so the graft union is 4 inches beneath the surface and the roots no more 12 inches. (See illustration). It doesn't matter that some of the stems are buried.

Water the root zone immediately after planting, and earth up the above-ground stems for a period of ten days to prevent desiccation while the fine root hairs are forming. As strong new shoots appear, prune away whatever stem remains above the shoot, and any dead or crossing branches. Keep the roots moist, but not saturated, throughout summer with the aid of a mulch.

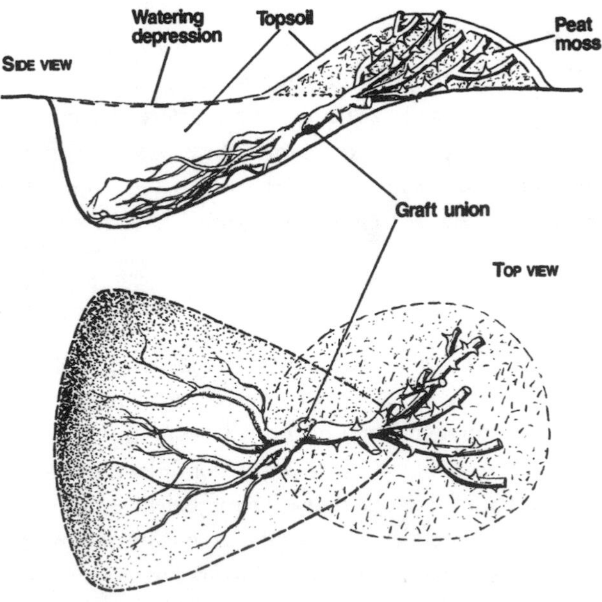

Careful planting and overwintering techniques can greatly improve winter survival rates of tender roses. Dig a pie-shaped hole 12 inches deep at the deepest point, with one side angled up to the surface. Plant the rose bush with the graft union 4 inches beneath the surface, leaving a watering depression. After planting, mound the exposed tops for ten days to pervent drying while roots become established. Cut back tops at the end of the growing season and mound again for winter protection.

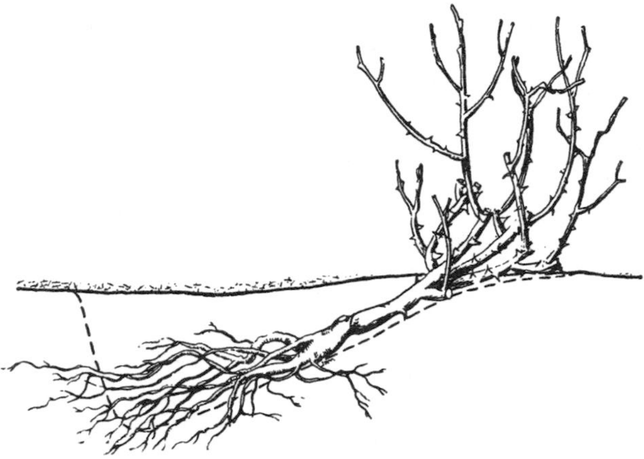

After one season, a tender rose bush planted on the slant will start to grow upright shoots from both above and below the surface, and the root system will begin to expand.

Before snow comes to stay for winter, and preferably after the ground starts to freeze, cut the tops back by half and remove entirely any soft new shoots. Then mound up with pulverized dry peat to a depth of 8 inches plus and sprinkle a little dry soil over the mound to keep the peat moss dry and in place.

Gradually uncover the roses in spring when native trees first start to show signs of bud break, and prune away dead stems when new shoots appear. Don't be too impatient to discard tender roses that appear to be killed down to the ground. With the slant method of planting, there is a good chance that new shoots will grow from the underground part of the rose above the graft, and they will recover and flower before the season is out.

Once you have a few of the famous roses like 'Peace,' 'Love,' 'Double Delight,' 'Iceberg,' and 'Europeana' showing off in your garden, you may wish to learn more than the basics of rose growing. If so, consider joining the American Rose Society; they will welcome your membership.

CHAPTER VII

Conifers

THE PROS AND CONS OF CONIFEROUS TREES

The "evergreen" or "Christmas" tree is an established part of our northern landscape. It is much admired by those from milder climates, where many people would give any number of orange trees to be able to grow, for example, a majestic Colorado blue spruce. The big bonus that comes with spruce, pine, and other conifers is their constant green foliage; and in a country that experiences at least six months of garden dormancy every year, that's worth considering.

Apart from their obvious winter charm (especially when adorned with a little sparkling snow), evergreen coniferous trees have practical uses. They provide the best windbreak to shelter home and gardens from the prevailing winds, and when planted on the south quadrant, ample shade to cool the home in summer. The density of conifers like spruce and white-cedar gives privacy where required or blocks an unattractive view. Their size and form provide a strong focal point as an alternative to less eye-appealing architectural features, and, when carefully placed, the coniferous tree serves to soften the otherwise harsh visual impact of buildings and other man-made structures.

Despite all these advantages to growing spruce, pine, white-cedar, and fir trees, they do have less congenial attributes, and the home gardener should consider both sides of the picture before making a decision on what to plant, and where. Too often, choosing an evergreen is as casual as accepting a seedling spruce presented to junior at school as an Arbor Day gift. We welcome the tiny potted plant into the family and wake up one morning to find that the cute little seedling now demands almost half the front lawn, and a part of the one next door. The first rule of selection is to check out the size of mature trees by looking at older residential districts that have been planted for at least twenty-five years. You will probably be surprised at the amount of room conifers take up if they aren't squeezed and deformed against a building, fence, or other trees. If planted in the open where they assume their natural form, any surrounding lawn grass will have to compete increasingly for available sunlight, moisture, and nutrients.

If a small tree is needed, plant one that will not outgrow its location, or be prepared to remove it once it grows too large. Pruning back large-growing conifers to keep them within bounds is rarely satisfactory, as they will show the mutilation however carefully it is done.

Another minor annoyance associated with coniferous trees is the dropping of cones that have to be picked or raked up. On larger properties where a row of conifers is to be planted as a windbreak, avoid planting them on the windward side of a path or driveway. Snow accumulates more on the leeward side of a shelterbelt, resulting in more snow removal chores.

What Are the Choices of Conifers?

When it comes to shape or form, evergreen coniferous trees that grow on the plains as ornamentals can be grouped into three categories: the dense form and spirelike growth habit of the spruce, fir, and Douglas-fir; the more open-textured, round-headed appearance of pine; and the narrow, pillarlike form of the upright white-cedars. (The larch or tamarack could be grouped with spruce, but because these conifers are leaf losing, they are better included with the deciduous trees.)

While the average town or city garden will accommodate only one or two evergreen trees, and often gets by without any at all, their smaller counterparts are almost essential in the plains garden design. In addition to miniature forms of spruce, fir, pine, and white-cedar, there is an impressive variety of junipers and the occasional yew. Look for suitable cultivars.

"Cultivar" is the correct term for fancy-named cultivated varieties of plants. (The term "variety" is now properly reserved for natural variations of wild species.) Once a plant is selected as distinct enough to be named and propagated as superior and garden worthy, it becomes especially deserving of consideration. In the case of evergreens, the ornamental cultivars are usually selected for their attractive foliage, compact and symmetrical habit, or dwarf stature—sometimes for all three. If they are forms of hardy species already being grown, they too are likely to be suitable for prairie conditions.

PLANTING AND TRANSPLANTING

The planting and transplanting of evergreen trees and shrubs calls for special care. While bare-root storage and planting works well for deciduous trees as long as they are dormant, evergreens are never entirely dormant and will not survive bare-root conditions once they are past the early seedling stage. Conifers must retain a ball of soil around the root in order to survive. Never accept conifers with bare roots.

Conifers are suitable for planting only if the soil around the roots remains intact. Nurserymen achieve this by wrapping the soil ball securely in burlap (listed in catalogs as "B & B" for "ball and burlap") or by growing them in containers. Both methods are satisfactory when properly carried out, but there can be problems. Ball and burlap material must have a solid soil ball, moist and firm. Refuse any that are obviously broken up or dried out. When you obtain ball and burlap conifers, be aware that they have recently been dug from the nursery row and that a portion of their roots has been severed and left behind in the process. Ball and burlap plants should therefore be planted with very little delay and with no further disturbance of the soil ball.

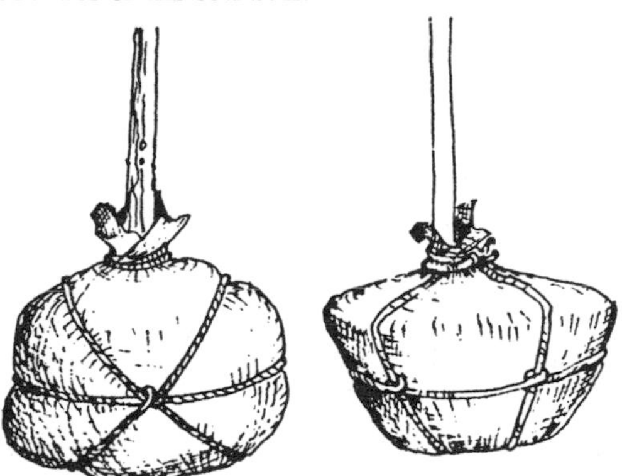

Although container-grown plants are becoming more commonly offered, coniferous trees and shrubs may still be sold with a secure covering of burlap around the soil ball.

Nowadays, plants are usually sold in temporary pots of polyethylene or treated cardboard. In such cases try to determine if the plant is really growing in the pot or if it has been recently stuck bare root into the container of soil. A firm, well-settled soil in the container is a good sign, while plants in loose soil should be viewed with suspicion.

Timing Your Transplant

The best time to plant or transplant conifers on the plains is very early in spring, as soon as the frost is out of the ground. This allows almost a full season of root development before the evergreen has to face the long, desiccating winter. Late summer is a second-best choice, as the roots will have a few weeks in which to settle before the ground freezes. Late fall transplanting is often done, but it is not recommended because the roots are severed just as the plant is heading into winter and no new root growth can take place until the ground thaws the following spring. The worst time to transplant conifers is in late spring and early summer, during the period of rapid top growth.

Transplanting Tips

When you have your specimen home, keep it watered but not saturated and leave it in the shade until you have the planting hole prepared. Avoid planting during hot and dry windy weather if you can, but don't delay more than a few days getting conifers into their home ground. Dig the hole a little deeper than you think necessary, as it is easier to add more soil to the bottom once the plant is in the hole than it is to lift it out again to dig deeper. The less the plant is handled, the better the chance of keeping that all-important soil ball intact.

If you have referred to the chapter on fertilizing, you will note that root development is enhanced by fertilizers relatively high in phosphorus—such as 11–48–0. When adding your fertilizer at planting time, neither line the hole with it nor place it at the bottom; instead, blend it throughout the soil going into the root zone. In this way you avoid a toxic concentration of chemical in contact with the roots. Also, a little fertilizer is better than a lot; for example, add a very small handful for a plant with a root ball of about 8 inches and twice that amount for a 12-inch root ball.

Resist the temptation to pour water into the hole just before planting; this just makes for a muddy mess. The soil will not be in a condition suitable for firming around the roots, and the water may cause that all-important soil ball to disintegrate. If the subsoil is very dry, you can fill the hole with water the day before and let it soak away before planting.

Some people spray an antidesiccant on evergreens just before planting to reduce the risk of the plants drying out. Recent reports suggest that, although antidesiccants do aid in the rooting of cuttings, they are of no benefit at planting time or for winter protection. In my experience, the foliage of sprayed plants remains paler than normal for several years, and growth is slower than untreated plants.

With the hole prepared, you are now ready to take the plant out of its mobile home and into your garden. Despite the fact that the burlap around ball and burlap stock will rot away in time, it is a good idea to remove it if you can do so without breaking up the soil ball. Otherwise, untie it and peel it back so no burlap protrudes above the soil surface after the hole is filled in. Exposed burlap acts as a wick to evaporate water around the roots where moisture is so essential.

Remove container-grown plants from the containers, cutting the pots if necessary. Now you are faced with something of a dilemma. While much emphasis has been placed on keeping the soil ball of conifers intact, container-grown conifers may well have been in the container long enough to have developed a constricting mat of fine roots around the inside of the container. Unless this twisted root system is corrected at planting time, it will persist to the later detriment of the plant. Some of the outer roots may have to be disturbed after removal from pots so they will grow out into the surrounding soil. Without breaking the moist soil ball, see if you can pry any major spiralling roots free of the soil before planting. If unwinding the roots is not possible without breaking up the soil, it is better to cut the roots in three or four places (with hand pruners) to encourage new roots to grow out into the surrounding soil.

Before filling in the hole, check (using a horizontal stick at ground level if you like) to see that the soil ball will be just slightly lower than ground level (an inch or so). Once the plant is in place, the easiest way to fill in the hole is to use the spade to slice from the surrounding soil, levering it towards the roots, firming the loose soil with your feet. Finish by adding some of the soil first taken from the hole. The soil should not be raised any higher up the trunk than it was before transplanting, and you should end up with a shallow, saucerlike depression in the soil around the roots to hold water.

With the conifer in its new home, it should now receive a thorough watering at the roots to settle the soil. As soon as the water has soaked in, some of the loose dry soil should be raked over the surface to serve as a mulch to conserve soil moisture.

After this first watering, don't water every day or you risk inducing a terminal condition by oxygen starvation of the root system. Instead, wait until the soil shows the first signs of drying and then apply a second soak. In short—water infrequently, but well.

To cut down transpiration from certain newly planted conifers, it is a good idea to shear them lightly to reduce the foliage by up to one-quarter. This can be done with junipers, white-cedars, and yews. Others should not be pruned, but if you want to pamper them, erect some temporary shade and protection from strong winds.

Transplanting Larger Trees

Transplanting semimature trees can be satisfying and economical if you are relocating valuable specimens before they become overcrowded and spoiled, or if you wish to create a mature landscape in a newly developed area. If the conifer is much taller than you are, a move with an adequate soil ball calls for more muscle than most of us can muster. You have probably seen trucks equipped to move and replant with no setback except for the loss of the outlying root system. The biggest problem with most mechanical tree

A temporary screen erected to protect a newly planted conifer on an exposed site. The arrows indicate the direction of the prevailing winds.

spades is that they need a lot of room to extend the hydraulic spades in order to excavate or plant a tree, and your selected tree or planting site may not be accessible to the heavy machinery. Even so, for the big jobs I suggest that you contact professional tree movers for their opinion and estimates on the proposed move.

A Mistake to Stake?

Conifers moved with an adequate soil ball should not need to be staked to prevent them leaning with the prevailing wind. If the site is particularly exposed to strong winds, it would be better to erect a temporary wooden screen resembling two sides of a long box to windward. If a dense conifer still tends to tilt like a sailing boat on tack, then it might be best to thin the branches. Remove some of the smaller branches back to the trunk, allowing air movement through the tree.

If staking tall conifers is really necessary, proceed with care and inspect the ties periodically so trunks are not strangled by the growing tree or damaged by bonds rubbing the bark.

The recommended method of supporting evergreens is to use three guy wires or cables extending in three different directions to angled stakes in the ground. To prevent damage to the bark, the wires must be encased in a soft material, such as rubber garden hose, where they loop the trunk, and the wires must not be too tight.

CARE OF CONIFERS

Once you have made a home for your conifer, invest in its future to keep it in top shape year-round through some simple maintenance considerations.

Watering and Washing

To some degree all conifers lose moisture through transpiration year-round, so your most important concern for evergreens should be water. A lack

of soil moisture in late summer or fall will result in conifers entering the long winter season too dry. Then, before the the soil thaws in spring, the needles of recent growth will start to turn yellow, then brown, and fall off. (A certain amount of spring shedding of older needles back from new growth is quite normal.)

When watering, soak the root area around and just beyond the drip-line, and never allow the root area beneath the surface to dry out completely. (The drip-line is the area of the soil beneath the outer reach of the branches.) Frequent light waterings are unsatisfactory as they serve only to bring the roots closer to the surface where they are more subject to drying out. Use a mulch if necessary to retain soil moisture.

Sprinkling the foliage during hot sunny weather is of no benefit and may cause needle burn because of the lens effect of the water droplets. However, a wash-down in the spring and at any time there's an accumulation of grime on the foliage will be of benefit. A tablespoon of mild dishwashing soap in a hose-end sprayer bottle will help remove the dirt and should be rinsed off to complete the job.

Fertilizing Conifers

Heavy fertilizing of evergreens is neither required nor desirable. If your conifers are surrounded by lawn, they will receive adequate supplemental fertilizer from whatever is not utilized by the grass—assuming, of course, that you fertilize your lawn. (Three or four applications of fertilizer during the growing season are recommended for lawns.) If not surrounded by lawn and if your soil is of average fertility, conifers will do very well with a single application of nonorganic fertilizer each spring as soon as the frost is out of the ground.

As a rough guide, your fertilizer analysis should be higher in phosphorus than in nitrogen and potash. Quantity will depend upon your soil fertility and choice of fertilizer, but no more than three or four cups full will be needed for a large tree—spread evenly around the drip-zone, worked into the surface, and watered in.

Pruning Conifers

White-cedar and yew cultivars respond well to a light shearing of the most vigorous branches in the spring (and perhaps once more in late summer) to keep them compact. This is not required if you plan an informal garden. Junipers may be sheared very lightly or weak branches pruned back to the main stem. If not overdone, this will keep the plants dense without destroying their natural appearance. Mugho pines can be kept neat and compact for years by nipping in half the elongating growth candles in mid-May to early June.

For all other conifers of our area, pruning should be limited to the removal of weak or bare branches, or a few lower branches to improve access for maintenance. When removing branches, cut them off flush with the trunk or next heavy branch. Never shorten growing branches back to bare twigs, as these will not regenerate like those of deciduous trees and shrubs. Lower branch removal often improves the look of pine trees, but a spruce looks more graceful with a full-length skirt.

Some gardeners clip spruce to produce formal and unnatural shapes; but once started this practice must continue for the life of the tree or shrub, or the result is very untidy. Personally, I think that as a general rule, the less pruning performed on conifers the better.

Winter Protection for Conifers

Winter hardiness of conifers should be a major consideration at selection and planting time. There are those who bundle their favorite cedars and upright junipers in cardboard and burlap all winter, but considering the length of our winter season, this practice is unacceptable. Conifers should be enjoyed as a living, breathing part of our winter landscape. Any that will not survive without being mummified half the year should be replaced with hardier kinds.

Some people use antidesiccants to reduce transplanting setback and drying of conifers; however, the thin "plastic" film changes the natural color of the foliage to some extent. The best way to ensure that your conifers overwinter is to limit yourself to those that have been proven hardy for your area, and see that they don't go short of water.

SELECTING A CONIFER

The following evaluation of evergreen conifers has been divided into two sections, trees and shrubs. Some advantages and disadvantages are mentioned to help you decide which will be most suitable for your garden. All should be available, if not locally, then through the mail-order trade.

Coniferous Trees

The two most important groups of coniferous trees are spruce and pine. Conifers that will reach a height of 30 feet or more are identified as tall growing; those referred to as "small" trees will attain less than that size. The spruce trees available and mentioned here are all thoroughly hardy (A), with the possible exception of *Picea amorika*, the tall-growing Serbian spruce (B). Like the pines, spruce trees are reliable and popular subjects for the home garden, although both groups are likely to become too large for the average property after some thirty or forty years and may then need replacing. One or possibly two conifers are all that an average city lot can hold, and good neighbors keep them away from the property line, where they might become a nuisance.

The most popular representative of the spruce group is *Picea pungens*, the Colorado spruce, and its blue-needled variant *Picea pungens glauca*; both are tall growing. The wavy-margined cones are decorative, the needles very rigid and sharply pointed, and the form of the tree most formal. Seedlings vary in the degree of glaucous blue present on the needles. This bloom often disappears entirely after a setback such as transplanting, but future growth retains the desired color as long as the trees are kept healthy. Some of the better selections of Colorado blue spruce have been named and are kept true to form through grafting to preserve their distinctive characteristics. These include 'Hoopsii' (dense growth and a little smaller than most), 'Koster' (zigzag trunk), and 'Moerheimii' (a good cultivar with a tiered effect). The price for any cultivar will be several times that of a seedling Colorado blue spruce.

Picea glauca, the native white spruce, makes a tall, satisfactory specimen if not crowded by other trees, and its cultivar 'Densata' (known as the Black Hills spruce after the nursery that introduced it in 1920) is slow growing with small, dense needles. I would like to see 'Densata' more widely available.

Other tall spruce species grown on the plains include *Pica abies*, the Norway spruce, with long ornate cones; and the graceful Serbian spruce, which has purple immature cones.

While the spruce are spirelike in form, the pines are more round headed and their larger needles present a softer look. They do best on a well-drained site, are fast growing, and attain a tall stature once established. The softest looking of all the pines grown in our area is *Pinus cembra*, the Swiss stone pine (C). It produces fine, graceful long needles in bundles of five. Another attractive pine for sheltered locations is *Pinus ponderosa*, the ponderosa or three-needle pine (C).

The hardiest of all pines (A) have needles in pairs, including *Pinus contorta latifolia*, the lodgepole pine. *Pinus resinosa,* the red pine (B), usually develops a form and density superior to the native jack and lodgepole pines; and *Pinus sylvestris*, the Scotch pine (A), is a fast-growing specimen with orange-brown bark as it matures.

Pinus uncinata is today's botanical name for what has been known as *Pinus mugo rostrata,* the tall mugho pine or Swiss mountain pine (A). In general appearance it is similar to the well-known mugho pine of foundation plantings, but it grows to small tree size and spreads too wide for the average city lot.

Occasionally planted, *Abies*, the true fir trees, are attractive when young with smooth, grey bark and whorled branches. The needles are flat, and the cones disintegrate rather than falling whole. With age, the firs lose their compact form and become tall and quite open and ragged. *Abies balsamea*, the balsam fir (B), is native to the boreal forest. *Abies concolor,* the silver fir (D), is superficially similar to the Colorado blue spruce, but it has softer needles and a less formal appearance. Some good specimens of silver fir have been established in the region, but most succumb to our cold, dry climate.

The *Larix* (larch and tamarack) are also true conifers, but because they are deciduous, they have been included in the preceding chapter.

Coniferous Shrubs

While the spruce and pines dominate the landscape as trees, it is the variety of junipers and white-cedars that gives us the majority of useful and attractive coniferous shrubs. The junipers prefer sun and good soil drainage, while *Thuja occidentalis*, the white-cedar or arborvitae, do best in more sheltered and moist shady locations.

No conifer covers the ground with a dense mat like *Juniperus horizontalis*, the creeping juniper (A). Native to parts of our region, it spreads along the ground, rooting as it goes. Many named selections are offered, including the low-spreading *Juniperus horizontalis* 'Douglasii,' the Waukegan juniper, with grey-green foliage; and *Juniperus horizontalis* 'Plumosa,' the Andorra juniper, with a more ascending branch habit. Selections of creeping juniper with silver to blue-green foliage include 'Hughes,' 'Wiltonii' (or the "blue rug" juniper), 'Yukon Belle,' 'Blue Chip,' and 'Dunvagan Blue.' Dark green foliage is found in such selections as 'Emerald Spreader,' 'Prince of Wales,' and 'Wapiti.'

A juniper with soft foliage often used as a vase-shaped foundation plant is *Juniperus sabina,* the savin juniper (B). Common selections of the savin include 'Arcadia' and 'Skandia,' as well as the green and white 'Variegata' and the greyish blue 'Blue Danube.' Perhaps the most popular savin is *Juniperus sabina tamariscifolia*, the tamarix juniper, frequently used as a foundation plant for its low mounds of soft green foliage.

A little less hardy is *Juniperus chinensis*, the Chinese juniper group (C). The most frequently seen of these, again for foundation planting, is *Juniperus chinensis* 'Pfitzeriana,' the pfitzer juniper, together with the compact 'Pfitzeriana Compacta,' the yellow 'Pfitzeriana Aurea,' and the silver-blue 'Pfitzeriana Glauca' selections.

Junipers with an upright growth habit are found mainly among the *Juniperus scopulorum*, Rocky Mountain juniper group (C). Named cultivars of these, all with a degree of blue-green or silver-green color, include 'Blue Heaven' (often listened as "Blue Haven") 'Grey Gleam,' 'Grizzly Bear,' 'Medora,' 'Springbank,' and 'Wichita Blue.'

More tender than the Rocky Mountain junipers, but often doing well once established, are the *Juniperus virginiana* or Eastern red-cedar selections (D). 'Grey Owl' is one of these cultivars with soft, silver-grey spreading branches and a growth habit similar to the pfitzer, while 'Skyrocket' displays an exceptionally narrow pillar form.

Juniperus communis, the common juniper, is a sharp-needled shrub (C) locally available in the Scandinavian selection 'Suecica.'

Choice among the slow-growing and dwarf junipers are 'Blue Star' and 'Meyeri' (both B). These are cultivars of *Juniperus squamata*, best planted in the alpine garden.

The soft appearance of *Thuja occidentalis* cultivars, the white-cedar (generally B), endears them to gardeners everywhere. Success with these depends very much on local climatic conditions. They are, for example, difficult to maintain in chinook regions. When positioned on the south side of a building where they are warmed into premature growth in early spring, they will likely suffer sooner or later from severe browning. But if they are positioned in a less exposed site with shelter from the prevailing wind, no supplemental screen or special winter care should be necessary other than a good fall soaking of the soil. The flattened, fanlike foliage can be kept trimmed to a hedge or formal shrub, and most need very little shearing to maintain a neat appearance. Some good examples of columnar white-cedar cultivars are 'Brandon,' 'Fastigiata' ("Pyramidalis"), and 'Skybound.' Another of the same type but with finer foliage is 'Smaragd,' locally listed as 'Emerald' or 'Emerald Green' (C).

'Techny' is a robust cultivar with dark green foliage, and 'Woodwardii' has a fine globose form. In contrast, the old 'Wareana,' the Siberian white-cedar (sometimes listed as "Robusta" or "Ware's Cedar"), has a coarse, open growth habit. There are any number of dwarfs, including 'Little Gem' and 'Holmstrup,' that are most effective when planted several to a group.

The other dwarf conifers are mutants of full-sized trees. These novelties are extremely slow growing and compact and are normally planted in the alpine garden or as a slow-growing foundation plant. Examples include *Abies balsamea* 'Hudsonia,' a dwarf balsam fir; *Picea abies* 'Nidiformis,' a dwarf Norway spruce commonly called nest spruce; and *Picea glauca* 'Echiniformis,' a dwarf white spruce known as the hedgehog spruce.

There are also two slow-growing forms of Colorado blue spruce currently available: *Picea pungens* 'Globosa,' with a growth habit to match its name (unless an unscrupulous supplier has trimmed an ordinary blue spruce to fill demand), and 'Montgomery,' of normal shape but very slow growing.

One dwarf spruce to avoid in all but the very mildest of sites is *Picea glauca* 'Conica' (also known as *Picea* "Albertiana Conica"). Although popular as a neat dwarf specimen in milder climates, on the Great Plains it is hardly ever satisfactory for long and must be rated no higher than D hardiness.

The most popular of the foundation plants is *Pinus mugo mugo,* the mugho or Swiss mountain pine (A). The neat round appearance can be assisted with the judicious pruning of "candle" growth each spring. Various cultivar names such as 'Compacta,' 'Pumilio,' and 'Montana' are used.

In more favored regions and in a moist and shady area with protection from drying winds, you might try *Taxus cuspidata* 'Nana,' dwarf Japanese yew (D). The dark, glossy green needles make a good contrast with other plants. The low bush has a straggly growth habit, calling for a light shearing each spring.

Among the many good conifers suited to our region there is likely to be at least one that fits your idea of what a conifer should be, and a place in your garden where it will feel and look at home.

CHAPTER VIII

Fruit

There is a certain satisfaction in producing fruit fresh from the home garden, but by and large it takes a little more space, effort, and patience to grow fruit than to grow flowers and vegetables. Strawberry and raspberry plants require some dedicated attention every season, or they will spread out of bounds and deteriorate with age. Also, many fruit bushes seem to attract more than their share of insect and other pests.

Even so, there are those who would not be without a strawberry patch, a clump of raspberry canes, a few currant bushes, or an apple tree and who feel that the extra attention these plants demand is well rewarded by the fresh fruit they provide.

STRAWBERRIES

Three types of strawberry plants are available, June bearing, everbearing, and day neutral. These last two extend fruiting into summer or fall, usually at the expense of the spring crop. Good June-bearing kinds for our region are 'Senga Sengana,' 'Protem,' and the slightly less hardy 'Redcoat.' The hardiest everbearing kinds are 'Ogallala' and 'Jubilee.' 'Hecker,' 'Aptos,' and 'Fern' are all day-neutral cultivars that show promise. They are not as hardy as some of the everbearers, but they will survive the Great Plains winter if well covered with a mulch of straw. These all produce young plants by runners; there are no runnerless strawberries yet recommended for our region.

Strawberries need a moist soil without standing water, as well as a growing season free of late spring frosts. The best site, therefore, is one that slopes gently to improve water and air drainage and faces north to reduce the risk of premature spring growth.

Before planting, clear the soil of all perennial weeds and add organic matter to clay or sandy soils. Obtain and set sturdy, virus-free plants as early as the soil can be worked in spring, and take care to set the crown at soil level—neither buried nor with any roots exposed. Be careful not to let the roots dry out while being planted. The rows should be spaced about 4 feet apart, and the plants 18 inches apart in the row. As long as the plants are not short of soil moisture, they will soon produce enough daughter plants to fill in a matted row about 2 feet wide.

The first season, resist the temptation to let the young plants fruit; instead, nip off the clusters of early blossoms. Encourage some shoots to root wherever there is space, using soil or wire pegs if necessary to hold them in position. With a bevy of daughter plants established the first season, you should welcome the ample crop from both mother and daughter plants the following year. After the third year (the second crop year), the mother plants will no longer be paying their way and should be removed. At this time of renovation you may wish to allow the matted row to move over and colonize new, clean land, removing the old plants and everything on the other side of that original row. With this system the colony gradually moves across the garden, the older plants being removed and runners filling in the gaps. Alternatively, start a new row every year, and limit the number of daughter plants to four per mother plant. Discard the oldest row after the second cropping year.

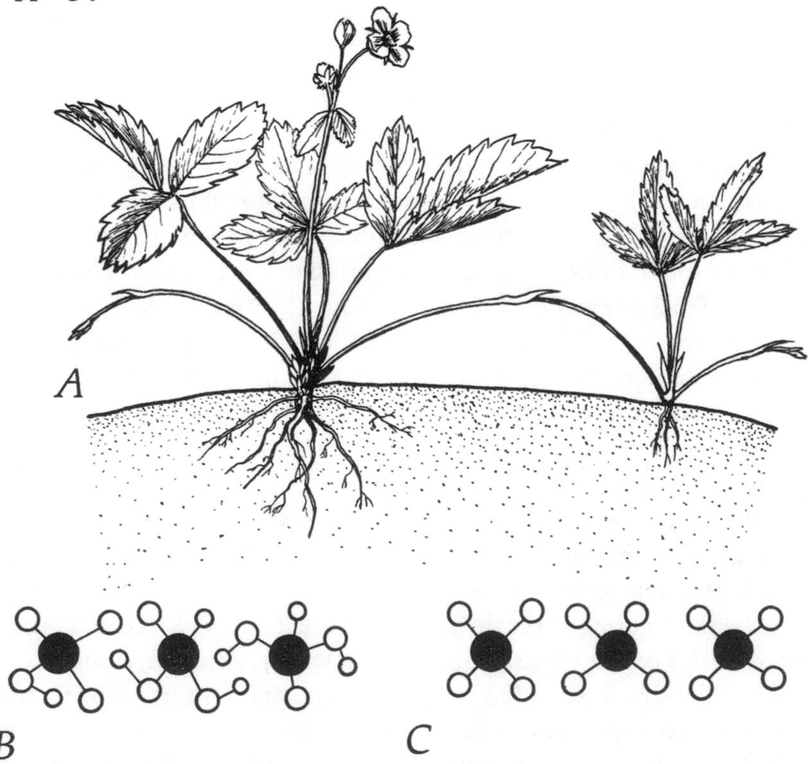

The kinds of strawberries that can be grown on the prairies spread by runners (A). You can either let the plants form matted rows (B), or you can start a new row each year and limit the number of daughter plants to four per mother plant (C).

Whichever system is used, it's a good idea to apply winter protection against repeated thawing and freezing. Each fall, after the ground freezes, apply a layer of straw about 2 or 2 1/2 inches thick. In regions where snow cover stays all winter, this may not be essential to plant survival, but you may consider it good insurance. Remove most of the straw as soon as growth starts in spring, preferably on a cloudy day to reduce the shock. Leave a little straw around the plants to mulch the soil.

Other materials, like wood shavings, are sometimes used for winter protection and mulch, but they tend to blow around. Most important, don't be tempted to use lawn mowings or leaves for the winter cover, as such materials become soggy before spring and smother the plants.

Gardening magazines often include articles on growing strawberries in barrels or tiered planters. The saving of space and the novel appearance of such structures may make this approach tempting, but there is a greater risk of the soil becoming hot and dry (hated by strawberries) and more likelihood of loss through winter-kill unless the planters are very well protected during the off-season.

RASPBERRIES

Raspberries also prefer a moist, organic soil with good air and soil drainage. Obtain well-rooted and disease-free canes from a reliable source. "Bargain" plants may be infected with virus diseases like leaf curl and mosaic that will not become apparent until well into the first or second growing season. There is no effective cure for such diseases and infected plants will have to be dug up and discarded.

Plant the canes in spring as soon as the ground can be worked, the rows 6 feet or more apart, 2 1//2 feet between plants in the row. They should be planted just a little deeper than originally planted, and the tops pruned down to 6 inches to promote early root development. They will need watering after planting and will respond well to at least one good soak (rain or irrigation) just after flowering.

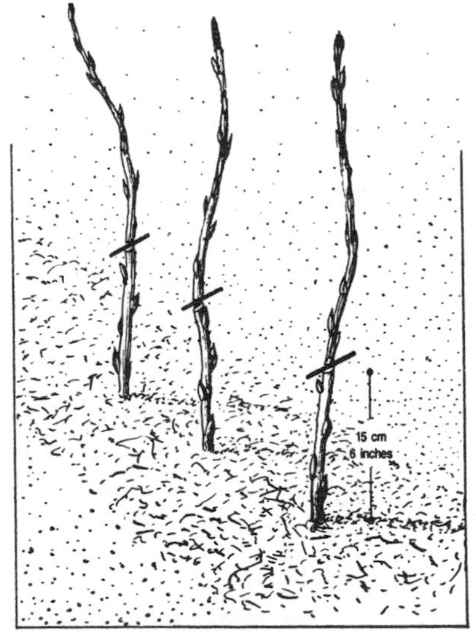

Newly planted raspberry canes should be pruned back to a height of 6 inches to promote root development.

A support will help keep rows of raspberry canes within bounds. In early spring, thin the canes and cut back the tops to remove winter die back.

The new shoots of raspberry canes (sucker growth) complete their growth in height in the first year. The second year these canes produce raspberries and die shortly after fruiting. Meanwhile, a new growth of canes takes their place. In the late summer, cut the old, spent canes down to about 12 inches and dispose of them. The remaining stumps will provide a little extra winter protection and help catch snow.

Early each spring, cut the remaining stumps of the old canes down to the ground. Then reduce the new canes to about ten per yard, first cutting out the weak or crowded ones. Complete the pruning by cutting the tops of the canes along the row to remove winter die back; this should be at about eye level if the length of the canes permits.

Keep the width of the row to no more than 2 feet by cutting off adventurous suckers anytime during the growing season. The row will be kept tidier if a support is made; the most common consists of wooden posts with cross-arms, and wire stretched between to embrace each side of the row.

Throughout most of our region, and certainly within the sheltered city environment, winter protection of hardy red raspberries is not necessary. Bending canes down in fall and covering them with soil is not my idea of fun, and may damage the canes. If even the small-fruited and hardy selection 'Chief' winter-kills more than once in your garden, I suggest that you put the space to other use.

Two raspberry cultivars that usually produce a heavier (but more acid) crop than 'Chief' are the selections 'Killarney' and 'Boyne.' 'Latham' is another good red, and 'Honeyqueen' a good yellow raspberry.

Purple raspberries differ from the red and yellow in more than just fruit color. Not as hardy, they do best in warm, sandy loam. As the fruit is produced on side branches of the previous year's canes, head the canes back to about 2 feet in spring to encourage the lateral branching. They do not sucker.

Some experimental work is being done to develop kinds of raspberries that fruit late in the season on new canes, but so far there are none that I can recommend with confidence.

BUSH FRUITS

The term bush fruits includes currants, gooseberries, saskatoons, bush cherries, and the cherry-plum hybrids. Many of these may be planted for their value as ornamental shrubs, as well as for the fruit they produce. In order to get the best results from your bush fruits, select hardy cultivars and healthy stock. The hardiness ratings A, B, C, and D given in this chapter are based on the principles outlined on pages 66–67.

Obtain one-year-old plants and space them at least 5 feet apart in a moist but well-drained soil high in nutrients, preferably on a gentle north-facing slope. Shelter from the south and west helps to delay spring blossoming and lessens the risk of damage from late spring frosts. Use a mulch to retain cool, moist roots, and use very shallow cultivation to avoid disturbing feeder roots.

Bush fruits generally need chemical sprays timed just right, or the fruit may well house tiny unwanted guests such as fruit flies, and the leaves are susceptible to such fungal diseases as powdery mildew. The chapters on insects and plants diseases give pointers on how to control these situations.

Pruning—The pruning of bush fruits is not difficult as long as the basic principles are understood. Briefly, red and white currants and gooseberries bear most heavily on short spurs on the two- and three-year-old branches. Each spring, cut out old, unproductive branches, saving some vigorous new shoots to take their places. Then cut back any long and straggly growth to keep the bush in shape and to encourage the development of fruiting spurs.

Black currants are pruned a little differently because most of the fruit is carried on stems from the previous season (one-year-old wood). In this case, retain only enough of the older wood to provide a framework for the bush, keeping only those branches that are producing vigorous young shoots. Unlike red and white currant bushes, the tips of black currant branches should not be cut back.

Black Currants

There are a number of black currant cultivars that do well in our region. Two of the hardiest are *Ribes* 'Albol' and *Ribes* 'Magnus' (both A). The 'Albol' currant is the larger of the two. This vigorous, drought-resistant shrub deserves to be more commonly available. It does have a tendency to sucker, but it produces an abundance of large mild black currants. The 'Magnus' currant also yields large quantities of good-quality fruit, but it is more subject to mildew. The slightly less hardy *Ribes* 'Willoughby' (B) is one of the few cultivars we can grow in our region that is resistant to this disease.

Of the other black currants you might encounter, all B, the low-yielding *Ribes* 'Boskoop Giant' produces fruit of an excellent processing quality; *Ribes* 'Consort' has been rated unacceptable because of its bitter fruit; and the old cultivar *Ribes* 'Buddenborg,' which produces a good yield of large black fruit that processes well, is rarely offered in our region.

Red and White Currants

The most popular red currant in our region is *Ribes* 'Red Lake' (A). This hardy currant produces an excellent yield of high-quality fruit that ripens over a long season but is subject to mildew. Less common are *Ribes* 'Stephens' (A), which produces a small but tasty fruit; and the slightly less hardy *Ribes* 'Perfection' (B). A good choice of white currant for our area is *Ribes* 'White Imperial' (B).

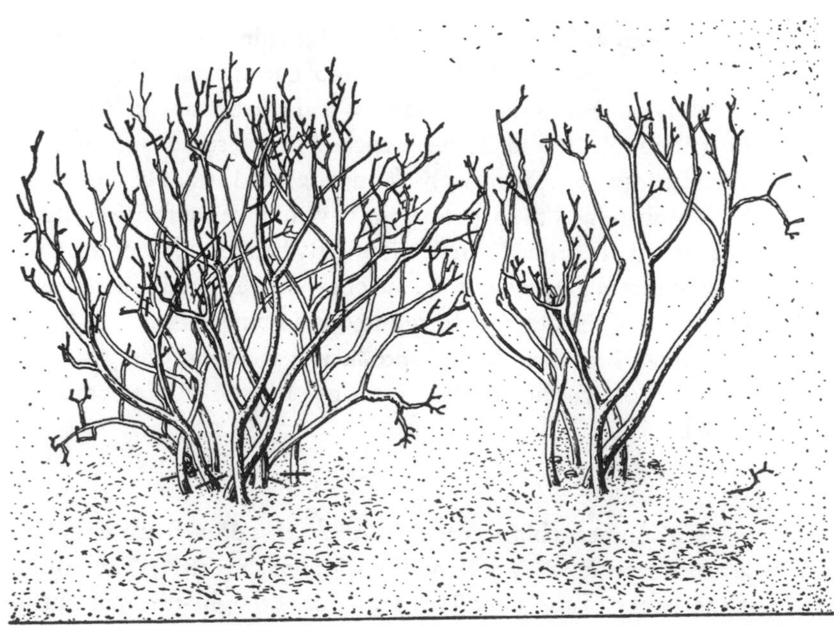

When pruning red and white currant bushes and gooseberry bushes, remove unproductive, old branches close to the ground, then cut back straggly growth from the remaining branches.

Gooseberries

The most commonly grown gooseberry on the prairies is *Ribes* 'Pixwell' (B), a shrub with relatively few thorns. The fruit is pinkish when ripe and of excellent quality and yield. The slightly hardier *Ribes* 'Pankiw' (A) has early ripening fruit of good size and quality. Its popularity has probably been suppressed by the fact that the fruit remains green when ripe. *Ribes* 'Pembina Pride' (B), together with the virtually identical *Ribes* 'Thoreson' is another gooseberry sometimes available. Fruit is of good quality, and the yield fair.

Bush Cherries

The term bush cherry is used loosely to include any of a number of shrubby *Prunus* species with cherrylike fruit. Many people find these "cherries" to be disappointingly small and sour, but they still find a place in jelly or wine making. There are possibilities for improvement through hybridization with less hardy but more palatable cherries—but that is for the future.

There are three bush cherries frequently grown, all B. *Prunus besseyi,* the western sandcherry, is a low, straggly shrub with black, astringent fruit. It is also grown as a pollinator for cherry-plums: A number of selections have been made for the prairies, but none are widely available. (See also the cherry-plum hybrids in the next section.)

Prunus fruticosa, the Mongolian cherry, is also a small shrub, suckering freely and producing red fruit used for pies and canning as well as for jelly and wine. The foliage is dark, glossy green. *Prunus tomentosa,* the Nanking cherry, is a taller shrub. The red (occasionally white) fruit is less astringent than the other bush cherries and is sometimes eaten fresh. Two or more plants are required to produce fruit.

Cherry-Plum Hybrids

The cherry-plums are hybrids of the sandcherry. The branches are too weak to hold a crop of fruit, so they are best trained up a fence or trellis for support. The fruit (about 1 1/4 inches) may be used for dessert but is more frequently used for canning or as a preserve. The ripe flesh of these cherry-plums is normally a very dark red to purple. However, the oldest, and possibly hardiest, is the 1908 introduction 'Opata' (A), which has green flesh when ripe. It is sweet and firm with a small pit. A cherry-plum with juicy yellow fruit is 'Convoy' (B). A productive shrub with many thin branches, it ripens in September.

'Manor' and 'Epsilon' (both B) have dark red flesh. 'Dura' (C) has fruit with a dull green skin, blotched purple. Ripening in late August, the fruit will hang on the branches into October. 'Sapa' (C) has fruit similar to its 'Sultan' plum parent, purple with a bluish bloom.

FRUIT TREES

Fruit trees are often grown with good results on the prairies. There are a number of things to bear in mind when considering whether to plant fruit trees. The number of trees (fruit or otherwise) that can properly be accommodated on the average city lot is one or two, and even one will reduce the quality of most other plant life in the vicinity. When growing plums, unless neighbors also have plum trees for cross-pollination, you will need to plant at least two trees of different cultivars to aid fruit set. Apples also need cross-pollination, but there are usually enough apple trees growing in a town or city so you don't have to consider pollination for fruit set. Pears are somewhat self-fertile but will bear more heavily if two cultivars are used.

Learning from the triumphs and mistakes of early settlers and from thousands of gardeners who have since accepted the challenge of growing fruit trees in our region, we know that it is not practical to attempt to grow them on a site exposed to high winds. Fruit trees need sunlight to do well, so the site should be a compromise between shelter from prevailing winds and too much shade from buildings or other trees.

The trees will be more productive if allowed adequate root space (for approximately the eventual height of the tree in all directions), without competition from other trees. For the first few years it also helps to keep the grass or weeds away from the root zone area beneath the outer reach of the branches. Occasional watering during dry spells will help, as will a thin mulch to conserve moisture. Avoid constantly wet soil conditions and the use of high nitrogen fertilizers.

Fireblight (a bacteria) can sometimes take heavy toll of mature pear trees. Silver-leaf (a fungus) can attack plums. Both may infect mature apple trees. The chapter on diseases lists these problems and how best to deal with them.

Pruning—No discussion of fruit trees would be complete without some mention of the pruning that is needed to develop a properly branched and productive tree.

"When pruning, cut as flush as possible to the trunk or larger branch" goes the normal advice to the novice pruner. Unfortunately, the flush cut often means a larger area of cut surface that has to heal; thus, the entirely flush cut is no longer recommended by the International Society of Arboriculture. A smaller cut surface heals faster, so leave the shoulder bulge at the base of

the cut to keep the cut surface area to a minimum.

"Then paint all cuts over 1 inch in diameter with pruning paint." Wrong. Painting the cuts may do something for the satisfaction of the gardener, but it does nothing for the health of the tree. Decay organism are undaunted by paint or dressing of any description, and the cosmetic may in fact delay healing.

Entire books have been written on pruning, but the basic principles are as follows. First, cut out any dead wood without leaving a stump. Remove all sucker sprouts from the base and any long, soft shoots (water sprouts) sprouting from the trunk or old branches; then cut out any other rubbing or crossing branches. A little more thinning of crowded branches in the center of the tree may be needed; then stand back to see if the tree looks reasonably well balanced. Finally, cut back a portion of the previous season's growth, leaving the end bud pointing in the direction that you would like the branch to grow—normally away from the center of the tree. Once a strong framework of branches has been developed with a central leader, a regular light pruning each spring is all that will be required.

Beware. The pruning of fruit and ornamental trees can become addictive. Learn to walk away just before you have reached perfection, or there may be no tree left to prune next year!

Choice of tree—Selecting a cultivar that has been proven satisfactory to your own district is essential to success, and for this information you would do well to contact your local extension agent.

The fruit trees mentioned here are included because they are frequently commercially available in Canada. The letters A, B, C, and D again refer to the hardiness ratings introduced in the earlier chapter on trees and shrubs.

Apples

Apples are of the genus *Malus*, where they may be found listed in some plant catalogues. At one time it was a simple matter to classify apples as either crabapples or standard apples. Crabapples (or crabs) were those producing small, tart apples useful for jelly making, canning, or apple sauce. The larger dessert and cooking apples were classified as standard apples. As a result of the many hybrids between the two types, a new classification, the apple-crabapple (or applecrab) came into being. Hybrids between the apple-crabs and the other classifications result in offspring that are not readily categorized. The result is that one cultivar may appear in one catalogue as an applecrab, for example, and in another catalogue as a crabapple. As a general

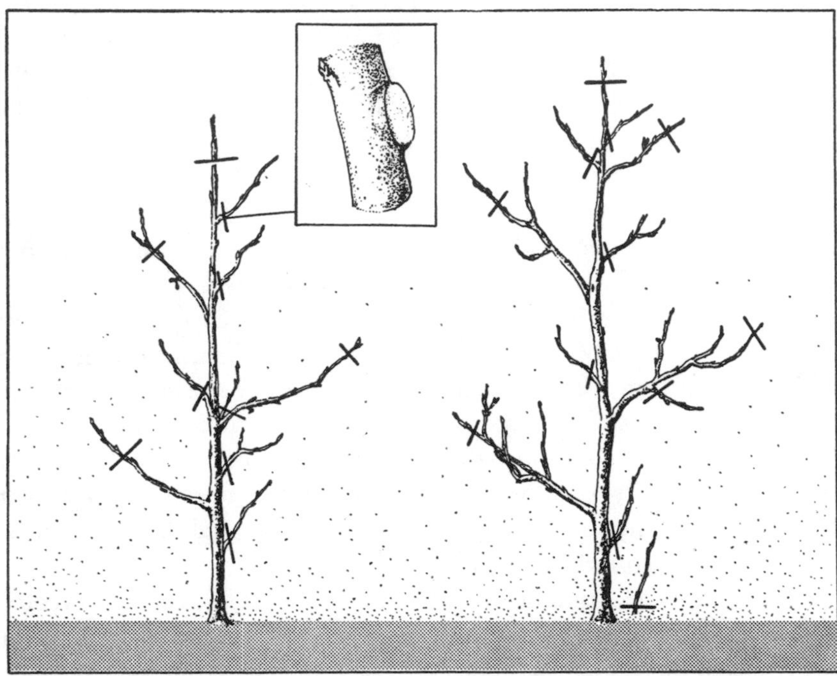

Second- and third-year apple trees showing typical pruning locations. Pruning cuts should not be flush with branches or with the tree trunk. The inset shows an appropriate pruning stump.

guide, those with fruit over 2 inches in diameter may be considered standard apples, and the smaller ones that are used mainly for jelly and jam are considered crabapples. Apple-crabapples are somewhere in between.

Crabapples—The introduction of locally grown dessert and cooking apples has not banished the small, tart crabapple into history as a cultivated fruit tree. Those with high pectin content and good rosy flesh color are ensured a place in the gardens of those who value home-grown preserves. Good quantity usually compensates for the smaller size of the fruit.

Our most popular crabapple is 'Dolgo' (A/B). This cultivar was introduced to the United States from Russia in 1917. The name means "long," in reference to the fruit shape. The skin is purple-red with a heavy blue bloom. While not a good keeper, it is productive and excellent for jelly.

'Osman' (A) has stood the test of time since 1911. Its physical appearance is not its strong point, with a red-brown skin and some seasons with splits and checks. However, the fruit ripens in August, and it is of

excellent quality for jelly and canning.

The fruit of 'Columbia' has a thick skin, pale green and washed with red. The yield is fair and the quality good. It is apparently susceptible to fireblight.

Local areas often have a fruit tree supplier who favors selections that are not widely grown. It sometimes pays to consult your local nurseryman before making a purchase that you will likely live with for many years.

Apple-crabapples—A step up in size from the crabapples, but with fruit generally less than 2 inches, are the apple-crabapples, or applecrabs. These were developed by hybridizing crabs with standard apples, the general aim being to produce a fruit with the size and quality of a standard apple, while still retaining at least some of the hardiness of the original Siberian crabapple. The resulting applecrabs differ in their hardiness, quality, and keeping potential. Some of the best available are included here.

The oldest selection still popular is the 1906 cultivar 'Quality' (A). Productive and good for both canning and cooking, 'Quality' has a pale yellow skin with red markings. The 1930s saw several applecrab introductions that have also stood the test of time. Tops among these in popularity is 'Rescue' (A), a high-yielding applecrab with a carmine skin, good for both canning and dessert. Its faults are an intolerance to chlorosis, a flesh that soon turns mealy, and a susceptibility to fireblight.

'Renown' (A) is a mild, sweet dessert, sometimes listed as a crabapple. The yellow fruit is splashed with red and is good for canning. It shows some susceptibility to fireblight.

Scarlet-colored 'Rosthern' (A) is early fruiting and keeps well. The yield is lower than for many other selections.

'Kerr' (A) was a welcome applecrab introduction of the 1950s with purple-red skin, the flesh yellowish and flecked with dark red. It is sometimes considered a large 'Dolgo' crab, but milder in flavor. 'Kerr' has good canning qualities, fair vigor, and good yield. It ripens later than some but will keep in storage until early January.

From the same decade comes 'Dawn' (A). Ripening to a light crimson in early August, it produces a heavy yield. Sometimes listed as a crabapple, 'Dawn' is best used for canning.

Into the 1970s and 1980s came several new introductions. It is still early to say which of these will stand the test of time. 'Trailman' (A) has fruit with a greenish ground overlaid with dull red, the flesh golden-yellow. Its flavor is spicy and slightly tart, and good for dessert or canning. The tree bears at an early age and is fireblight resistant.

'Rosybrook' (A) shows good promise. The pale green skin is mostly covered with red; the flesh is creamy white, firm, crisp, and sweet, with no trace of astringency.

Standard apples—The commercially produced dessert and cooking apples that we see in the grocery store, like 'McIntosh' and 'Granny Smith,' are not satisfactory in our area, but there are a number of other quite large apples that we can grow. Some have better flavor or are better keepers than others, and the comments that follow outline the main features of the ones you are likely to find offered for sale across the prairie. Here they have been divided into cooking, dessert and general purpose apples.

Cooking apples: The cooking apple most frequently grown on the prairie since 1940 is 'Heyer #12' (A). The tree survives neglect and dry, exposed sites, and (given half a chance) produces a heavy crop of tart yellow apples. The fruit breaks down quickly, so it should be picked just before it turns yellow. There are better cooking apples now available.

Another introduction from the 1940s is 'Battleford' (B). The fruit is pale green, striped red. 'Battleford' provides a moderate yield most seasons. It is susceptible to fireblight and slightly less hardy than the other cooking apples noted here.

You may come across 'Edith Smith' (A), introduced in the mid-1960s, an open-pollinated seedling of 'McIntosh' ('McIntosh' is the female parent; the other is unknown.) It is rather tough and pulpy, but satisfactory for cooking and keeping.

The mid-1970s saw the introduction of 'Noran' (A). Its fruit is green with a red blush on the sunny side. It ripens late in September and keeps well in storage until February.

Finally, in 1980, 'Westland' (B) was introduced as replacement for 'Heyer #12.' It is a pale yellow-green, washed and striped red.

'Milowski' is a new cooking apple not yet widely tested for hardiness.

Dessert apples: Developed in the mid-1950s, 'Harcourt' (A) is a good-quality dessert apple, blushed bright red. Unfortunately, it doesn't keep well.

In the 1960s, 'Carroll' (C) became popular in the less severe climatic regions, or for planting in sheltered places. Mottled and streaked rosy red, it has a very soft texture and good flavor.

'Luke' was introduced at the same time (C). Mottled dark red over green, it often matures too late for the shortest season, but when productive, it is noted for its large-sized fruit (3 1/8 or 3 1/2 inches) and good keeping qualities.

A dessert apple introduction of the 1970s, 'Norda' (B/C) is early ripening to a red overlay. It provides consistently good yields and keeps well.

Occasionally, an exceptionally good cultivar is overlooked by the trade, and this may be the case with 'Moris' (A). Although the thin skin is rather rough and greasy, this red apple keeps well in storage until February.

'Williams' is a newly introduced dessert apple not yet fully tested for hardiness.

General purpose apples: The oldest of the general purpose apples still frequently offered is the 1923 introduction 'Haralson' (A). The skin is brown-red; the flesh firm but tough; and it is good for dessert only after storage into the new year. It also tends to overproduce; therefore, the newly formed fruit need to be thinned.

'Breakey' (C), a red apple that keeps well, appeared in 1936.

'Collet' (C/D) is a light red apple introduced in 1948. Its quality is good, but fireblight and lack of hardiness have been problems.

Named in 1955, 'Goodland' (B) is a creamy green apple washed with red. It is late ripening and has no resistance to chlorosis.

In 1960 'Patterson' (A) was introduced and remains popular today. Blushed red over greenish yellow, the red is almost lacking some seasons.

'Parkland' (A) is red skinned and ripens about mid-August.

Three introductions of the 1980s will likely be A or B hardiness. These are 'Brookland,' a yellow-green apple, striped red, the flesh crisp and fairly sweet; 'Norland,' a red apple that drops when ripe in mid-August but keeps well; and 'Sunnybrook,' a yellow apple with red cheeks, a small core, and a slightly acid but sweet flavor.

Plums

Plums are of the genus *Prunus* and are sometimes included in catalogs under that name. They are mostly intersterile, and therefore not likely to set fruit unless two or preferably three different kinds are planted in the same or nearby gardens. There are three main types of plum for our area—those selected from the native plum (*Prunus nigra*), those from the Manchurian plum (*Prunus salicina*), and others that are hybrids between these and other kinds.

Early flowers are often spoiled by frost, resulting in little or no fruit set. Therefore, all should be planted in a protected site and mulched in the fall to retard flowering.

The native plum selections—While fairly hardy, three introductions of the 1930s and 1940s lack something in size and quality. 'Bounty' (B) has the largest fruit (1 1/4 to 1 1/2 inches), and thin skin dark red with dots and slightly bitter. The orange-yellow flesh is tender, juicy, and sweet. Although used as a dessert plum, it is most suited to jam making. It ripens in late August or early September.

'Dandy' (B) has a yellow skin, dotted and blushed red. The flesh is yellow, juicy, and mild flavored. The tree tends to overbear, so fruit should be thinned to maintain fruit size. It makes a good pollinator for other plums.

Ripening by mid-August, 'Norther' (C) has a bright red skin with a light grey bloom. The yellow flesh is juicy and sweet with a large flat stone. It is best used for dessert.

The Manchurian plum selections—The Manchurian plum selections (B) are generally superior in quality to those of the native plum, but the fruit is still rather small. The seed of *Prunus salicina,* the Asiatic plums, came to the prairies in 1939 from L. V. Ptitsin of Harbin, Manchuria. They were numbered under trial, and 'Ptitsin #5' with dull red skin is considered to be one of the best of its kind.

Two further selections of this kind were introduced in 1979. One was 'Brookgold,' with the fruit about 1 1/4 inches, skin golden-yellow with red on the exposed cheek. Ripening in mid-August, the flesh is sweet, yellow, free-stone, and good for dessert. 'Brookred' has large fruit about 1 1/2 to 2 inches, and dull, dark red skin. Ripening in late August, the flesh is pale orange. It is satisfactory for dessert use but better for jam.

Hybrid plums—The remaining plums you are likely to find offered for prairie gardens are nearly all hybrids of the native and the Manchurian kinds. They produce somewhat larger fruit, but some lack the hardiness of the parent species.

The oldest selection still around is the 1917 cultivar 'Pembina' (C). Fruit is thick skinned, red with a heavy bluish bloom. Flesh is bright yellow; good for dessert, fair for canning. Ripening in late August, it tends to be biennial bearing.

'Prairie' (B) has fruit of good size and quality, but with a rather tough and sour skin. 'Patterson Pride' (B) is a shrub unique in its untidy serpentine habit and low growth, rarely attaining much more than 24 inches in height. The fruit ripens deep red with a thin, tender skin; the flesh is yellow, juicy, and of good flavor. It ripens in September.

Also ripening in September, 'Perfection' (B) produces dark red fruit of good size and excellent quality but with a tough, astringent skin.

Apricots

The apricots hardy enough for trial in our area are all selections and hybrids of the Manchurian apricot *Prunus armeniaca mandshurica.* This variety is variable in quality and generally not as satisfactory as the following selections, which can be used as dessert or for jam, or canned. With the exception of 'Westcot' (possibly B), the small apricot trees are C hardiness.

'Scout,' introduced in 1937, is the oldest cultivar still available and differs from the others in its fruit not being juicy. Fruit shape is rather flattened, more or less heart shaped, and bronzy-gold in color.

The other old introduction is 'Morden 604,' or simple 'M604.' Flesh is deep orange, of very fine texture, sweet and juicy. Two recent and presumably superior selections are 'Brookcot' and 'Westcot.'

Pears

The pears are of the genus *Pyrus* and are sometimes included in catalogs under that name. There are about ten named pear cultivars available from time to time, but other than 'Ure,' they are suitable only for canning and sauce. They are all small trees. It appears that the hardiest cultivars are those introduced in 1960 'Andrew,' 'David,' 'John,' 'Peter,' and 'Phillip' (all B).

Introduced from Russia in 1940, 'Tioma' (C) has fruit about 2 3/4 inches long. The flesh is white, coarse, and moderately acid. It ripens in early September and can be stored for about two months. 'Olia' (D), introduced from the same place at the same time, is not recommended because it is only borderline hardy.

'Golden spice' (B) is also listed in catalogues. The flesh is light yellow, juicy, and the flavor spicy and tart.

CHAPTER IX

Bulbs and Plants with Fleshy Roots

SPRING BULBS

Because each blossom of early spring seems as precious as half a dozen flowers of midsummer, spring bulbs are well worth including in your garden. Not only do tulips, daffodils, and certain other bulbs extend our short flowering season, but they are also welcomed as a promise of warm summer weather to come. In order to enjoy spring bulbs in the home garden, we must prepare well ahead of time.

Though planning and planting comes naturally to most of us in springtime, planting bulbs in the fall for results the following year takes a large slice of faith. Bulbs should be planted as soon as they become available in the stores, in late August and throughout September. This early planting allows the bulbs time to put down roots before the ground freezes. Bulbs planted in October or later often do not have time to get established. However, bulbs can be planted anytime in the fall as long as the ground can be worked. While this difference in early or late planting may not be very evident when the bulbs flower the following spring, the late-flowering ones with poor roots will exhaust the bulbs as they flower and will normally fail to repeat bloom the following and subsequent years. Those well rooted, on the other hand, will be in a position to "recharge" the bulb immediately after flowering and will likely continue to flower for several years.

To be sure of planting at the correct time, buy locally. Mail-order bulbs can arrive late, allowing no time for bulb rooting once planted, or (unthinkable but not unknown) bulbs can arrive after the ground has frozen. I have yet to meet anyone, keen gardeners included, who enjoys having to chop through a crust of frozen soil to plant late-arriving bulbs.

If you should ever find yourself in the position of having bulbs to plant after the garden appears to be frozen, you may be able to find a one-season holding place by the side of the house where the ground is only just beginning to freeze. Allow such a planting to flower and continue to grow in the holding place the following summer, transplanting the bulbs to the preferred site in late August or early September.

A bulb order arriving after the snow has come to stay or when the ground has frozen hard as concrete does pose a problem. If you have a cool storage place (not higher than 40°F), you can try keeping the bulbs dormant in a medium such as dry peat until conditions permit planting out the following spring.

If there is no cool storage place to be found, you will have to make the best of a bad situation and pot them to prevent them from sprouting and wasting away in storage. Use a moist potting mix, keep as cool and dark as possible until the tops start to grow, and then move to a bright room to flower. Remove the spent flower stalks and keep the foliage growing, finally allowing the pots to dry out as the leaves start to yellow. They should then be left dry in the pots until planting time next fall.

The bottom line is this: if you don't appreciate tiptoeing through wall-to-wall tulips in your living room in the middle of winter, try to avoid accepting late bulb deliveries.

Selecting the Best

Quality bulbs are likely to be available from late August through September at your year-round garden center in town, as well as through mail-order supplies. When shopping locally, you can see what you are getting, which is nice, and a knowledgeable and reliable garden center will likely stock only those bulbs that will perform well for you. Before making your purchase, make sure the bulbs are firm with no soft spots or sprouts and free of mold and bad odor. They should feel heavy for their size.

The selection may be wider through a mail-order house, but unless you have prior experience or information, you run the risk of ordering some that are not satisfactory for your location. You also have to rely on the mail-order firms to deliver what they promise. Nevertheless, the mail-order trade currently supplies almost half the total dollar volume of bulbs in North America, so most customers are obviously well satisfied. If you do order by mail, it might be a good idea to stipulate a September delivery date and to state clearly that late deliveries will not be accepted.

"Bargain" bulbs are often purchased in bulk for supermarkets and department stores by people who have little knowledge of horticulture. They may not even be aware that cool, dry conditions are needed to prevent deterioration. On the other hand, as bulbs are perishable, good-quality bulbs are sometimes sold cheaply because they are unnamed, or because they have been overbought by the wholesaler, or because they are culls and too small to produce flowers the first year.

You might want to take a gamble on cheap bulbs if they appear to be of good quality, but the results of your bet will not be known until the following spring. Personally, if I am going to spend some time and effort planting bulbs, I don't want to risk wasting that effort and a full year for the sake of a few dollars' difference in price.

Getting Them into the Ground

Most books recommend an open, sunny site for the majority of bulbs. This is good advice for regions where the spring weather is cool, allowing the bulbs time to fatten up their reserves before the summer heat. But in our region we often leap from winter into hot, dry summer weather, a situation that promotes the development of many small bulbs where one large one was planted. This trend leads to a gradual decline in the quantity and size of the flowers.

Positioning the bulbs where they will receive spring sunshine without the blazing heat of early summer is a challenge, and often the best solution is to plant to the east or west of a building where there is shade for much of the day.

Naturalizing bulbs in grassy areas is also often advocated, but it poses problems of maintenance as the grass cannot be cut until the bulb foliage dies down in midsummer. Unless well irrigated, the grass steals most of the soil moisture and the bulbs fade away.

Bulbs look best planted in groups, rather than singly here and there. They also benefit from the addition of annual bedding plants in season to give them that needed shade. An alternative is to plant them among deciduous shrubs or ground covers—as long as soil moisture and nutrient level can be kept up.

For more than a handful of bulbs, the easiest way to plant is to excavate the entire bulb planting area to the required depth. Plant tulips with their bases 8 inches deep, spaced about 6 inches apart. In heavy clay soils, reduce the depth to 6 inches, incorporating coarse, washed sand at the bulb base to ease root penetration.

For other bulbs the rule of thumb is to plant four times as deep as the height of the bulb. Spacing between bulbs is done "according to taste," averaging about 6 inches apart, or closer for the small ones. If your soil is heavy clay, dig some coarse sand in where the bulbs will sit. You can also add a dusting of bone-meal—but not if you have inquisitive dogs in the neighborhood.

Once the bulbs are set out, you should cover them with soil free of big lumps, firm the soil by treading down lightly, and water the area thoroughly. No further water should be necessary before winter unless you have a particularly long, dry fall.

Bulb Care

After the bulbs have finished flowering in the spring, the spent flowers may be removed to prevent bulb energy being diverted to seed production. The foliage can be treated to moisture and a good bulb food to build the bulbs up for the following year's show. The tops should not be removed until they yellow naturally in midsummer.

Digging the bulbs after the tops die down and sorting, drying, and replanting the largest are frequently recommended. My experience, however, is that because bulbs on the plains don't have a long, moist summer in which to fatten up for the following season, it is best simply to add some good new ones to the group every year or so.

Some gardeners apply a mulch after planting to delay the freezing of the soil a week or two and so extend the period of fall root development. A mulch may also be of some benefit in places where the soil would otherwise warm up before spring and force premature sprouting. The disadvantage of a mulch is that it cannot be removed in spring without the risk of damaging emerging bulb shoots.

Bulb Tips

While some people in our region grow tulips and other bulbs successfully, others seem to get one year of good bloom, followed by several seasons of decline in both the number and the quality of flowers. This is not so much due to regional differences in climate as it is to the different cultural practices employed.

A bulb planting that is heading for failure has one or more of the following features.

- Bulbs of kinds not hardy enough to survive our winters;
- Bulbs purchased at a bargain price (often small or deteriorating because of poor storage facilities);
- Early-flowering kinds of tulips and daffodils used (likely to be damaged by late spring frosts);
- Bulbs planted late in the fall, shortly before the ground freezes;
- Bulbs planted under trees, where soil is usually dry;
- Bulbs planted close to the north or south side of a building (too shady or too hot);
- Soil waterlogged (poorly drained) or compacted (heavy clay);
- Bulbs crowded or planted at the wrong depth;
- Insufficient soil moisture and nutrients to keep the leaves growing after flowering;

- Leaves removed after the flowering season to keep the garden tidy.

It follows that your bulb investment will be more likely to blossom if you keep these points in mind.

- Purchase top-quality bulbs from a knowledgeable supplier;
- Ask for cultivars or species well proven for your area (late-flowering Darwin tulips are a safe bet);
- Plant as soon as the bulbs are available, early in September if possible;
- Plant where the bulbs will have adequate soil moisture and good drainage;
- Plant where the bulbs will be shaded for part of the day and not exposed to hot, dry conditions;
- Plant at the proper depth (see page 125);
- Continue to provide soil moisture and nutrients until the tops wither;
- Shade the soil of the bulb area from midsummer sun (low-growing annual plants serve well).

Tiny Tough Alternatives

While most of the bulbs grown in our region are tulips and some daffodils, there are several small but reliable bulbs that are excellent for sparkling up the ground with blossoms while other plants are just coming out of dormancy. My own choices, in approximate order of preference, are these.

Scilla sibirica, the Siberian squill. Blue hanging bells in May.

Tulipa tarda, a low species of tulip from Turkestan. Petals yellow and white. (A similar hardy species is *Tulipa kolpakowskiana.*)

Muscari, the grape hyacinths. Spikes of flowers like upright clusters of miniature grapes bloom in May or June. Available in different shades of blue and white. (The large hyacinths are not hardy enough to overwinter.)

Puschkinia scilliodes, the striped squill. Petals very pale blue with a deep blue midrib.

Chinodoxa luciliae, the glory of the snow. Violet to blue flowers with a white center.

Allium moly, the golden garlic. Bright yellow flowers in June on rather taller stems than the others mentioned here.

Bulbocodium vernum, the spring saffron. Lavender-rose flowers appearing very early and before their leaves.

Crocus vernus 'Purpureus Grandiflorus'. This is the only crocus that I have tried that does well for me, although other named selections of *Crocus vernus* should also be satisfactory. With the possible exception of *Crocus chrysanthus* 'E. A. Bowles,' the dainty crocuses don't survive long enough to make them worthwhile.

HARDY LILIES

Nearly all the lilies grown on the plains are hybrids of either martagon (Turkscap), Asiatic, Aurelian, or trumpet types. There are hundreds of named selections and dozens that are excellent for our region. In fact, a number of plains plant breeders have worked with lilies and produced world-class cultivars.

The lilies in the following table have all proven successful on the plains and may be considered top-rated cultivars.

White
'Snowbird' (upfacing)
'Snowdrop' (downfacing)
'Snowlark' (outfacing)
'Sterling' Star (upfacing)
'White Prince' (upfacing)

Cream/Ivory
'Dawn Star' (outfacing)
'Honey Queen' (outfacing)

Pink
'Carol Jean' (upfacing)
'Embarrassment' (outfacing)
'Pussy Cat' (outfacing)

Apricot
'Ambrosia' (outfacing)
'Maureen' (upfacing)

Red
'Firebright' (upfacing)
'Flaming Giant' (upfacing)

'Pirate' (upfacing)
'Red Carpet' (short, upfacing)
'Red King' (upfacing)
'Ruby' (upfacing)

Deep Red
'Towering Turk' (downfacing)

Bright Red
'Bold Knight' (downfacing)

Orange
'Alexis' (outfacing)
'Connecticut Yankee' (downfacing)
'Earlibird' (outfacing)
'Enchantment' (upfacing)
'Margie Wysong' (outfacing)
'Orange Light' (nonspotted, upfacing)

Yellow
'Ambassador' (upfacing)
'Connecticut King' (upfacing)
'Gold Rush' (upfacing)
'Golden Princess' (downfacing)
'Indian Maid' (outfacing)
'Nutmegger' (downfacing)
'Sonnentiger' (outfacing)
'Stuart Criddle' (upfacing)
'Sun Ray' (upfacing)

Bicolor
'Appleblossom' (pink/cream, upfacing)
'Cheerful Charlie' (wine/cream, outfacing)

Planting and Care

Lilies are an exception to the general rules for handling hardy bulbs. While the best time to transplant them is in the fall after the tops have withered, they cannot be allowed to dry out. Never expose lily bulbs to the dry air, and get them planted again as soon as possible. Plant at the original depth, carefully retaining any fleshy roots attached to the bulb. They must have good soil drainage, without standing water at any time.

Lilies are also offered for sale in the spring, and these should be planted as soon as the soil can be worked. Plant them with the tops of the bulbs covered 2 to 6 inches deep, the larger bulbs deepest. Many lilies have contratile roots that slowly pull the bulbs down to their ideal depth, thus the shallow planting. You might want to mulch newly planted lilies for the first couple of winters to be on the safe side; after that they will be settled in and satisfied without winter protection.

Don't expect fantastic results the first year from newly planted lilies. They need at least one season to build new basal roots while they live to a large extent on reserves stored in the bulb. Some lily gardeners plant newly acquired bulbs in a separate area for the first year in order to observe them for signs of botrytis. Plants afflicted with this disease develop wilting, shrivelled leaves from the bottom up during the growing season, spoiling the appearance and weakening the bulb for the following year. The chapter on diseases gives some advice on dealing with botrytis.

Once established, lilies will return like old friends to perform year after year. Lift and divide them only if, after several years, they seem to be declining despite adequate water and nutrients.

TENDER TYPES

There are a number of perennial plants with fleshy roots or stems that can be grown on the plains, but they need to be treated as annuals. Glads, begonias, and dahlias are all popular additions to the plains garden.

Glads

Gladiolus is Latin for a small sword, and in the past glads were known as sword lilies or corn lilies. Their sword-shaped leaves and spikelike cluster of flowers add variety and color to the garden without taking up much room. They are also excellent cut flowers because their individual flower buds open slowly from bottom to top.

The gladiolus stores its energy over winter in a corm. Superficially, a corm looks like a bulb, but if you cut a corm open you will see that it's solid—actually a modified stem. (True bulbs, like tulips and onions, have evolved from leaves and can be peeled apart.) The difference between a bulb and a corm is evident when gladioli are harvested in the fall and the old, withered corms are found attached to the bases of the fresh, newly developed ones. Incidentally, the clusters of small (pea-sized or smaller) cormels found

attached to corms at digging time would take two or more full growing seasons to reach flowering size, and they are usually discarded.

Gladiolus cultivars are classified by flower size, color, and season of bloom. Because of our relatively short season, grow only the very early to midseason kinds, avoiding the late midseason and late kinds (often abbreviated to LM and L in catalogs). The larger flower types are impressive in the garden, but small- and medium-flowered ones look best as cut flowers and in arrangements.

Several thousand selections have been named, dozens of which are available locally or from bulb and corm specialists. Flower colors range from white through yellow and buff, salmon, pink, and red to lavender and purple, with some smoky brown or green for those seeking the unusual.

Choose corms that are plump, not flat, and at least 1 inch or more in diameter. They can be planted in May, about two weeks before the last anticipated sharp frost. That way, by the time the shoots surface, they should be looking at mild weather. When grown as cut flowers, they are usually planted in rows for ease of cultivation. Try to rotate your glads to a different place in the garden each year, growing them in the same soil not more than once in four years.

Planting—Plant in a well-drained soil and a sunny location at a depth of about 4 inches—a little deeper for large corms and in light soils, less deep

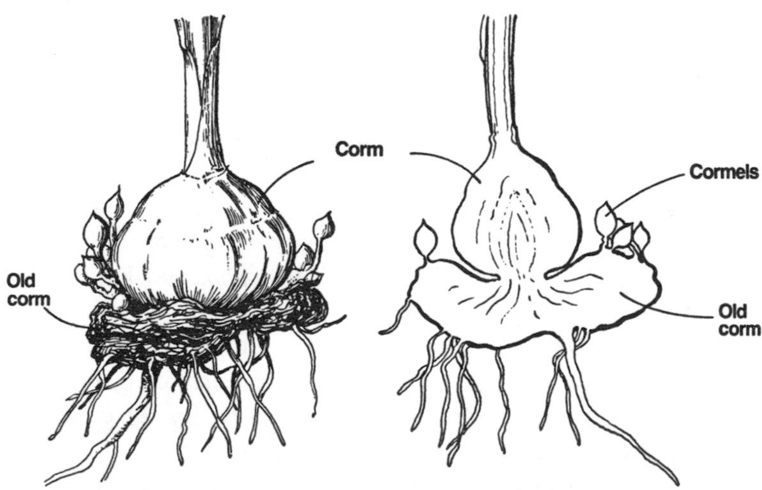

Gladiolus corm and cross section of the same corm, showing old corm and cormels.

in heavy clay. Bamboo canes and ties may be necessary to hold the tall spikes upright in the wind, and make sure the plants don't go short of water during the growing season. They need moisture at the roots—not applied by overhead sprinklers—and a side dressing of a high phosphorus fertilizer such as 11-48-0 once they are off and running.

Most of the flowering can be expected in late summer and fall, and if the corms get away to a slow start they may be hit by early frosts while still in bud. To give them a jump on the season and to encourage earlier flowering, you can plant the corms indoors in a flat (a wooden tray) of moist perlite or vermiculite a couple of weeks before the corms are normally planted outdoors. Once the roots are formed and the leaves emerge, plant them outdoors with the leaf tip just covered. Be careful not to break the brittle roots.

A recurring concern about glads is the mysterious change in flower color known as "reversion." I hear people complain that, for example, red flowering kinds do well for a few years and then suddenly flower white or yellow. Real color changes are extremely rare, with perhaps one or two flowers of a spike showing variation. What usually happens in the home garden is that some cultivars are more vigorous and persistent than others. A poor growing season or disease may eliminate the weaker kinds and, *voila*!, a change of color. In selecting the larger corms from your garden for replanting, you may unwittingly aid this natural selection. In order to give your glads the best possible chance of repeat blooming year after year, try not to take too many leaves when cutting flower spikes for indoors. If you remove too much foliage, you will have smaller corms and fewer flowers the following year.

Overwintering—If you intend to keep corms in storage for planting next spring, dig them on a fine day in early October, or after the first hard frost kills the tops, and cut off the tops close to the corm.

Cure them immediately for ten to fourteen days, until the new corm separates easily from the old one. Curing is simply a matter of spreading the corms out to dry in a warm place. A temperature of about 90°F is best, but 75°F will do.

Peeling off the old husk will reveal any rot and reduce the chance of overwintering insects and disease. After separation, discard the old corms and cure the new ones for another five or six days to dry the corm bases properly. They are then ready for dusting and storage.

Dust with an insecticidal-fungicidal bulb dust and store them in wire-mesh bottom trays all winter in a ventilated cold-room at about 40°F. Check

them once a month and remove any bad ones. An electric fan heater may be used briefly to reduce excess moisture. If suitable storage conditions are not available, I suggest that you buy new corms each spring.

Begonias

Tuberous begonias have gorgeous flowers, but they do demand attention and are recommended only for those who have time to fuss. The hot, dry prairie winds can be unkind to them, so they should be grown in semishade with some protection from the elements. They are much too tender to survive outdoors year-round, so they must be lifted and stored indoors over winter. These tuberous perennials should not be confused with the fibrous "wax" begonias (like *Begonia semperflorens*) that are throw-away annuals, nor with the "foliage" begonias (like *Begonia rex*) often grown in conservatories.

Tuberous begonias come in three different groups: those known as dwarf/multifloras that produce a short, bushy plant covered in a mass of small blooms; the large-flowered hybrids; and the pendula group suitable for hanging baskets.

The flowers show tremendous variety of form. Not only are there single, semidouble, and double-flowered kinds, they may be of camellia form, rose form, ruffled, or picotee with marked petal edgings. The color range is also extensive, from white, yellow, and pink to flamboyant reds and orange. The California hybrids are popular because of their sturdy growth and large flowers.

Unlike tulips and other hardy bulbs that are planted outdoors in the fall, the tuberous begonias needed to be started indoors in late March or early April, placing them, depressed side up, in an organic potting compost. If the soil mix is kept moist and the temperature maintained at 61 to 68°F, they will start to sprout in abut six weeks. Avoid rot by keeping water out of the center of the tuber and by maintaining a moist, not wet, soil.

Using a pot about three times the diameter of the tuber, the sprouted tubers can be planted in 5- and 6-inch pots with good drainage. Weak sprouts should be broken off to allow one or more strong shoots to produce larger flowers. When all danger of frost is passed, they may be left outdoors (re-

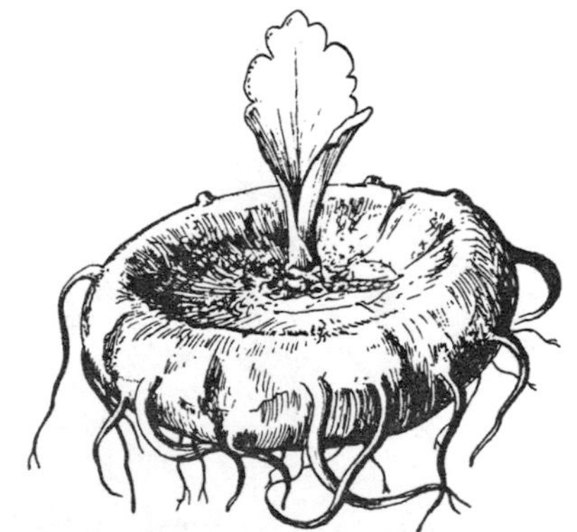

A sprouting tuberous begonia.

maining in their pots or transplanted) in a spot that is not cooked by the midday sun. They enjoy bright light without direct sunlight. Use green bamboo stakes and string to tie the taller soft stems, as they are easily damaged in rough weather. Tuberous begonias look especially impressive in window-boxes, patios, and hanging baskets on a protected porch. If the smaller (female) flowers can be picked off and the faded flowers regularly removed, the plants will bloom flamboyantly all season.

After the first fall frost, let the potted tuberous begonias mature by withholding water, or dig those that have been planted out, keeping as much soil as possible at the roots. After about three weeks the tops will be wilted and can easily be pulled off near the tuber in preparation for storage. Keep over winter in the pot or in dry vermiculite or peat moss in a basement cold-room held at about 40 to 50°F.

If you don't find the price too off-putting, you can avoid some of the fuss and still enjoy these exotic plants by purchasing your tuberous begonias already in bloom when you pick up your spring bedding plants.

Dahlias

There are sizes and colors of dahlias to suit every taste, but again, only those who have the time and interest to store roots over winter will persist with these tender perennials. For large gardens there are the spectacular giants of 5 feet or more in height, and smaller ones—down to dwarfs—for smaller spaces. They do well in sun or a little shade and a well drained, fertile soil.

Dahlia tubers are planted outdoors in May, a couple of weeks before the last anticipated spring frost. Plant horizontally in a 8-inch hole with the sprout up. It is recommended that the support stakes for the taller dahlias be tapped in place at this time, as stakes driven in later could hurt more than their feelings. The planted tuber is covered by about 2 1/2 inches of soil. Then gradually fill in the hole over the next few weeks as the sprouts grow. Dahlias respond to feeding with a fertilizer high in phosphorus, good soil moisture (not wet), and tying to prevent wind damage.

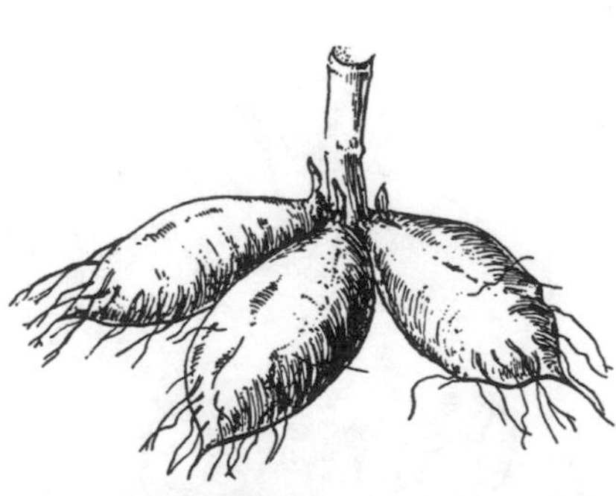

Plant dahlia tubers horizontally with the sprout pointing up.

The main stems are usually cut back early in the season to induce branching, and enthusiasts may also pinch out still-small buds to direct energy into the remaining flowers. This is a trick used by those who like to compete at horticultural shows.

As the season ends, allow the tubers to dry out if possible and be ready to dig them up about ten days after the first frost blackens the foliage. Cut the tops off, and dig to retain as much soil around the tubers as possible. These encased roots can then be stored in boxes in a basement cold-room, at 35 to 50°F . If the soil falls away from the tubers, they should be left indoors to dry for a week or so. Remove the stems. Discard any tubers with signs of rot, dust them with sulphur or a commercial bulb dust for sanitation, and store in boxes of dry vermiculite, peat moss or sawdust. This packing material should be kept moist enough to prevent the tubers from emerging from winter shrivelled like King Tut, but not so moist that they rot and start to sprout in storage. If a heated greenhouse is available, you can resurrect the tubers in early March; otherwise, plant outdoors in May as discussed earlier.

CHAPTER X

Herbaceous Perennials

The term "herbaceous perennial" refers to the many plants that die down to the ground each season and sprout again each spring. In the gardening sense, this term refers to such plants grown for their ornamental value. Catalogs often include them as either "perennials" or just "HP."

PREPARATIONS

Choosing a Site

Perennials are often used to provide patches of relief in shrub borders or foundation plantings, or as occasional flowering plants grouped here and there around the home and yard. They are most effective, however, when used as a mass display. This can be either as an island bed or as the more traditional perennial border. The advantage of an island bed is that it can be appreciated from all sides. The disadvantage is that it can easily look like a ship adrift on an open sea of green. As a general rule, I would suggest keeping such plantings off the front lawn and using them only if they can be balanced visually with other prominent landscape features such as a specimen tree or shrub, a mellow brick wall, or a stone ornamental feature. Perennials really come into their own when they are used as a backdrop for family activities in the private area of the property.

In selecting a location for a typical group of perennials, try to find a sunny spot. A good site is often found along a fence or garden wall, leaving a little space at the back for maintenance access. If space permits, the border should be at least 6 1/2 feet wide to allow for the most flattering arrangement of plants. The site should not be crowded by trees and shrubs, which might cast unwanted shade or sap valuable nutrients from the soil.

Color through the Seasons

One of the nicest things about herbaceous perennials is that they return like old friends year after year. They also arrive in the same sequence, turning the garden into a giant calendar as they announce the passing seasons. From springtime on, a series of herbaceous perennials produces a continuous parade of color until the ground freezes in the autumn. But contrary to popular belief, this does not mean that you can have a season-long mass of bloom from herbaceous perennials. Rather, you have two choices. Either plant those that flower all at the same time to obtain a solid show for a limited period, or plant an assortment that provides some color (but not a solid show of color) from spring to fall.

If you opt for some color all season, spring-flowering attractions like giant rockfoil or lungwort will continue to take up space long after their early but brief spring performance. The foliage may be satisfactory, but that space will not produce color again until the following year. Likewise, fall-flowering goldenrods are just patches of green promise all season as they await the shortening days of late summer.

To obtain that dashing picture-postcard show of solid color that most gardeners hope for, you must sacrifice season-long color and opt for a collection of perennials that bloom together all at the same time. Such a display is easiest to arrange for peak bloom in July. So you still want the best of both worlds? Then plant one area to give that photogenic display in midseason, and plan to have separate places for both spring- and fall-flowering perennials. The early- and late-flowering plants can be given visual support during the nonflowering part of the season by adding spring bulbs and annual bedding plants.

Early-flowering perennials
Bergenia cordifolia (giant rockfoil or heartleaf bergenia)
Centaurea montana (mountain bluet)
Convallaria majalis (lily-of-the-valley)
Primula auricula (auricula)
Pulmonaria saccharata (lungwort or Bethlehem sage)
Saponaria ocymoides (rock soapwort)

Late-flowering perennials
Achillea millefolium (yarrow)
Aster hybrids (aster)
Gyposphila paniculata (baby's breath)
Saponaria officinalis (bouncing bet)
Solidago (goldenrod)

Color Combinations

The first rule when arranging plantings for effect is to use bold blocks of color rather than a patchwork of many different colors. Having said this, I must quickly add that your personal preference is more important than any rule. As you stop to notice other gardens and illustrations of herbaceous plantings, you will increasingly develop a feel for the color arrangement and combinations of plants.

In the herbaceous border where many kinds are to flower simultaneously, you can use the general principles of color theory to provide a pleasing picture. Plant flowers with complementary colors side by side. Some planning ahead on paper helps to avoid a *faux pas* such as orange in combination with bright pink, salmon, or magenta.

There is no last word on color preferences and combinations. Some people wrinkle up their noses at a planting of pink-flowered sweet Williams next to yellow-flowered stonecrop, yet others enjoy the striking effect of that same yellow and pink combination. You can always plant the border experimentally and watch to see if anything cries out to be moved.

The herbaceous border can reflect the design of the garden as a whole to give an impression of either vitality or tranquillity. Use bright flower colors such as yellow, orange, and scarlet to produce a vibrant effect. Alternatively, restrict your selection of flowers to the more subdued tints and shades such as mauve, purple, and the tans and mahogany (found in some of the daylilies) to produce a feeling of serenity. In either situation, a scattering of white-flowering plants is a good idea, as white highlights the subdued flower colors and prevents monotony, and in a bright border it tends to separate clashing colors.

Don't forget that warm colors like red, pink, and especially orange appear to come closer, while cool colors like blue and lavender appear distant. Using this to your advantage, you can plant yellow, orange, and white to make a distant section of the border appear closer; use soft blue, mauve, and blue-grey foliage to create visual distance.

Plant Patterns

The obvious advice in arranging herbaceous perennials is to group the larger specimens to the rear and center of the border. However, if this arrangement is followed without variation, the effect can be rather monotonous. Try to group upright plants among those with rounded forms, without hiding the smaller ones from view.

Keen plantsmen are most likely to fall into the habit of using all available space to grow as many different kinds as possible. This "plant zoo" approach may lead to an interesting plant collection, but it is not the way to achieve a satisfying landscape design. To avoid that spotty and disjointed look, plant at least three or five of most kinds of plants to form groups. Then, if space allows, repeat the same arrangement several times to create a pattern.

The Casual Approach

An alternative to doing a lot of reading and preliminary planning before planting your perennial border is to try the method of gradual acquisition, purchasing a small assortment of readily available perennials each spring. After all, this is the way thousands of amateur gardeners get started. The idea is to gradually introduce an assortment of these ornamentals into your garden over a period of several seasons. You may not always know what to expect, but your interest will be sparked by an element of uncertainty.

Warning. Although this blind planting method allows you to skip the initial planning stage, the time will come when plants have to be moved to create the best effect. This is much like rearranging furniture and is a practice common to all gardeners, whether they start with a well-considered plan or not.

It's a good idea, especially when "planting blind," to keep labels with the plants so you know later which plants did or did not provide the desired effect. White plastic labels marked with pencil last for several seasons. Push them into the center of the plant just beneath the soil surface at planting time.

After a few seasons you will become your own expert. You will know which of the tall ones are best suited to the middle or back of the border, which flower colors go well together, and which should be planted here and there throughout the border to provide variety in form and foliage texture. By exchanging divisions or cuttings of your successful plants with neighbors and friends, you can soon develop an interesting collection.

SPECIAL PLANT GROUPS

Some gardeners love to specialize and build up a fine collection in one genus, like the lily, daylily, or peony. I advise such enthusiasts to join a society specializing in the plant of their choice. Your botanic garden or other horticultural facility should be able to provide you with an initial contact. Other gardeners specialize in groups of perennials suited to special situations.

The Rock Garden

Rock gardens are becoming popular with owners of small city lots because they need not take up much space and yet they still give the gardener the satisfaction of a growing a wide variety of different plants. The dwarf perennials suited to rock gardens are known as alpines.

Choose a sunny, sheltered location for your rock garden, in a place where there is good snow cover. Although alpines are adapted to long, cold winters, they do not appreciate the extremes of temperature (winter or summer) that we often get on the plains: winter snow cover and shelter from desiccating winds will help moderate the extremes. The site must also be well drained, as alpines are subject to root rot.

Dwarf perennials come in a number of forms that are suited for rock garden plantings. Maiden pinks and saxifrages develop into compact cushions of foliage covered with delicate flowers. Creeping plants such as rock soapwort and certain stonecrops carpet soil and rocks. For variety, Carpathian bellflowers provide neat tufts of green with a long season of dainty bell flowers. Moss pinks (a creeping phlox) serve to link soil and stone by embracing both as they slowly advance, and dwarf iris offer their fans of pointed leaves in a show of individuality.

Some perennials for the rock garden

Alyssum saxatile (madwort or perennial alyssum)
Anemone pulsatilla or *Pulsatilla vulgaris* (pasqueflower)
Artemisia schmidtiana (silver mound)
Campanula carpatica (Carpathian bellflower)
Cerastium tomentosum (snow-in-summer)
Dianthus deltoides (maiden pink)
Geranium sanguineum prostratum (Lancaster geranium)
Gypsophila repens (creeping baby's breath)
Heuchera hybrids (coral bells)
Iris pumila (dwarf iris)
Phlox subulata (creeping phlox or moss pink)
Saponaria ocymoides (rock soapwort)
Saxifraga paniculata (saxifrage or rock foil)
Sedum (stonecrop)
Sempervivum (hen-and-chicks)
Veronica repens (dwarf speedwell)

Ground Covers

Lawns, a mass of annual bedding plants, and inert matter like bark bits and granite chips are all ground covers, but what we usually mean by the term is a growing mat of plant material that spreads, trails, or creeps over the soil. Although some ground covers are conifers (such as the low-growing junipers) and woody climbers such as clematis can be trained over the ground just as easily as on a support, the majority of ground covers grown in the home garden are herbaceous perennials.

Some perennial ground covers are more aggressive than others. Fast-spreading plants are an advantage at first in covering and stabilizing the soil, but they may create a maintenance problem when they refuse to stop where you would like them to. Lethargic plants, on the other hand, are not likely to push their way into the territory of an adjacent plant, but they take longer to fill in the bare spaces. But you never know; slow plants in one garden may be quite active in another, not only because of climatic differences from region to region but also because of microclimatic factors such as soil, soil moisture, and exposure. As a general rule, ground covers spread very rapidly when reasonably satisfied with their situation, so they are best used in areas where they can easily be contained—such as along the side of a building with a path or other kind of root barrier on the other side.

One thing is certain. The term "ground cover" should never be equated with "weed killer." Ground covers may help suppress annual weeds, but if ever a determined perennial nuisance like thistle or quack grass enters the scene, you will likely have to renovate the entire area by clearing and replanting. Before planting ground covers, then, it pays to leave the land fallow long enough to ensure that all perennial weeds are gone.

Ground covers for shady locations

Aegopodium podagraria variegata (variegated goutweed)
Convallaria majalis (lily-of-the-valley)
Glechoma hederacea variegata (variegated creeping Charlie)
Hosta (plantain lily)
Lysimachia nummularia (creeping Jenny or moneywort)
Vinca minor (periwinkle)

Ground covers for sunny locations

Cerastium tomentosum (snow-in-summer)
Dianthus deltoides (maiden pink)
Eriogonum umbellatum subalpinum (umbrella plant)
Glechoma hederacea variegata (variegated creeping Charlie)
Phlox subulata (creeping phlox or moss pink)
Saponaria ocymoides (rock soapwort)
Sedum (stonecrop)
Sempervivum (hen-and-chicks)
Thymus serpyllum (mother-of-thyme)

GROWING TIPS

The soil at the site chosen for your perennial border should be in good tilth, and it is most important to see that all perennial weeds are removed before planting time. A low retaining wall can be used to create a raised planting area for sites that have cold and poorly drained soil. Two or three weeks before planting, the soil should be treated to a helping of fertilizer high in phosphorus (such as 11-48-0) mixed well into the soil by digging or rototilling.

Seed for herbaceous perennials may be gathered from garden plants or purchased. Home-grown seed will often produce good results, but some complex hybrids, such as Russell lupins, should be grown only from seed offered by the better seed houses. Not all herbaceous perennials are satisfactory when grown from seed. Seed of some plants can be difficult to germinate or may take a long time to produce a mature plant. Some herbaceous perennials have been carefully selected from a complex genetic background and should be grown from root division or cuttings to maintain the superior type. Some others (like the cushion mums) do not produce seed. Many perennials are therefore set in the ground as plants.

As individual herbaceous perennials become established, many can be divided and replanted as two or more plants. In general, planting and division of herbaceous perennials is best accomplished in the early spring, before new growth commences, or in late summer, after all top growth has ceased for the season. Peonies do best if transplanted in the fall, after the first hard frost. At these times it is often easy to separate roots by teasing them into two or more pieces before replanting or (if they don't separate easily) by slicing fibrous clumps with a sharp spade or knife. Early spring is also the time to cut back any of last year's growth that was left on plants to catch snow for winter protection. A few perennials like columbine, baby's breath, and some pinks have a tap-root, and division of these is not satisfactory. If you need to increase your stock of such plants and seeding is not an option, you will have to propagate by cuttings rooted in moist sand—or leave the job to nurserymen.

Should you miss out on the spring transplanting season, don't despair. If necessary, most perennials can be transplanted with care at any time during the growing season. Just remove any flower stems, cut the plant back by half, and dig to retain a ball of soil around the roots. Once in its new home—with a slight depression around the root area to hold water—soak once and maintain some soil moisture for a few weeks without overwatering. To be on the safe side, you might want to screen the tops for a week or so until they can take the sun and wind again without wilting.

WINTERING

Herbaceous perennials are not as vulnerable to our wild winters as are the woody trees and shrubs, mainly because they don't stick their necks out. The tops of most herbaceous perennials naturally die off each winter, producing fresh growth each spring. As long as the below-ground parts are kept snug, all is well. At least some of the plant top should be left on during the winter to catch drifting snow. Exceptions are peonies and lilies, which might be infected with botrytis disease; in such cases the tops are removed to the ground and disposed of.

Where there is reliable snow cover throughout the dormant season, overwintering of perennials poses no problem. But in places where snow protection is uncertain or where warm chinook weather stays long enough to interrupt dormancy, you should protect the plants with a material like flax straw, light strawy manure, wood chips or discarded Christmas trees. Avoid nonbreathing materials such as plastic, or anything like grass or leaves that mat down when wet. Place the protective covering after the soil has frozen down an inch or so. Once in place, the mulch will prevent significant temperature fluctuations at the root zone.

SELECTING SUITABLE PERENNIALS

First of all, consider the kind of habitat you have to offer your perennials. In many cases where herbaceous perennials have been written off by plains growers as being "not hardy," the difficulty has been in discovering and providing a suitable microclimate (including soil), according to their needs. *Primula* (primroses of various kinds) are a good example. A number of different primrose species and cultivars have survived without winter-kill throughout the region. The organic soil where they grow is cool and moist, and they enjoy a blanket of snow for most of the winter. Losses would more likely be expected during the hot, dry conditions of summer. You may have to remind yourself as well that, while some of the old-fashioned kinds of *Hemerocallis* (daylily) and *Iris* (bearded iris) are as tough as you please, there are named selections of these same plants that have been developed for gardens in other climates that are not likely to do well here.

Consider too the amount of time you have to invest in your garden. Some perennials demand more than their share of attention. While *Paeonia* (peony) and *Dicentra* (bleeding heart) are examples of those that may be left undisturbed from one human generation to the next, many other perennials must be dug and divided or they deteriorate. Tall plants may need staking. Examples of the more challenging herbaceous perennials include the outdoor cushion type of chrysanthemum needing frequent division and the *Chrysanthemum x superbum* (shasta daisy) group, which are often short lived here. *Lupinus* hybrids (lupins) are also short lived and need to be replaced often. Many of the tall *Delphinium* hybrids are top heavy, and fit to be tied. Invasive subjects such as *Aegopodium podagraria variegata* (goutweed) and *Lysimachia nummularia* (creeping Jenny) need to be contained in their allotted space or they will attack and choke their neighbors.

The following reference list includes many of the herbaceous perennials advisable and satisfactory for the plains garden.

HERBACEOUS PERENNIALS FOR THE PLAINS

Those plants marked with an asterisk (*) will thrive in a variety of soils and situations. The remainder should be planted in their preferred situation of soil, moisture, and light intensity. All plant dimensions are average and will vary according to microclimate and cultural conditions.

* ***Achillea millefolium*** **(yarrow)**—The common yarrow is a wild plant with flat heads of whitish flowers. The hardiest garden kinds are 12 to 24 inches tall and have rose-pink flowers that bloom from July to August. 'Cerise Queen' and 'Fire King' are satisfactory cultivars. The large-flowered yellow hybrids such as 'Coronation Gold' need a sheltered site. All prefer well-drained soil.

* ***Achillea ptarmica*** **(sneezewort)**—The double-flowered form called 'The Pearl' is popular. It reaches a height of 24 inches and blooms from June to September. Best lifted and divided every year or so, sneezewort is valued for its drought tolerance. It can be invasive.

* ***Aconitum x bicolor*** **(monk's-hood)**—Two-tone blue and white flowers in July and August. These tall plants (3 to 4 feet) prefer rich, moist soil and may need staking. All parts are poisonous if eaten.

* ***Aegopodium podagraria variegata*** **(variegated goutweed)**—Light green and cream foliage. A useful ground cover under 12 inches for shady and difficult sites, but extremely invasive if the root system is not contained.

Alyssum saxatile **(madwort or perennial alysum)**—'Silver Queen' is a low (under 12 inches), very compact cultivar with lemon-yellow flowers from late May through June. Drought tolerant, madwort is especially good in rock gardens. It can be grown from seed and does best in well-drained soil.

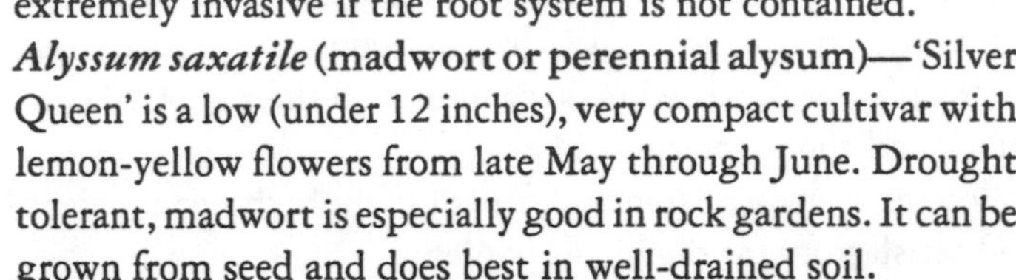

* ***Anchusa azurea*** **(Italian bugloss)**—The coarse foliage and floppy habit are overlooked when the true blue flowers are displayed from late June through early August. Italian bugloss does best in well-drained soil and will reach 2 to 3 feet. Deadhead (remove spent flowers) to prevent unwanted seedlings. One of the best named cultivars is 'Loddon Royalist.'

* ***Anemone pulsatilla*** **or *Pulsatilla vulgaris*** **(pasqueflower)**—Similar to our native prairie crocus, flowers purple to pink and white in April and May. Plants are usually raised from seed, doing best in well-drained soil, and often the seeds come true to flower color. Pasqueflowers generally grow to a height of 8 to 12 inches and are suitable for rock gardens.

* ***Anemone sylvestris*** **(snowdrop anemone)**—The single white flowers bloom in June and July and show up well in shade. Snowdrop anemones can be grown from seed. They need a rich, moist soil and will reach a height of up to 24 inches.

* ***Anthemis tinctoria*** **(golden Marguerite)**—Cheerful yellow flowers bloom in August and September like small, single mums. Good for hot, dry sites and poor soil conditions, golden Marguerite reaches 2 to 3 feet. Divide good selections every year or so and weed out seedlings. Named selections have much superior flowers.

* ***Aquilegia*** **hybrids (columbine)**—The bicolored and spurred columbines are favorites in the flower border. Columbines may bloom from May to August and attain heights ranging from under 12 inches to 3 feet. Easily grown from seed, but often short-lived, and not easily transplanted once established. The 'McKana's Giant' and 'Biedermeier' hybrids are popular. A dwarf form, *Aquilegia alpina*, is suitable for half-shaded spots in rock gardens.

Armeria maritima **(thrift or sea pink)**—Pink flowers from June to August, held above cushion tufts of green about 6 inches high. Named selections are offered. Must have sun and well-drained soil.

Artemisia schmidtiana **(silver mound)**—'Silver Mound' is one of the more popular cultivars, the name describing the cushions of silvery foliage up to 8 inches high. The plants are much more compact if sheared lightly before the insignificant flowers develop. They are very popular for rock gardens, preferring well-drained soil. Divide every three years or whenever the mound starts to get ragged.

Aruncus dioicus **or** ***Aruncus sylvester*** **(goat's beard)**—From June through July, white flowers in plumelike panicles, leaves divided, on 2- to 4-foot plants. The slightly smaller 'Knifii' has finely divided, lacy foliage. Goat's beard requires rich, moist soil.

Aster **hybrids (aster)**—Appreciated for their pink to purple flowers at the end of the season, asters prefer moist soil and reach 12 to 24 inches. Most showy ones dislike the hot plains summers and not all will survive the winters. Others are highly susceptible to mildew, especially in dry soils.

* ***Bergenia cordifolia*** **(giant rockfoil or heartleaf bergenia)**—This and similar species (*Bergenia crassifolia*) and hybrids are very reliable in plains gardens. Green rhubarblike leaves turn reddish in fall. Pink flowers on fleshy stems about 18 inches high in early spring. Tolerates most soil conditions.

* ***Campanula carpatica*** **(Carpathian bellflower)**—Attractive mauve, purple, or white flowers bloom from July to September. Easily raised from seed and grows to 12 to 24 inches. Divide every three or four years. Avoid very dry or very wet sites. The neat tufts of green with a long season of dainty bellflowers add variety to the rock garden.

* ***Campanula glomerata*** **(clustered bellflower)**—Clusters of purple or white flowers from July to September on plants up to 24 inches tall. Clustered bellflower is too boisterous and invasive for most gardens. Divide or reduce every year or so.

* ***Campanula persicifolia*** **(peach-leaved bellflower)**—One of the most hardy and desirable candidates for the herbaceous border. Purple-blue or, occasionally, white flowers from June to August. One to 3-foot plants. Divide every three or four years.

* ***Centaurea montana*** (mountain bluet)—A coarse plant, 12 to 24 inches, with blue flowers in May and intermittently through to September. An occasional plant is useful in large borders as filler material. Very hardy, even in poor soil, but needs good drainage. The same can be said for the taller growing *Centaurea macrocephala*, with large, yellow, thistlelike flowers.

Cerastium tomentosum (snow-in-summer)—Thick, silvery green mats about 6 inches high, well covered with starry white flowers in spring. A useful ground cover and trailing plant in the rock garden, as long as soil is well drained. Divide and replant if vigor declines.

Chrysanthemum coccineum (pyrethrum)—Single or double daisy flowers in pink, red, or white in June and July. Foliage finely divided, and plants attain 12 to 24 inches. There are many attractive cultivars, all of which require rich, well-drained soil. Good as cut flowers.

* ***Chrysanthemum maximum*** (shasta daisy or daisy chrysanthemum)—Single white flowers with a yellow center from June to August on 12- to 24-inch plants. This and the similar oxeye daisy enjoy rich, moist soil and are very hardy. They tend to become weedy in borders and lawns if not kept within bounds. Many of the fancy shasta daisy hybrids (*Chrysanthemum x superbum*) are not hardy enough, but try 'King Edward VII' and 'Sedgewick.'

Chrysanthemum morifolium (outdoor mums)—Appear similar to the Mother's Day pot plants. The hybrids developed for the plains are compact plants, up to 12 inches, covered with well-formed flowers in a good range of colors. They bloom from June to September and prefer rich, well-drained soil. To survive more than a season or two, they must be divided in the fall after blooming.

* ***Convallaria majalis*** (lily-of-the-valley)—This well-known ground cover, happy in shady places, may reach up to 12 inches. It needs to be divided and replanted every few years in enriched soil or it soon fails to bloom. The fragrant, white, bell-shaped flowers appear in May and June.

* ***Coreopsis verticillata*** (threadleaf coreopsis)—Deep yellow flowers from July to September; foliage finely divided into

linear segments. Threadleaf coreopsis will attain 12 to 24 inches grown in moist soil. Most other species are less satisfactory on the plains.

Delphinium hybrids (delphinium)—The common delphinium with true-blue flowers on tall spikes is a tenacious plant, frequently self-seeding in a moist shady soil. The more choice delphiniums, however, like the tall Pacific Giant hybrids (3 to 4 feet or more), and the shorter (about 30-inch) Connecticut Yankees hybrids, are more difficult to satisfy. When they do perform they make up for their fussiness with large flowers in June and July in a good range of colors. In general they are short lived, lasting from three to six years. Seed saved from your own plants of these special selections will be less satisfactory as subsequent generations show characteristics of their more primitive ancestors. Therefore, it's wise to obtain your plants and seed from a reliable grower. All the tall delphiniums need to be staked and tied before the first summer squalls throw them down. If you take time to cut out all but four or five of the new shoots in spring, the remaining stems will be more sturdy, but they will still need to be tied. Some perfectionists like to nip out all the flower buds from delphiniums the first year to allow the plants to build strong reserves of energy; this can pay off with sturdier plants and more flowers in future years. The pink-flowering hybrids are less robust than the blues and whites. The need to remove spent blooms and protect against insects and diseases makes these "high maintenance" plants. Rich, moist soil is also necessary for delphiniums to thrive.

* ***Dianthus deltoides*** (maiden pink)—Dense mats of green with dozens of small, bright, single flowers in red, pink, or white make welcome additions to the rock garden or as a cheerful ground cover. Self-seeding but easily hoed out where not required. A number of cultivars are offered, reaching heights of up to 12 inches and flowering in June and July.

Dianthus gratianopolitanus (cheddar pink)—Fragrant pink carnation like flowers in June and July, held above tufts of grey-green foliage up to 12 inches high. Requires well-drained soil.

* ***Dicentra spectabilis*** **(bleeding heart)**—A favorite garden perennial, well known for its heart-shaped, rosy flowers hanging on gracefully arching stems in May and June. The 2- to 3-foot plants need rich, well-drained soil. White-flowered forms are less robust. *Dicentra eximia* and *Dicentra formosa* are similar but smaller plants with more finely textured foliage and longer periods of bloom.

Doronicum cordatum **or** ***Doronicum caucasicum*** **(leopard's bane)**—Rather coarse plants, 12 to 24 inches tall, valued for their yellow daisylike flowers early in the season. Best planted in rich soil with a mulch to keep the roots cool.

Echinops ritro **(globe thistle)**—Globe-shaped, thistlelike heads of silvery blue from July to September. Used for dried flower arrangements. These tall, 3- to 4-foot plants are often short lived in our region, although they can self-seed. They require a rich soil to thrive.

* ***Erigeron*** **hybrids (fleabane)**—Named divisions of these pink- and mauve-flowered, daisylike hybrids are of more value than those grown from seed. They bloom from July to August and will perform better in well-drained soil. Suitable cultivars include 'Amity,' 'Charity,' and 'Dignity.' Fleabane generally attain 12 to 24 inches.

Eriogonum umbellatum subalpinum **(umbrella plant)**—Although not commonly available, the umbrella plant is one that I would like to see promoted. This ground-hugging plant spreads slowly, rooting across the ground on short woody stems, creating a dense mat of small, firm leaves. Early in the season it sends up short stems 8 inches tall with flowering clusters spread at the top in a way that suggests an umbrella. The flowers are cream in color when fresh, drying with rosy tints as they hang on into summer. This ground cover plant native to the Rocky Mountains does well on sandy soils, spreading steadily but without excessive vigor.

* ***Eryngium planum*** **(sea holly)**—Relatively small blue flower heads (flowering from July to September) are subtended by rather spiny collars. The young stems and leaves are also metallic blue and retain their color and form when air dried. Plants, which reach 2 to 3 feet, will tolerate poor soil as long as drainage is good.

* ***Euphorbia cyparissias*** (cypress spurge)—Spreading by creeping roots, this low plant, under 12 inches, is useful as a soil stabilizer. It has dense clusters of greenish yellow flowers in May and June, but it is grown primarily for its crowded, finely textured foliage. Its delicate appearance is deceptive, and it should not be planted close to other plants or in rock gardens, where it can become a weed. It will do well in most soils, provided drainage is good.

Euphorbia epithymoides (cushion spurge)—Very uniform plants 12 to 24 inches tall with long-lasting and showy golden early flower bracts. Hardy in well-drained sites.

Gaillardia x grandiflora (blanket flower)—Several excellent selections of this plant can be grown from seed, including 'Burgundy' (deep red flowers) and 'Goblin' (red petals tipped yellow). Flowering periods vary from July to August, and heights from under 12 inches to 3 feet. All need well-drained soil but are short-lived even under ideal conditions.

* ***Geranium ibericum*** (crane's bill)—Informal but reliable perennials with rather small purple, mauve, or white flowers from June to August. Not to be confused with the common garden geranium. Good selections include 'Johnson's Blue' and 'Album.' *Geranium endresii* is another rugged perennial of this same group with the cultivar 'A. T. Johnson' (light pink). Selections need well-drained soil and attain heights varying from under 12 inches to 24 inches.

Geranium sanguineum prostratum or ***Geranium sanguineum lancastriense*** (Lancaster geranium)—A choice crane's bill with soft-pink flowers veined crimson from June to September. Low growing, 6 inches, and more compact than other types. Needs well-drained soil.

Glechoma hederacea variegata (variegated creeping Charlie)—This low-growing ground cover has obtained a bad name where allowed to colonize lawns, alpine gardens, or other choice plantings. But in areas where root berries can be used, in sun or shade, this green or yellow foliage plant can be relied upon to succeed.

* ***Gypsophila paniculata*** (baby's breath)—This species is drought tolerant and hardy enough that it has become naturalized on sunny slopes. Once established, it is difficult to

transplant because of the tap root. It flowers from July to September and reaches 3 to 4 feet. Two of the more desirable cultivars are 'Bristol Fairy' a double-flowered white, and 'Compacta Plena' a more compact plant, 15 inches tall, with double white flowers fading to pale pink.

Gypsophila repens **(creeping baby's breath)**—A more dainty and trailing form of baby's breath, suitable for use as a ground cover, and in rock gardens. Low plants, under 12 inches, they require well-drained soil, and the white flowers bloom in June and July. 'Rosea' is a pink-flowered cultivar.

Heliopsis scabra **(orange sunflower)**—Used as an accent plant and for cutting, this tall species will reach 2 to 3 feet. Obtain plants of cultivars, as they are much superior to the variable species. Orange sunflowers require rich, moist soil and flower from July to early September. 'Golden Plume' is a satisfactory cultivar with double flowers.

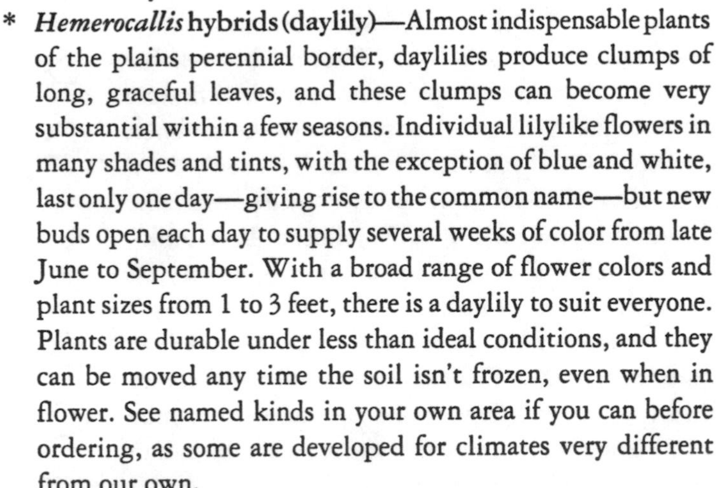

* ***Hemerocallis*** **hybrids (daylily)**—Almost indispensable plants of the plains perennial border, daylilies produce clumps of long, graceful leaves, and these clumps can become very substantial within a few seasons. Individual lilylike flowers in many shades and tints, with the exception of blue and white, last only one day—giving rise to the common name—but new buds open each day to supply several weeks of color from late June to September. With a broad range of flower colors and plant sizes from 1 to 3 feet, there is a daylily to suit everyone. Plants are durable under less than ideal conditions, and they can be moved any time the soil isn't frozen, even when in flower. See named kinds in your own area if you can before ordering, as some are developed for climates very different from our own.

Heuchera **hybrids (coral bells)**—Most coral bells cultivars are too tender for Great Plains plantings, but a few suitable ones have been developed for our climate, including 'Brandon Glow,' 'Brandon Pink', and a recent red-flowering hybrid, 'Northern Fire.' Although they tolerate dry conditions, coral bells do best in moist, well-drained soil. They can reach heights of up to 24 inches when in bloom, but the cultivars available for rock gardens, such as 'Brandon Pink,' are shorter (15 inches).

Hosta **(plantain lily)**—The small white or lavender flowers may be quite attractive in June and July, but the plantain lily is usually most prized for its distinctive and attractive foliage. Leaves are variously ribbed, wrinkled, and variegated with white or yellow marks or edgings, while some are blue-green in color. Plants are 12 to 24 inches tall and need rich, moist soil. Named ones that have done well in our region include *Hosta fortuei* 'Aureo-marginata,' 'Honeybells,' *Hosta fortunei, Hosta sieboldiana*, and *Hosta undulata.*

Iris **(iris)**—Although many iris are flamboyant and spectacular when in bloom, their flowering period is quite short. By planting early-, mid-season-, and late-flowering kinds the iris season can be extended a little. It is still a good idea, however, to mix them in with other flowering plants (without crowding them) where their foliage will make good contrast during the nonflowering season. The following selections are suitable for plains gardens.

Iris x germanica **(bearded iris hybrids)**—A wide range of sizes (1 to 3 feet), soft flower colors and bicolors, and large elegant flowers ensure that the bearded iris will retain a strong following among hobby growers. In the average home garden they may look a little out of place unless included in a formal border. Detractors also point to their short flowering season in the month of June and susceptibility to foliage tip burn and diseases. As clumps decline after several years, they should be lifted and divided in midsummer. Need well-drained soil.

Iris pumila **(dwarf iris)**—A wide array of colors and bicolors have been developed in these low (under 12-inch) plants. Dwarf iris look very much at home at the front of a flower border or in the rock garden, provided soil is well drained. They bloom in May. The line between these and the bearded iris hybrids becomes blurred as the two types are hybridized further to produce intermediates.

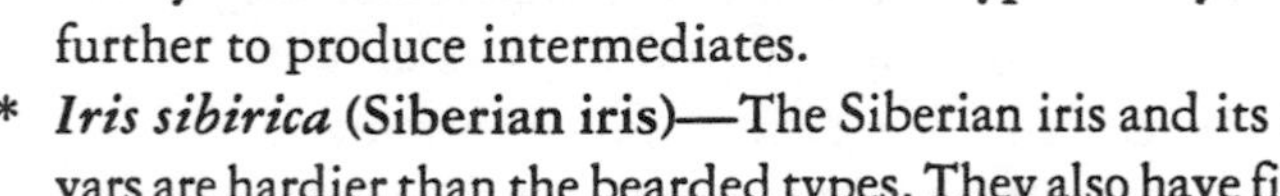

* ***Iris sibirica*** **(Siberian iris)**—The Siberian iris and its cultivars are hardier than the bearded types. They also have fibrous roots rather than rhizomes, but, with the exception of water, are not as demanding in their cultural requirements. Blooms appear in June and July; flower colors are generally limited to purple through mauve to white; size ranges from 2 to 3 feet.

* ***Liatris spicata*** **(spike blazing star)**—Strong flower spikes of rosy purple or white flowers, normally opening from the top down in August and September. The strong flower color may clash with nearby flowers but goes well with mauve or light yellow. 'Kobold' has darker flowers, 'Alba' white. Plants reach 2 to 3 feet in well-drained soil.

Ligularia dentata **or** ***Ligularia clivorum*** **(golden groundsel or ragwort)**—Bold, tall (3 to 4 feet or more) plants for the back of moist borders. They take up lots of room with their large, heart-shaped leaves. "Elephant Ears" is another common name. Flowers orange-yellow late in July to early September. 'Desdemona' is a frequently seen cultivar. Several other *Ligularia* species are satisfactory in the right location, notably *Ligularia przewalskii, Ligularia vietchiana,* and *Ligularia wilsoniana*. Availability may be a problem.

Limonium latifolium **(common sea lavender)**—Lavender sprays similar to baby's breath flower in August and September, and are popular for drying and use in winter bouquets. Also known as "perennial statice." Rather slow to become established and not easily transplanted. Prefers moist, well-drained soil; reaches 12 to 24 inches in height.

Linum perenne **(flax)**—Sky blue flowers remain closed in shade and on cloudy days. Plants reach 12 to 24 inches. Easily grown from seed in well-drained soil, they also self-seed. Plants cut back immediately after the May-June flowering tend to repeat bloom until fall.

Lupinus polyphyllus **hybrids (lupin)**—Thick spikes of flowers in many subtle colors in the range of pink, red, blue, purple, and yellow, plus white and cream. Must have a deep, moist soil in light shade. Seed in April where they are to bloom; they resent being transplanted because of their long tap root. Lupins are notoriously difficult plants to grow on the plains as they cannot stand alkalinity, and their roots easily dry out if not shaded or mulched. Recommended only for those willing to devote extra time and attention to their needs. Plants will grow to heights of 3 to 4 feet or more.

* ***Lychnis chalcedonica*** **(Maltese cross)**—Known by pioneers as "scarlet lightning," the magenta flower color of July blooms may clash with other flowers. Very hardy, thriving in rich,

moist soil and often becoming naturalized in abandoned garden sites. Reaches 2 to 3 feet. The larger and even brighter flowered *Lychnis x arkwrightii* is a nice alternative.

* ***Lychnis viscaria*** **(German catchfly)**—Narrow leaves, sticky stems, and a good show of rose-red flowers from May to July. Needs rich, moist soil and grows to 12 to 24 inches. 'Splendens' is offered, as well as the double-flowered, 'Splendens Flore Pleno.'

Lysimachia nummularia **(creeping Jenny or moneywort)**—A prostrate plant up to 8 inches valued for its success as a ground cover in moist areas. In such locations it will spread very rapidly by creeping stems. Flowers are bright yellow in midsummer. Propagate by division.

* ***Lythrum*** **hybrids (purple loosestrife)**—These upright, resilient flowers may be grown on even the most difficult of sites as long as they have adequate moisture. 'Morden Pink' and 'Morden Gleam' are well known on the plains, but others are likely to be just as satisfactory, even in shady areas. Flowering period is July to September; mature height, 2 to 4 feet.

* ***Matteuccia struthiopteris*** **(ostrich fern)**—Perhaps the hardiest of the ferns under general cultivation on the plains as long as they have adequate moisture. The dark, fertile fronds that grow from the center of the (3- to 4-foot) clump are sometimes mistaken for diseased material, and they may be cut out. Invasive by spreading roots.

Monarda **hybrids (bee balm or bergamot)**—The species *Monarda fistulosa* (often known as wild bergamot) with white or pink flowers is hardy and tolerates drought, but it is not particularly desirable as a garden plant. It bears most of its leaves on the top half of tall stems and therefore appears to be top-heavy by the time it flowers. The more select and garden-worthy hybrids include 'Souris' (red-purple), 'Cambridge Scarlet' (bright red), and 'Croftway Pink.' These are tender and short lived, and therefore require frequent division and replanting. They are very susceptible to mildew, flower from June to September, and attain heights of 2 to 3 feet. Under ideal conditions, they may become invasive.

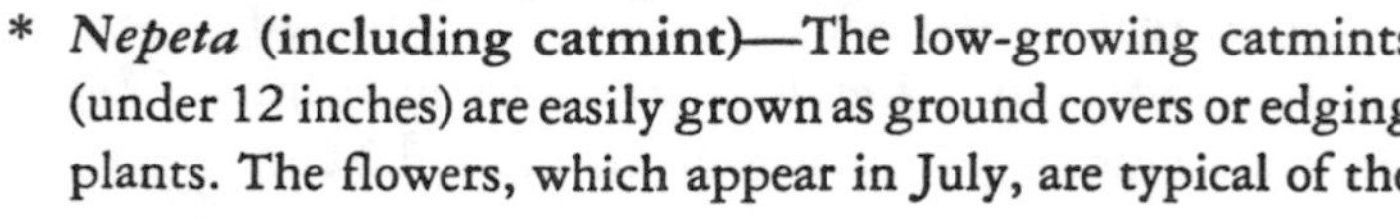

* ***Nepeta*** **(including catmint)**—The low-growing catmints (under 12 inches) are easily grown as ground covers or edging plants. The flowers, which appear in July, are typical of the

mint family: blue with white spots, 1/2 inch long, in loose, elongated clusters. The sterile *Nepeta faassenii* is the more choice plant, although most of those available are *Nepeta mussinii* from seed. The true catmint *Nepeta cataria*, growing to 3 feet, is attractive to cats but is not ornamental.

* ***Paeonia*** (peony)—Hebaceous peonies are the mainstay of many plains flower gardens. There are many cultivars available in a variety of types and colors and sizes from 1 to 3 feet. Other than the tree peonies (which are not hardy enough) almost any of the species or named selections are worthwhile. Cultivated selections have largely superseded the smaller-flowered single-peony species. *Paeonia tenuifolia*, the fernleaf peony, has attracted a lot of attention, but supply has not kept up with demand. Its foliage is finely divided, the plant is smaller than the *Paeonia* cultivars, and it flowers several weeks earlier than the normal June to July. The recommended planting time for peonies is late August or early September in rich soil. When planting, ensure that the buds of the fleshy root are covered no more than 2 inches deep. Deeper planting may result in a lack of flowers. Another cause for failure to bloom is a location close to buildings, where they are sheltered by overhanging eaves and receive insufficient moisture. Once established, peonies will be happy if left alone for many, many years.

Papaver orientale (oriental poppy)—Single bright scarlet flowers with a dark purple blotch at the base of each petal in June and July. The named selections of this striking flower include soft colors and doubles. All require well-drained soil and reach heights from 2 to 3 feet. Planting and transplanting time is critical and should take place after flowering—August on the plains. Spring planting should be limited to container-grown plants; disturb the roots as little as possible. Divide every five years or so.

Penstemon (beard-tongue)—Most are short-lived plants, not well suited to the plains garden. They flower in July and August and grow to 12 to 24 inches. 'Prairie Fire' with its scarlet red tubular flowers on upright stems is worth trying in a protected site where the soil is well drained.

Phlox paniculata (garden or summer phlox)—Short-lived perennials on stems 2 to 3 feet long available in many hybridized colors. Phlox require rich, well-drained soil. Many

are not hardy enough, but the short-growing 'Marlborough' (rose pink with a darker eye) and the taller and pristine 'White Admiral' are among the more successful ones, flowering in July and August.

Phlox subulata **(creeping phlox or moss pink)**—Its shockingly bright pink flowers in May are enough to awake anyone from the winter doldrums. More in keeping to complement other plants in most gardens are the softer colors of some of the named ones. Try 'Blue Hills,' 'White Delight,' and the bright rosy red 'Temiscaming.' Useful rock gardens plants 4 to 6 inches high requiring well-drained soil.

* ***Polygonum*** **(knotweed)**—Many knotweeds are wild or weedy plants, but the following are hardy and worth garden space: *Polygonum affine* 'Darjeeling Red' is a good ground cover with bright red poker flowers; it grows no taller than 12 inches. *Polygonum bistorta* 'Superbum' flowers pink and needs adequate moisture to reach 2 to 3 feet. Both flower over a long season, June to August or September.

Potentilla **hybrids (herbaceous cinquefoil)**—The hybrid potentilla 'Gibson's Scarlet' with blood red flowers is one of the more satisfactory herbaceous potentillas for the garden. In well-drained soil, it flowers in June and July and grows to 12 to 24 inches. Most others are either very borderline hardy on the plains or weedy without a saving grace.

Primula auricula **(auricula)**—These are the low primroses (under 12 inches) with smooth, firm leaves and early flowers that are so perfect they seem almost artificial. They may be grown from seed and they are not nearly as fussy as some people believe, provided they have rich, moist soil. Many other fine primroses will overwinter well in a moist, organic soil, semishade. A 2-inch winter mulch may be needed where snow cover is minimal. In a suitable place, grow *Primula denticulata, Primula florindae, Primula japonica, Primula x polyantha, Primula sieboldii,* and *Primula vulgaris.*

* ***Pulmonaria saccharata*** **(lungwort or Bethlehem sage)**—The lungworts are appreciated for their early spring flowers, drooping clusters of blue bells on 12- to 24-inch plants, and large, pale-blotched leaves. *Pulmonaria officinalis* is a coarse plant with pink flowers in bud, opening to blue.

* ***Rudbeckia*** **(coneflower)**—Several rambunctious plants with cheerful yellow flowers that bloom in summer and fall are grouped under this name. The flower heads of *Rudbeckia fulgida* (orange coneflower) are nearly 1 1/2 inches across. The yellow rays have orange bases, the eye is purplish black. 'Goldsturm' is a good cultivar. Easily grown from seed, coneflowers are very hardy in rich, moist soil and most range in height from 2 to 3 feet. *Rudbeckia laciniata* 'Golden Glow' is very tall, over 6 feet.

* ***Saponaria ocymoides*** **(rock soapwort)**—A creeping-plant about 6 inches high with pink flowers, particularly appreciated in rock gardens. The cultivar 'Splendens' has larger, deeper pink flowers. Soapworts flower from May to July, and none are successful in alkaline soils.

* ***Saponaria officinalis*** **(bouncing bet)**—The wild species flowers from July to September and is little more than weed. However, the white, pink, and red cultivars, 'Albo Plena,' 'Roseo Plena,' and 'Rubra Plena' are much more garden worthy. The plants reach heights of 12 to 24 inches. Not for alkaline soils.

Saxifraga paniculata **(saxifrage or rock foil)**—Ideal for miniature and rock gardens. Most are tight rosettes of tiny leaves under 12 inches tall. The dainty white flowers with purple markings bloom from May to August. This and many other species of saxifrage survive well where there is winter snow cover and well-drained soil.

Scabiosa caucasica **(blue bonnets)**—Beautiful powder blue or white flowers from July to September. Good for herbaceous borders and for cutting. Attain heights of 2 to 3 feet. 'Clive Greaves' is lavender-blue; 'Alba,' white. Need rich, well-drained, nonacid soils.

* ***Sedum*** **(stonecrop)**—The stonecrops are a good choice for dry, sunny sites where watering is not possible. Their fleshy leaves carry them through to the next rainfall. The dwarf kinds can be used in rock gardens as ground covers. Several hardy species and their cultivars are available. Look for the following: *Sedum acre* is distinctive with its very small, light green leaves hugging the ground. *Sedum kamtschaticum* is very hardy and shows mounds of green about 6 inches with yellow flowers in summer and early fall. *Sedum spectabile* is a taller (over 12 inches), upright species with flat-topped flower clusters in the

fall. Not quite as hardy as some of the other species, but selections such as 'Autumn Joy' are worth growing for their late rosy pink flowers. For winter interest, leave the spent flower head on until the following spring.

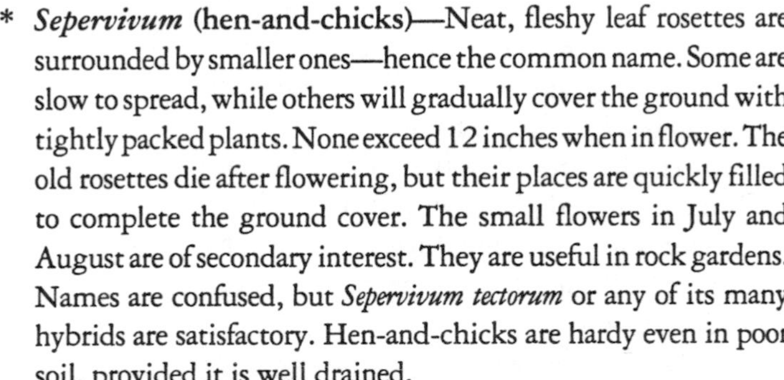

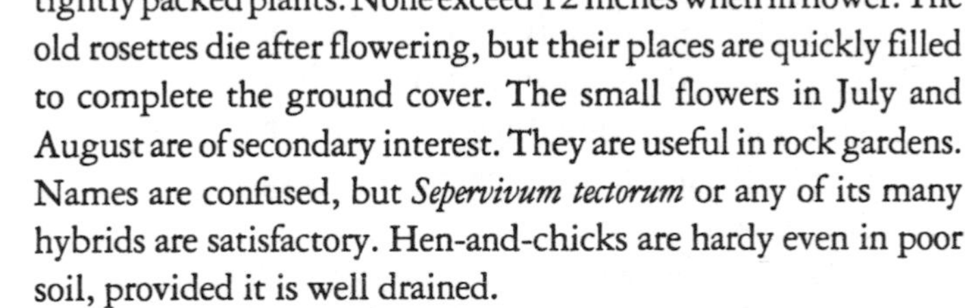

* ***Sepervivum*** **(hen-and-chicks)**—Neat, fleshy leaf rosettes are surrounded by smaller ones—hence the common name. Some are slow to spread, while others will gradually cover the ground with tightly packed plants. None exceed 12 inches when in flower. The old rosettes die after flowering, but their places are quickly filled to complete the ground cover. The small flowers in July and August are of secondary interest. They are useful in rock gardens. Names are confused, but *Sepervivum tectorum* or any of its many hybrids are satisfactory. Hen-and-chicks are hardy even in poor soil, provided it is well drained.

* ***Solidago*** **(goldenrod)**—Well known in the wild, goldenrods have a place in the plains garden for their yellow flowers at the end of the season. Named ones are more compact than the species and retain their flowers well. All prefer moist soil to thrive. Good examples of garden goldenrods, ranging from under 12 inches to 24 inches, include 'Cloth of Gold,' 'Crown of Rays,' 'Lemore,' and 'Peter Pan.'

* ***Thalictrum*** **(meadow rue)**—Distinctive for their foliage which resembles the maidenhair fern. The small summer flowers may be attractive in season, although in some species they are insignificant. Many species are hardy and suited to shade, but will tolerate sun. All do best grown in rich, moist soil. *Thalictrum aquilegifolium* is reliable, as is its cultivar 'Atropurpureum' with purple flowers. It is 3 to 4 feet tall. *Thalictrum dipterocarpum* 'Hewitt's Double' is smaller, 12 to 24 inches, with mauve flowers. *Thalictrum flavum* 'Glaucum' has pale yellow flowers and blue-grey leaves and is very tall, over 4 feet.

* ***Thymus serpyllum*** **(mother-of-thyme)**—Tiny leaves form a close carpet under 12 inches tall over the soil, which makes it useful for soil stabilization. It may be too much of a good thing in the well-drained rock garden, where its seedlings can crowd out more choice specimens. For variety it comes in several types, including white, pink, and red flower forms, and blooms from June to August. A lemon-scented kind is available as 'Citriodora.'

* ***Trollius*** **(globeflower)**—As long as the soil is moist, the globeflower is not particular as to sun or shade so it usually gets planted in the shade where few other plants are content. The round, shiny yellow flowers early in the season remind us of large buttercups (which is just about what they are). They vary from pale primrose yellow to deep orange. More than a score of named cultivars, ranging from 1 to 4 feet, are available from time to time, and any are worth having.

* ***Valeriana officinalis*** **(valerian)**—Another subject for moist, shady places, this old-fashioned plant, with its rather inconspicuous but fragrant sprays of pink flowers in July and August, makes a reliable filler for the large herbaceous border. Valerian is very tall, over 4 feet.

* ***Veronica*** **(speedwell)**—Slender, poker-shaped flowers of blue (sometimes pink or white) in the summer make the speedwells useful accent plants in the flower border. They do best in well-drained soil and vary in size from 12 to 24 inches. The most frequently grown are *Veronica incana*, with the added attraction of silvery grey foliage. *Veronica latifolia* or *veronica teucrium* may have a floppy habit in flower, but several good cultivars exist, including 'Crater Lake Blue' and 'Shirley Blue.' *Veronica repens* (creeping speedwell) is a creeping, almost mosslike species under 12 inches with shiny leaves and small rose pink to bluish flowers in July. It is good as a low, spreading foliage plant in rock gardens where snow cover is reliable, otherwise too tender for the plains. *Veronica spicata* (spike speedwell), together with *Veronica longiflora* (and hybrids of the two), gives us some more hardy speedwells, including 'Barcarolle' (rosy-pink), 'Blue Spire' (deep violet-blue), and 'Icicle' (white). These cultivars have a longer flowering period and vary from under 12 inches to 24 inches. All the speedwells prefer well-drained soil.

Vinca minor **(common periwinkle)**—The trailing roots and stems make periwinkle a useful ground cover, under 8 inches, for shade. It comes through the plains winter in green condition, but may suffer with late spring frosts. Prefers moist soil conditions. Bright blue flowers in spring and sporadically later in the season.

CHAPTER XI

Annuals

I use the term "annual" very loosely to include all those plants that are sown in the garden or set out as seedlings in spring, enjoyed for one season, and then discarded after the first killing frosts of autumn. Plants with fleshy roots that are planted annually and discarded or stored over winter (such as dahlias and tuberous begonias) are found in chapter nine.

VERSATILITY

Annuals are among the most versatile plants that we can grow. Dwarf annuals or those of a compact stature can be used to edge a path or a perennial border and can make colorful seasonal space fillers in a rock garden. Many of the dwarf annuals perform well in containers such as tubs and window-boxes and in hanging baskets. Containers and hanging baskets should be placed in sheltered locations, out of the wind. Because of their exposure, the plants will need watering more often than if planted in beds and they should be checked daily. A complete soluble fertilizer in diluted form might be beneficial once or twice during the season as well. Some of the low-growing annuals tough enough to withstand the stress of a container environment are marked with an asterisk in the following list. These annuals are either low growing or there are low-growing selections available.

Popular low-growing annuals

*_Ageratum houstonium_ (floss flower)
*_Antirrhinum majus_ (snapdragon)
*_Begonia x semperflorens_ (wax begonia)
*_Calendula officinalis_ (pot marigold)
Callistephus chinensis (China aster)
*_Centaurea cineraria_ (dusty miller)
*_Coleus_ hybrids (coleus or flame nettle)
Consolida ambigua or _Delphinium ajacis_ (rocket larkspur)
Coreopsis tinctoria (calliopsis)
*_Dianthus barbatus_ (sweet William)
Dimorphotheca sinuata (African daisy or Cape marigold)

**Dorotheanus bellidiformis* (Livingstone daisy or ice plant)
Eschscholzia californica (California poppy)
Iberis amara (rocket candytuft)
**Impatiens wallerana* (impatiens or patience plant)
**Lathyrus odoratus* (sweet pea)
**Lobelia erinus* (edging lobelia)
**Lobularia maritima* (sweet alyssum)
Nemesia strumosa (nemesia)
Nicotiana x sanderae or *Nicotiana alata* (flowering tobacco)
**Pelargonium x hortorum* (geranium)
**Petunia hybrids* (petunia)
**Phlox drummondii* (annual phlox)
**Portulaca grandiflora* (portulaca or moss rose)
**Salvia splendens* (scarlet sage)
**Sanvitalia procumbens* (sanvitalia or creeping zinnia)
**Tagetes* (marigold or French marigold)
**Tropaeolum majus* (nasturtium)
**Viola cornuta* (bedding viola or tufted pansy)
**Viola x wittrockiana* or *Viola tricolor hortensis* (pansy)
**Zinnia* hybrids (zinnia)

Relatively few annuals are tall. Some, such as hollyhocks, annual larkspur, and common sunflowers, are planted at the back of an annual border; others are useful as seasonal climbers to break up a large expanse of fence or wall, to hide unsightly objects, or to provide color and shade on an arbor or trellis. Most annual climbers, marked with an asterisk in the list that follows, will need supports such as wire, netting, or string.

Tall annuals

Alcea rosea (annual hollyhock)
Amaranthus caudatus (love-lies-bleeding)
Cleome hasslerana (spider flower)
**Cobaea scandens* (cup-and-saucer vine)
Consolida ambigua (rocket larkspur)
Cosmos bipinnatus (cosmos)
Dahlia (dahlia)
**Echinocystis lobata* (wild cucumber)
Helianthus annus (common sunflower)
**Lathyrus odoratus* (sweet pea)

Lavatera trimestris (annual mallow)
**Phaseolus coccineus* (scarlet runner bean)
Salpiglossis sinuata (salpiglossis)
Tagetes (marigold or French marigold)
Tropaeolum majus (nasturtium)
Zinnia hybrids (zinnia)

DIFFICULT SITES

Most annuals grow best in full sun; others are quite tolerant of partial shade and these are noted in the descriptive list at the end of this chapter. A few annuals thrive under moist, shady conditions and will do poorly in bright sunlight. These are ideal for borders with northern exposures or those under continuous shade.

Annuals that do well in shade

Begonia x seperflorens (wax begonia)
Coleus hybrids (coleus or flame nettle)
Impatiens wallerana (impatiens or patience plant)
Viola cornuta (bedding viola or tufted pansy)
Viola x wittrockiana or *Viola tricolor hortensis* (pansy)

Sites with poorer sandy soils and southern exposures are often difficult to deal with. Choosing plants which are native to similar conditions will ensure a higher success rate. Some popular heat-loving annuals are listed below. Others may be found in the plant listings.

Popular heat-loving annuals

Centaurea cineraria (dusty miller)
Centaurea cyanus (bachelor's button or cornflower)
Coreopsis tinctoria (calliopsis)
Dimorphotheca sinuata (African daisy or Cape marigold)
Dorotheanus bellidiformis (Livingstone daisy or ice plant)
Eschscholzia californica (California poppy)
Gaillardia pulchella (annual gaillardia)
Iberis umbellata (globe candytuft)
Kochia scoparia (summer cypress or burning bush)
Pelargonium x hortorum (geranium)
Petunia hybrids (petunia)
Portulaca grandiflora (portulaca or rose moss)

Sanvitalia procumbens (sanvitalia or creeping zinnia)
Tagetes (marigold or French marigold)

TRANSPLANTING OR SEEDING?

Because of our short growing season (usually fewer than a hundred days) here in the plains states, the vast majority of annuals are grown from seed under lights in advance of the season, or purchased as bedding plants. A few are seeded directly where they are to grow, either because they come into flower very quickly or because they are difficult to transplant.

Annuals, such as rocket candytuft, that are difficult to transplant can be seeded indoors into individual biodegradable peat pots which are then planted out (pot and all) without disturbing the young plants. If this method is used, it is important to cover the rim of these containers with soil when setting them out. Otherwise, the peat pots themselves will act as "wicks," carrying soil moisture to the atmosphere and drying up both peat pot and plant.

Most home gardeners are content to purchase plants ready for setting outdoors when spring temperatures moderate. Whether you purchase bedding plants from a local nurseryman, or prestart your own annuals indoors, it is important to "harden off" your transplants before planting them out. Young seedlings started under ideal conditions of uniform heat and humidity must be gradually acclimatized to changeable outdoor conditions. Begin the hardening off process by setting the plants outdoors in the daytime and bringing them into a sheltered location (somewhere cool like an unheated garage is ideal) at night. After about a week of increasing intervals of time spent outdoors, your transplants will be ready for the transition of planting out with a minimum of trauma. In the descriptive list beginning on page 166, it is assumed that all annuals are set out as young plants unless stated otherwise.

PLANTS FOR SPECIAL NEEDS

Your choice of annual flowers will be influenced by factors other than their adaptability to your garden.

Many annuals are fragrant. Plant those close to paths, patios, decks, porches, and open windows to best appreciate their sweet scent.

Fragrant annuals

Cleome hasslerana (cleome or spider flower)
Dianthus barbatus (sweet William)
Dianthus chinensis (China pink or dianthus)
Laythrus odoratus (sweet pea)

Lobularia maritima (sweet alyssum)
Malcomia maritima (Virginia stock)
Matthiola longipetala or *Matthiola bicornis* (night-scented stock)
Nicotiana x sanderae or *Nicotiana alata* (flower tobacco)
Petunia hybrids (petunia)
Tropaeolum majus (nasturtium)
Verbena hybrids (garden verbena)

You may wish to emphasize the importance of flowers for cutting. As will be seen in the descriptive notes, a great many annuals are excellent as cut flowers. While most of these are used in fresh arrangements, some are valued as "everlastings" and can be dried and used as winter bouquets. In a climate such as ours, with such a reduced growing season, it might be worth growing these. One has the double pleasure of seeing the flowers both in the garden and months later, as part of a dried arrangement.

Everlastings
Celosia cristata (cockscomb)
Celosia cristata plumosa (feathered celosia)
Centaurea cyanus (bachelor's button or cornflower)
Consolida ambigua or *delphinium ajacis* (annual or rocket larkspur)
Gomphrena globosa (globe amaranth)
Gypsophila elegans (annual baby's breath)
Helichrysum bracteatum (strawflower)
Helipterum roseum (acroclinium)
Limonium sinuatum (statice)
Rudbeckia hirta pulcherrima (gloriosa daisy or annual coneflower)
Salvia splendens (scarlet sage)
Scabiosa atropurpurea (sweet scabious or pincushion flower)
Xeranthemum annuum (immortelle)

Some annuals are valued mainly for their foliage, their flowers being small or insignificant. The dusty millers are known for their finely cut, silver-grey leaves and are often planted between groups of brightly colored annuals to soften what might otherwise be clashing colors such as orange and red. In contrast, coleus, another foliage plant, has leaves with a wide range of exotic colors and is often used to brighten up an annual or perennial border.

Annuals valued for their foliage

Centaurea cineraria (dusty miller)
Centaurea gymnocarpa (dusty miller)
Coleus hybrids (coleus or flame nettle)
Kochia scoparia (summer cypress or burning bush)
Ocimum basilicum 'Dark Opal' (ornamental basil)
Senecio cineraria (dusty miler)

SELECTION

I personally find the most enjoyable method of selecting annuals is to visit the nearest horticultural facility during the flowering season. Check with your nearest university, cooperative extension service or botanical garden for any "open day" events in your area. (See Recommended Reading.) City parks departments as well often have excellent displays of flowering annuals—especially on the grounds of state capitals. (If they are not labelled, you could do horticulture in your area a big favor by encouraging them to do so.) But don't try to emulate any large public display. Bear in mind that, especially in small gardens, the most pleasing appearance is attained using mostly low plants and generally limiting the colors to two or three in any one area of the garden.

Once you know what kinds of annuals you would like to grow, consider which of the many cultivars (cultivated varieties) of the species would be best. Some cultivars do better than others, but by and large selection is just a matter of personal taste.

Rather than try to describe a multitude of annual cultivars within these pages, it is enough to bring to your attention the special work of the All-America Selections. This nonprofit association has been in operation for more than fifty years and, through a network of professional judges at horticultural research stations across North America, has turned the spotlight on dozens of superior annual selections. Especially noteworthy All-America Selections can be found in the individual plant listings.

You may wish to keep up to date by reading the annual seed catalogs. Hardly a year goes by without some new selections becoming available that could add extra sparkle to your garden for a modest cash outlay.

ANNUALS FOR THE PLAINS

The most popular annuals in the following list are marked with an asterisk (*).

Full sun 

Partial shade 

Full shade

* ***Ageratum houstonium*** **(floss flower)**—Low-growing annuals of 5 to 10 inches traditionally used for edging borders and in containers. Floss flowers have a long flowering season and are available in blue, pink, and white. 'Midget Blue' is a 1940 All-America Selection.  

Alcea rosea **(annual hollyhock)**—Tall plants of up to 8 feet, hollyhocks are best placed at the back of the border. Colors include white, yellow, pink, and red with single, semidouble, and fully double flowers. Hollyhocks are "heavy feeders" and do best in rich soil with adequate moisture. They are susceptible to rust diseases. All-America Selections include 'Majorette' (1976), 'Silver Puffs' (1971), and 'Summer Carnival' (1972). They sometimes reseed themselves yearly. 

Amaranthus caudatus **(love-lies-bleeding)**—The common name is taken from the blood-red flowers, which droop in tail-like spires from 2-foot plants. Tolerant of poor soil and drought, love-lies-bleeding may be subject to root rot under conditions of excessive moisture or poor drainage. May be seeded outside in favored areas; disturb as little as possible if transplanting.  

* ***Antirrhinum majus*** **(snapdragon)**—Native to the Mediterranean region, snapdragons are available in white, yellow, orange, pink, red, and salmon, in heights ranging from dwarf 6-inch plants to taller cultivars of about 3 feet. Pinch young plants to encourage bushiness. Noted for their long flowering season, snapdragons are useful as cut flowers and in containers. Recent All-America Selections include 'Little Darling' (1971) and 'Madam Butterfly' (1970). 

* ***Begonia x semperflorens*** **(wax begonia)**—Native to Central and South America, wax begonias are noted for their preference for cool, moist, shady conditions and long flowering season. Some of the new hybrids are tolerant of sun. They are well adapted to containers and can be utilized as house plants through the winter. Colors include white, pink, and red, as 

well as bicolors. The more popular kinds are compact dwarf cultivars 6 to 8 inches tall. The term "wax" refers to the shiny leaf texture.

Brachycome iberidifolia **(Swan River daisy)**—Tiny single, daisylike flowers in blue, pink, and white, 10 to 18 inches high make for a charming display. Bloom is usually limited to three or four weeks. They may be seeded outdoors in favored areas and can be used in containers and for cutting.

Browallia **(bush violet)**—Lovely deep blue flowers with white eyes bloom profusely until frost. *Browallia americana* is 12 to 18 inches tall with bell-like flowers an inch or so long. *Browallia speciosa* is shorter (about 8 inches) with larger flowers. 'Heavenly Bells' is a popular compact cultivar. Used extensively in containers, hanging baskets, and as bedding plants. Bush violets are best grown in partial shade with adequate moisture in rich, peaty soil.

* ***Calendula officinalis*** **(pot marigold)**—Chrysanthemumlike flowers in shades of yellow, orange, and apricot are borne on 1- to 2-foot stems. Pot marigolds may be seeded outside in the spring as soon as the ground can be worked. To obtain large flowers the plants must be kept moist. They have a long flowering season, and are excellent as cut flowers. Flowers are sometimes utilized as a dye.

* ***Callistephus chinensis*** **(China aster)**—Large flowers in white, yellow, pink, red, and blue resemble those of chrysanthemums. Heights range from 6 inches to about 3 feet. China asters have a long flowering season and are excellent as cut flowers. Avoid disturbing roots when transplanting. To control wilt diseases, use resistant cultivars and plant in a different location each year. Also susceptible to aster yellows disease, which is spread by sucking insects such as leaf hoppers.

Celosia cristata **(cockscomb)**—Annual noted for its crestlike flowers resembling sea coral or the comb of a rooster. Both dwarf, 6-inch, and taller, 2-foot, cultivars are available in crimson, salmon, gold, white, pink, orange, and bicolors. Foliage can be green or bronze. Excellent as cut or dried flowers. Transplant carefully to avoid root disturbance. Prefer moist, fertile soil high in organic matter. 'Fireglow' (1964) and 'Toreador' (1955) are a couple of choice All-America Selections.

* ***Celosia cristata plumosa*** (feathered celosia)—Flowers are plume shaped, loose, and feathery, and available in red, pink, yellow, gold, orange, and apricot. Height of plants ranges from 10 inches to 2 feet. Good for cut flowers and air drying. Same care as *Celosia cristata.* 'Apricot Brandy' (1981) and 'Century Mixed' (1985) are a couple of All-America Selections.

* ***Centaurea cineraria*** (dusty miller)—Grown for its felty silver grey foliage, the name is derived from the "dusty" appearance of the miller who was always covered with flour dust. Plants range from 5 to 16 inches in height and are heat and drought tolerant. Flowers are best removed as they detract from the general tidiness of the foliage. Useful as an edging plant, in containers, and as a foil between groups of brightly colored or clashing annuals.

* ***Centaurea cyanus*** (bachelor's button or cornflower)—An old-fashioned garden flower native to Europe, cornflowers are available in blue, red, pink, and white, on stems ranging from about 15 inches to 3 feet. They transplant with difficulty, so are best seeded directly outdoors after first prechilling seed for five days at 40°F. Tolerant of poor soil. Excellent as a cut flower and for air drying. 'Jubilee Gem' (1937) is a well-loved All-America Selection.

Centaurea gymnocarpa (dusty miller)—Similar in culture and use to *Centaurea cineraria* but with leaves twice cut into narrow segments. It is generally taller as well, 18 to 24 inches or more.

Chrysanthemum carinatum (painted daisy)—Large, single, daisylike flowers in shades of red, pink, purple, white, bronze, and yellow on 24-inch stems. Excellent as cut flowers.

Chrysanthemum parthenium (feverfew or matricaria)—Masses of small, 1-inch, double flowers with tiny yellow centers. Plants range in height from 6 to 24 inches. Tolerant of poor soil and drought. Excellent as cut flowers. The name "feverfew" comes from the belief in ancient times that the plant had medicinal use.

Chrysanthemum segetum (corn marigold)—Profusely branched plants of 18 inches, corn marigolds produce large yellow, daisylike flowers. Excellent as cut flowers.

* ***Clarkia amoena*** (godetia or satin flower)—The term satin flower refers to the shimmering texture of the petals. Flowers

are white, pink, red, and purple, borne on moundlike plants of 12 to 24 inches. May be difficult to transplant and could be sown directly. The seeds need light to germinate so they should not be planted too deep. Used as cut flowers. They flower best when crowded, well watered, and in a cool, semi-shaded location.

* ***Clarkia unguiculata*** (clarkia)—Clarkias tend to be taller and more erect than godetias, with 2-inch double flowers carried on 3-foot plants. Flowers are white, red, orange, pink, and purple and are useful toward the back of the border and for cutting. Like godetias, they transplant poorly. May be sown indoors in individual biodegradable peat pots or directly where they are to grow.

Cleome hasslerana (cleome or spider flower)—The fragrant flower heads are 6 to 7 inches across and produce long seed pods that radiate from the stem like the legs of a spider. Plants begin producing flowers in white, pink, rose, and purple when they reach 3 feet and continue until frost. Mature height is 3 to 4 feet. Useful at the back of the border and as cut flowers in large arrangements, cleomes are heat and drought tolerant and attractive to bees.

Cobaea scandens (cup-and-saucer vine)—A climbing annual with attractive compound leaves and tendrils, and 2-inch, bell-shaped flowers in blue and white that are surrounded by saucerlike bracts, hence the common name. The seed pods remain attractive, and the foliage takes on a purplish tinge in early fall. Only successful if vigorous plants can be established in June.

* ***Coleus*** hybrids (coleus or flame nettle)—Along with impatiens and wax begonias, coleus is one of the more popular choices for the shaded annual border. Grown for its brilliant foliage, coleus is available in a dazzling range of color and leaf shape, from 12 to 24 inches in height. Flowers are inconspicuous, blue, and best removed as they detract from the foliage. Although at least partial shade is recommended, some selections will tolerate sun as long as the soil is uniformly moist and high in organic matter. Pinch to encourage side branching. Coleus is useful in shaded beds, containers, and hanging baskets.

* *Consolida ambigua* or *Delphinium ajacis* (annual or rocket larkspur)—Cousins of the delphiniums, annual larkspurs are somewhat shorter, with smaller flowers in white, pink, and various shades of blue and purple. Heights range from 14-inch kinds to taller ones of 4 feet. Need fertile, well-drained but moist soil. The taller ones are useful toward the back of the border. Popular in fresh or dried arrangements.

* *Coreopsis tinctoria* (calliopsis)—Daisylike, free-blooming flowers in yellow, orange, and red, as well as bicolors. The calliopsis reaches heights ranging from 1 to 3 feet and is tolerant of poor soil and drought. Useful as cut flowers. Plants produce volunteer seedlings.

Cosmos bipinnatus (cosmos)—This native of Mexico produces large, single, daisylike flowers up to 4 inches in diameter, in white, pink, and red. Heights vary from 1 to 3 feet. Tolerant of poor soils as well as drought and heat. Useful as cut flowers. In favored areas, can be seeded outdoors. Many self-sow.

* *Dahlia* (dahlia)—Although the majority of dahlias grown today are purchased as mature tubers, these annuals are also available as bedding plants started from seed. Seed grown kinds vary from 12 inches to 4 feet in height, but most are dwarf plants used for bedding in white, yellow, orange, and purple, pink, and red. Plant in fertile but well-drained soil. Dahlias demand uniform moisture, as irregular watering often checks flowering. Taller kinds will require support. Excellent as cut flowers. The 1975 All-America Selection 'Redskin' is a choice selection.

* *Dianthus barbatus* (sweet William)—An old-fashioned, fragrant garden flower, grown for over four hundred years in Europe, sweet William forms a compact plant of 12 inches with flowers in white, pink, purple, red, and variations thereof. Plant in fertile, well-drained, but evenly moist soil. Useful as edging plants, in containers, and in rock gardens. Although some of the newer dwarf kinds can be treated as annuals because they flower the first year if started early from seed, sweet Williams are biennials. Often they will not flower until their second growing season.

Dianthus chinensis (China pink or dianthus)—A native of China as the name implies, dianthus form dwarf compact plants of 12 inches. They have fragrant flowers with fringed petals in white, red, pink, purple, and bicolors. Tolerant of poor soils and drought. Useful as edging plants, in rock gardens, and in containers. Excellent as fragrant cut flowers. There are a number of very good All-America Selections available including 'Magic Charms' (1974), 'Queen of Hearts' (1971), and 'Snowfire' (1978).

* ***Dimorphotheca sinuata*** **(African daisy or Cape marigold)**—Single daisylike flowers in white, yellow, salmon, pink, and orange with darker centers are borne on plants 12 inches high. Drought tolerant, but regular watering will promote more continuous bloom. Flowers close in dull weather and at night.

Dorotheanus bellidiformis **(Livingstone daisy or ice plant)**—Sometimes listed as *Mesembryanthemum*, these succulent plants from South Africa are commonly known as ice plants because of the icelike crystals which cover the fleshy leaves. Dwarf in stature, ranging from 8 to 12 inches, with crimson, white, pink, purple, yellow, and orange daisylike flowers with dark centers. Drought tolerant. Useful for edging and in rock gardens and containers.

Echinocystis lobata **(wild cucumber)**—A rather coarse vine with hairy leaves and long sprays of creamy white, lacy flowers. These are followed by papery, spiny pods that somewhat resemble cucumbers. Grows to 20 feet and is useful for covering unsightly areas. Plants produce volunteer seedlings.

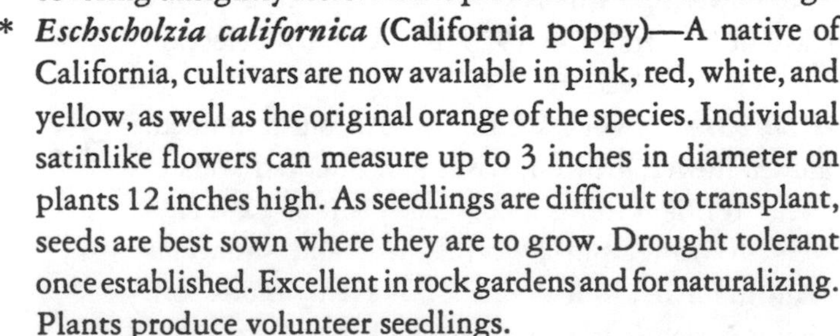

* ***Eschscholzia californica*** **(California poppy)**—A native of California, cultivars are now available in pink, red, white, and yellow, as well as the original orange of the species. Individual satinlike flowers can measure up to 3 inches in diameter on plants 12 inches high. As seedlings are difficult to transplant, seeds are best sown where they are to grow. Drought tolerant once established. Excellent in rock gardens and for naturalizing. Plants produce volunteer seedlings.

* ***Gaillardia pulchella*** **(annual gaillardia)**—These plants with daisylike flowers are native to North America. Cultivars are available in autumn colors of red, orange, and yellow, often with dark, contrasting centers, in both single and double forms. Gaillardias are drought tolerant and some reach a height of 3 feet. They will also tolerate some frost and have a

long flowering season. Useful toward the back of flower beds, for naturalizing, and as cut flowers.

Gomphrena globosa **(globe amaranth)**—Spreading plants of 6 to 30 inches in height with cloverlike flowers in white, yellow, orange, pink, and purple. Flowers are 1 inch in diameter with an almost papery texture. Tolerant of heat, drought, and poor soil. Useful for dried flower arrangements.

Gypsophila elegans **(annual baby's breath)**—The botanical name *Gypsophila* means "love of chalk" and refers to the plant's preference for alkaline soil, which explains why the baby's breath thrives on most plains soils. A myriad of tiny white or pink flowers are born on 2-foot plants. Tolerant of poor soils and drought. Useful in both fresh and dried arrangements, baby's breath is usually sown outdoors where it is to bloom.

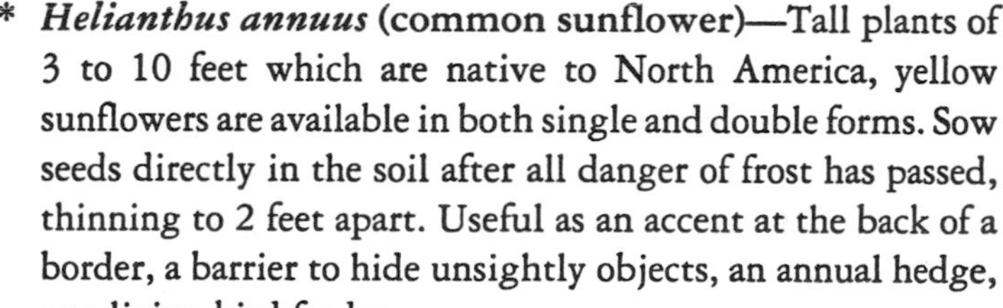
* ***Helianthus annuus*** **(common sunflower)**—Tall plants of 3 to 10 feet which are native to North America, yellow sunflowers are available in both single and double forms. Sow seeds directly in the soil after all danger of frost has passed, thinning to 2 feet apart. Useful as an accent at the back of a border, a barrier to hide unsightly objects, an annual hedge, or a living bird feeder.

Helianthus debilis **(dwarf sunflower)**—Similar in culture to the common sunflower, the dwarf kind is multibranched and only 4 to 6 feet tall. The many flowers that form the head are purplish brown: the rays are yellow.

Helichrysum bracteatum **(strawflower)**—Among the most popular annuals used in dried arrangements, strawflowers are native to Australia. Long-stemmed daisylike flowers available in red, yellow, white, pink, orange, salmon, and purple are up to 3 inches in diameter with a shimmering texture. Plants reach a height of 2 to 3 feet. Heat and drought tolerant but flower more profusely with regular watering during dry spells. Excellent for both fresh and dried arrangements.

Helipterum roseum **(acroclinium)**—Flower heads daisylike, white to pink, and easily dried for winter bouquets—for which they are normally grown. Leaves very narrow on a plant attaining some 2 feet. Culture similar to strawflowers.

* ***Iberis amara*** **(rocket candytuft)**—Dwarf plants of 12 inches with racemes of large white fragrant flowers. Usually

sown outdoors where they are to bloom, or can be prestarted in individual biodegradable peat pots.

* ***Iberis umbellata*** **(globe candytuft)**—Compact dwarf plant of 12 inches with a profusion of white, pink, purple, and crimson flowers. Drought tolerant once established. Can be sheared to encourage further bloom once first flush has passed. Powdery mildew is sometimes a problem. Useful as edging plants, in rock gardens, and for dried arrangements. Seeding and planting as for *Iberis amara.*

Impatiens balsamina **(garden balsam)**—An old-fashioned annual with double flowers of up to 2 inches in diameter in white, yellow, pink, red, and purple. Plants reach 1 to 3 feet. Plant in light, well-drained soil with high organic content. Keep uniformly moist.

Impatiens glandulifera **(policeman's helmet or tree-orchid)**—This distinct botanical is gaining popularity as a robust and reliable feature for moist and shady locations near buildings. Growing to 6 feet or more in height, and with the base of the reddish stem as thick as your wrist, the clusters of orchid-like pink (occasionally white) flowers come as quite a surprise. You may need to stake plants against gusty weather. The touch-me-not exploding seed pods are an irresistable temptation. Be prepared to hoe out dozens of surplus seedlings the following spring.

* ***Impatiens wallerana*** **(impatiens or patience plant)**—One of the best annuals for continuous bloom. Many single flowers in white, pink, salmon, red, and purple, as well as bicolors with white centers. Heights range from 1 to 3 feet. Impatiens demand cool, moist soil high in organic matter; the addition of peat moss is helpful. Excellent in containers and hanging baskets. 'Blitz' (1981) is a recent All-America Selection.

* ***Kochia scoparia*** **(summer cypress or burning bush)**—The common name burning bush refers to the red coloration taken on in fall by the foliage. Native to Mexico, summer cypress is often used as an annual hedge, or as a tall accent plant in a bed of mixed annuals. It is valued for its light evergreenlike foliage. Plants average 2 to 3 feet in height and about 2 feet in width. Tolerant of poor soil and drought. The cultivar 'Childsii' is an improved selection, and 'Acapulco Silver' is an

All-America Selection from 1983.

* ***Lathyrus odoratus*** **(sweet pea)**—A long-time favorite in European gardens, sweet peas were one of the earliest flowers brought by colonists to the New World. Heights now vary from dwarf kinds of 12 inches suitable for bedding to taller types up to 5 feet which are climbers and require support. Colors range from white through pink, red, orange, purple, blue, and bicolors. Sweet peas are usually seeded directly into the soil where they are to be grown. Although they enjoy cooler weather, soil temperature should be at least 50°F at seeding time to avoid seed decay. Seeds may be soaked overnight in lukewarm water prior to planting. Plant 1 inch deep as germination requires total darkness. Perform best in well-drained soil rich in organic matter with uniform moisture. Powdery mildew and root rot are sometimes a problem. Hot weather can check flowering although heat-resistant cultivars are now available. Excellent as fragrant cut flowers and climbers and in containers.

Lavatera trimestris **(annual mallow or tree mallow)**—A tall plant of up to 4 feet producing large solitary pink or white flowers with maplelike leaves. Difficult to transplant so best sown directly where plants are to be grown, or indoors in individual biodegradable peat pots. Soak seeds overnight in lukewarm water before planting to speed germination. Thin to 1 foot apart. Susceptible to rust diseases. Useful toward the back of the border, as accent plants, or for cut flowers.

Limonium sinuatum **(statice)**—Along with strawflower, statice is one of the most popular of the "everlastings," which are dried and used as winter bouquets. Plants are 2 1/2 feet high and produce masses of white, yellow, pink, blue or purple flowers. Needs fertile well-drained soil. Heat and drought tolerant but flowers more profusely if not allowed to dry out. Excellent for fresh and dried arrangements. Robust plants must be set out as soon as danger of frost is past in order to achieve flowering by the end of the season.

Linum grandiflorum **(flowering flax or scarlet flax)**—A native of Algeria, scarlet flax produces bright red 1 1/2-inch flowers and is easily naturalized. Can be seeded directly. Each of the numerous flowers lasts only one day.

* ***Lobelia erinus*** **(edging lobelia)**—Dwarf, free-flowering plants of 4 to 6 inches traditionally used for edging paths and borders. Although most often seen in blue, lobelia is also available in white and red. Will benefit from a mulch and cool soil during hot weather. Excellent for edging and use in containers and hanging baskets. 'Blue Butterfly' is a heat-tolerant cultivar with unusually large flowers. Other cultivars should be treated to semishade.

* ***Lobularia maritima*** **(sweet alyssum)**—Another dwarf annual long used for edging paths and borders, alyssum forms mounds of 3 to 6 inches covered with masses of small white, pink, or purple fragrant flowers. Plant out (or seed in favored areas) in well-drained soil. Excellent in rock gardens, containers, and hanging baskets. One of the last annuals to succumb to frost. Two good All-America Selections are 'Rosie O'Day' (1971) and 'Royal Carpet' (1953).

Malcomia maritima **(Virginia stock)**—An edging plant also used in rock gardens, Virginia stocks are 6 to 12 inches high with a profusion of small, fragrant white and pink 1/2-inch flowers. Most stocks will cease flowering during hot weather. Require light, fertile, well-drained soil with even moisture. Susceptible to root rot. Can be seeded outdoors.

Matthiola incana **(ten-week stock)**—An old-fashioned, fragrant annual of 12 to 30 inches with single or double flowers in white, yellow, rose, and purple. Excellent for cutting. Culture similar to Virginia stock.

Matthiola longipetala **or** ***Matthiola bicornis*** **(night-scented stock)**—An old-fashioned annual whose flowers open and become fragrant in the evening and close during the day. Ideal near patio and decks. Small lilac flowers on 2-foot plants. Excellent for cutting. Culture similar to other stocks.

* ***Nemesia strumosa*** **(nemesia)**—Tubular flowers 2 inches across in red, yellow, orange, pink, white, and blue somewhat resemble pansies. Plants are 12 to 24 inches high and free flowering. Plant in fertile soil with uniform moisture. Good for edging and rock gardens. Hot weather will check flowering.

Nemophila menziesii **(baby-blue-eyes)**—This dwarf 9-inch moundlike plant is a native of California, producing masses of sky-blue, white, or purple flowers. Water during dry periods.

Excellent plant for edging or in a rock garden. Produces volunteer seedlings.

* ***Nicotiana x sanderae*** or ***Nicotiana alata*** (flowering tobacco)—An old-fashioned, sweet-scented plant. Newer improved cultivars are more compact, and their shimmering 2-inch flowers remain open all day. Available in white, green, yellow, pink, red, and purple on 1 1/2- to 3-foot plants. Needs uniform moisture. Excellent for cutting. 'Nicki Red' is a 1979 All-America Selection.

Ocimum basilicum 'Dark Opal' (ornamental basil)—An edible ornamental for the flower border valued for its glossy purple-bronze foliage. Plants are 18 to 24 inches with tiny white, rather inconspicuous flowers. Plant in well-drained soil high in organic matter. Useful in containers.

Papaver rhoeas (Shirley poppy or corn poppy)—Similar to the perennial Iceland poppy, Shirley poppies are available in white, pink, purple, red, and salmon with single or semidouble flowers up to 3 inches in diameter on 2- to 3-foot plants. As they do not transplant well, seeds should be surface sown where they are to grow when soil temperature has reached 60°F. Useful for naturalizing. If using as cut flowers, pick when still in bud and seal stem ends with a flame to prevent rapid wilting and petal loss.

* ***Pelargonium x hortorum*** (geranium)—Second only to petunias in popularity in North America, geraniums are available in white, pink, rose, red, crimson, orange, and bicolors, many with decorative "zonal" leaves. Plants are 10 to 20 inches high and need well-drained soil. Drought tolerant, though watering in dry periods enhances flowering. Tolerates some frost. Poor drainage and overwatering can lead to stem rot. Useful in containers and hanging baskets.

* ***Petunia*** hybrids (petunia)—The most popular annual grown in North America, petunias are fragrant, free flowering, and available in a wide range of colors including white, red, purple, blue, yellow, and many bicolors, both single and double. Heights are 12 to 15 inches. They will tolerate some frost. Plant in well-drained soil. Fairly drought tolerant. Excellent for massing in borders, containers, and hanging baskets.

Phacelia campanularia **(California bluebell)**—Dwarf annuals of 9 inches with lovely blue flowers enhanced by contrasting white stamens. Excellent for edging and containers. Seed outdoors where they are to be grown.

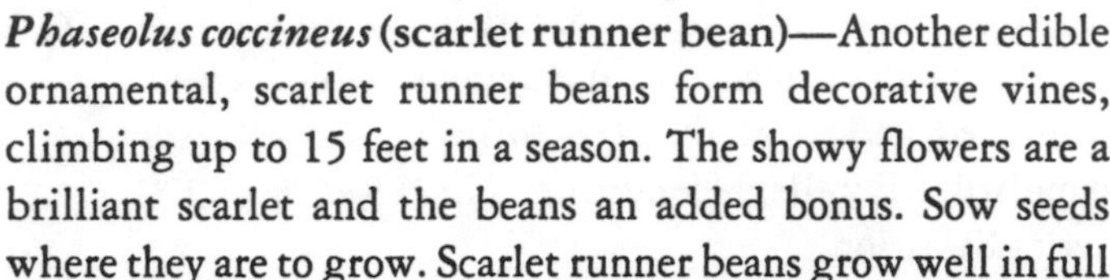

Phaseolus coccineus **(scarlet runner bean)**—Another edible ornamental, scarlet runner beans form decorative vines, climbing up to 15 feet in a season. The showy flowers are a brilliant scarlet and the beans an added bonus. Sow seeds where they are to grow. Scarlet runner beans grow well in full sun, but tolerate shade part of the day. Shade also helps the set of pods as very hot conditions cause the blossoms to drop.

* ***Phlox drummondii*** **(annual phlox)**—Clusters of single white, blue, red, pink, and bicolor flowers on mound-shaped plants of 8 to 15 inches. Needs fertile soil and even moisture. Tolerates some frost. Useful for massing in beds, as edging, in rock gardens and containers, and as cut flowers. 'Twinkle' (1957) is a good All-America Selection.

* ***Portulaca grandiflora*** **(portulaca or moss rose)**—One of the most useful annuals for hot, dry areas, portulaca is a dwarf succulent of 6 inches producing masses of 2-inch white, yellow, orange, red, and cream flowers in single or double form. Flowers close at night and on cloudy days. Excellent as an edging plant, in rock gardens, and in containers. Can be seeded outdoors in favorable areas.

Rudbeckia hirta pulcherrima **(gloriosa daisy or annual coneflower)**—Selections have enormous flowers, up to 5 inches in diameter, in yellow, orange, bronze, and mahogany held on 2- to 3-foot stems, in both single and double form. Can be seeded outdoors in favorable areas. Excellent cut flowers for fresh and dried bouquets. 'Double Gloriosa Daisy' is the All-America Selection from 1961.

Salpiglossis sinuata **(salpiglossis or velvet flower)**—The common name refers to the velvety texture of the flower petals. Large 2 1/2-inch trumpet-shaped flowers are produced in an exotic array of colors including red, white, yellow, blue, purple, and beautiful shades of brown, on plants 2 to 3 feet high. Require well-drained soil high in organic content. Water regularly. Taller kinds demand a sheltered location and should be staked. Excellent for cutting.

* *Salvia splendens* (scarlet sage)—Brilliant red spikes with masses of small tubular flowers on plants 1- to 30-inches high. Also available in pink, salmon, dark purple, and white. Plant in fertile, well-drained soil and water regularly. Tolerates some frost. Dwarf kinds are useful for edging and in containers. Flowers used in dried arrangements. Plants are attractive to hummingbirds.

Sanvitalia procumbens (sanvitalia or creeping zinnia)—Dwarf 6-inch plants with masses of tiny yellow flowers resembling zinnias. Heat and drought tolerant. Can be seeded outdoors in favorable areas. Useful as a ground cover and for edging, rock gardens, containers, and hanging baskets.

Scabiosa atropurpurea (sweet scabious or pincushion flower)—Called pincushion flower because the silver stamens resemble pins sticking out of the globular, cushionlike, double 3-inch flowers. Scabious is available in white, pink, red, and blue. Plants are 3 feet in height. Tolerates some frost. Excellent as cut flowers in fresh or dried arrangements.

Schizanthus pinnatus (butterfly flower)—Orchidlike flowers in white, yellow, orange, pink, and purple with yellow throats on plants 12 to 24 inches high. Plant or seed in fertile soil high in organic matter and water regularly. Hot weather checks flowering. Useful for cutting.

Senecio cineraria (dusty miller)—Another silver-grey foliage plant with deeply cut leaves useful as a foil between groups of more brightly colored annuals. Grows to 2 1/2 feet high with pale yellow flowers.

* *Tagetes* (marigold or French marigold)—Long a North American favorite, marigolds are available in white, yellow, orange, and mahogany, with single or double flowers. Vary from dwarf plants of 6 inches to taller ones of 3 feet. They may be seeded outdoors and are tolerant of some frost. The pungent odor of the leaves is believed to have insect repellent properties. Heat and drought tolerant but need well-drained soil. Dwarf kinds are excellent for edging and containers while taller ones are best toward the back of the border.

* *Tropaeolum majus* (nasturtium)—Types range from vines to compact dwarf plants of less than 12 inches. All have large, trumpet-shaped flowers available in white, yellow, orange,

red, pink, and mahogany. The flowers are good for cutting and some are scented. Nasturtiums thrive in poor soil. Richer soils or fertilizer may result in lush leaf growth at the expense of flowering. As they will not tolerate cold soil or light frost, it is important to wait until early June before sowing them outdoors. Dwarf kinds are excellent as ground covers and for edging, containers, and hanging baskets. Two gold medal winning All-America Selections are 'Golden Gleam' and 'Scarlet Gleam,' both from 1935.

Verbena **hybrids (garden verbena)**—Dwarf plants of 6 to 12 inches with primroselike flowers in red, white, pink, and blue with white centers. Somewhat susceptible to chlorosis. Verbena have a long flowering season and tolerate some frost. The fragrant flowers are excellent for mass display, as edging, in rock gardens, and in containers. Although they tolerate some shade, they do best in full sun in a rich but well-drained soil. 'Ametheyst' (1966), 'Blaze' (1968), and 'Trinidad' (1985) are three All-America Selections worth considering.

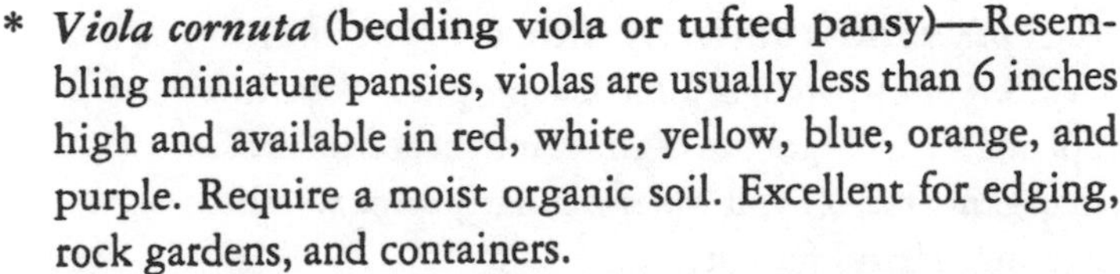

* ***Viola cornuta*** **(bedding viola or tufted pansy)**—Resembling miniature pansies, violas are usually less than 6 inches high and available in red, white, yellow, blue, orange, and purple. Require a moist organic soil. Excellent for edging, rock gardens, and containers.

* ***Viola x wittrockiana*** **or** ***Viola tricolor hortensis*** **(pansy)**—Red, white, blue, yellow and orange flowers, many with black "faces" and some measuring 4 inches in diameter on plants only 6 inches high. Like cool, moist soil with high organic content. Useful in shady beds, as edging, and in containers and hanging baskets. Three All-America Selections are 'Imperial Blue' (1975), 'Majestic Giant' (1966), and 'Orange Prince' (1979).

Xeranthemum annuum **(immortelle)**—An "everlasting" flower excellent for cutting for fresh or dried arrangements. Daisylike flowers are 1 1/2 inches in diameter in white, purple, pink, and rose, in both single and double form. Plants are 2 to 3 feet high with silver-white foliage. The seeds need light for germination. Grow in individual biodegradable peat pots or sow seed where they are to be grown.

* ***Zinnia*** hybrids (zinnia)—The most popular flower grown from seed in North America, zinnias are available in white, yellow, orange, red, pink, purple, and green, in heights ranging from 6 inches to 3 feet, in both single and double form. They do not transplant well and are best sown where they are to be grown or seeded in individual biodegradable peat pots. Light improves germination. Avoid wetting leaves when watering as zinnias are highly susceptible to mildew. Dwarf kinds are useful for edging and in containers while taller types make excellent cut flowers.

CHAPTER XII

Meadow Gardening

Building on the current momentum of the green movement, and widespread concern for the environment, the "wildflower meadow" might well be the next significant development in home garden design. By definition, this new art form may be considered a horticultural style somewhere between the old cottage garden and the alpine garden.

The cottage garden (nowadays infrequently seen) would include such persistent stalwarts as *Tanecetum vulgare* (tansy), *Hesperis matronalis* (Dame's rocket), *Saponaria officinalis* (soapwort), and *Helianthus annuus* (sunflower). Such plants would be too large and obstreperous for the meadow garden.

The alpine garden has several attributes in common with the meadow garden, including plants selected for their low stature, and by the gardener's attempt to caricature nature by naturalizing plant colonies to complement each other. The alpine garden may differ from the meadow garden in its need for good soil drainage and, of course, the presence of at least a few rocks. The alpine garden has a concentration of bloom early in the spring, with less interest for the remainder of the season.

The meadow garden, as it appears to be evolving, includes plants that provide some ground cover, produces a series of flower color all season, and often includes annuals that will self-sow or otherwise naturalize to give the look of a "controlled wilderness."

Due to climatic differences, the meadow garden will certainly vary from one part of the country to the other, but in the Great Plains and prairie region this latest evolution of the home garden will include both herbaceous perennials and annuals of medium to low stature, tolerant of heat and drought.

If you are contemplating the addition of a meadow garden or the conversion of some lawn area to a "wildflower mix," be aware of the challenge. A meadow is not for those who simply wish to retire the lawn mower and sit back to watch nature perform. To be successful, the meadow takes planning, site preparation, and ongoing maintenance. It is anything but an easy release from lawn mowing and other garden maintenance.

Another common misconception is that the "wildflower meadow" consists of wild flowers. A few purists may limit their meadow inventory to plants strictly native to the region in which they live, but unless carefully researched, even these are likely to include flowers originally introduced from other floristic regions.

The more eye appealing meadows will consist mainly of exotic flowering plants suited to the site. The following (native and introduced) species have proven satisfactory in our region.

PLANTS SUITED TO THE MEADOW GARDEN

(A) = annual (in our region)
(B) = biennial
(P) = perennial

Anemone pulsatilla—(P) prairie crocus
Aquilegia alpina—(P) alpine columbine
Campanula carpatica—(P) Carpathian bellflower
Campanula rotundifolia—(P) harebell
Centaurea cyanus (dwarf form)—(A) bachelor's button
Dianthus deltoides—(P) maiden pinks
Clarkia amoena—(A) godetia
Coreopsis lanceolata (dwarf)—(P) dwarf lanceleaf coreopsis
Coreopsis tinctoria (dwarf)—(A) dwarf plains coreopsis
Erysimum capitatum—(B) coast wallflower
Eschsholzia californica—(A) California poppy
Gaillardia pulchella—(P) annual gaillardia
Gypsophila elegans—(A) annual baby's breath
Iberis umbellata—(A) candytuft
Layia platyglossa—(A) tidytips
Linaria maroccana—(A) spurred snapdragon
Linum lewisii—(P) blue flax
Lotus corniculatus—(P) bird's-foot trefoil
Papaver nudicaule—(P) Iceland poppy
Papaver rhoeas—(A) corn poppy
Phacelia campanularia—(A) California bluebell
Viola tricolor—(A/P) Johnny-jump-up

The meadow menu listed above is intended as a guide to getting started, and by no means excludes other low growing taxa. If you are ever bitten by the "meadow bug" you will want to experiment with other low growing plants such as *Cerastium tomentosum* (snow-in-summer), *Antennaria parviflora* (pussy toes), or selections of *Sedum* (stonecrop). Only be aware that some plants will tend to take over more than their fair share of the world, at the expense of the "shrinking violets."

Wildflower seed mixtures are available, but I prefer to order the separate species that promise to do well on a particular site. Mixtures often include some kinds that are too weedy for the location, or too temperamental to share a place on the wild meadow stage. Two well established wildflower seed companies that I have dealt with are Applewood Seed Co. of Arvada, Colorado; and Clyde Robins Seed Co., Castro Valley, California. Aside from wildflower specialists, you could order a good selection of suitable seed from regular mail order seed houses.

To reduce the number of flowering species, or to add a meadowlike base, you may wish to add a turt grass. *Festuca ovina* (sheep fescue) is appropriate, and by all means avoid the creeping grasses commonly used in lawns.

MEADOW MAKING

The establishment and maintenance of the meadow garden will likely remain an imprecise art for some time to come, with various individuals trying different methods and materials. For this reason I would not be surprised to see the formation of a number of specialist garden societies catering exclusively to the art and science of meadow gardening. For the benefit of all members, such societies will accept and distribute suitable seed through an annual seed list, and circulate a newsletter describing the various approaches to meadow gardening.

Meanwhile, a few general guidelines might be in order. Rule number one, the establishment of the meadow must follow the same thorough site preparation and eradication of all perennial weeds as if preparing to seed a lawn. You will find that most of the flower seed is very small, and before sowing it should be mixed with at least five parts by volume of coarse sand to improve even broadcast distribution. The seeded site is then raked lightly once over, and the area kept moist until the young plants are casting shade. Strictly limit the use of fertilizers; we are not aiming for lush growth.

MEADOW MAINTENANCE

Maintenance consists of identifying seedings at an early stage—an education in itself—and pulling them promptly to allow the fast development of the seeded crop. As the meadow comes into flower it is also necessary to pull some of the more successful flowering plants in order to maintain balance and species variety.

No matter what, your meadow will be one of a kind, the result of several variables: the particular climate of your garden; the choice of seed mix; the ratio of those seed; the pattern of their distribution; and the personal biases and preferences that will impel you to add certain new elements and reduce or discard others. In my meadow garden I was too lavish with both spurred snapdragon and bachelor's buttons, and reduced them to limited areas by the end of the first season to allow a wider diversity.

Weeding must be ongoing. I inadvertently introduced the weeds *Linaria vulgaris* (toad flax) and *Chrysanthemum leucanthemum* (oxeye daisy), as an adulterant in other seed, and spent the next two seasons removing these on sight.

The end of the summer cutting back of the meadow and the disposal of the tops can be the major chore of the season. Indeed, this work may be enough to discourage some homeowners to the point where traditional lawns are looked upon as an easy alternative. One approach to this problem is to use a good string trimmer to pulverize the tops, and to rake away any surplus vegetation not needed as a winter mulch. (In the future, outdoor power vacuums could make the job easier.)

Your meadow garden will differ each season, at first because the easy annuals will give up some ground to slow starters and herbaceous perennials; and later as a direct result of your additions, reductions and deletions. It is interesting to keep a photographic record of the meadow at different phases of its development. That way, when someone visits and appears less than impressed, you can always hasten their departure by threatening to bring out your photograph album.

CHAPTER XIII

Vegetables

"PUTTING IN A GARDEN"

It's a reminder of our very recent pioneer history on the Great Plains that, to most people, "putting in a garden" still means growing vegetables, just as the first settlers did in order to survive. Times have changed and growing vegetables is normally no longer a matter of survival; however, fresh produce from the home garden can still deliver the sort of quality that makes you feel smug as you pocket the small change that would otherwise have gone to the local supermarket.

Another big attraction of vegetable growing is that it allows us to change our minds at least once a year. Aside from such solid citizens of the vegetable community as asparagus and rhubarb, most vegetables are treated as annuals, leaving us free to invite something new into the garden each year. The old switcheroo doesn't work very well in the landscape, where trees and lawns appreciate a few years to grow and mature. But in the vegetable garden we can be as fickle as kids in a candy store, and every new season is a brand new start.

So, how do you go about planning a vegetable garden that will compare favorably with those on the other sides of the fence? Taking a step-by-step approach (but not necessarily in this order), you need to:

- Select a suitable site;
- Decide what to grow;
- Form a general strategy;
- Prepare the soil;
- Purchase seed;
- Sow according to package directions;
- Plant seedlings, tubers, and sets;
- Control pests;
- Thin seedlings, weed, and water;
- Harvest;
- Store and enjoy fresh.

MAKING THE MOST OF IT

We can count on only three months of the year frost-free—June, July, and August. Seasoned growers may casually add (I think with a touch of pride at their own endurance), "Of course, we sometimes get a late frost early in June, and the first sharp frost of September can come before the end of August." Add to this shocker strong winds and scarce moisture, and we start to wonder if vegetables can be grown at all in the plains region. But every August, at horticultural shows all across the plains, there is ample proof that we can not only grow vegetables, we can grow superb vegetables.

The positive factors are good soil, long summer days, bright sunshine, and ever-improving cultivars developed for short season conditions. Sunshine, shelter, water, and good timing are the main steps to growing good veggies, so first choose or create a sunny location. Any slope in the land should fall to the south to make the most of warmth and light—particularly important early in the season. Then provide shelter. If you have planned your grounds according to chapter three, the garden area will probably be tucked away behind the home, protected from raiders and screened from northwesterly winds by a fence or hedge—preferably a fence. Avoid any site close to trees if at all possible, as they not only cast shade but also rob the soil of moisture and nutrients for a surprising distance all around. The soil in your vegetable garden should be the best that you can muster. The chapters on soil and fertilizers earlier in the book will help you get a good start.

"Home-grown" is not a guarantee of quality, and under adverse conditions it is quite possible to grow tough vegetables with poor flavor. Of prime importance is water. Without a reliable supply you are taking a gamble that the rains will come at the right times. If you lose that bet you suffer either crop failure or at least a poor return for your efforts.

WHAT TO GROW

There are those who dream of going back to the early days when every gardener tried to grow all the vegetables needed by the family, both in season and for storage. But changes in modern homes and the small size of lots have changed the situation so there is a new approach to the types and quantities of vegetables grown in today's home garden. The basement may now house the home furnace, making it too warm for good vegetable storage. Instead, the home freezer has become a common appliance, accommodating quality, fresh-frozen produce without the mess and bulk of installing a root cellar. Considering the present day availability of fresh and fresh-frozen vegetables at reasonable prices year-round, most of us utilize the home vegetable patch to produce only choice produce in season.

Even so, there are still two basic approaches to vegetable growing, depending upon whether you are a hobby grower at heart or a subsistence gardener. We will take a quick look at each approach, and you can decide which best suits your own situation and temperament.

The hobby grower tends to try for a wide range of vegetables, mainly for the pleasure of seeing and tasting a little of everything that can be grown in the home garden. Typical crops from this garden are asparagus, Brussels sprouts, celery, sweet corn, eggplants, peas, tomatoes, and perhaps early potatoes. Such vegetables are available in season at reasonable prices, or they are needed in relatively small quantities so price is not an important consideration. Although the economics of growing such vegetables in the home garden is questionable, the advantage that often outweighs any monetary consideration is the quality of the produce when picked and used fresh from the garden.

At the other extreme, the true subsistence gardener considers economics first and will always limit production to the vegetables easily grown in quantity and readily stored or preserved. Rhubarb is typically productive. Carrots are a good example of a money-saving crop because of their nutritional value and the fact that they comprise a regular part of most good diets. Main-crop potatoes represent another food staple, well worth growing if there is space enough without limiting a variety of other crops. Beans are a good bet for return on investment, and Swiss chard for early and repeat greens. Don't forget beets for canning, rutabagas or swede turnips suitable for storing, and cabbages for cold storage and sauerkraut.

You will find a significant difference in the rate of maturity, texture, and flavor among vegetable cultivars, so be discriminating when you select your seed or transplants. Named vegetables come and go, and some old soldiers just fade away, but you can keep up to date by checking your local catalogs and newspaper gardening columns. Here are some of the top vegetable selections currently recommended for plains conditions.

Asparagus—'Mary Washington,' 'Viking'
Beans, broad—'Exhibition Long Pod,' 'Windsor'
Beans, green bush type—'Bush Blue Lake,' 'Contender,' 'Tendercrop'
Beans, runner—'Blue Lake,' 'Kentucky Wonder'
Beans, yellow bush type—'Gold Crop,' 'Sungold'
Beets—'Formanova,' 'Ruby Queen'
Broccoli—'Green Comet,' 'Premium Crop'
Brussels sprouts—'Jade Cross'

Cabbage, Chinese—'Spring Time'
Cabbage, early—'Golden Acre,' 'Stonehead'
Cabbage, keeping—'April Green,' 'Storage Green'
Carrots—'Scarlet Nantes,' 'Spartan Bonus,' 'Touchon Deluxe'
Cauliflower—'Snowblanche,' 'Snowball'
Celery—'Tendercrisp'
Corn, sweet —'Golden Beauty,' 'Northern Vee,' 'Seneca Star,' 'Sunny Vee'
Cucumber, pickling—'Earli Pik,' 'Pioneer'
Eggplant—'Black Bell,' 'Dusky'
Kale—'Dwarf Green Curled,' 'Green Curled Scotch'
Kohlrabi—'Early Purple Vienna,' 'Early White Vienna'
Leek—'Titan,' 'Unique'
Lettuce, head type—'Buttercrunch,' 'Ithaca,' 'Great Lakes'
Lettuce, loose leaf—'Grand Rapids'
Muskmelon (cantaloupe)—'Alaska,' 'Maine Rock,' 'Northern Queen'
Onion, bunching—'Evergreen Bunching,' 'Japanese Bunching'
Onion, cooking—'Autumn Spice,' 'Early Yellow Globe'
Onion, pickling—'White Barletta,' 'White Pearl'
Parsley, leaf—'Champion Moss Curled,' 'Curlina'
Parsnip—'All American,' 'Hollow Crown'
Peas—'Jade,' 'Lincoln,' 'Little Marvel,' 'Sugar Snap,' 'Olympia'
Peppers, hot—'Hungarian Wax,' 'Red Cherry'
Peppers, sweet—'Ace,' 'Castle,' 'Gypsey'
Potato—'Carlton,' 'Norland,' 'Norgold Russet,' 'Russet Burbank' (also referred to as "Netted Gem"), 'Yukon Gold'
Pumpkin, bush—'Spirit'
Radish—'Champion,' 'Cherry belle'
Rhubarb—'McDonald,' 'Valentine,' 'Honeyred'
Rutabaga—'Altasweet'
Salsify—'Mammoth Sandwich Island'
Spinach—'America,' 'Long Standing Bloomsdale'
Squash, summer—'Ambassador,' 'Gold Neck,' 'Zucchini Select'
Squash, winter—'Buttercup' (bush type), 'Golden Delicious' (vine)
Swiss chard—'Fordhook Giant'
Tomato, bush-determinate— 'Rocket,' 'Sub-Arctic Plenty'
Tomato, staking-indeterminate— 'Ultra Girl,' 'Ultra Boy'
Turnip, summer—'Tokyo Cross'
Vegetable marrow—*See* squash, summer
Watermelon—'Early Canada,' 'Stokes Sugar Hybrid'

FORM A GENERAL STRATEGY

It often seems that we are either waiting for a crop to mature or harvesting so much all at once that it can't be used or given away fast enough. Beginning gardeners are inclined to underestimate the quantity of vegetables produced by a small packet of seed, but a season or two will tell how much space you should devote to each crop. A 20- to 30-foot row of any one vegetable should provide more than enough for the average family—especially when it pleads to be picked and eaten all in the same week.

The first season you should plan to space the rows according to packet directions and take note at the end of the season whether or not you could have brought the rows a little closer or would have preferred a wider spacing. You will find that rows can be about a yard apart for substantial vegetables like cabbage, half that distance for smaller vegetables like carrots and beets, and wider for the real space gobblers like cucumbers and squash.

After a season or two of using standards rows, you might like to try a few different methods. Instead, you could broadcast certain vegetables such as carrots, beets, and lettuce in broad bands. Band sowing has the advantage that the crop shades the soil as it grows, which conserves soil moisture and tends to suppress weeds. However, more care is needed in thinning the

Raised soil beds are often used by advocates of intensive vegetable gardening. They must be watered frequently to prevent them from drying out.

seedlings so plants don't overlap or start to compete strenuously with one another. Such overcrowding can result in lower yield, although when carefully tended the band method actually increases crop production.

The crowding of vegetables can be taken to extreme in a technique known as the intensive method. Advocates of this system use raised soil beds, usually supported all around with a wooden plank retainer wall. The soil outside the planking is turned inside to raise the level of the planting bed 12 inches or so and is mixed with as much coarse sand, organic matter, and fertilizer as necessary to give the sort of high-quality planting medium usually reserved for container plants. The raised beds result in an aerated root run twice the normal depth, and the soil warms up much faster—a significant advantage in much of our short-season gardening region. The vegetables respond to this special attention by outdoing themselves in both quantity and quality.

Caution: Part of the babying process is that you must be on stand-by with the watering hose because raised beds can dry out rapidly. Also, because plants are generally more crowded in raised beds, there is a greater risk of disease, especially in wet weather.

Planning on Paper

Once you have decided on the system to be used—traditional rows, broad band seeding, raised beds, or a combination of these—you are ready to put a plan on paper. Measure your vegetable plot and draw it to scale on graph paper. Draw in the rows of raised bed locations to scale, and make your decisions on quantity and variety based on what will fit into the allotted space.

While putting your plan on paper, try to arrange to have perennial vegetables like rhubarb and asparagus at one end, leaving the rest open for ease of cultivation. Mark in any area of your vegetable garden that is in the shade for more than half the day during the growing season. Crops that will tolerate some shade are beets, broccoli, leeks, lettuce, parsnips, peas, and spinach. Others need full sun.

Plan to have your tall vegetables to the north where they will not cast unwanted shade on their lower brethren. Some growers like to run the rows north and south to reduce the problem of shading, but the advantage is very slight. Tomatoes should be given lots of room, as they need full sunlight and their root systems are wide spreading and greedy.

You can save space by growing some kinds of vegetables up fences around the boundary of the vegetable garden or by erecting special contraptions of poles, wires, strings, or netting. Runner beans are obvious candidates for climbing, and the system works well with peas and cucumbers. In fact, any plant that sprawls across the ground can be trained up supports; the trade-off is that the root zone of upright plants dries out faster than plants that are allowed to trail along the ground and a soil mulch may be needed to conserve moisture.

The first year of planting you will probably want to keep things simple, but later you might start considering companion crops, those that get along well with each other when grown side by side. For example, lettuce and spinach, with shallow roots, will not compete seriously for moisture and nutrients with deep-rooted vegetables like beets, carrots, or parsnips. For the same reason eggplants and celery are recommended companion plants.

A great advantage of planning on paper and keeping your plan for future reference is that you will be able to keep track of where each crop was planted from year to year. One of the most important aspects of insect and disease control is to avoid planting the same or similar crops in the same location every year. By returning a crop to the same part of the garden only once every three or four years, you will make it more difficult for pests and disease organism to reach serious proportions. There is more on pest control later in this chapter (pages 207–9) and in chapter sixteen.

Many gardening books advocate sowing a succession of vegetables to prolong the harvest season, but experience in this country leads me to believe that we should get on with seeding and planting as soon as the soil and weather conditions permit. Lettuce, for example, tends to bolt to seed and become bitter if grown in midsummer heat. Only crops such as corn, tomatoes, cucumbers, and squash relish the hot weather, and they usually require a full Great Plains season to mature. They should be sown or set out as transplants as soon as the soil has warmed up in early June. Radishes are generally considered a good repeat crop, but even for this short-season vegetable I don't recommend that you delay the last succession planting more than a month after the first suitable seeding date. Enthusiasts sometimes

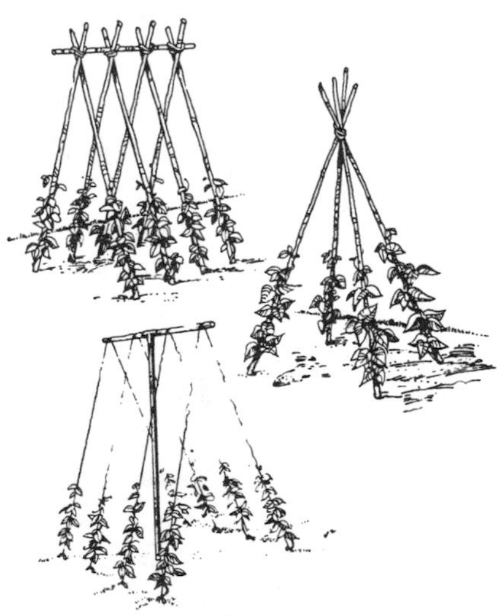

A number of different kinds of supports can be used in the vegetable garden for climbing plants such as peas, beans and cucumbers.

seed radishes and leaf lettuce in late summer to take advantage of the cool autumn season, but this practice doesn't work very well over much of our region because of the uncertain date of the first sharp fall frost.

Once you have everything you want to grow (or have room for) included on your plan, you are ready to move onto the land—ready, that is, just as soon as the calendar and soil conditions are right. Having spent some time on drawing up a suitable plan, try to keep to it as far as possible, but if you change your mind when it is time to put the garden in, make the changes on paper too. Kept on file, it will be useful for future reference, not only to aid crop rotations but also to remind you of what was or was not successful. For this reason it is most desirable to add notes at harvest time regarding the quality and degree of satisfaction you obtained from each crop.

SITE PREPARATION

The garden site should preferably be dug over in the fall in preparation for planting the following spring. Older books on this subject advocate double digging of the vegetable garden every year. I performed this time-consuming feat when working on a private garden estate in England soon after leaving school. It's a somewhat tedious form of exercise, and I don't know of anyone of this time and place that still digs "two spits deep." If you have a deep layer of topsoil, double digging will certainly do no harm, but the trade-off is that other jobs don't get done.

There are times when deep digging is advisable. Those who grow sweet peas for the show bench, for example, will still take time to place manure well below the surface at that location. But unless the gardening bug really bites, be miserly with your time.

Most people just churn the top few inches of soil with a rototiller once a year. This pulverizes the soil and doesn't reach down to aerate the layer where most of the roots should be. I compromise between double digging and tickling the surface by digging one full space depth, maintaining a trench as I go. If you follow the same exercise, pause at the end of each row to fill the bottom of each furrow with compost or similar organic matter before covering it with the next row. Incidentally, this is also a good time to add phosphorus and potash fertilizer. Nitrogen fertilizer is best broadcast over the surface in the spring, just before raking the site level in preparation for seeding. More information on suggested formulations of fertilizer and application rates can be found on pages 114–19. If, after all your digging and raking, the soil is still lumpy, refer back to the soil chapter and plan for the addition of more organic matter and coarse sand.

Weeds are discussed in chapter fifteen, but I should mention here that the time spent digging out perennial grasses—the ones with the long, stringlike roots—will pay off in time saved later on. Cutting off perennial weeds at the soil surface will not contain them for long, and as soon as you turn around, they will be competing with your vegetable crops again. However, annual weeds germinating from seed can be easily dispatched with a sharp hoe. If you are not sure which are perennial and annual weeds, the perennials will soon let you know by sprouting from the root within a week or so of being cut down.

If you are faced with an extreme situation where the vegetable patch is a wild tangle of weeds, it is a practice of long standing to plant a crop of potatoes rather than leave the soil dormant for a whole season. The competition from the smothering potato tops, together with your regular hilling or moulding of the tubers with the hoe, suppresses persistent grasses and other perennial weeds to the stage where they are more easily eradicated during the fall digging.

If you intend to use the raised-bed method of vegetable gardening, spring is the time to raise those flat-topped ridges. This should be done as soon as the soil is dry enough that you can walk on it without compacting it.

SEEDS

The Seed Market

Just like your site preparation, seed purchases may cover a period of several weeks. Start early in the new year by sending away for two or three free seed catalogs. They are one of today's rare bargains and contain a wealth of information that will help your decision making. You should order from one or more catalogs as soon as you have decided what you need, and beat the spring rush.

If you plan to deal with local seed suppliers, you should still shop early in the new year to assure the best selection as well as more professional advice. Those who leave their seed purchases until seeding time may face shortages of certain popular kinds, and perhaps only the harried advice of seasonal sales staff less knowledgeable than the full-time professionals.

Have your list or garden plan with you when you buy because it is so easy to be tempted by extras. We are all limited by either the size of the garden, the time and energy available to maintain it, or the amount of produce that we can use and give to neighbors. So every time we yield to the temptation to grow something not on our original list, we must be prepared to strike off something else.

If you are like me, you will soon accumulate an assortment of half-used seed packages. If so, it's a good idea to write the year of purchase on each packet of seed as you buy it because the life expectancy of seed is limited. When writing my shopping list for fresh seed, I rummage through the old packets to see if I still have some of what I need. Old onion and parsnip seeds are not likely to be much good, but a left-over packet of cucumber seeds may be worth dusting off. Seed lasts longer if kept in a reasonably well-sealed can and stored in a cool place just a little above freezing. The table on pages 200–201 contains information on the number of years seeds can be expected to survive under favorable storage conditions.

If you think some left-over seed might be worth trying, run a germination test in late winter by putting a few of the seeds between constantly moist paper towels in a saucer of water. If the seeds sprout after a few days, the package is still good. (See the table on pages 200–201 for the approximate number of days to germination.) Seed is still a minor cost in the home garden, so there is a good case for applying the adage, "If in doubt, throw it out."

A Time to Sow

The annual ritual of sowing seed outdoors commences as soon as the ground can be worked in the spring. Most of the seeds to be sown in the plains garden can be put into the soil once the frost is out of the ground and the surface is dry enough to walk on without compacting it. This is normally about a month before the last anticipated spring frost, which translates as late April for most of the plains region. Remember to allow for local variations in the onset of spring when you use the table on pages 200–201 for the timing of seeding. The weather may not feel like spring, but if the soil is ready, it is up to you to get things started to make the most of our short plains growing season.

Hold off on seeds of more tender plants such as bush and runner beans, and cold-sensitive plants like cabbage and cauliflower until the time of the average last killing frost (usually sometime during the latter half of May). If reviews of gardeners in your neighborhood are favorable, you might like to try seeding some tender types such as corn and cucumber as the soil warms up and the risk of disruption by frost becomes minimal—about two weeks after the beans and beets.

In our region a number of vegetables are planted out as young plants instead of being grown from seed. This applies to those that need a long season in which to mature. Likewise, warm-season crops that have to wait until June before they can see the garden have a much better chance of maturing if they also make their debut as young plants. The table on pages 200–201 and the section on transplants cover these vegetables.

Fall seeding of vegetables is not a common practice here but is quite suited for Swiss chard, head lettuce, Spanish onions, and parsnips. Fall seeding of these vegetables can result in earlier maturity, higher yield, and frost tolerance. Best results are obtained on a light sandy soil and in a sheltered spot where all-winter snow can be expected. You should sow the seed as late as possible, before the soil freezes, and water them in the spring when the temperature rises above 40°F. Carrots are sometimes fall seeded too, but they show uneven germination (more seed needs to be sown), and although they will be ready for harvest earlier than those sown in the spring, the summer harvest reduces flavor quality. If fall-seeded carrots are left in the ground until the following fall, they tend to bolt to seed.

Suggestions for Seeding

With the vegetable plot raked smooth, choose a calm day to start your outdoor spring seeding. For those early seedings, the soil is usually moist enough just beneath the surface thanks to snow melt, but as the season progresses, you might have to add moisture to get new seed to germinate. Rather than watering after the seed is in the ground, which tends to develop a hard soil crust at the surface that is difficult for sprouting seed to penetrate, you can either sprinkle the area a few days before seeding or trickle water on the open furrow shortly before seeding.

One method of sowing pea or bean seeds is to plant them in a miniature trench in a pattern that resembles double-fives in dominoes.

Measure off one row at a time. Place small marker sticks at both ends of each row and a label (pencil on plastic or wood) to identify each. Unless you have planned to have all your early-seeded plants together, you will be returning in a few weeks to seed the missing spaces.

Stretching the garden line firmly to mark a row, draw the corner of a chop hoe carefully alongside the string to open a shallow furrow. Use enough seed to allow for some lack of germination and for hungry birds and bugs; but try to avoid the beginner's common error of thick sowing, as this increases the labor of thinning the seedlings later on.

Tiny seeds like carrots should be barely covered with fine soil. In this case, all that is needed is the back of the rake tapped down along the row to firm and fill the groove or, for the perfectionist, a light covering of soil shaken through a fine garden sieve.

Large seeds like peas and beans will need to be planted deeper—as per package directions—about four times deeper than the thickness of the seed. I like to place my pea seeds in a miniature trench, spaced in a pattern resembling double-fives in dominoes. However, this layout doesn't seem to affect the flavor of the crop much one way or the other.

TRANSPLANTS

Putting in a garden often involves more than sowing seed. In a short-season vegetable garden such as ours, setting out young plants as an alternative to seeding and waiting for germination can spell the difference between a good harvest and no harvest at all.

Seed catalogs put out by companies such as Burpee, Parks, and Garst often list the days to maturity from seed for different vegetable cultivars. The early-maturing cultivars are the ones most suitable for growing in the plains garden. Check the number of days to maturity of any given vegetable seed; if it exceeds the number of frost-free days in your area, you will need to get a jump on the season by setting out seedlings instead. Crops such as Brussels sprouts, celery, and leeks that take a long time to mature are often set out as transplants; however, it is when using transplants for tender vegetables such as eggplants, peppers, tomatoes, muskmelons, cucumber, squash, watermelons, and pumpkins that we really gain. These softies do not tolerate frost, and cannot be planted out too early in the season. Small container plants purchased from a greenhouse and then planted out in early to mid-June will give these plants the best chance to mature before the killing fall frosts.

If you miss the early spring seeding dates, you can often turn to transplants instead to make up the lost time. Then again, some people prefer to buy transplants instead of packets of seed. About ten cucumber seedlings started in a greenhouse will cost more than a packet of several hundred seeds, but a few plants are all that you can likely use. Buying transplants also gives

you the opportunity to experiment with a few plants of a number of different vegetables. The only constraint with transplants is that our choice is limited to those vegetables that transplant well—buying sweet corn seedlings is not an option even though seeding of this tender vegetable must be delayed until all danger of frost is past. The table on pages 200–201 will help you decide which vegetables to seed and which to set out as seedlings.

Nursery Transplants

If your district is like mine, you will probably find that seedling quality varies among growers from year to year, so you might want to visit more than one outlet before making your purchase. Indications of well-grown plants are uniform size of plants in each pack, fresh green color, and most importantly sturdiness. Avoid those pale and spindly ones that stretch appealingly towards the light. Never, ever buy plants because you feel sorry for them; it takes too long for them to get established, and they never catch up.

Usually the stocky and robust little transplants have been acclimatized to outdoor conditions after their initial time in the greenhouse. But if the sales staff is hesitant in assuring you that the seedlings are hardened off, you should look elsewhere or be prepared to nurse them along yourself by protecting them from frosty nights, sunscald, and chilly winds.

If your plants have come straight from a greenhouse, you can help their transition to the real world by exposing them gradually to outdoor conditions. This can mean postponing the planting for several days, leaving them outdoors but sheltered from direct sun and wind. This hardening-off process also provides some insurance against late frost, because plants in flats and containers are more readily covered overnight or moved into an unheated building when outdoor temperatures fall near freezing. The roots of plants in containers dry out rapidly, so remember to check them for water at least twice a day.

DATES FOR SEEDING AND SETTING OUT TRANSPLANTS

Years to keep seed	Type of Vegetable	One month before last anticipated spring frost —late April	Time of average last killing frost —later half of May	Two weeks after last killing frost—early June
3	* Bean, broad	seed (63-65)		
3	* Bean, bush type		seed (40-55)	
2	* Bean, runner		seed (55-65)	
4	* Beet	seed (48-65) and/or	seed (48-65)	
3	* Broccoli	seed (70-93)	set out seedlings	
4	* Brussels sprouts		set out seedlings	
3	* Cabbage		seed (61-99) or set out seedlings	
3	* Carrot	seed (49-70) and/or	seed (49-70)	
4	* Cauliflower		seed (47-72) or set out seedlings	
1	Celery			set out seedlings
2	Corn, sweet			seed (56-94)
5	Cucumber, pickling			seed under protection (45-75) or set out seedlings
4	Eggplant			set out seedlings
4	* Kale	seed (55-65)	set out seedlings	
3	Kohlrabi	seed (45-55)	set out seedlings	
2	Leek	seed (70-105)	set out seedlings	
3	* Lettuce (head)	seed (80-98)	set out seedlings	
3	Lettuce (loose-leaf)	seed (45-50) and/or	seed (45-50)	
5	Muskmelon (cantaloupe)			set out seedlings
1	Onion	seed (76-120) or set out seedlings		
-	Onion sets	set out sets (65-100)		
1	*Parsley	seed (72-78)	set out seedlings	
1	*Parsnip	seed (120)		
3	*Pea	seed (55-70) and/or	seed (55-70)	
2	Pepper			set out seedlings
-	*Potato		set out tubers (90-130)	
4	Pumpkin			seed (100-120) or set out seedlings

Years to keep seed	Type of Vegetable	One month before last anticipated spring frost —late April	Time of average last killing frost —later half of May	Two weeks after last killing frost—early June
5	*radish	seed (20-30) and/or	seed (20/30)	
4	Rutabaga			seed (90-92)
1	Salsify	seed (115+)		
3	Spinach	seed (43-53)		
4	Squash			seed under protection (47-110) or set out seedlings
4	* Swiss chard	seed (55-60) and/or		
4	*Tomato			seed (48-80) or set out seedlings
4	*Turnip, summer	seed (30-60) and/or	seed (30-60)	
4	Watermelons			set out seedlings

Key
Table assumes that the last killing frost of spring occurs the last week in May or first week in June. Please adjust according to your own location.
Numbers in parentheses give an indication of the number of days to maturity from seed.
* Plants marked with an asterisk are recommended for the beginner.

Home Transplants

It is sometimes tempting to sow your own seed indoors a few weeks before planting-out time, getting a jump on the season and saving the expense of nursery-grown transplants. It can be done, but the average home gardener finds that it is hardly worth the trouble and mess. Try indoor seeding only if you have a cool, light room with rather high humidity, and above all, avoid the common error of germinating seeds too soon. There's nothing more frustrating than having young plants ready for transplanting or putting outdoors for hardening off, only to have an April blanket of snow covering the still-frozen soil.

Be especially aware that the small containers in which you sow the seed will soon be outgrown and the seedlings will need to be transplanted into flats or individual pots—all demanding more space than most of us are able to find. If, despite the difficulties, you would still like to raise vegetables from seed without a greenhouse, you will find that these procedures are no different for plains gardens than for milder climates; standard seeding and transplanting methods are described and illustrated in more specialized gardening books.

The date to sow indoors will depend upon three things: your average last spring frost date, the length of time needed for a particular kind of seed to germinate, and the time required for the seedling to mature to the planting-out stage. (Germination may take anything from three days to three weeks, and the growing to transplant stage another three to twelve weeks depending upon the type of vegetable.) By counting backwards from the date you wish to plant outdoors, you can figure the appropriate indoor seeding date.

If indoor conditions are less than satisfactory for seedling growth, you will want to avoid seeding vegetables like celery and leeks in the home; a period of up to three months in the wrong environment spells disappointment. In a home environment that is perhaps a little too warm and too dry for optimum plant growth, try the easier ones first, like lettuce, tomatoes, and members of the cabbage family.

GREENHOUSE (AND SUNNY PORCH) SEED SOWING DATES

Vegetable	Days to germination	Indoor seeding date	Weeks to transplanting indoors	Outdoors transplanting date
Broccoli	3-10	mid-April	5-6	early/late May
Cabbage	4-10	mid-March	5-6	mid-May
Cauliflower	4-10	mid-March	5-6	mid-May
Celery	9-21	late February	-	early June
Cucumber	7-14	early May	-	early June
Eggplant	7-14	late March	6-7	early June
Leek	7-12	early March	-	late May
Lettuce	6-10	mid-March	4-6	mid-May
Parsley	14-28	mid-March	-	mid-May
Peppers	10-20	mid-March	6-8	early/mid-June
Pumpkin	7-14	early May	-	early June
Tomato	6-14	mid-March	5-7	early June

Note: Outdoor seeding dates will vary from season to season depending on weather conditions.

TUBERS AND SETS

April is the time to start sprouting potatoes indoors. If you buy only certified seed pieces or eyes (buds), they should be disease free. You might get away with using ordinary market potatoes, but this is not recommended as they often carry scab or ring rot and may be chemically treated to retard sprouting. It is always best to stick with potatoes sold for planting.

It is quite in order to simply plant the seed potatoes and let nature take its course, but you can speed the process by presprouting them. Either way, the tubers should be set out in the garden in the latter half of May. Before planting out or presprouting, be sure to remove any long, pale sprouts that have appeared in dark storage as these are useless.

Egg cartons make good sprouting trays, and the sets should be placed with the rose end up (that's the end where the eyes are most crowded). Keep them in a bright but cool and frost-free place. Wait five or six weeks for them to produce good firm sprouts 1 1/4 inches long, ready for planting out in the garden. When fully sprouted you can cut any sets larger than a goose egg into two pieces by slicing lengthwise so both parts have a couple of strong sprouts at the rose end. Rub off the remaining sprouts and plant your seed potatoes 14 inches apart and 4 inches deep, being careful not to damage the young sprouts.

In our region, onions raised from seed or seedlings often do not grow very large before the end of the growing season. Certainly, if the first killing

Potatoes can be presprouted in egg cartons. Before planting the sprouted potatoes out in the garden, cut any large ones in half lengthwise leaving at least a couple of strong sprouts on each piece.

frost arrives in late August or early September, the plants will not have had time to mature. This is why onion sets are so popular on the plains. These minibulbs have had a previous season to make their initial growth, and they get off to a good start if you plant them outside as soon as the soil can be worked in April or May.

PERENNIAL VEGETABLES

This part of the chapter cannot be concluded without praise for the two perennial vegetables mentioned in passing earlier, namely, rhubarb and asparagus. Both have a place in my own garden and are appreciated for their durability. In appearance these two odd fellows are the antithesis of each other, one with large heavy leaves and thick succulent stalks, the other with delicate ferny and needlelike foliage, more graceful than most ornamentals.

Contrasting plants, yet with similar needs, both can be grown from seed but are normally set out as plants. Both respond with amazing vigor and productivity if treated to extra moisture and nutrients. Deep digging and enrichment of the soil before planting pay off. Both need a few seasons to become well established before harvesting. Both are best harvested in the spring and then left to grow and recuperate for the remainder of the season. Finally, it is invasion by grasses and other perennial weeds that usually spells the end of a planting, but weed free they will thrive and produce for fifteen years or more without division.

Asparagus

Incorrectly called "sparrowgrass" by some, asparagus is usually planted as two-year or older transplants, 'Mary Washington' being the common and preferred cultivar. A recommended method of planting is to row them out in a trench excavated to about 6 inches deep, covering the crowns with no more than 2 inches of soil, and gradually filling in the trench as the shoots grow well above the surface. This should be done as soon as the ground dries sufficiently in the spring.

Allow the new plants a couple of years in which to get properly established before starting to harvest, and even in the third year be sparing in the number of spears taken. Then, when there are a good number of thick shoots about 4 to 8 inches tall, some may be cut off an inch or so beneath the soil. Take care not to damage adjacent budding shoots.

When cutting, cease harvest by mid-June, allowing the remaining shoots to develop and provide strength for the following year. The tops should be allowed to grow and mature until late fall, although I must admit to cutting a few small sprigs to add to vases of cut flowers. In November I place the cut tops over the row to reduce repeated thawing and freezing during the dormant season. An annual top dressing of manure worked into the soil each summer assures a good picking of tender spears each spring.

Rhubarb

It is the leaf stalk of the rhubarb plant that is used (the leaves are poisonous), and the plant is traditionally included in lists of vegetables. Personally, I think of rhubarb as a fruit. I well remember a long and animated discussion in a horticulture class in which the students attempted to decide the place of rhubarb in the grand scheme of things. At length an acceptable definition received the blessing of the instructor. It had nothing to do with the part of the plant being used but was simply this: If you normally add salt to the dish, then the subject is a vegetable; if you add sugar, it's a fruit.

Fruit or vegetable, rhubarb must be one of the easiest plants to grow. So easy, in fact, that it is often ignored year-round until spring harvest time. Although the plant will tolerate this neglect, it responds rapidly to additions of manure or compost, watering, and feeding.

Plant the root divisions in early spring, the buds just covered beneath the surface. Resist the temptation to harvest the first year and pull very sparingly the following two years. Promptly remove any seed heads that appear. The cultivar 'McDonald' is popular and productive, and 'Valentine' and 'Honeyred' both score high in taste tests.

OUTDOOR PLANT PROTECTION

Some people like to get their seeds off to a fast start by sowing them under the protection of a glass or plastic cold frame. If you do not have a cold frame, storm windows can also be used for this purpose. Have the frame face south, and set it up a week before seeding under it to allow soil warming. Cosy though the cold frame may be when the sun shines, it cools off quickly at night because glass and plastic are such poor insulators. Old carpet helps if rolled over the frame in the evening, but the best advice is to postpone seeding into a cold frame until you would be seeding outdoors without protection. The warmer soil and higher humidity inside the frame will still bring your plants along well ahead of those grown without protection.

Temporary protection can also be used to enhance the growth of seedlings planted out in the vegetable garden. The advantages and disadvantages of using plastic for earlier and heavier yields of warm-season crops will continue to be argued over the garden fence. But advocates of the system

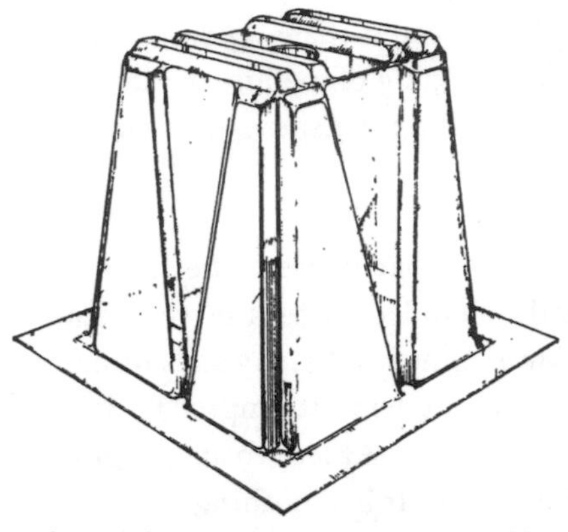

Plastic plant protectors can get vegetable seedlings off to a good start.

point out that tomatoes, eggplants, and peppers do very well when started under the cozy environment of tentlike plant protectors, while vine crops (cucumbers, melons, pumpkins, and squash) do best when covered with plastic tunnels. One advantage of the plastic tunnel is that it spans twice the width and is half as high again as the typical tent-type protector. With this system the plants don't overgrow their accommodations too soon and thus benefit longer from their sheltered environment.

One argument against the use of plastic in the vegetable garden is the expense and bother of replacing it every season. Even though a good crop may more than compensate for the initial outlay, the difference may not justify the extra time and labor involved. The other negative aspect of plastic tunnels and mulches is the messy appearance of plastic on the ground and the clean-up chore after harvest. True, there are some plastics that are biodegradable in sunlight, but even this material does not disappear where it is shaded by leaves or tucked into the ground.

If you plan to use clear plastic tunnels, you should first lay down a layer of 5 mil thick, black plastic mulch to retain soil moisture. It comes in rolls about 4 feet wide. (Clear plastic mulch is preferred by commercial producers, but black plastic with its weed-control property is best in the home garden.) Lay it down on soil that has been finely worked and firmed and is quite moist without being wet. About 10 inches at each edge of this groundsheet should be buried to keep it in place. Cut slots when you plant through the plastic, and you are then ready to erect the clear plastic tunnel over the mulch and newly planted seedlings.

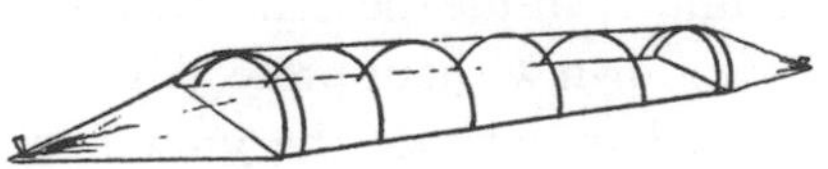

Plastic tunnels are simple to construct and modify the climate for vine crops such as cucumbers and squash.

The clear polyethylene sheeting should also be 4 mil thick, and when erected over wire hoops should stand 20 inches high and 30 inches wide at the base. You can buy tunnel kits, or you can make your own for about one-third the cost.

The do-it-yourself tunnel maker will need No. 9 wire to make the support hoops. Cut lengths of this wire about 6 1/2 feet long and bend them into a U shape. The hoops are then pushed into the ground to span the strip of black plastic mulch. The hoops can be 6 1/2 feet apart, but both the end ones should be supplemented by an additional hoop 12 inches away to add extra support near where the plastic tunnel will be anchored.

Angle a strong stake securely into the ground at each end of the black plastic mulch. Tie one end of the clear plastic to one of these stakes at ground level; unroll the plastic and cut it about a yard beyond the far stake.

Bunch the end of the plastic like a rope and pull it as tight as you can (a warm day will help soften the plastic) and then tie it down to the end stake. Now form the tunnel by pulling the plastic over the hoops and burying the edges. It helps to anchor one edge first and then pull the other side taut. A nice tight tunnel is less subject to wind damage.

As soon as the tunnel is finished, use a sharpened piece of dowelling about 1 inch thick to punch holes all over the tunnel at intervals of about 8 inches in all directions. Speed is important here, or the plants can cook in the heat buildup within the tunnel before the ventilation is complete. Cutting slots with a blade instead is not satisfactory as this tends to induce tearing and eventual destruction by the wind.

By early July you will recognize that it is time to remove the tunnels, as the plants will outgrow their space and wilting or leaf burn may become evident because of high midday temperatures. When flowers start to appear on the crop, they will need to be exposed to the outdoors for pollination—another indication that the tunnels are no longer needed.

Two questions frequently arise when tunnels are tried for the first time. Is it all right to plant earlier than normal when the crop is protected by a tunnel? And how can the soil be watered under the tunnel and mulch?

To the first query I suggest that you resist the temptation to plant those warm-season crops any earlier than the first frost-free week. Plastic is a very poor insulator. Blankets draped over the plastic on cold nights might be a feasible approach, but I doubt that this would influence the earliness or yield of the crop enough to make it worth the trouble. As for the watering, if the soil is quite moist at the time the mulch is put down, the plants will manage well enough until their roots extend to the outer edges of the plastic to take up natural or artificial irrigation.

PESTS AND DISEASES

The basics of controlling plant diseases are covered in chapter seventeen, but this is an opportune moment to mention a nuisance that is sooner or later encountered by all indoor growers of seedlings. The menace is called "damping off," a term applied to the sudden death of young seedlings caused by one of several fungi. A black or brown line is evident on the stem at the soil line, and the seedling falls over. Unless it is spotted quickly and the healthy seedlings are removed from the container, damping off will spread within a few days to kill all plants in the container.

To lessen the risk of damping off, avoid overwatering and crowding of seedlings, and limit fertilizers—especially nitrogen. Use a light soil mix. Some ready-packaged potting and seeding soils are not as sterile as they claim to be, so you might want to sterilize your own. This can be achieved by baking in a 200°F oven for 45 minutes. First make sure that the soil is just moist and seal it in a plastic cooking bag to reduce the earthy aroma.

Once past the small seedling stage and hardened off (acclimatized to outdoor conditions), the next period of risk occurs at outdoor planting time.

For seed sown outside there is an exciting time of two or three weeks following germination when your crop is most vulnerable to a variety of pests.

When the cutworms slice off tender young seedlings overnight, I often think of the fellow who purportedly made a fortune advertising an infallible bug killer. Those who sent their money received two blocks of wood and an instruction sheet—"Place insect on Block A and strike sharply with block B." This principle is still one of the best for the small home garden, used in conjunction with crop rotation and garden sanitation. By poking into the soil around the base of a fallen seedling, you will often find the offending cutworm and can treat it as you see fit. Surviving seedlings can be protected by improvising small collars from old cardboard milk cartons or similar material. Keep a collar around each seedling until the chomping season is past.

Flea beetles are an example of a different kind of menace. They appear by the hundreds, each making a small hole in seedling leaves before the plants can get established. Trying to catch these sprightly pin-head-sized creatures is out of the question, so a dusting of fresh rotenone is a more practical solution.

Birds may claim a share of the seeds you sow. They may be kept away by whirling windmills and bits of flapping material that add a touch of springtime festivity to the garden, and strings or nets over the seeded rows act as a further deterrent. Usually, however, it is less trouble to sow a few extra seeds. If you watch carefully, you will often see that the birds are more interested in insects and worms than in your newly sown peas.

Knowing how to deal with these three examples (cutworms, flea beetles, and birds) is your secret to keeping control of the pest problem in your vegetable garden during the first critical two or three weeks when the plants are particularly vulnerable. Keep a daily watch on both seedlings and transplants, and be ready to protect them in the most time- and cost-efficient means available. More on pests in chapter sixteen.

THINNING AND GENERAL MAINTENANCE

Many kind-hearted folk have a natural aversion to pulling healthy young vegetable seedlings out of the ground and throwing them away. It does seem a shame, but thinning the crop to package recommendations will give the remaining plants room to develop properly. The favored plants are likely to experience some root disturbance during the thinning operation, so I like to choose a day with the sort of weather that is easy on the surviving seedlings. The soil should be slightly moist (water the row the day before if necessary) and the weather reasonably calm and overcast.

There are a couple of good reasons why thinning should be done at intervals of a couple of weeks rather than all at once. Later thinnings of, say, radishes and lettuces are likely to be large enough to use. More importantly, if you were to thin a crowded row to the ultimate spacing all at once, you might well be faced with unnecessarily wide gaps and wasted space if something untoward happens to some of your remaining plants.

Thinning time presents an ideal opportunity to hand weed the rows. Weeds between rows can easily be sliced off with a sharp hoe on a dry sunny day, but weed seedlings that come up with the crop should be left until thinning time as they provide a little shade and protection during the first week or so after germination.

Later, to save water and maintain a more even soil moisture supply for your crop, you can add a thin mulch—a soil surface cover—adjacent to the plants. The mulch will prevent evaporation from the soil and may consist of organic material like manure, compost, leaves, peat moss, or chopped bark, or inorganic material like polyethylene film. However, just as the mulch prevents moisture escaping, it also prevents moisture from the outside reaching the plant roots. If you use a mulch, remember to soak the soil under the covering from time to time. Because the mulch tends to keep the soil cool as well as moist, it is best to apply it after the soil has thoroughly warmed up (mid-June or later in much of our region), or growth could be slowed.

A supplemental side dressing of a fertilizer high in nitrogen will be beneficial for all the leafy crops and should be applied before any mulching, as some of your soil nitrogen is lost in the natural breakdown of the mulch. See chapters one and two for more on soils and fertilizers.

A garden that relies on natural rainfall in our area will often go thirsty. If at all possible, have supplemental water available and be ready to soak the ground as soon as the soil starts to dry beneath the surface. The most critical times for water in the vegetable garden are at germination or transplanting time when root systems are small and shallow, and again shortly before maturity.

PICKIN' AND PACKIN'

Harvesting is a satisfying part of gardening and poses few problems, but don't wait too long. Bigger isn't necessarily better when it comes to quality. Overmature corn, peas, beans, and other vegetables are likely to deteriorate, making up in toughness what they lose in flavor and nutritional value.

Some people joke about having the water ready and boiling on the stove before they run to pick their fresh cobs of corn. Why not? It isn't often that you'll have the pleasure of savoring vegetables so fresh, and I think you will notice the difference.

One crop gets more than its share of abuse at harvest time, so I'll take time here to put in a kind word for the potato. As they are harvested, they should not be left exposed to sunlight or toxic greening may occur, so choose a cloudy day for digging. First cut and remove the tops (hedging shears are useful here), leaving stumps to indicate the center of each potato hill. After you have sliced or spiked a few tubers, you learn to start removing soil far enough away from the clump so they are not damaged. Handle those spuds lovingly to avoid bruising them—I've known some people who delight in tossing them into a pail as if it were a fairground game of skill, a practice that can reduce their keeping qualities considerably.

Wipe off excess soil without washing them, and if you are digging the main crop in late fall, bring them under cover so they don't get frosted overnight. Damaged and bruised ones should be set aside for immediate use.

Carrots and beets should be dug carefully and the tops cut off with a thin slice of the root. Wash them and store in coarse sawdust without drying. They last best in the sort of cool, dark, humid place that we try to banish from our homes. Until recently, the recommended temperature for the storage of root crop vegetables was 45°F. Now the optimum temperature for carrots and beets has been found to be 32°F with total darkness and a humidity level of 90 percent; for potatoes, 35 to 37°F. The old-fashioned underground root cellar was often just about ideal for the storage of root crops, but most of us have to use our ingenuity to approximate the best storage conditions in a warm, dry home.

Perhaps you are able to erect two insulated walls in one corner of a basement, fit an insulated door and ceiling, and make a vent to the outside. Partially close the vent as the cold-room temperature drops low enough, and regulate the temperature with the aid of a thermometer and a daily check.

Less work is an old refrigerator with the door completely removed, kept within the insulated storage room. Sophisticated equipment is available to control temperature and humidity levels within predetermined levels, but if the economics of the game are of concern, check the cost of the set-up against possible future savings and convenience.

Vegetable storage tips keep appearing in newspaper advice columns, and most are based on sound principles and tested by time. For example, if you use plastic bags to store potatoes, make sure there are enough air holes, as lack of oxygen causes rapid crop deterioration. Stored carrots last longer when placed together in a brown paper bag inside a plastic bag; change the moist paper bag if it becomes wet. If you make sure all tomatoes are harvested before the temperature falls close to freezing, they will keep much longer, and green ones will ripen at normal room temperatures. Surplus tomatoes at the end of the season can be washed and sealed in plastic bags, and kept in the deep freeze at about 0°F for later use in omelets, soups, and stews.

There's no getting away from it: heavy crop surpluses can cause storage problems. But you can bet there are people who would just love to have that sort of problem.

CHAPTER XIV

The Home Greenhouse

Once you cross the threshold from basic home gardening to owning a greenhouse, you are entering the world of the dedicated hobby gardener. It is a commitment that most people are not prepared to make. But there may come a time when you wonder if a greenhouse would be an enjoyable or profitable addition to your house or garden. Is a greenhouse for you? To help you decide, here are some aspects of greenhouse ownership on the Great Plains, both the pros and cons.

A greenhouse will require someone to look after the task of daily watering as long as plants are growing in it. Ventilation must be attended to several times a day under changeable weather conditions. You could, of course, install automatic venting and heat controls, even automatic drip watering to minimize the chores of greenhouse sitting, but such accessories add substantially to the building costs and never entirely free the owner from the responsibility of plant watching. If price is no object, you could hire a horticulturist to tend the greenhouse for you—a situation beyond the range of this book.

To be brief, although immensely gratifying to some, the investment of time and money involved in owning a greenhouse should not be undertaken lightly. First, you should ask yourself whether your aim is to avoid some of the expenses associated with buying bedding plants and starting vegetables, or whether you would be willing to take some of the money you now use for other things in order to extend the growing season.

If the savings and convenience are a deciding factor, a greenhouse is not for you. The plants that you grow will not come cheap. If, on the other hand, the extra time and expense involved are no deterrent, then you are a hobby gardener. Read on.

CHOOSING A SITE

There are a number of factors to weigh when selecting a spot suitable for a greenhouse in your garden.

Location

The first consideration is to find a sunny location. Unless the greenhouse receives sunshine all day, you will be limited in the range of plants that you can grow, and for some, like cut flowers, you will need supplemental lighting. (Light fixtures further cut down on the amount of natural sunlight reaching the plants.)

So a south-facing or open location is by far the best, free from shading by other structures or trees. A straightforward method of checking to see if your greenhouse site is suitable is to stake out the path of shadows cast by adjacent buildings and trees during the season that you plan to operate the greenhouse. You can speed up the process by referring to special greenhouse books that include tables based on the angle of incident light at different times of the year. These tables are used in conjunction with latitude to determine where shadows are cast at any time of the year.

Shelter

Shelter from the north is desirable in our prairie climate to reduce wind-related heat loss from the greenhouse. A wind-break of shrubs or fencing will provide some protection. Tall shrubs are excellent for this purpose, but large trees often lack dense lower branches and have the disadvantage of competing with other garden plants for water, light, and nutrients.

Water and Air Drainage

Consider both water and air drainage at the site. Avoid locating the greenhouse in a depression where water may accumulate, and be sure that the soil is porous enough to permit good penetration and dispersal. Soil drainage may be improved by working in coarse sand (see chapter one on soil), but in extremely waterlogged places it will necessary to install drainage tiles around, and leading from, the site before the greenhouse foundation is built.

Good air drainage is often overlooked when selecting a greenhouse site. A gradual slope (land slightly higher on one side of the greenhouse than the other) will allow the natural flow of the cold air downhill. There should be no solid barrier to this air flow within about 6 yards downwind from the site, or the cold air will tend to back up like water at a dam.

Utilities

The closer your structure is to existing utilities, the better. You will need water, electricity, and another source of heat, such as natural gas, to supplement the heat of the sun.

Water is of prime importance, both in quantity and quality. Up to about 4 gallons per square yard of greenhouse area will likely be needed.

Water quality is especially important if you plan to grow plants in pots or other containers. The accumulation of certain chemicals in a small quantity of planting medium can have rapid and tragic effects on container grown plants. Before you proceed, I strongly recommend that you have a sample of your water supply analyzed. Water from a pond or dugout may be quite suitable, but it is sometimes subject to chemical pollution, such as that from pesticides or fertilizer residues. Check with your local extension agent to determine the best location for submitting water samples and whom to contact to help you assess the results. The testing lab normally provides official forms and sample containers on request.

Before leaving the subject of water, I should mention that it should be about 72°F in cold weather. A fairly constant water temperature can be maintained by using an appropriate electrical element and thermostat.

You will probably want electricity for lighting, and it can also be used either to heat the whole greenhouse or to supplement another system. Electricity is clean, and the installation costs are often cheaper than for fuel systems such as natural gas, propane, or fuel oil. However, electrical energy can be much more expensive per unit of delivered heat, and you may find that natural gas is a much more economical alternative.

To evaluate the cost of different heat sources, you could use the old Btu (British thermal unit) to compare them. One Btu will raise the temperature of one pound of water one degree Fahrenheit (specifically from 59°F to 60°F). The capacity and heat loss of furnaces are usually given in Btu's per hour, while the heat output of an electrical baseboard radiator may be described in so many Btu's per foot per hour.

Orientation

Once you have chosen a suitable site, you can determine the best orientation for your greenhouse to take advantage of available sunlight. If you intend to use the unit all winter, the best orientation is to have the ridge of the greenhouse running east-west. If your greenhouse will be used mainly to extend the season in early spring and late autumn, a north-south orientation is preferable.

SELECTING A PLAN

Once you have determined the best location for your greenhouse, you will have to consider a number of design options before settling on a plan.

The Lean-to Design

Your choice of site may dictate whether you build a lean-to design or a greenhouse that is free-standing. Lean-to units are built for entry from the home (or other building, such as a garage) or from outdoors or both. Access from the home is a convenience in bad weather. Another advantage is that a lean-to greenhouse may be included in the interior design of the home and residence utilities may be easily extended. Lean-to models have the advantage of saving up to one-third the heating costs of a free-standing unit because of the solid wall and wind protection. Also, the cost of construction is lower than for the free-standing kind.

There are two or three notable problems associated with the lean-to design. Insect pests can invade the home at will, and chemical fumigation cannot be used or the home would be contaminated. There is also the question of access for bulky soil and plants. These problems could be overcome by having access only from outdoors, but this decision must be weighed against the difficulty of serving the unit in bad weather. If the greenhouse is used all winter, there will be days or weeks when simply opening the outside door to enter or leave could result in a sudden and severe temperature drop. In a small greenhouse, this would severely damage or kill the plants. Any winter-operated greenhouse with an outside door only should be designed with a double entrance to provide an airlock.

Common sizes of prefabricated lean-to greenhouses are from approximately 6 x 8 feet to 8 x 12 feet.

The Free-standing Design

Free-standing, even-span greenhouses are generally larger than lean-to types, and they are obtainable in sizes from 8 x 8 feet up. The main advantage of this type of unit is that maximum light and ventilation are possible when it is located on a suitable site away from buildings. Also, the free-standing unit can be more readily oriented to the desired axis than the lean-to. Furthermore, with no adjoining building, the danger of airborne contamination is eliminated.

Disadvantages are that utilities must travel farther. With access only from outdoors, free-standing units may be more difficult to service during bad weather. They should certainly be screened from the prevailing wind, but even then they cost up to one-third more to heat than the lean-to kind.

So Which Greenhouse is Better?

In the debate about which type is better, it seems that the lean-to has the advantage where there is a suitable south-facing wall available and if the unit is to be a small one, up to 8 square feet. Anything larger, and the free-standing unit looks increasingly more economical and convenient, especially if you may wish to add on later. You should consider using a design that allows for easy extension, just in case.

Materials and designs being equal, larger greenhouses are cheaper to build per growing area unit than smaller ones. Bear in mind that a very small greenhouse of, say, 6 square yards is much more difficult to manage than one four times larger. The small house heats up and cools off much more rapidly with variable outdoor conditions, making it difficult to maintain the desired growing conditions.

As you consider a do-it-yourself plan or a prefabricated unit, bear in mind the durability of the construction materials and whether or not the design is functional for the purpose you have in mind. Will there be room for benches of the desired size and height? If plants like tomatoes and cucumbers are to be grown in floor beds, are the side walls high enough to accommodate them as they reach mature size? Is the door wide enough for your wheelbarrow? You will find that the recommended roof angle for year-round operation is a 30- to 35-degree slope. If the concern is for optimum light in midwinter, then a 60-degree slope is best.

There is no one greenhouse that will suit all people and locations. Perhaps more than with any other aspect of gardening, the consideration of a greenhouse calls for reading a variety of literature on the subject, talking to those who have hobby greenhouses, and shopping around to evaluate what is currently on the market. I'm sure that you will find the traditional designs are generally the cheapest and more satisfactory than the avant-garde.

If you are building the unit yourself, good plans are essential to avoid costly mistakes in construction. For example, a design using corrugated panels will show the fastening holes drilled in the ridges, not the troughs, of the panels. Mastic sealant is needed between overlapping panels. Special installation methods are needed for some plastic panels because of thermal expansion and contraction. Good plans explain exactly what special molding strips, spacers, and fasteners are available for the type of greenhouse covering material you are using.

As with so many other first-time jobs, you will be an expert on the construction of your own type of greenhouse, but only after you have completed the job. Unless you are an experienced builder, try to obtain the advice of someone who has recently built a greenhouse of the same kind.

SOLAR GREENHOUSES

If you have ever been in an unheated greenhouse on a sunny winter day, you will know how surprisingly warm it can get, even when outside temperatures are low. When the sun clouds over, the temperature starts to fall, and at night the heat is soon lost because a greenhouse is a very poor insulator. The objective of those who build a "solar" greenhouse is to use sunlight not only for growing plants but also as a significant source of heat.

In that sense, all greenhouses are "solar," but the designs that have become more common with the rising costs of heating fuel aim to store some of the free energy from sunlight and use it to maintain a minimum temperature when needed. (This is not to suggest that the use of sunlight as an energy form is free, or necessarily cheap.) See also the section on heating, page 225.

When you consider the storage of collected solar heat, bear in mind that you will need about 800 pounds of rocks or 10 gallons of water per 10 square feet of glazed surface.

A *passive* system uses mass such as rocks or water to soak up excess heat on sunny days and then releases the heat by natural circulation (air or water) as the greenhouse temperature falls. An *active* system works on the same principle as the passive, except supplementary energy, such as electricity, is used to operate fans or pumps to aid the collection, storage, or delivery system.

Considering the present state of solar technology and the extremely low winter temperatures that are common in our region, solar energy can be expected to provide only a portion of our greenhouse heat requirements. This is not to say that the principles of capturing and retaining heat generated by sunlight cannot be applied. On the contrary, we should keep abreast of recent developments in solar technology and apply them whenever we can. Just avoid too much emphasis on this particular aspect of greenhouse heating, for it may swallow up more money than is warranted by the savings. In short, don't overlook the law of diminishing returns.

One good idea already proven satisfactory on the plains is the Brace Research Institute Greenhouse. The design features an insulated north wall to reduce heat loss. The inside of the north wall is painted with a flat white finish to reflect light. Another design on the same principle is the pit-type greenhouse, as illustrated on the next page.

As with our homes, the first, and usually most cost-effective, method of improving the efficiency of our heating systems is to cut down on heat loss.

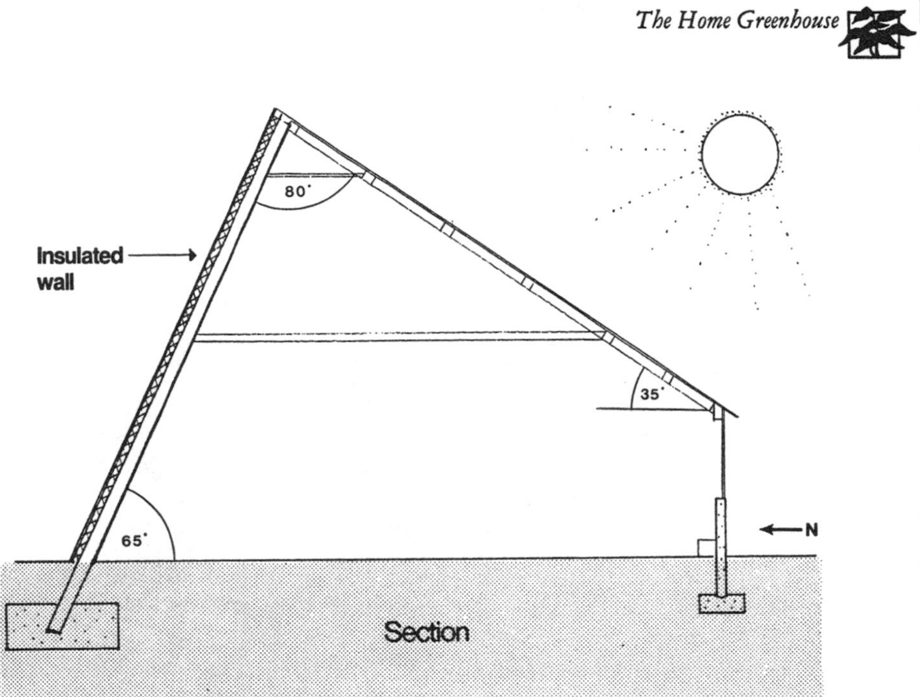

The Brace Resarch Institute greenhouse design, pictured here, has proven satisfactory on the plains and upper Midwest. The combination of a tall south-facing roof and an insulated north wall makes the most of winter sunlight.

CONSTRUCTION

The cost of building a greenhouse includes much more than the basic structure. Be sure to consider preconstruction expenses like extending utilities to the site—as well as the foundation, heating and lighting systems, and interior furnishings—to arrive at a realistic estimate.

Source of Supply and Cost

Prefabricated greenhouses may be purchased from greenhouse construction firms, building supply stores, or department stores. The price tag on a greenhouse is not likely to include anything more than the basic structure. Costs can be reduced if you are prepared to build your own. If this is your intention, then I strongly recommend that you obtain a good plan.

Foundation

One important feature of the foundation has already been mentioned: that it must provide good drainage. Not only is this important during the rainy season, but a well-drained site is less likely to heave during shut-down

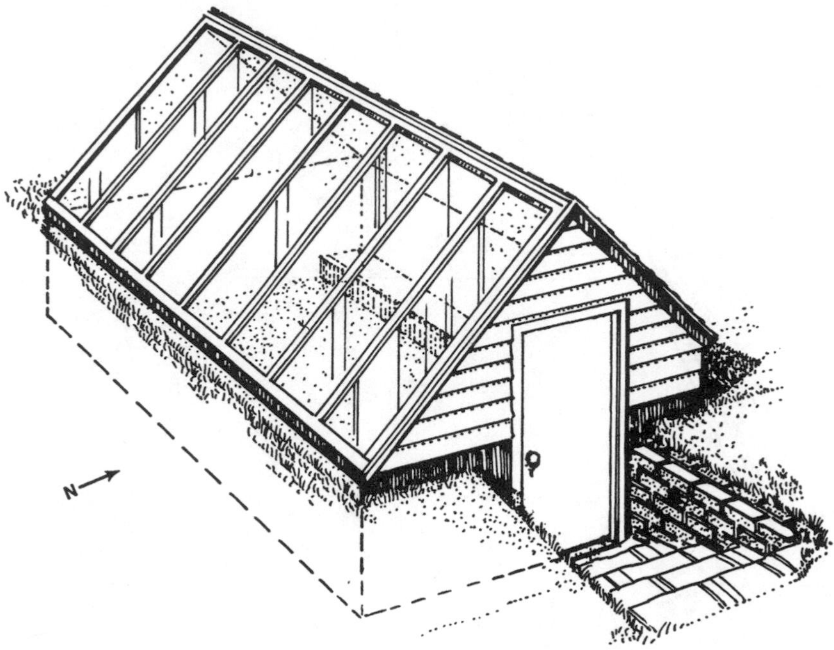

The northern slope of the roof of this pit-type greenhjouse is shingled. The use of shingles on the north side and the sunken design help reduce heat loss.

periods in midwinter. Two other important factors are insulation of the foundation and firm attachment to the upper structure.

Either wood or concrete is used for building the foundation. Use wood that has been pressure treated with a water-borne, salt-based preservative such as acid copper chromate, chromed copper arsenate (CCA), chromate zinc chloride (CZC), or flouride chromate arsenate phenol (FCAP). Avoid creosote or pentachlorophenol preservatives, which are toxic to plants.

Pressure-treated wood may cost two or three times as much as untreated lumber but it is well worth the extra expense considering its extended life. Painting or spraying untreated wood with preservatives is not very effective, as the treatment is only as good as the amount of preservative that is retained in the wood. Several coats of preservative brushed in are better than no treatment at all, but not nearly as satisfactory as the pressure-treated wood.

The wooden wall (or post-pier) foundation is built much as you would construct a fence, first sinking the posts and then attaching the sides and top rail. Instead of spacing the rails as you would for a fence, the foundation sides should be butted close, preferably interlocking with tongue and groove edges, the tongue edges up. At this stage, 2-inch rigid foam slab insulation can be secured to the inner wall using contact or linoleum cement.

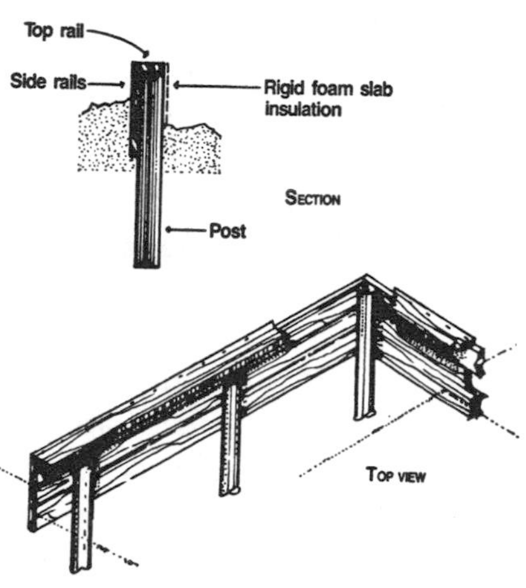

Post-pier greenhouse foundations are constructed in much the same way as you would construct a fence with horizontal rails.

When using concrete for the foundation, include two reinforcing rods all around to help prevent frost cracks. Bend and overlap the rods about 15 inches at the corners. The foam slab insulation should be set inside the forms before pouring the concrete, and it will be firmly bound to the inside walls once the concrete hardens. Soon after the concrete is poured, set bolts in it to hold the wooden sill plate.

After the concrete forms are removed, you may face the foam insulation with thin panels to preserve and protect it from damage. See your building supply dealer for a suitable and inexpensive product.

The Frame

The material normally used for framework in the prefabricated greenhouse is an aluminum alloy, and there are good reasons for its popularity. It requires little or no maintenance. Also, because it is a strong material, the frame needs smaller and narrower supports than wooden structures, casting less shadow. Disadvantages of aluminum alloy are its relatively high cost and the fact that it is a poor insulator.

Do-it-yourself plans often incorporate steel pipe for the framework. Very strong, the pipe allows maximum light into the greenhouse, but it will need to be painted and maintained with a metal paint or it will soon rust.

Wood is the most popular frame material with the do-it-yourself hobby greenhouse builder. It's easy to work, not too expensive, and because it is a much better insulator than metal, fluctuations of the inside temperature are more gradual than with metal frame structures.

Cedar and redwood are easier to work with than hardwoods and are more resistant to decay than cheaper lumber. Again, to ensure durability, pressure-treated wood is a good investment. Remember to use the non-phytotoxic, water-based, salt-type preservatives mentioned earlier

Covering Materials

It is only in the last couple of decades that "greenhouse" and "glasshouse" ceased to be synonymous, but nowadays there are several alternatives to glass for greenhouse construction. The firm plastics include polyethylene, co-polymere, and vinyl films. Examples of rigid plastics include PVC (polyvinyl chloride), clear acrylic, and fiberglass.

Each of these materials has its advantages and disadvantages as a greenhouse covering, and your choice will be based on initial cost, maintenance costs, and durability.

If a relatively cheap material is used, there will be recurring maintenance and replacement costs. The more expensive covering materials will last longer and be less expensive to maintain. Whatever your choice of covering material, make sure that it has been designed for this purpose.

Greenhouse covering materials must allow good transmission of light. Some diffusion of the transmitted light, resulting in weak shadows, is also desirable. All the materials that I will mention permit good light transmission.

As a general rule, the quality of the light passing through the material is important for proper plant growth, especially a balance of the red and blue portions of the spectrum. Colored covering material is not satisfactory because it limits light transmission of certain beneficial wavelengths. Avoid translucent forms of PVC and fiberglass, as they significantly reduce the amount of light transmitted.

Materials also differ in their capacity to retain heat within the greenhouse. Polyethylene and vinyl films allow rapid heat loss; fiberglass, clear acrylic, PVC, and glass are relatively good insulators. Another important point is that the material should be resistant to deterioration caused by ultraviolet (UV) light or it may quickly decay in sunlight. Here are the main greenhouse covering alternatives.

Glass—If a neighbor plays ball within throwing or batting distance of your greenhouse site and you still opt for standard glass, be ready with a replacement pane. Hail is an even greater risk in many locations and every few years large hailstones leave greenhouses looking as if they had been built in a war zone.

Even so, glass is still the most popular cover for permanent greenhouse structures. More people are turning to tempered glass (double or triple strength) and frosted or hammered panes that spread the light rays more evenly. Glass is installed on special frames, using special nonhardening putty, rolls of mastic glazing tape, or caulking compounds formulated for this purpose. Glazing nails will hold the glass in place, but using rafter caps will result in a neater finished appearance.

Polyethylene film (UV treated)—Regular polyethylene film is not recommended because of its very short life span. The ultraviolet light-treated poly, on the other hand, is often used as an inexpensive, one-season cover. A 4-mil thickness is satisfactory, but 6-mil is much stronger. Sometimes a second layer of polyethylene is used to reduce heat loss (by about 40 percent), but it seals the greenhouse so tightly that condensation becomes a problem. When two layers of poly are used, they are often separated by the air pressure of a small fan to give additional stability.

Polyethylene films come in rolls from 3 to 40 feet wide and 50 to 200 feet long, depending on type. Polyethylene film is much easier to work with during warm and calm weather. Stretch the material over the frame just enough to prevent sagging, allowing for some contraction when cold.

When covering a wooden frame with plastic film, first cover the end walls, then the sides, and finally the roof. Bury the end of the poly about 6 inches into the ground, lap the material 6 inches on the vertical studs, and cover the laps with wooden lath strips as wide as the studs.

Stretch the plastic from eave to eave, secured with lath at each rafter; preferably use double-headed nails for easy removal.

Once you have erected your own polyethylene version of the Crystal Palace, it is distressing to see cracks appearing in your masterpiece as the plastic gradually deteriorates and becomes ragged. Little can be done to extend its life, but avoid using folded sheets (plastic first tears on the folds), and try to reduce excessive rubbing and stretching where the material comes into contact with the supporting frame.

Well-installed UV-treated poly will last one or two years. The same kind of material reinforced with a glass or acrylic fibre mesh will last a little longer, but still less than three years. Your local garden center is likely to have some in stock, but for the less common materials and sizes you will have to plan ahead and talk to your supplier about a special order long before construction time.

Polyvinyl fluoride—These films are excellent and may last seven or eight years. But they are still too expensive compared to other suitable films and not as readily available. The 8-mil weight is sometimes used, but all polyvinyl fluoride films tend to attract dust because of an electrostatic charge.

Polyvinyl chloride (UV) treated)—Only the UV-treated PVC panels (lasting about six years) are recommended, as the untreated product soon darkens with exposure to ultraviolet light. PVC comes in flat, ribbed, or corrugated panels of various sizes. It expands and contracts with temperature changes, so bear this in mind during installation. Avoid using the translucent kind as the visible light transmission is as low as 77 percent. The transparent kind allows close to 90 percent light transmission.

Clear acrylic—Acrylic has the advantage of being half the weight of glass and highly impact resistant, and it lasts about twenty years.

With trade names like Perspex, Plexiglass, and Transpex, clear acrylic is available in UV-resistant, antistatic-treated, and scratch-resistant kinds. There are even double-walled panels with air traps to reduce heat loss. All are quite expensive.

Like PVC panels, clear acrylic expands and contracts with temperature changes, so it should never be nailed down. It also attracts dust.

Fiberglass (clear and UV treated)—Use only the clear and UV-treated fiberglass. Others yellow and progressively reduce the transmission of light each year. While fiberglass is lighter and stronger than glass, resulting in fewer supports being needed, it has several disadvantages.

If not kept clean, a bloom may cover the fiberglass surface, reducing the amount of light passing through the material. Weathering will result in the exposure of fibers. The surface should therefore be coated with a clear acrylic fiberglass refinisher every four years or so, extending the life of the material to ten or twenty years.

The best cover?—Taking everything into consideration, tempered glass is a good choice for a permanent greenhouse, but more recent developments like PVC should be considered as an alternative if you are prepared to replace the material after about five years. For coverings intended to last one season, or two at the most, the UV-treated poly films are a less expensive method.

THE INTERIOR

Plan your greenhouse interior at the same time as you plan the basic structure. Then, once construction is complete, you can turn your attention to inside furnishings and flooring.

Planting Beds and Benches

You can use ground beds for indoor landscaping directly into the soil, or use raised benches, which are easier to manage. Benches should be about 3 feet high, a little more or less depending on your own height, and about the same width if placed against a side wall. Center or island benches can be as wide 5 feet, just as long as you can reach the center easily from either side.

Your benches can be designed to hold containers, or a bed of soil or other planting medium. For container benches, spaced slats of cedar or redwood are satisfactory. Galvanized metal mesh, such as plasterer's lath, is also long lasting and allows good air circulation, but it must be supported by a framework of wood or perhaps angle-iron so it doesn't sag.

Your soil benches must have drainage holes covered by a shallow layer of drainage material such as pea gravel to provide good water drainage without allowing the soil mix to wash through. You will need about 1 foot of soil depth for root development.

Flooring

Most floors, such as ready-mix concrete, wood, interlocking bricks on a sand base, and stepping stones, tend to get slippery with algae and moss. While the brick and stepping-stone floors are attractive when first installed, they have a tendency to tilt and become unstable. Wood soon rots unless pressure treated, and it harbors disease organisms.

Nonskid alternatives for flooring are pea gravel, porous aggregate, and porous concrete. The pea gravel is somewhat soft for easy walking and rolling wheelbarrows. Porous aggregate is pea gravel mixed with epoxy resin and comes in a choice of several colors. It can look very attractive. Porous concrete is a quick-draining, nonslip alternative to ready-mix concrete. Mix one sack of Portland cement with 440 pounds of 1/2 inch crushed rock. Gradually mix in 4 US gallons to make a porridge, and pour into forms to a depth of about 3 inches. Finish by using a fine rake, not a shovel or trowel, to level the surface.

HEATING

If you plan to use your greenhouse to extend the growing season in spring and autumn, all you need is a small space-heater to take the chill off on cold nights. But for year-round use, you need to determine the required size of heater by calculating the heat loss from your greenhouse. Planning a heating system that is to function during the winter calls for technical assistance

Your options for heating are several, but gas, fuel oil, or propane are probably the best for value and efficiency. The final choice will depend on the price in your area.

Electricity is generally too expensive for anything except minor supplemental heating, such as for heating cables beneath a propagating bed. Kerosene space-heaters that do not need venting to the outside are satisfactory only for occasional use, as they give off fumes that are toxic to plants. Hot water circulatory systems are fine for very large greenhouses, but they are too bulky (and expensive) for the vast majority of home greenhouses—unless run directly from an adjacent residence.

Gas, fuel oil, and propane must be properly vented. The heat should be distributed with the aid of an electric fan, positioned so warm air is not blown directly onto the plants. Locate the thermostat away from the heat source.

The use of solar heat is worth considering in the planning stages, but for the foreseeable future there will be no such thing as a totally "solar greenhouse" for year-round use—at least not in our climate.

Emergency Heating

If your heating system fails at night or during cold weather, the greenhouse temperature will drop rapidly and your plants will be in serious danger. You should install an alarm system to alert you if the temperature falls below a set minimum and have a good back-up system on standby. Portable electric heaters, a kerosene or propane stove, or a standby electric generator could save the plants until your main system is restored.

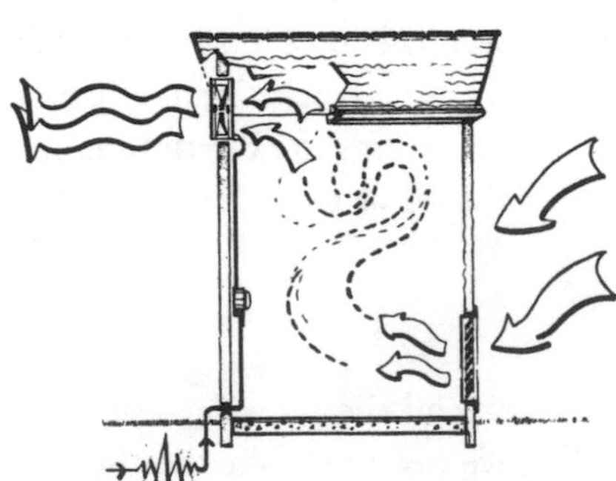

Proper ventilation is important in greenhouses. In this system. a fan expels the stale air as it draws in fresh air through wall vents. The operation of the fan is controlled by a thermostat.

VENTILATION

You might perhaps think that a greenhouse should be bottled up like a terrarium, an enclosed environment to retain as much warmth and humidity as possible. Not so. Ventilation is needed not only in warm weather to remove excess heat and humidity but year-round for fresh air exchange. Either vents (windows designed to open) or a fan, and preferably a combination of both, will keep your greenhouse properly ventilated.

The two-speed or variable-speed electric fan, or fans, should be set high in an end wall and have the capacity to exchange the total volume of air in the greenhouse from one and a half times to twice every minute.

The intake vent is normally positioned low down at the end of the greenhouse opposite the fan. It should have movable horizontal flaps that swing open to allow fresh air to enter whenever the fan is working. A thermostat regulates the fan operation.

This exhaust fan and louvred-shutter venting system also works well when set up in reverse, that is, with the fan drawing in the fresh air and forcing the stale air out.

Roof vents set at the ridge of the greenhouse are commonly included in prefabricated units and greenhouse plans. Sidewall vents are also popular. A gear wheel and handle is often incorporated to allow fine adjustment of the vents from wide open to the slightest chink. An added refinement that might be well worth the extra expense is an automatic vent-opening and vent-closing motor, triggered by a thermostat set at the desired temperature.

A less precise vent-opening device works on the principle of expanding and contracting liquid in a tube. Your greenhouse supply dealer will bring you up to date on such innovations and their relative costs. An automatic vent-opening system pays for itself by trapping daytime heat when the temperature drops and is a great personal saver of time, patience, and shoe-leather.

COOLING AND HUMIDITY

Often visitors and new residents of the Great Plains are surprised by how hot our summers can be. Winter frequently turns to scorching summerlike days without pausing for spring, and a greenhouse turns into an oven. Temperatures of 86°F (30°C) or more can have an adverse effect on many plants, so cooling is necessary.

It helps to wet the floor and benches to cool the greenhouse through evaporation or to set up an automatic mist from nozzles near the ridge line of the building. The misting system may be activated by a humidistat switch.

Automatic cooling can be accomplished through the addition of a unit called a Swamp Cooler. This machine incorporates an electric blower, a water-circulating pump, and excelsior pads. As its thermostat calls for cooling, the unit is automatically switched on, and water drips down the pad as the fan is activated—providing both cooling and increased humidity.

Another system, working on the same principle as the Swamp Cooler, can be purchased in separate parts. The pads are normally installed along one wall, with a circulating water pump to keep them wet: about 17 ounces of water per minute per lineal yard of pad. The exhaust fans serve to draw outside air in through the wet pads.

Without a cooler or an automatic misting system, you should spray or wet the greenhouse floors and benches now and then to aim for a daytime humidity level of about 70 percent. An overnight humidity level of about 50 percent is best to reduce the risk of disease problems, so ventilate accordingly.

WATER

A garden hose is commonly used for watering. Check that the temperature of the water is not extreme before applying it. A hose that has been lying in the sun can heat the first water to a surprising degree. To take the chill off water used during the colder months, you can run a supply into a barrel inside the greenhouse, and it will warm to air temperature overnight. The ultimate approach to controlling water temperature is to use a hot water line and mixing valve.

There are several automatic watering devices worth considering if you are often away from home for more than a day or so at a time. A solenoid valve controls the watering frequency, and the delivery system may be in the form of spaghetti tubes to each pot. There is a mat designed to provide water through capillary uptake, or you could use a system of spray nozzles.

Systems should include an in-line strained to filter out dirt. If nozzles still become blocked because of impurities associated with hardness, carbonates, or bicarbonates, you should have the water analyzed to determine what additives are needed (and in what quantities) to overcome the problem.

SHADING AND LIGHTING

As a general rule, plants shut down their growth system in full sunlight and perform best under somewhat reduced levels of light intensity (depending upon the plant species and other growing conditions). Shading of the greenhouse can adjust the amount of light to provide something like the optimum light value to keep the plants growing and at the same time reduce the risk of extreme temperature buildup.

Wooden lath or aluminum lath blinds can be secured to the outside, but light-weight metal blinds have a tendency to rattle in the wind, and heavy wooden ones are often difficult to roll up or otherwise adjust.

Glass houses seem to need shading more than film or rigid plastic houses, and many owners whitewash the outside of the glass instead of using blinds. A commercial whitewash formulated for greenhouse use is available from suppliers, but you can also use a diluted white latex paint. A paint roller (made to fit an extension handle) is a reasonably good method of application, faster than a brush and less messy than a paint sprayer. The stuff is usually applied in May, and whatever remains by the end of August is then washed or scraped off.

Shade cloth is a good alternative inside the greenhouse. It is available in a variety of mesh sizes for different degrees of shading and can be draped over a frame inside the greenhouse to reduce the light intensity for groups of plants such as cyclamen and primulas.

If your greenhouse is to be kept running during the winter, you should consider the addition of supplemental lighting. Only by increasing the day length and the intensity of light can plants continue to function during the deep winter months.

The most suitable artificial light for a hobby greenhouse is the fluorescent tube light. An ordinary incandescent light bulb would have to be placed so close to the plant that there would be too much heat for proper growth, or the proximity might even cause burning of the leaves.

In the 1970s fluorescent lights became widely accepted as the best means of illuminating plants, both in the home and in the hobby greenhouse. At first, five percent incandescent light was recommended in conjunction with the tubes to provide the red end of the light spectrum so beneficial to plant growth. But the bulbs gave off so much heat and cost so much more to operate that special fluorescent "plant growth" tubes were introduced.

While the quality of light for plant growth was improved by the use of Growlux and similar fluorescent lights, the light intensity was diminished, which tended to cancel out the advantage. Until you are ready to experiment with a variety of light fixtures, including the more recent incandescent grow-light bulbs, I recommend the use of warm-white fluorescent tubes side by side with cool-white tubes (one of each in a two-tube fixture). Economy and efficiency increase with longer fixtures, so avoid the short tubes and opt for the 4- or 8-foot long fixtures.

The enthusiast might like to investigate high-intensity-charge (HID) lights. The fixtures cost about ten times as much as fluorescent fixtures, but they are twice as economical in their use of power. The metal halide type of HID gives a white light close to that of daylight and is usually preferred to the sodium type with its yellowish glare.

Don't try to make the lights elegant by hiding the tubes behind lenses and screens; just leave the tubes naked, use a white reflector above the lamp, and paint all surfaces in the vicinity with a flat white finish to reflect all available light. (The flat paint reflects light more efficiently than silver paper or mirror surfaces or even high-gloss paint.)

CHAPTER XV

Weeds

As a general rule, weeds should not be tolerated among cultivated plants; they not only advertise a neglected garden but also sap valuable-moisture and nourishment from the soil at the expense of the plants we try to encourage. Nevertheless, in a few instances weeds are of limited value to the gardener. Some indicate a soil that is too alkaline, such as blue lettuce (*Lactuca pulchella*), blueweed (*Echium vulgare*), chicory (*Cichorium intybus*), heart-podded hoary cress (*Cardaria draba*), and povertyweed (*Iva axillaris*). Red samphire (*Salicornia rubra*) and wild barley (*Hordeum jubatum*) are a sign of saline soil, while acid soils welcome corn spurry (*Spergula arvensis*) and orange hawkweed (*Hieracium aurantiacum*). It may be of some comfort to know that lamb's quarters (*Chenopodium album*), redroot pigweed (*Amaranthus retroflexus*), and perennial sow thistle (*Sonchus arvensis*) are among the common weeds that indicate a good rich soil. To give weeds their full due, they quickly move in and stabilize disturbed soils and prevent erosion. Annual weeds may also serve a temporary but valuable service in shading seedling grass in a newly seeded lawn and will then disappear once mowing is commenced and the lawn fills in.

KEEPING THE WEEDS AT BAY

No area of the garden is sacred from attack by weeds, but there are some general strategies you can follow to make life more difficult for them, especially for those whose seeds drop uninvited from the sky.

Keep the lawn thick with proper watering, fertilizing, and cutting. A healthy stand of grass will make it more difficult for weeds to get started. In ornamental and vegetable plantings, mulching will prevent the establishment of many weeds that arrive by seed, and if any should get a root-hold, they are more easily pulled out of the loose mulch before they reach terra firma. Traditional mulches are best—organic materials such as wood chips, short straw, and well-rotted compost; anything, in fact, that does not look out of place, will not blow away, and will eventually break down in soil. Plastic put down as mulch looks untidy and, even when buried just beneath the soil surface, will likely cause more problems than it solves. Plastic prevents the natural exchange of water and air from the surface to the root zone. Today there are sheets of fine mesh plastics that do allow the roots to breathe, but only time will tell if this innovation will be worthwhile in the home garden.

Despite your best efforts, weeds will arrive and will have to be dealt with.

Coping with Annual and Biennial Weeds

Annual and biennial weeds will move in to the home garden and surreptiously produce seed almost overnight. Let one annual weed go to seed and you are inviting hundreds of seedlings to appear. And they don't necessarily germinate all at the same time for your convenience, but may pop up over a period of several years. Examples of common annual and biennial weeds include chickweed (*Stellaria media*), flixweed (*Descurainia sophia*), lamb's-quarters, (*Chenopodium album*), common peppergrass (*Lepidium densiflorum*), purslane (*Portulaca oleracea*), redroot pigweed (*Amaranthus retroflexus*), shepherd's purse (*Capsella bursa-pastoris*), and stinkweed (*Thlaspi arvense*). All have a short life cycle of one or two seasons; some species may overwinter as immature plants and produce flowers and seed the second season. All annual and biennial weeds depend absolutely on seed production for the survival of their species. Consequently, all we have to do as gardeners is to see that annual and biennial plants never reach the seed-forming stage.

When it comes to keeping a small home garden free of annual weeds, the old traditional methods are still hard to beat. Slicing off annual weeds with a hoe at the seedling stage, before they can set seed, is a simple and practical solution. Shallow cultivation with a sharp hoe cuts the weeds instead of transplanting them root and all farther down the row, and it avoids damage to the roots of the cultivated plants. It also reduces the number of weed seeds brought to the surface for germination. Most gardeners then like to rake off all weeds for the sake of appearance and for prevention of their becoming reestablished. Succulent weeds like purslane should always be removed, as fragments will often reroot and go on to seed.

You will find that, in time, virtually all the annual weed seeds in your garden will have germinated, and control becomes limited to pouncing on the few seedlings that develop from airborne seeds distributed by winds and by thoughtless birds. Chemical control of annual weeds in the home garden should never be necessary.

Coping with Perennial Weeds

Perennial weeds are rather more trouble than the annual and biennial

varieties. The worst perennials are those either with deep tap-roots (dandelion, *Taraxacum officinale*, for example) or with wide-spreading underground roots (quack grass, *Agropyron repens*; Canada thistle, *Cirsium arvense*). I probably don't need to remind you that if a part of the tap-root or piece of the spreading rhizome is left in the ground after digging, the perennial weed will spring up again, seemingly invigorated by your earlier attention.

Perennials with spreading root systems such as sow thistle, bromegrass (*Bromus*), stinging nettle (*Urtica dioica*), and leafy spurge (*Euphorbia esula*), must be dug out before the garden is planted. Any roots left behind will be difficult to remove from cultivated plants later, so time spent in preparing a soil free of such perennials is time well spent. Once the garden is clear of the aggressive perennials weeds, you will have to watch for any stealthy advances from adjacent properties. If possible, keep clear a narrow no man's land around the perimeter. Any creeping roots that send shoots up into this strip

When digging out perennial weeds, whether they have spreading roots like quack grass (left) or long tap-roots like dandelions (right), it is important to remove as much of the root as possible.

may then be removed before they become established in your cultivated plantings.

Certain other perennials, such as prostrate knotweed (*Polygonum aviculare*), broad-leaved plantain (*Plantago major*), and the ubiquitous dandelion, arrive by seed and may pass as annuals until you notice that the hoe does little to discourage regrowth. These must also be dug out, or (where digging is not practical) treated with a herbicide.

The answer, then, appears to be very simple—dig as much of the root as you can; if the weed grows back, dig down immediately to get the remainder. The problem with perennial weeds is that the patches may be extensive or they may get mixed with desirable plants (such as dandelions in a lawn). With modern technology at hand, digging is not a popular activity, and we are tempted to try a less physically demanding and less time-consuming approach. Before considering chemical warfare, however, be sure that you have done whatever you can to make the battleground as inhospitable to the enemy as possible.

HERBICIDES

In the home garden we often grow several different kinds of vegetables and ornamentals in a relatively small area. To use a variety of chemical herbicides that would kill an assortment of weeds, and still leave all the cultivated plants unharmed, is a task that is frankly more trouble than it is worth. To apply the correct rate of chemical on a small scale is not easy; and the herbicide may leave residues that can injure your plants in the current or following years. In short, it makes more sense to take every opportunity to weed by hand, by hoe, or by spade, and enjoy the fresh air and exercise that is one of the benefits of the gardening game. Weeding the old-fashioned way gives the perfect excuse (if one is needed) to get out into the garden and appreciate its development throughout the growing season.

The joys of hand weeding aside, there are times and place where herbicides, properly applied, can be a practical solution. The most common are the control of broadleaf weeds such as white clover (*Trifolium repens*), plantain, and dandelion in a lawn and the eradication of well-anchored weeds from noncultivated areas such as patchwork paving and gravel driveways. Finally, herbicides may be useful for the eradication of perennials (such as quack grass) from areas where the roots are entangled with those of cultivated perennials and digging would do little for your plants and your disposition. (Note that this difficult situation is not likely to occur if soil preparation has been thorough.)

All herbicides can be grouped into one or more or three different categories—soil sterilant, pre-emergence, or post-emergence. Herbicides are also either selective or nonselective in their action. Nonselective herbicides are indiscriminately toxic to all plants (both broad-leaved and narrow-leaved), while at recommended rates and concentration, the selective herbicides will kill certain kinds of plants and leave others to survive.

Before you buy a herbicide:

- Know what chemical you need. Read the small print to see what chemical is in the product. There may be a dozen different names for the same chemical, depending on the formulation and the chemical company that is marketing the product. The common chemical 2,4-D, for instance, is sold under at least fifteen different brand names.
- Know which formulation of the chemical is best for your needs. Herbicides are marketed in a variety of formulations including emulsifiable concentrates, which need to be diluted with water before use, and wettable powders, which may be mixed and agitated in water long enough to be applied by sprayer. Some herbicides come in granules, crystals, dust, or aerosol cans.
- Remember that while not as toxic to humans as some insecticides, herbicides can be hazardous to your health if not handled with care.
- Once home, store the herbicide in a safe place away from frost and out of the reach of children and pets.
- Remember that all chemicals have the potential for injuring all plants at certain concentrations, depending on application conditions, so follow label directions and safety precautions carefully.
- If you use a sprayer to apply the chemical, do not use that sprayer for insecticides or for any other purpose.

Soil Sterilants

The most effective of the nonselective herbicides is the soil sterilant. These "vegetation killers" are usually advertised for the complete eradication of weeds from paths, patios, and driveways. Disliked by most gardeners, these chemicals provide indiscriminate destruction of plant life and leave the soil barren for one or more years. Because the soil sterilant often spreads out from the area of application and roots of trees and shrubs enter the area from some distance away, the desolation frequently spreads to neighborhood gardens.

I have seen the consequences of a soil sterilant used along a back yard fence to eradicate thistles: resulting in the death of several fine Colorado blue spruce trees some distance away. It is not always evident that the roots of all trees and shrubs may travel at least twice the height of the plant laterally in all directions. What makes matters worse is that mature trees may be joined by natural root grafts, and soil sterilants are then translocated from tree to tree until the problem is recognized and the poisoned trees removed.

In my view, the soil sterilant has no place in the arsenal of the town or city gardener. Chemicals such as atrazine, borax, bromacil, prometon, simazine, and sodium chlorate should be avoided at all costs. Driveways, fence lines, and other noncrop areas are just too close to cultivated land to avoid injuring your own and your neighbor's gardens.

Pre-emergence herbicides

Pre-emergence herbicides such as chloramben, dichlobenil, and trifluralin are generally cultivated or watered in weed-free soil in an attempt to keep it that way. In the home garden I usually advise against the use of pre-emergence herbicides. I suggest you first take preventive action and then wait and see what weeds will show themselves before you consider how to deal with them. A regular light hoeing may be all that it takes to keep under control those that do appear.

Post-emergence herbicides

These are the herbicides most commonly used by home gardeners. They are applied once the weeds are up and growing and can be either selective or nonselective in their action.

Nonselective post-emergence herbicides will kill any growing plant they come into contact with, whether it is a weed or not.

Glyphosate (commonly sold under the trade name Roundup) is an example of a nonselective post-emergence herbicide that is frequently used in the home garden. Glyphosate is sold as a soluble solution, that is to say as a concentrated liquid that needs to be diluted just before use. Although it is rated as nontoxic, it may cause eye irritation. Glyphosate is very effective on annual weeds at any stage of growth and also controls perennial weeds, including grasses and thistles. As it is not very effective if applied to the young growth of perennial weeds, it is best applied at the four- to eight-leaf

stage. Rainfall within six hours of application reduces its effectiveness. Do not cut the treated foliage or cultivate the treated area for two weeks after application. The chemical breaks down rapidly in the soil, so there is no residual action and plants that have not been hit by the spray will be unaffected.

As glyphosate is nonselective, it is useful for treating driveways and pathways where you wish to eradicate all vegetation. Glyphosate diluted according to label directions can also be used for spot treatments where digging is not practical, such as on quack grass in the lawn or weeds entangled in the roots of ornamental planting. Keeping the chemical off your skin, wipe it carefully on the leaves of the plants to be eliminated, using a rag or glove. It will kill only plants it comes into contact with.

Selective post-emergence herbicides. The most well-known of the selective herbicides is 2,4-D, a chemical that kills most broadleaf plants while leaving narrow-leaved plants (monocots) relatively unharmed. That is why 2,4-D is so useful in eradicating broadleaf weeds like dandelions from lawns, and it does not accumulate in the soil from year to year. 2,4-D is not very effective on mature weeds or foliage, and it is toxic to humans if ingested.

Application methods vary, but here are a number of options currently available for those applying 2,4-D. In choosing the most appropriate application method for your own situation, you will want to consider convenience, time, and expense. It is best to apply 2,4-D at temperatures between 50° and 90°F (10° and 30°C) on calm days when weeds are actively growing.

- **Liquid concentrate** The liquid concentrate needs to be diluted according to label directions and is then sprayed or watered onto the lawn. The foliage should be wetted to the point of runoff. Once you have a sprayer that is used only for herbicides, this may prove to be the most economical method of application. Several disadvantages of the liquid concentrate are the time needed to prepare the solution, the danger of mixing the wrong concentration, and the risk of spray drift damaging neighboring plants. Low pressure sprays should be used to reduce the mist. The highly volatile ester formulations of 2,4-D are not suitable for home garden use, and their fumes travel much more readily than low-volative amine formulations of 2,4-D, which are suitable and generally available.

Another method of applying the liquid concentrate is with a 1 fluid ounce hypodermic animal syringe. This is a convenient and safe method for eradication of persistent broadleaf weeds (such as Canada thistle) when they are growing among ornamentals or in your vegetable garden. A few drops of the 2,4-D concentrate are easily deposited on the thistle leaves and rosette by syringe without risk of getting chemical on the soil or desired plants. A similar but messier system works by wiping individual plants with a solution, using a thick glove. The hand must be protected by plastic to avoid skin contact.

- **Solid tablet.** A solid tablet form is available that is dissolved in a tube of water at the time of application and used for spot treatment of individual weeds. One trade name for this kind of applicator is Killer Kane. Its advantages over the liquid concentrate are that there is far less risk of making a mistake in application rates, less risk of damage from drift, and less time needed for cleanup of equipment afterwards. While useful for small areas, there is little point in attempting to use this spot treatment on large lawns where it is time consuming and difficult to find and squirt every individual weed. It is useful for small lawns only.
- **Impregnated wax bar.** The impregnated wax bar is quite popular and is easily dragged across a medium-sized lawn to control broadleaf weeds. One trade name example is the Weedex Wonder Bar. Advocates of the weed bar point out that the chemical is already mixed, so there is little or no time wasted in preparation and cleanup. One disadvantage is the greater persistence of the herbicide in the wax once applied. For this reason it is wise to be especially careful not to use the clippings from treated lawns as mulch in the rest of the garden or to use them in the compost heap. While the best time to control weeds is while they are young and fast growing during the spring weeks, the weed bar is best used on fairly warm days when the wax is soft. As with all applications of 2,4-D, fumes may drift to desired plants. Use with caution, and don't drag the weed bar anywhere near your tomatoes or petunias.
- **Granules or crystals.** There are granular or crystal formulations mixed with fertilizer to feed and weed the lawn at the same time. One trade name for such a product is, rather obviously, Weed 'n

Feed. This dry material is applied by pushing a wheeled applicator hopper that deposits a measured quantity of the mixture over the lawn as you go. The big advantage of this type of preparation is the ease of application. If put down close to the ground with a calibrated fertilizer applicator as suggested, the material may be applied on days with a slight breeze that would be unsuitable for mist applications. However, broadcasting with spreaders that fling material out with a spinning disk action, including the hopper-on-wheels type of Cyclone spreader, is not practical at any time because of the very dusty nature of the formulation. Only the drop-type spreaders should be used.

Warning. While suitable for open grass areas well away from trees, shrubs, and other ornamental plantings, when using these weed and feed products in small gardens there is a distinct possibility of herbicide damage occurring on cultivated broadleaf and evergreen garden plants. Remember that tree roots run under the lawn not far from the surface; 2,4-D is taken up by the roots, often with very detrimental results to the woody plants.

- **Aerosol spray** An effective but expensive method of applying herbicide is with an aerosol can. If the spot treatment is so limited in scope that an aerosol will do the job, then I suspect that hand weeding would be cheaper and more efficient.

BE PHILOSOPHICAL—HOE IN HAND

Weeds are the successful opportunists of the plant world, species that have been devising ways of populating your garden path long before you and I started thinking of ways to keep them out. Weeding may be kept to a minimum once your garden is relatively weed free, but my best advice is to check your garden frequently rather than let weeds gain a head start or go to seed.

Use preventive methods and garden tools to physically discourage weeds before considering chemicals, and if you do decide to use herbicides as well as cultural controls, know exactly what you expect of the herbicide before making a purchase. Then, buy only enough for the job on hand. Follow label directions and safety precautions carefully, and if you do have left-over chemicals, keep them stored away safe from frost and out of the reach of children.

CHAPTER XVI

Insect Pests

THE CASE FOR INTEGRATED PEST MANAGEMENT

The modern approach to insect control makes use of current chemicals and technology but uses these weapons only after the life cycles of the pest and its natural controls are considered. This is called integrated pest management. We have to remember that some insects are on our side. Bees and wasps help pollinate plants. Lacewings, ladybugs, and syrphid fly larvae help keep aphid numbers down, and ground beetles prey on caterpillars. Tacinid flies, chalcid wasps, and ichneumon wasps devour caterpillars. A chemical attack on insect pests without understanding the side effects of the treatment can lead to higher pest populations as natural predators of the pest are reduced. Furthermore, applying an unsuitable chemical, or applying a suitable chemical at the wrong time, is an obvious waste, and both actions can do more harm than good.

First, consider the consequences of leaving an insect infestation untreated. Will the infestation kill the host plant or merely make it less attractive? You might sometimes turn the other cheek when you see some insects heartily enjoying your plants. Take the birch leaf miner. The chemical treatment of young or recently established birch trees, or repeated annual applications of pesticide, can cause more deterioration of the tree from your good intentions than from the work of the leaf miner. The tree would be best helped by your attention to water and nutrients.

You can also ignore the caterpillars of the cabbage white butterfly that feed on the outer leaves of your cabbage, if you so choose. The creatures are not damaging the head that you will harvest. Centipedes and millipedes look dangerous to plants but are not likely to cause damage. Leaf cutter wasps scissor out neat circles of leaves for nests, but healthy plants shrug off such small losses as being all in day's work. Plant galls are a sign that tiny creatures are using a plant as a nest, but if you can accept some malformed stems or leaves, your plants will hardly notice the intrusion. Besides which, by the time you see the galls, the adults are gone and the offspring are safely encased—or perhaps already grownup and away on business.

Even those insects whose natural appetites make it hard for us to overlook their garden activities can have their uses. Many people believe that an insect infestation on a tree must endanger the health and possibly the life of the tree. This is not generally true. Sometimes, in fact, the insect can even be of benefit, as in the common case of aphid infestation on maples. According of Jeff Cox in Organic Gardening, the fallen honeydew excreted from the aphid stimulates nitrogen-fixing bacteria in the soil, thus turning excess sap production to the plant's benefit. Most extension horticulturists agree that insect infestations are more likely to be "people" problems than plant problems.

First, then, consider whether or not measures need to be taken against any insect intruders in your garden. If you decide to do battle, try cultural controls before you take the pesticides down from the shelf. Only when nonpesticide methods won't work should you consider a chemical: one that is as specific as possible to the pest and least harmful to beneficial organisms, to ourselves, and to our environment.

CULTURAL CONTROLS

If we accept the principle of integrated pest management, we must also accept a certain amount of pest injury and develop an attitude that blemish-free plants are rarely necessary. The biological and cultural approach to pest control incorporates several policies, and these may be summarized as follows:

- Choose plants that are suited to your particular environment; plants growing under stress are more subject to pest problems.
- When available, grow selections with built-in pest resistance. These have long been developed for essential crops and are available for some garden plants.
- Grow your plants under the most favorable conditions possible; healthy plants often show more tolerance to attack.
- Avoid growing similar vegetables side by side; make the pests search for their supper.
- Rotate vegetable crops annually; insect and disease pests tend to increase wherever the same crop is planted in the same location year after year.
- Clear away garden litter and till the soil in fall or early spring to expose pests to predators and harsh elements.
- Intervention can be as simple as a strong jet of mild, soapy water from a hose-end sprayer; this treatment will keep down the numbers of aphids and mites.

- Hand picking of large insects in limited areas is usually far easier and faster than using a pesticide spray.
- Barriers made from such materials as tar-paper, waxed milk cartons, and fine window screening can be effective against root maggot flies.
- Traps are effective against a number of pests. (See the discussion on slugs and fall cankerworms.)
- Removing badly infested plants reduces the chance of infestation spreading to healthy ones; burn or bury deeply any such refuse. Prune off or remove overwintering caterpillar eggs where practical.

CHEMICALS

Insecticides work in one of several ways. Most are either taken into the insect on contact and destroy the nervous system of the pest, or work through stomach action when ingested. Some chemicals, therefore, may be sprayed onto the plant parts that are being eaten, while other chemicals must make body contact before they will take effect.

Chemical contact is not easy when the pest is feeding inside leaves or stems, or protected within the leaves that they distort. There is normally some stage in their life cycles when these insect pests must relinquish the safety of their leafy environments, even if it is only for a short while, and this is the time to catch them with a contact spray. Alternatively, leaf miners and other hard-to-reach pests are frequently controlled with a systemic chemical. These chemicals, when taken up into the system of the plant, make the plant toxic to sap-sucking insects. Such formulations can be applied to the leaf or stem of a plant but are often best assimilated when applied as a soil drench to be taken up through the roots. Note that systemics are not as reliable in their action when used against leaf-feeding insects, and they are toxic to quite a variety of plants. As always, a label check before use is very important.

Three products should be mentioned that are distinctive in their composition or action. These are baits, dormant oils, and microbials.

Baits are edible products (such as bran) that attract the pest and are laced with an appropriate poison. Care must be taken to ensure that birds, pets, and other nontarget life do not fall victim. Baits often have a short shelf life.

Dormant oils (also called miscible, mineral, or petroleum oils) are specially formulated to be sprayed only on woody plants without leaves during the dormant season. The oil film suffocates overwintering creatures such as scale, mites, and moth eggs. Dormant oils need to be applied during the winter or in very early spring (they are very toxic to all green foliage), yet they must be applied when the temperature is above 40°F . This often poses a problem on the plains. Also, oils can injure the plants under less than ideal conditions; and while insects have not developed a resistance to oils, insect toxicity is not particularly high.

Microbials are disease organisms that are parasitic upon the pest. The first common microbial to be made commercially available was Bacillus thuringiensis (often abbreviated Bt), used to control caterpillars. The product is sprayed on the foliage of a host plant so that it is ingested by the caterpillar. Timing of the application is critical or results are disappointing. Spray too early and the product will be gone by the time all the eggs are hatched; too late and the larger caterpillars will not cease feeding until the damage is done. Rain soon after application will reduce or entirely negate the effectiveness of this microbial. Unfortunately, while initially acclaimed as the ideal pesticide, it is now evident that caterpillar strains are evolving that are resistant to the disease, just as surviving generations build resistance to chemical poisons.

Garden pesticide chemicals come in five common formulations: aerosol cans, dusts, emulsifiable concentrates, granules, and wettable powders.

Aerosol formulations are convenient to use but an expensive way to buy a product. They are practical for very limited applications only, and consequently are hardly ever suitable for garden use. They should not be sprayed directly onto a plant, as the aerosol carrier can cause foliage burn.

Dust formulations are ready to use without mixing, but they don't stick well to dry foliage. Also, much of the chemical is lost by drift so dusts should be applied only during calm weather.

Emulsifiable concentrates (often abbreviated EC) are most suitable for use in sprays. The concentrated liquid is diluted with water just before use, according to label directions.

Granule formulations are a convenient means of controlling soil insect pests. The dry, free-flowing particles are easily placed, and most useful in releasing systematic insecticides for uptake by host plants.

Wettable powders are, as the name suggests, powders that are mixed with water before use. They need to be agitated constantly in the sprayer to prevent settling, and sprayer nozzles and screens frequently become clogged.

Pesticide Application Suggestions

If you plan to use chemical pesticides in your garden, first know which pest is involved, then select a suitable pesticide to do the job. Your regional horticultural extension people (department of agriculture or university) can help identify pests and answer questions you might have about pesticides. Remember, pesticides can be harmful to certain plants, as well as to pests. Always read the label carefully before making your purchase.

Obtain small quantities of a chemical so you won't have to store it for decades. (It's a good idea to mark the date of purchase on the label.) Most are formulated to remain in good condition for at least two or three years under proper storage conditions. Store pesticides in cool, dry conditions where children can't get at them.

Remember that the product label is the final authority; general application directions may change from time to time. For this reason, never store pesticides in other than original marked containers. Note in particular the waiting period from the last treatment to harvest of edible crops, and always wash treated produce before consumption.

Keep a separate set of measuring utensils for pesticides, and mix no more than you need to do the job. If you end up with a surplus of mixed pesticide, never pour it down the drain; instead, pour it into a hole at least 3 feet deep. (Where there is a high water table this will not be possible.) Deeply buried, the pesticides recommended in this chapter will break down relatively quickly in the soil. If you have a quantity of concentrate to dispose of, check with your local department of agriculture.

Choose a calm day for spraying or dusting, and avoid spraying blossoms where bees visit—or apply early morning or late evening when they're not around. Check any temperature restrictions on the product you are using.

Use separate sprayer units and measuring utensils for weed killers; herbicide residues can be very harmful to some plants.

When spraying, first direct the spray up under the leaves, then finish off by spraying from the top. When dusting, the air should be relatively still and the leaves slightly damp.

Avoid breathing dusts or inhaling vapors, and don't allow concentrates to touch the skin. Wear old clothing and rubber boots and gloves. Wash with soap and water immediately after spraying, and wash the clothes. Don't eat or smoke while working with pesticides.

After spraying, flush the tank and lines with clean water. It's a good idea to remove the nozzle and dry it separately to avoid corrosion.

A few words on some common insect pests and their feeding habits and life-styles might help you find them, identify them, and decide whether or not to fight them.

SOME PEST *CURRICULA VITAE*

Ants are not a direct threat to plants, but they often spread other problems by "ranching" aphids. The ants feed on the honeydew secreted by aphids and carry these "cows" to other plants to start new aphid colonies. Apart from the ranching habits of ants, anthills are rarely appreciated as part of the garden landscape.

One interesting story is that ants must swarm on peony buds before the flowers will open. This is not true, but the myth is understandable because ants are attracted without fail to the sugary excretions of the fat, healthy flower buds.

Pouring boiling water onto the ant colony is an old remedy, and various physical traps have been devised. But poison baits and boracic acid work best of all. Diazinon, a contact spray sometimes used for ants, kills only the ants in contact with the chemical, while the poison bait is carried by foraging ants to the entire colony. Bait must be fresh.

Aphids, also known as plant lice, could take the prize as plant pest number one. Gardeners know them by their small, soft bodies and their insatiable thirst for sap. Typically, they are pale green and wingless, but they also come with wings and in an assortment of colors including yellow, red-brown, and black.

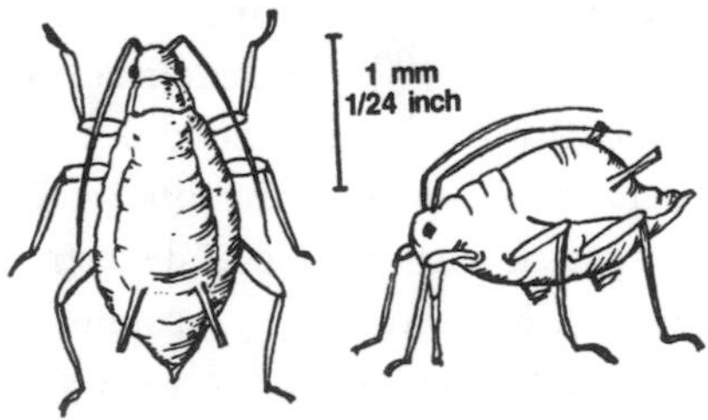

Top view of aphid and view of aphid feeding.

Some species feed openly on leaves and stems; others live inside curled leaves or galls. The insects create these galls by salivary secretions of the adult. There are several hundred different aphid species in our region. Most overwinter here as eggs on perennial plants and hatch as wingless females in spring. Populations can soon build to tremendous proportions.

At first an infestation of aphids may have little obvious effect, but as their numbers increase, the plants lose vigor, and leaves and stems become deformed, mottled, and dried out. The honeydew from the aphid gives the plant a sticky and disagreeable appearance and serves as a medium for a sooty mold fungus. As if this is not enough, aphids are carriers of plant diseases transmitted while feeding.

Light infestations may be held in check by natural enemies of the aphid such as ladybugs and lacewings, but a rapid buildup of the pests will call for intervention. Sometimes a whole colony can be removed by nipping off a terminal shoot. On house plants, rinse the visitors off with warm, soapy water, paying special attention to the undersides of leaves and new stem growth. Outdoors, a soapy spray under pressure may solve the problem. If not, a wide range of pesticides are effective, including dimethoate, resmethrin, and rotenone. (See also conifer woolly aphids.)

Blister beetles are bright red with three broad black stripes. The small black larvae tend to remain below ground during the day and feed on leaves at night. They enjoy cabbages, turnips, and related plants and sometimes gather in numbers on ornamentals.

Rotate vegetable crops each year so emerging beetles or larvae do not find their food supply nearby. Hand picking is one option, but wear plastic kitchen gloves as protection against the oily substance they exude when disturbed. It can raise painful blisters on sensitive skin. If you have to resort to chemical control, try carbaryl, methoxychlor, or rotenone.

Birch leaf miner sawflies insert eggs into the leaves of birch trees, and the resulting maggots feed and fatten between the upper and lower leaf surfaces. They then drop to the ground to pupate for two weeks and either emerge as adult sawflies to repeat the cycle or remain until the following year, depending upon species. The adult sawflies are so small that they are rarely noticed. The foliage of birch trees becomes severely blotched and brown by midseason. Although this will not kill an otherwise healthy tree, it will spoil its ornamental value.

Control is not easy, as contact sprays don't work on the maggots inside the leaves, and there are no natural predators or parasites. As a result, the number of birch trees being planted is decreasing in areas where the pest is most prevalent.

The systemic insecticide dimethoate has proven effective, but is phytotoxic to young or recently established birch trees, or even to mature trees when used year after year. Bark and foliage applications of this chemical are not as effective as a soil drench applied as soon as the leaves start to open.

Undiluted dimethoate (23.4 percent emulsifiable concentrate) is applied at a rate of 1 3/4 ounces for each 1 inch of tree trunk diameter (as measured about 40 inches above the ground). Water the soil well immediately after application. One treatment lasts the full season.

Contact sprays with malathion (and other contact pesticides) may be of some help if applied to the foliage or used around the base of the tree when adult sawflies are seen.

Bronze birch borers have recently advanced west through the plains states. The adult is a bronze-colored beetle about 3/8 inch long. The heads of the females are copper colored, the heads of the males green.

Birch trees host this insect, and it is interesting that it is the trees already under stress of some kind that are normally attacked. The cut-leaf weeping birch in particular, and trees weakened by annual attacks from other insects such as leaf miner and aphid, are especially prone to damage.

By late June the adults appear, and the female soon deposits eggs in cracked and loose bark high in the tree. The larvae (known as "flathead borers" for the broad second segment of the thorax) feed just beneath the bark, starting on branches about 3/4 inch in diameter. The location of the tunnels may be readily seen as the bark is raised by the boring activity. The larvae may take more than one season to mature, attaining barely half the length of the adult beetle and pupating in the spring.

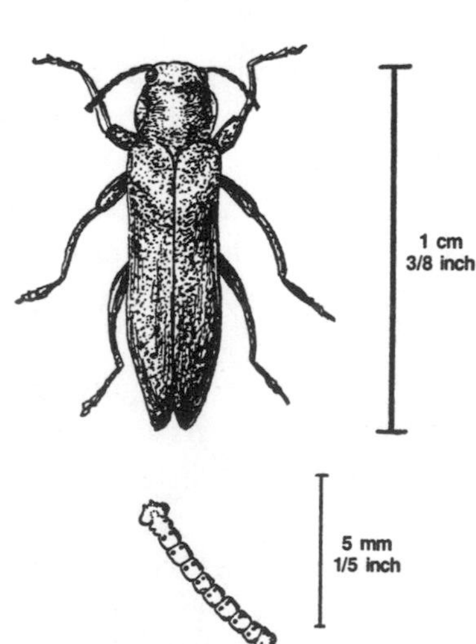

Bronze birch borer and larva.

There is no easy solution, but the first line of defense against birch borers is to see that your birch trees don't suffer stress from lack of water. At the first sign of die back, the damaged branches should be cut out and either burned (if local bylaws permit) or cut and bagged for disposal.

Chemical control is hardly a practical solution, but if the adults are positively identified, some advantage might be gained by spraying them with carbaryl or methoxychlor. The option of using the systemic dimethoate against the feeding borer should be considered with caution because its repeated use could weaken the tree, making it more prone to further attack. Woodpeckers and other natural predators of the borer, together with good cultural practices, are currently the best means of control.

Bugs, a term often used for all insects, is best reserved for a group of beetlelike, sap-sucking insects with "broad shoulders." Some species are shaped like a shield, and all emit a bad smell. They may be called shield bugs, stink bugs, or just plant bugs.

The tarnished plant bug is common and feeds on a wide variety of plants, including most vegetables. Adults are about 1/4 inch long, usually mottled bronze in color, and the wingless nymphs are yellowish green. Adults overwinter in garden debris and lay eggs in plant tissue in spring. Leaves, buds, and flowers are distorted by the feeding of nymphs and adults.

The boxelder bug is red and black, and it feeds mainly on female trees of maples. Red eggs are laid on the leaves and bark, and these hatch into red nymphs which moult several times as they change to the winged adult form.

Damage is not usually severe to the trees, but the nymphs may become a nuisance in the fall as they congregate in large numbers, often seeking refuge in houses.

Sprays are unnecessary to control these migrations as few nymphs survive the winter in hibernation. Better to spray in spring if their numbers still warrant intervention. A vacuum cleaner takes care of any that appear indoors. Carbaryl, dimethoate, malathion, and trichlorfon are some of the chemicals available for controlling heavy outdoor infestations.

Caterpillars are well known as the larvae of various butterflies and moths. One of the more regular visitors to the vegetable garden is the cabbage white butterfly. Every time a female flutters down to a leaf, she leaves an egg, and the cabbage worm that hatches a few days later is a slow-moving eating machine with a velvet coat the color of a cabbage leaf. These caterpillars grow to 1 inch long while they feed ravenously on the leaves,

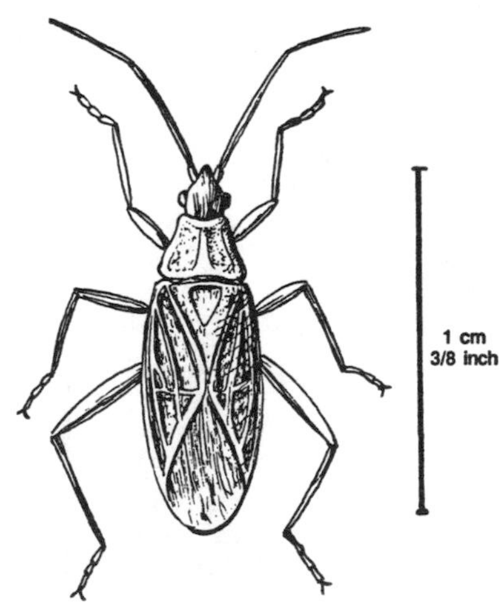

Adult boxelder bug.

and deposit dark green droppings in exchange.

As a lad, one of my duties on a private garden estate was to go down the rows of cabbages and cauliflowers rubbing out the eggs with my thumb. It was a distasteful job, but worse yet, the eggs that I missed hatched into cabbage worms that had to be squashed the same way. I remember being quite squeamish, and the smell was obnoxious. In view of this personal experience, I can hardly recommend enthusiastically that you follow that example, although the method is effective when done every day. Cutting off badly infested leaves is a reasonable alternative. Fortunately, the cabbage worms concentrate on the outer leaves, so the damage is not as serious as you might expect.

Carbaryl, dimethoate, and methoxychlor are a few of the insecticides that may be used. Avoid using them close to harvest time, and always wash your harvested vegetables well. The bacterial organism *Bacillus thuringiensis* is also used against caterpillars.

The mature caterpillars pupate above ground on walls and fence posts, and may achieve a second generation. Few pupae survive our winter, but butterflies migrate into the area each season. (See also corn borers, cutworms, fall cankerworms, forest tent caterpillars, sod webworms, spruce budworms.)

Centipedes and millipedes are well known for their long yellow-brown bodies and more legs than they appear to need. (Centipedes move fast and have one pair of legs per body segment, while millipedes are slower and have two pairs per segment.)

Centipedes feed on other crustaceans and small insects, while millipedes live on decomposing organic matter. Some people say that millipedes nibble on the tender roots of young plants, but I have never caught them at it.

Centipedes like to overwinter indoors if permitted, and they seek humid conditions and good hiding places such as stacked firewood in basements. Discourage them by keeping your home well caulked around windows and doors and by restacking stored materials away from walls. (See also symphylans.)

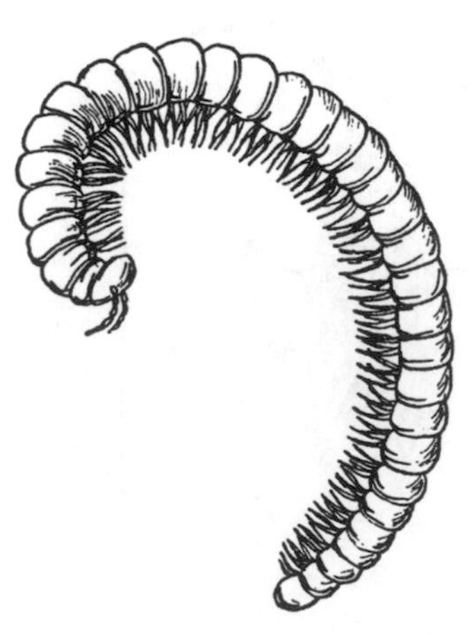

Millipede.

Colorado potato beetles can be recognized by their black and yellow longitudinal strips. They are most likely to be found on potatoes, tomatoes, and eggplants. This pest has a history of causing crop failure and famine, and more recently has demonstrated an ability to quickly develop immunity to all kinds of chemical controls. The beetle passes the winter beneath the soil and emerges just as your potatoes are starting to grow. Female beetles lay clusters of orange-colored eggs—mostly on the undersides of leaves.

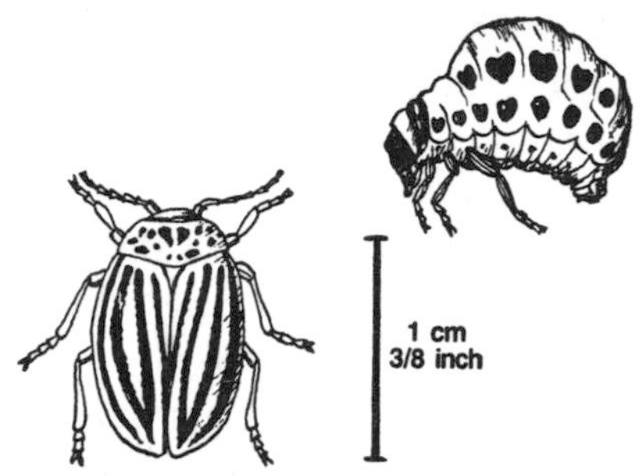

A Colorado potato beetle and larva.

The hatching larvae are reddish with two rows of black spots on each side. After chomping foliage for a couple of weeks, they pupate in the soil and emerge sometime later as adult beetles.

There are some years when field potato crops are almost completely destroyed by this insect. In the home garden where the number of plants is fewer, hand picking the beetles and larvae is the most practical solution. For larger plantings, use sprays or dust. Carbayl, methoxychlor, and rotenone are among the suitable chemicals available. A strain of *Bacillus thuringiensis* called M-one has been tested throughout the world on the Colorado potato beetle and has proven very effective.

Conifer woolly aphids are not true aphids; they are members of a small related group called adelgids. They become evident as small tufts of waxy cotton on conifer needles. The most common of these is the Cooley spruce gall aphid, particularly partial to the Douglas-fir trees.

The complete life cycle of conifer wooly aphids is not fully understood, but some species evidently use more than one host tree species. Apart from the cotton stage, the most evident signs of their presence are conelike galls on spruce trees. The

Gall of a Cooley spruce gall aphid, one of the conifer woolly aphids.

galls created by the salivary secretions of the adult adelgid, are home for feeding nymphs. The galls turn reddish purple and later dry up and open slits to release the fully developed nymphs. These moult into winged adults and move on to another host.

The cotton tufts of early spring and the small galls are unsightly, but they don't seem to seriously affect the health of mature trees.

It is not practical to control conifer wooly aphids when they are enclosed in the waxy cotton or the gall, so application of any pesticide spray has to be carefully timed to catch the exposed nyphs. Control of gall makers is best undertaken at the time the buds are opening. The other time for spraying is about seven to ten days after the cottontufts appear; three applications are usually necessary for control. Carbaryl, diazinon, dimethoate, and malathion are all appropriate insecticides, although dimethoate would be my first choice.

On small spruce trees you may reduce the pest population by removing and burning unopened galls early in the season.

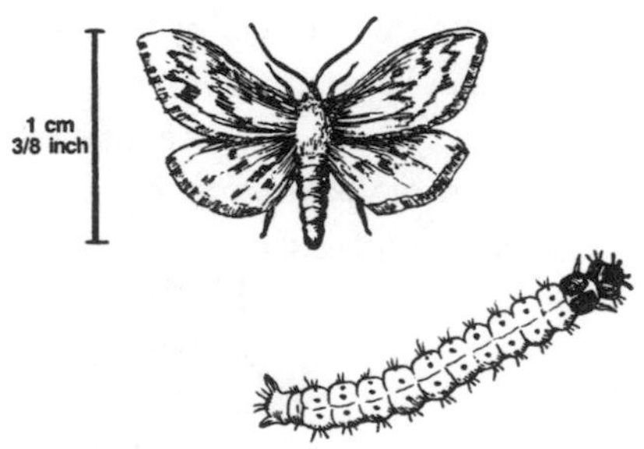

European corn borer moth and larva.

Corn borer The European corn borer moth prefers a higher humidity than we have to offer, but will accept our dryer conditions if tempted by a good crop of sweet corn. Soon after mid-July, look for the eggs which are laid by overlapping clusters of fifteen to thirty on the undersides of corn plant leaves, usually near the midrib.

A few days later the eggs hatch into larvae that feed on the upper side of the leaf, working their way down between the leaf sheath and the stalk where they bore into the stems. Mature larvae are light brown (paler underneath) with rows of brown spots and a dark brown head.

Manual control or applications of carbaryl or malathion should be timed to catch the young larvae before they seek refuge inside the stems.

Currant fruit flies appear about the time fruit bushes are coming into flower. The insects are rarely noticed as they hide under the leaves of the host shrub for a couple of weeks until the fruit is half developed. This is the stage at which they are vulnerable to chemical sprays. They are smaller than a house fly, yellow with dark markings on clear wings.

The eggs are laid one to each fruit, leaving a discolored scar on the skin of each infected currant or gooseberry. Some of these fruits will ripen prematurely and fall to the ground, while other maggoty fruit will remain until harvested.

The small white maggots pupate in the ground under the shrubs and emerge as adult fruit flies the following year.

Cultivating under the shrubs in the fall will tend to expose the pupae and help to reduce the fruit fly population. If your soft fruits were wormy the previous year, spray the undersides of leaves with methoxychlor or malathion when most of the fruit has set, and again about a week later. Spraying in the evening is recommended to avoid killing pollinating bees.

Cutworms are the larvae of the miller moths commonly seen in late summer and fall evenings fluttering around lights. The moths lay between 500 and 3,000 eggs, depending upon species, and these hatch and overwinter in the soil, awaiting the growth of tender seedlings.

Cutworm.

They fatten up in May and early June by chewing the stems at or near ground level, and even if the plant is not entirely severed, it cannot survive the damage.

Where cutworms are a problem in the vegetable garden, try to rotate crops, and seed a little heavier than normal. Put off thinning vegetable seedlings to their ultimate spacing in case the cutworms do the job for you. Each morning, stir the soil around the fallen victims to find the culprit, and deal severely with those discovered digesting their meal.

For valuable transplants, improvise wax carton collars around the plants and push well into the ground, or apply diazinon granules at planting time.

Earthworms are sometimes called dew-worms, angle-worms, or night-crawlers. There are several kinds, but all are much alike from the gardener's point of view. It has often been stated that earthworms do wonders for the garden. Compacted soil goes in at one end, aerated soil comes out the other, the worms working away like little rototillers to improve tilth. Although soil aeration is a factor, it appears that earthworms in the clay soil of many prairie gardens use up its organic matter. The fine casts (earth excreted by the worms) may increase the tendency of the soil to pack down, and they can be messy on a trimmed lawn.

Regardless, earthworms don't molest plants, and their presence in the garden does not personally offend me. In a plant pot they are certainly a nuisance and should be removed by immersing the pot in water to flood them to the surface. A heavy summer rain will often flood their outdoor burrows and bring them to light, where they are appreciated by many birds. Where a chemical control is felt to be necessary, carbaryl is the insecticide of choice. Incidentally, there is no evidence to support the story that a worm severed into two parts can become two viable worms.

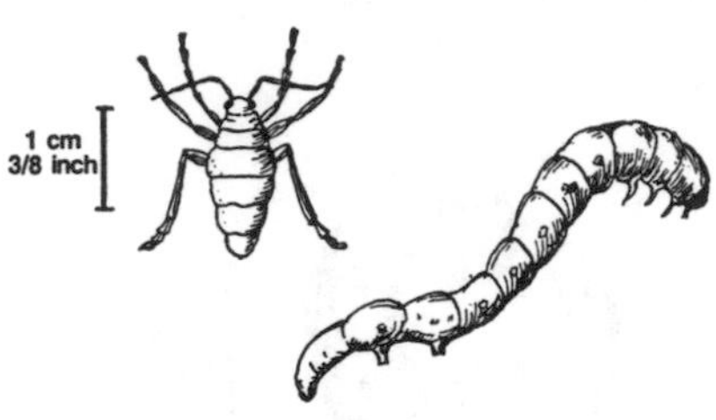

Fall cankerworm larva and adult female wingless moth.

Fall cankerworms are "loopers," small, thin caterpillars that characteristically loop and arch their bodies as they move. They feed on the foliage of almost any broadleaf tree or shrub but prefer elm, maple, apple, and basswood. Their feeding produces a shothole effect on foliage. They disperse by dropping on silken threads whenever disturbed or when food runs short. At maturity they are about 1 inch long, green with a dark stripe down the back.

If you are repeatedly troubled by this pest, and your trees are sufficiently isolated to prevent reinfestation by wind-blown larvae, there is an interesting method of control called banding. Because the female moths are wingless and have to climb the tree of the trunk of a tree to lay eggs near the leaves, they can be foiled by sticky bands. In September place a 4-inch band of glass wool insulation, paper side out, around the trunk about 5 feet above the ground. smear an adhesive such as Tree Tanglefoot (obtained from garden suppliers) over the paper to trap crawling insects, and keep it tacky until mid-November. Available chemical controls include carbaryl, diazinon, methoxychlor, and rotenone.

Flea beetles are dark dots about 1/8 inch long. They are hard to find because their powerful hind legs allow them to jump away as you approach. You will guess that they are around when you see tiny holes in the first leaves of seedling radishes, turnips, cabbages, and other members of the cabbage family.

Root feeding by the larvae and fall feeding by new adults are not likely to cause noticeable loss in plant vigor, but the pin-head-sized feeding holes in new leaves can wipe out an entire crop before the seedlings can become properly established.

The flea beetle is one good reason for checking your vegetable garden every day at the seedling stage. At the first indication of flea beetle damage, dust along the row with a preparation containing carbaryl, methoxychlor, or rotenone.

Forest tent caterpillars are among those insect visitors viewed with particular distaste by gardeners—especially by those living surrounded by aspen trees.

The light brown moths lay their eggs during July and August in grey bands glued around twigs. The tiny black caterpillars hatch about the time the aspen leaves unfold the following spring, and immediately commence feeding. They grow to about 2 inches long and can then be recognized by their dark brown color with a blue stripe down each side and a row of pale keyhole-shaped marks along the back. About six weeks after hatching, they pupate in silken cocoons and emerge as adult moths some ten days later.

Although unsightly, infested trees will lose vigor but will not be killed —even by repeated attacks. You may prune off the caterpillar clusters soon after they hatch or use malathion or the bacterial organism *Bacillus thuringiensis*—or better still, if you can, remove the egg bands in the fall.

Infestations of forest tent caterpillars tend to occur in cycles of several years, and in due course the populations decline (without our intervention) through disease, parasites, and climatic conditions.

Fungus gnats are tiny, long-legged flies, about 1/9 inch long, with a bouncy flight. They are often seen hovering around the soil and foliage in greenhouses and of house plants.

During her life span of one week, the female produces about 150 eggs, laying them into the soil in clusters close to the host plants. These eggs hatch in five days as tiny maggots with transparent bodies and black heads. They feed for a week or two on the roots and underground stems. They reach a mature size of about 1/4 inch and then pupate on or in the soil, emerging within a week as adult fungus gnats. They thrive in moist, organic soils.

The root and underground stem feeding by the maggots cause plants to lack vigor, wilt, and turn yellow. The remaining roots are then subject to rot.

Immerse the pot in tepid water to just above the soil line and leave it for six to eight hours to drown the maggots, or apply a soil drench of diazinon. You may have to use an aerosol containing malathion or pyrethrin and specified safe for plants to get rid of the adult flies. You can also try reducing the peat content of the soil, using perlite or vermiculite instead.

Pine cone gall on willow.

Gall insects of various kinds stimulate plants to create distinctive galls to serve as nurseries for the immature insects. Poplars, willows, and roses frequently act as unwilling hosts, but the damage is usually not serious. Removing and burning unopened galls is a helpful practice. Chemical controls are not generally recommended, a possible exception being control of the conifer woolly aphid. (See pages 251–252) Dispose of roses that develop crown gall—woody knots that develop at or just beneath soil level.

Leaf hoppers are like tiny grasshoppers, light green wedge-shaped insects about 1/4 inch long. Jumping from plant to plant, the nymphs resemble the adults except for their smaller size and lack of wings.

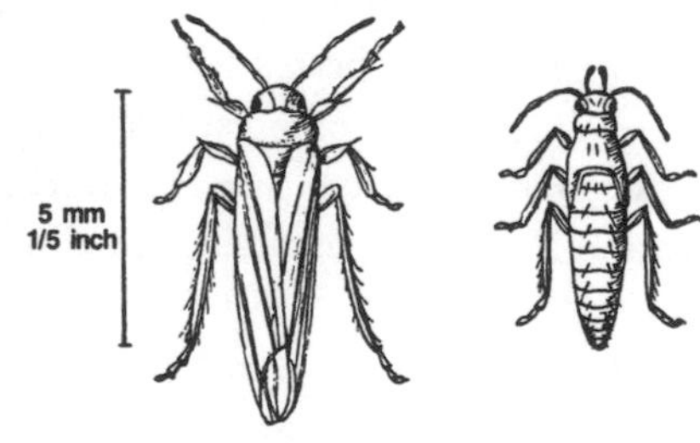

At leaf hopper and nymph.

Adult females lay eggs in host plants, and there may be two or three generations each year. Eggs laid in the fall to overwinter may not survive in the north, but new adults are usually blown in on southerly winds early in the season.

Leaf hoppers cause the pale mottling of foliage by sucking sap and also transmit plant diseases as they feed. Young leaves become curled, and the plant is weakened by heavy populations. Plants commonly attacked include roses, hops, cabbage, potatoes, lettuce, and celery.

A wide range of insecticides, including carbaryl, diazinon, dimethoate, malathion, and rotenone, can be used against leaf hoppers. Use the recommended chemicals carefully, and only when necessary.

Mealy-bugs are first noticeable on house plants as bits of white fluff. Microscopic investigation may reveal that these are egg masses protected by waxy cotton and that the insects are fringed scales, also with a white waxy coating. The scales move extremely slowly, stopping to suck plant juices. They favor the undersides of leaves and leaf axils, and like true scale insects and their allies, they excrete honeydew.

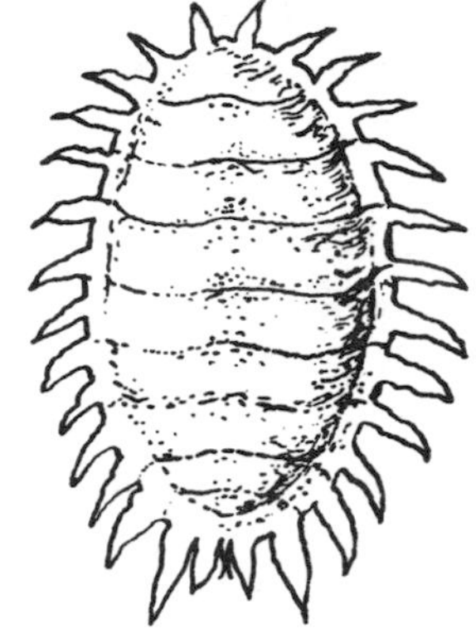

Mealy-bug.

Heavy infestations of mealy-bugs can severely weaken or kill the host plant. Pick off as many of the pests as you can with tweezers. Spray or bathe the plant with warm, soapy water to soften the wax. Use pesticides such as dimethoate, malathion, or miscible oil and repeat several times at weekly intervals to catch newly hatched nymphs. Incidentally, ferns are not tolerant of malathion, so they have to be treated with a systemic insecticide like dimethoate. This should be applied in the spring or early summer, if possible, when growth is most active.

There is much to be said for the policy of discarding badly infested house plants and starting again later with clean ones.

Oystershell scale is a descriptive name. These insects may infest a number of trees and shrubs including apple, birch, cotoneaster, dogwood, elm, lilac, mountain-ash, poplar, and willow. Look for brownish grey, shell-like humps on twigs and branches.

The insects winter as eggs under these scales and hatch in May. The crawlers disperse and the young females find permanent residence elsewhere on the plant. The males remain mobile. The cycle is completed as the female assumes the scale form and lays eggs beneath its protection.

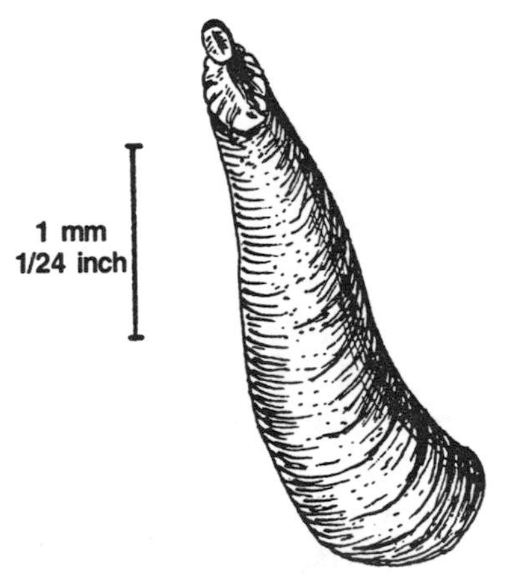

Adult female oystershell scale.

A branch of a woody plant weakened by this sap-sucking insect may be dead by spring, and if the infestation continues unchecked, it can spread and kill the entire tree or shrub.

Time your applications of carbaryl or diazinon to coincide with the vulnerable stage of the life cycle—when crawlers are on the move—usually late May in the north. Use miscible oil in early spring on the mature scales while the woody plants are still dormant.

Pear slugs are the larvae of a sawfly that deposits eggs in the leaf tissue of certain trees and shrubs, especially those of the rose family. Favorite targets include cherries, cotoneaster, pear, plum, and hawthorn.

The tiny larvae, 1/2 inch long, resemble tiny, dark green slugs covered with slime. They feed by scraping away the upper leaf surface and can quickly spoil the appearance of an ornamental. When mature, the larvae turn yellow and drop to the soil where they pupate and emerge as adult saw flies. Damage from a second generation is often more severe than the first.

Pear slugs are not considered a life-threatening menace, but if you have had previous problems with this insect, check the foliage in July for the larvae or any evidence of their feeding.

A strong spray of soapy water from a hose-end sprayer may be sufficient to keep the pest under control. If you do resort to chemical control, malathion and rotenone are the insecticides of choice, although carbaryl and pyrethrin may also be used. Exercise care when using chemicals and note that malathion should not be used when the temperature is lower than 68°F.

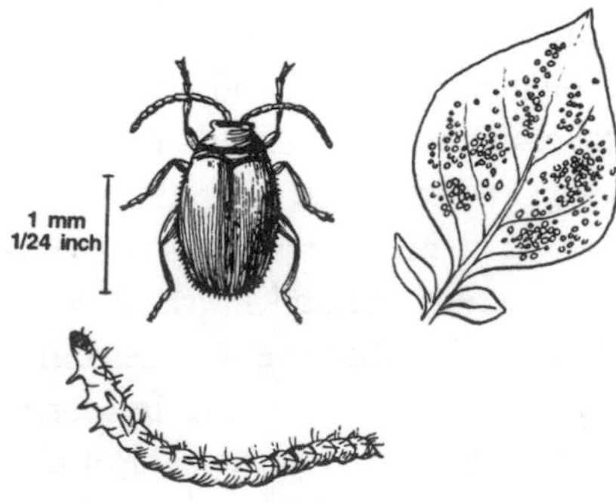

A potato flea beetle and larva. The potato leaf shows the shot-hole injury caused by the adult beetles.

Potato flea beetle larvae feed on potato tubers, leaving surface tracks and tiny, shallow tunnels. Like other flea beetles, the adults leave a shot-hole feeding pattern in the foliage. It is at this beetle stage that they are best controlled with rotenone dust, before they lay their eggs.

Root and onion maggots are the larvae of several species of flies closely resembling house flies. As your garden vegetables appear in the spring, the flies lay eggs on or close to the plants—onions, turnips, cabbage, cauliflowers, radishes, and other members of the cabbage family. Small, white, legless maggots from the eggs feed on the bulbs and roots, and may move from plant to plant down the row.

When the maggots are mature, they pupate in the soil. Onion maggots produce two or three generations in one season, while the others complete only one. Overwintering is in the pupal stage.

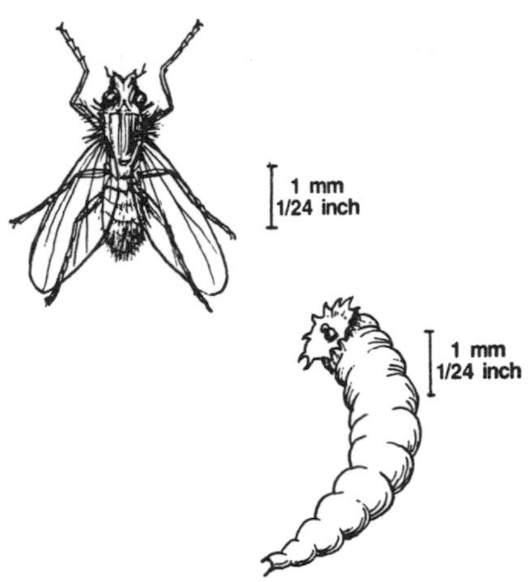

Cabbage worm fly and root maggot.

Seedlings wilt under attack, the damaged areas decay, and the seedlings usually die.

An old but laborious method of thwarting root maggot flies is to fit tarpaper disks around each plant, ensuring that they fit close to the ground. Epsom salt sprinkled down the row at seeding or planting time is said to protect the plants during those first critical weeks. Nowadays, the usual recommendation is to use either diazinon granules at seeding time (follow label directions) or a drench of that chemical soon after planting.

Rose weevils, also known as curculio, are red snout beetles about 1/4 inch long. They bore into rose-buds, and the damaged flowers either fail to open or are ruined by holes. The whitish grubs develop in the hips, fall to the ground when mature, pupate in the soil, and emerge the following spring as adult weevils ready to repeat the annual cycle.

Hand pick the adults daily, and pick off damaged buds. Spray if necessary with carbaryl and rotenone. Diazinon, malathion, or methoxychlor could also be used.

Sawflies may be a problem in the larval stage as small, false caterpillars. There are species that feed on the foliage of soft fruits and ornamental trees, including spruce, fir, larch, willow, and birch. They are smaller and thinner than the typical caterpillar.

The adult of the yellow-headed spruce sawfly looks like a small wasp. It lays eggs at the base of new spruce needles. The emerging larvae are pale green with a yellow head that turns reddish as they reach a mature length of

3/4 inch. Another species of sawfly has a shiny black head.

Mature spruce sawfly larvae fall on the ground, where they pupate until the following spring. Fruit sawflies also pupate in the soil, but they manage to emerge as adults the same season in time to complete a second generation.

Raking up and disposing of fallen leaves under fruit bushes will take care of some of the pupae in their cocoons. When the sawfly larvae are first seen in spring, you can prune off the clusters or use malathion when the temperature is 68°F (20°C) or warmer. (See also birch leaf miner sawflies and pear slugs.)

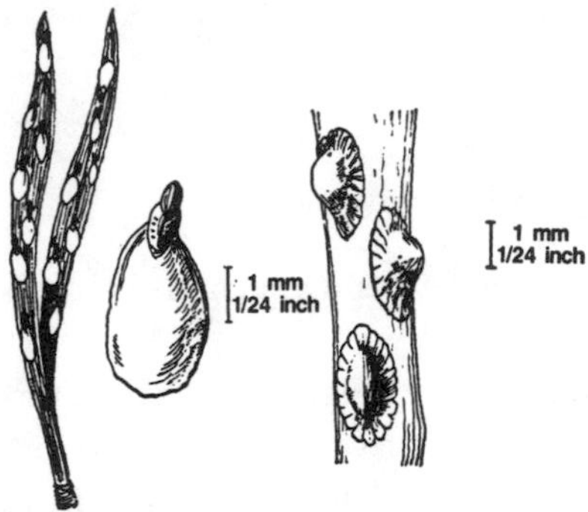

Scale-infested pine needles and close-up of adult female scale (left) and adult female lecanium scale (right).

Scale insects (such as pine needle scale and lecanium scale) look something like miniature flattened sea shells, but often go entirely unnoticed as they appear to be natural protrusions of the stem and leaf. The female holds fast to the plant with her mouthparts and forms a shield under which to lay her eggs. She then dies, and in time the young (crawlers) move out from the shield to disperse and set up shop for themselves.

Plants attacked become weak as the sap is sucked from stems and leaves, causing stunted and distorted foliage. A sticky residue is exuded on which thrives a black fungus growth, giving the plant a dirty appearance.

Scales on house plants and greenhouse plants are of waxy texture and soft enough to scratch off with a finger-nail. Try washing and rubbing them away with warm, soapy water and a soft tooth-brush. If chemicals have to be used, the washing treatment is still a good preliminary, as it softens the wax so pesticides are able to penetrate. Treatment is most successful at the crawler stage. Try carbaryl or diazinon on the crawlers and dimethoate, malathion and mild detergent soap, miscible oil, or pyrethrin on the adult scale insects. (See also oystershell scale.)

Slugs thrive in shady and poorly drained sites, devouring young leaves and shoots at night and hiding under garden debris during the day. They particularly appreciate ripe strawberries. Plant damage may not always indicate the source of trouble, but the tell-tale slime tracks they leave behind will warn you that they are lurking not far away.

Keep all garden litter cleared away so hiding places are scarce. There are several innovative methods for trapping slugs. One popular idea is to leave empty half rinds of grapefruit or oranges around the garden to serve as citrus igloos for the shade-loving molluscs. Another is to set out beer in shallow containers at ground level so the creatures might drink and become woozy. Check these resorts each morning and dispose of the clientele as you see fit.

Because slugs are soft-bodies creatures, they avoid sharp objects that bruise or irritate their unprotected flesh. You might take advantage of this situation by spreading sharp rock chips around your prize plants.

If using poison bran bait such as metaldehyde or methiocarb, place it in the evening under boards or tiles where the slugs will find it and the birds won't. The bait soon deteriorates in storage, so always obtain a fresh supply. Metaldehyde is suitable for use in the vegetable garden, but methiocarb is for ornamental plant areas only.

Sod webworm caterpillars live in silk-lined burrows in lawn soil or thatch. They are about 3/4 inch in length, off-white or tan in color, with a dark brown head, a few long hairs on the back, and sometimes rows of dark spots.

They feed at night, pulling grass blades into their tunnels, and by late summer the damage becomes evident as uneven brown patches in the lawn. They overwinter in the soil, pupate in the spring, and emerge as tan-colored moths about as large as your little fingernail. At rest, these tiny moths appear almost cylindrical with their wings folded round the body. When disturbed by mowing and when laying eggs during the warm evenings of May and June, they zigzag in short, erratic flight patterns close to the grass. The eggs hatch in six to ten days.

A healthy stand of grass can withstand a moderate infestation, so water and fertilizer for your lawn may be all that is required. If chemical control becomes necessary, apply carbaryl or diazinon two weeks after the moths first appear. The lawn should be trimmed and clear of clippings before treatment. As always, follow the label directions. You will find that diazinon should be watered well into the lawn, but that carbaryl should not be watered in after treatment. (See also white grubs.)

Sow-bug is a name applied to several similar crustaceans, the most memorable of which roll themselves into a pill when disturbed. Outdoors they are found under rocks, enjoying the cool damp. Indoors they may be found in damp, poorly ventilated basements. They do little damage to plants, but if they are found in a plant pot, you can be sure that they are taking at least an occasional nibble at the roots. Hand picking under such circumstances should be enough to clear them away.

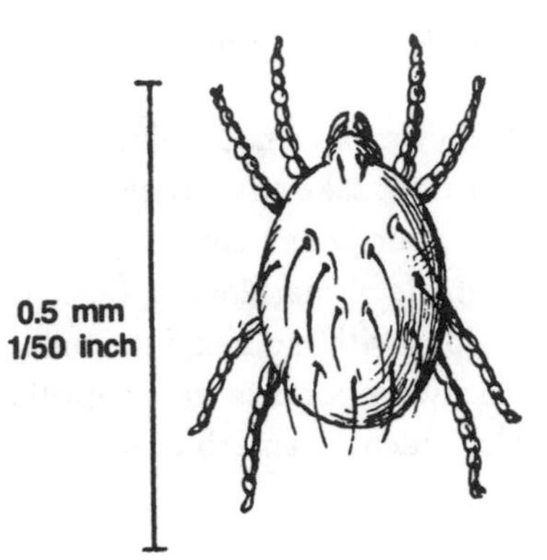

Spider mite.

Spider mites are one of the most persistent and annoying of plant pests. They are so small that it takes a practiced eye or a 10-power hand lens to see these tiny eight-legged creatures moving on the undersides of leaves. Their presence is usually first noticed by a mottling of the foliage caused by the sucking of sap and the death of some of the plant tissue. If spider mites are not controlled, you can expect a mass of fine webbing, drying of entire leaves, and premature leaf drop.

Hot, dry weather suits the mites very well, and under such conditions the life cycle can be completed in as little as seven days. Each female lays 100 to 200 eggs.

The two-spotted spider mite is the species usually found on house plants. Check your plants frequently, and keep new plants in quarantine for a week or so to make sure that they are free of this nuisance before adding them to your collection. Spider mites are highly mobile and accept a wide range of host plants.

Wash off infested plants daily, using warm, soapy water alternating with dicofol and malathion.

Outdoor damage by various mites is more likely to occur during hot, dry weather. Plants attacked include ornamentals, fruit trees, raspberry plants, and some vegetables—eggplants and peppers.

The spruce spider mite causes discoloration of the needles, turning them first speckled and then yellow before the needles fall. New needles will not replace those that have fallen, but in spring a spruce will normally put out healthy new growth at the branch tips, hiding the bare branches closer to the trunk.

Control of spider mites outdoors is accomplished through washing down with soapy water as soon as the pest is noticed and alternating sprays of dicofol and malathion as long as the problem persists. See that plants do not lack for moisture and nutrients during this time of stress.

Springtails can pose a mystery in greenhouse or house plant containers. You may notice that plants are not thriving or that there are small holes in leaves. Eventually, you will see a swarm of something minute jumping about the surface when the pots are flooded.

These tiny, wingless insects, 1/24 inch long, also feed on roots. On the surface they propel themselves through the air with their tail-like appendages.

Like fungus gnats, they thrive on organic and overwatered soils, so if possible let the pots dry out somewhat between waterings. Control measures are the same as for fungus gnats.

Spruce budworm can be a serious pest of spruce and fir. The adult, a small brown moth, lays clusters of green eggs on the undersides of needles in midsummer. The resulting larvae hibernate in webbing shelters on the tree, and in spring feed on needles and within the fattening buds. By late June, these brownish caterpillars are about 3/4 inch long and ready to pupate on the tree.

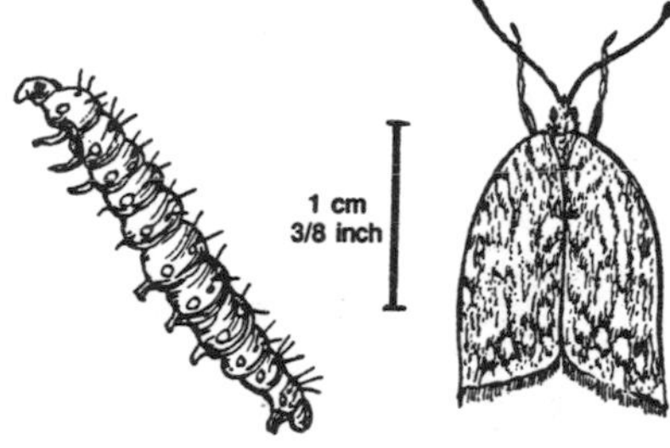

Spruce budworm larva and moth.

New shoots of the host are destroyed, needles drop, and trees take on a dirty look with webbing and a characteristic red-brown color. Several years of heavy infestation will kill the trees.

Hand picking of larvae from small trees will help where this is practical. If climatic conditions and other natural controls fail to prevent a buildup to epidemic proportions, chemical sprays or the bacterial organism *Bacillus thuringiensis* should be applied whenever larvae are noticed. Recommended chemicals include carbaryl, dimethoate, malathion, and trichlorfon.

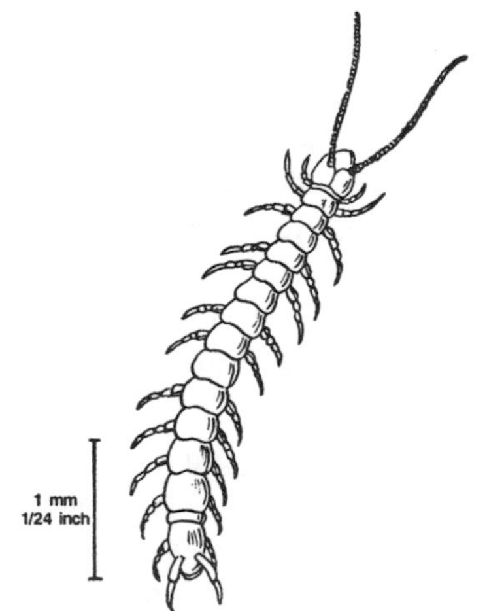

Symphylan.

Symphylans are small crustaceans that live on plant roots (and centipedes often get blamed for their crimes). In our region symphlans don't survive outdoors but may occasionally evoke consternation when found in greenhouse and house plant pots. At 1/4 inch in length when fully grown, they are only a third the size of the centipede. Symphylans have vibrating antennae instead of pincer jaws.

Should you ever find these tiny creatures feeding on the roots of your potted plants, you might use a soil drench of malathion to solve the problem or wash all soil off the roots and repot in a fresh soil mixture.

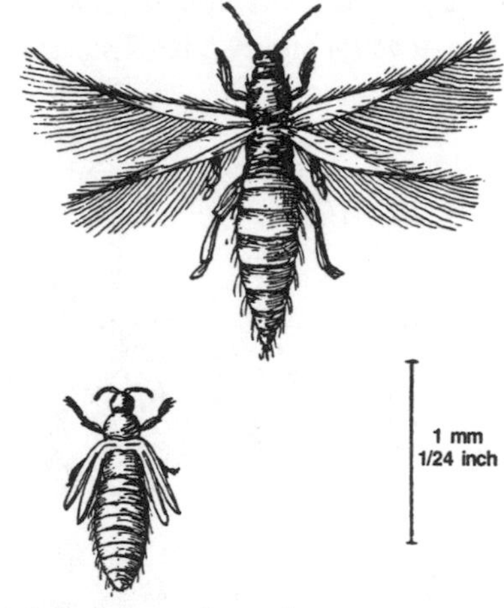

Adult thrips and nymph.

Thrips is a minute insect 1/24 or 1/12 inch long, and is very hard to see as it flies around on feathered wings. It feeds by rasping or piercing foliage, turning it grey, speckled, or streaked. Adults may overwinter in garden debris and other protected places and lay eggs in plant tissue in spring.

The resulting nymphs are small, wingless versions of the adults, and when mature they moult in the soil. A life cycle from egg to egg-laying adult may be completed in two weeks under ideal hot and dry conditions, resulting in a fast buildup of this serious pest.

The gladiolus and onion are particularly susceptible, but these insects enjoy a varied diet of flowers, fruit plants, and vegetables. Buds are frequently targeted for attack, resulting in malformed and spotted flowers. Leaves become silver spotted and may twist as they dry up.

Treating stored gladiolus corms with a suitable bulb dust is an important measure to prevent thrips overwintering indoors. Treat infested plants with dimethoate, malathion, or resmethrin, and destroy all infested plant parts at the end of each season.

Weevil pests of the garden are often known as snout beetles. Root weevils are very tiny and leave a characteristic notched feeding pattern on the leaf edge of strawberries and many herbaceous perennials. The grubs feed on the roots and burrow into the crown.

Spraying with carbaryl, malathion, or methoxychlor when fresh notching is seen will afford some control. There are also special weevil baits available containing 5 percent sodium fluosilicate for placing around the base of plants. (See also white pine weevil and rose weevil.)

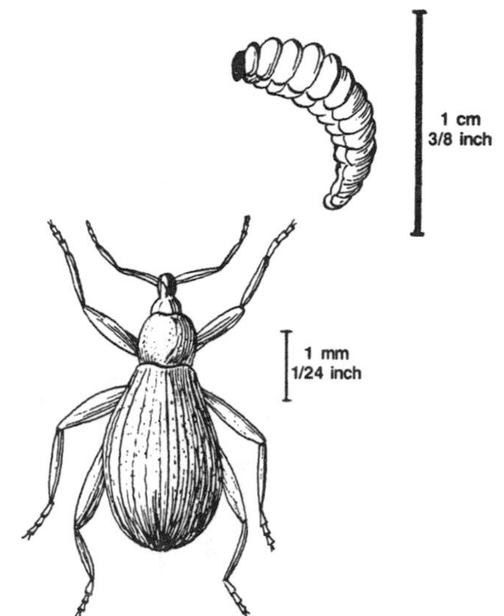

Adult root weevil and larva.

Western ash bark beetle, a recent pest of our region, is expanding its range north and east from the olive groves of California. Here the tiny pinhead size beetles invade ash trees, usually those trees that have been under drought stress for two or three seasons. Use a magnifying lens to see the dark "stick man" pattern on the back of the beetle that confirms its identity.

An attacked tree may show sap stained branches,with some branches with yellow leaves by late June or early July. A closer inspection shows pinhead size holes in the cracks and crevices, with an accumulation of boring dust beneath.

The life cycle of the western ash bark beetle varies considerably over its geographic range, but it appears that the best nonchemical control is to supply the trees with adequate soil moisture, and if an outbreak occurs in your area, consider placing Tanglefoot strip barriers near the base of the trunk. (See "Tree Tanglefoot" under the entry on fall cankerworm.) The barrier is applied in late summer, before the fall migration to their over-wintering sites.

White grubs are the larvae of the June beetle, a large, reddish brown beetle 3/4 inch long with clubshaped antennae. The beetles lay eggs in grassy areas in June and early July. These hatch into the destructive white grubs, which continue to root feed for two or three season, attaining a size of more than 2 inches. These fat, C-shaped grubs are cream in color with brown heads. They have three pairs of prominent legs on the thorax, and their fat bodies are thicker at the "tail end."

Plants are damaged by grubs feeding on the roots or main stems or by their burrowing into tubers and fleshy roots. Plants favored include deciduous trees and shrubs, potatoes, corn, and small fruits. Lawn grasses may die out in patches.

White grubs are numerous only where the soil was recently in grass, and damage ceases after the two or three seasons that it takes the grubs to mature and pupate.

Where sod land is being broken for planting, cultivate in spring to expose larvae to natural predators and parasites. In lawns where chemical control is necessary, spring treatment of the soil with an application of diazinon is a practical solution.

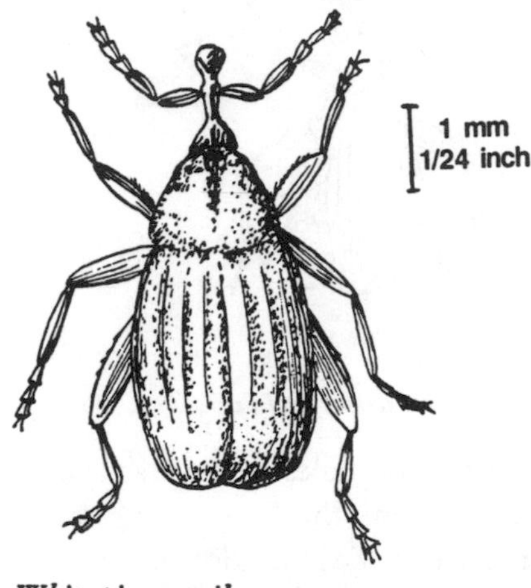

White pine weevil.

White pine weevil damage often goes unnoticed until the top growth of spruce or pine wilts and dies. Two or three seasons of growth may be lost, and a close examination reveals tunnels beneath the bark where maggots are working their way down the main stem. Punctures and oozing resin may also be evident where the adult weevils fed and inserted eggs in late May. The larvae are about 3/8 inch long when fully grown, white with a red head. After five or six weeks of feeding, they pupate and emerge in August or September as adult weevils. They overwinter in the soil.

It is the vigorous young spruce and pine trees that usually fall victim to this serious pest. With the leader shoot destroyed, a side branch takes over, but a crooked stem or bushy top is likely to be evident for several years.

As soon as you notice wilting of the leader, prune out the damaged section down to the topmost healthy side branches. Burn the infested section. This surgery must be completed by late July to prevent the emergence of a new generation of adult white pine weevils.

The strongest of the upper side branches will develop as the new top leader, and this development is encouraged by cutting the tips off any competing side branches.

If seen in May, the weevils may be sprayed with a contact insecticide such as carbaryl or methoxychlor, but chemical controls are rarely recommended.

White flies are only too common on greenhouse and house plant collections, but they often go unnoticed until one day you move a plant and a small cloud of tiny, mothlike insects swarm in the air and quickly settle again. These "flying dandruff" like to congregate on the undersides of the leaves where they lay eggs. The eggs hatch as pale, wingless nymphs, tiny sap-sucking creatures, each covered by a protective scale. At one stage they exude a sticky residue that serves as a medium for a sooty fungus growth. A new generation of white flies may appear every five days.

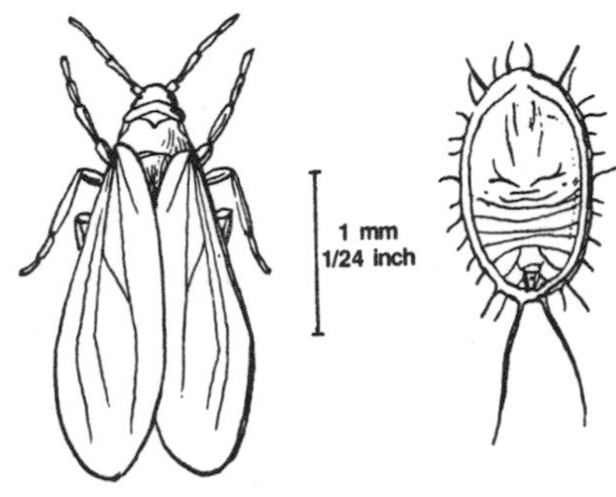

Adult white fly and larva.

As a result of repeated infestations, plants become weak, pale, and stunted.

Control is very difficult once these insects are well established, so do all you can to keep free of the menace. Isolate all new plants coming into the home or greenhouse for a week or so to ensure that they are not infested. At the first sign of trouble, wash the leaves with warm, soapy water and rub or brush off the scales. Repeat every five days for three weeks, finishing each wash with a spray of malathion. Bright yellow boards smeared with oil will attract and trap some adults.

In the greenhouse you may use the smelly systemic insecticide dimethoate. In the home I believe that it is far better to immediately discard all infested plants (unless you have a treasured family heirloom) and start afresh with clean stock in a pest-free environment.

Wireworms in the larval stage damage plants by feeding on bulbs, tubers, or roots, and sometimes burrowing up into the stem. They have straight, slender, hard bodies and are yellowish in color and very shiny, as if varnished. They are slow moving and also take their time to mature, remaining five to ten years in the soil before pupating. At maturity they reach about 1 inch in length.

The adult, a click beetle, is so named for its acrobatic method of springing away with a clicking sound. Dark in color, it reaches about 3/38 inch in length.

Plants attacked by wireworms become weak and stunted. There is little that can be done to control wireworms other than to avoid planting in land recently broken from grass cover. Diazinon is the insecticide of choice, although carbaryl can also be used. Wireworms rarely remain persistent in heavy clay soils.

A FINAL WORD

In recent years most people have come to the realization that chemicals are not going to rid the world of insect pests. Pesticides may control their numbers when used with care, but the use of stronger concentrations only hastens the time when, through unnatural selection, super-resistant insect populations evolve to replace the ones destroyed. Meanwhile, the more chemicals we use, and the stronger they are, the greater the risk to ourselves and the entire ecological system. Fortunately, we are beginning to exercise more discretion in the use of these chemicals.

Since Rachel Carson's book *Silent Spring* appeared in 1962, not only has DDT become virtually obsolete in our region, but several other long-residual chlorinated hydrocarbons (aldrin, diedlrin, endrin, and heptochlor) are considered inappropriate for home garden use. Two others, lindane and chlordane, are also being deregistered or restricted. As recently as 1977, public confidence was shaken once more when it was revealed that the results of some official pesticide safety tests were highly suspect.

In light of these circumstances and a continuing concern that the long-term side effects of many chemicals are as yet unknown, I have limited the chemicals included in this chapter to those pesticides that appear to be reliable and safe when used as directed. With the occasional exception, I have refrained from giving specific rates of application, as concentrations may vary from one brand name to the next. Far better that you read the label directions and follow them carefully.

Alternative methods of insect control are becoming more and more sophisticated. There are now several predator and parasite species commercially available that control populations of aphids, white flies, spider mites, and mealy-bugs within controlled environments such as greenhouses. A study at Simon Fraser University shows promise for using a certain nematode (microscopic worm species) that carries bacterial disease fatal to root weevils.

Another interesting approach that will bear more study is the use of pheromones. These chemicals, emitted by certain insects to attract the opposite sex of their species, have now been produced synthetically. It is therefore quite possible that pheromones will become increasingly important weapons against insects—not necessarily to lure them into death traps, but rather to permit sterilization and release of large quantities of males. This is not something that home gardeners will want to play with (the use of pheromones can attract high populations of a pest into your area from miles around), but I for one look forward to following such developments with interest.

The ultimate control against insect pests is of course to avoid growing plants that are constantly infected. This may seem defeatist, and perhaps you prefer to do battle every year, but if you waste no time in removing plants that cease to give you pleasure, you will be following the lead of some eminent gardeners of the past. Once you admit to yourself that some plants are not worth the trouble to keep them insect and disease free—and do something about it—the more you will come to enjoy a greater control over your environment. Be the master, not the slave.

SOME COMMON GARDEN PESTICIDES

Chemical	Selective?	Formulation	Action Mode	Residue	Comments
Bacillus thuringiensis THURICIDE DIPEL	yes—caterpillars	aqueous concentrate, wettable powder			biological control; nontoxic to all other life forms
boracic acid (boric acid)	yes—ants and cockroaches	aerosol and dust	contact stomach	long shelf life; once applied does not break down if kept dry and undisturbed	slow acting, derived from borax
carbaryl SEVIN	no	dust, emulsifiable concentrate, granules, wettable powder	contact and stomach	1 to 3 weeks	toxic to bees and fish
diazinon DIAZINON	no	aerosol, dust, emulsifiable concentrate, granules, wettable powder	contact and stomach	2 to 3 weeks	may be absorbed through the skin; toxic to bees, birds, and fish
dicofol KELTHANE	yes—mites	dust, emulsifiable concentrate, wettable powder	contact	long residual action	toxic to fish

dimethoate CYGON 2E LAGON	no	emulsifiable con-centrate, granules, wettable powder	contact (used as a systemic	short residual action	easily absorbed through the skin; toxic to many plants, as well as to bees, birds and fish
dormant oil GREEN CROSS DORMANT OIL	yes—aphids, mealy-bugs scale, mite white fly larvae	miscible oil (to be mixed with water)	contact	moderate to long residual action	application temper-ature limitations; discolors some plants and toxic to many others
malathion MALATHION CYTHION	no	aerosol, bait, dust emulsifiable con-centrate, granules wettable powder	contact	1 to 2 weeks in soil	application tempera-ature limitations; low mammlian toxicity; very toxic to bees
methaldehyde METALDEHYDE	yes—slugs	bait, dust, pellets	stomach	nonresidual; shelf life of only a few months	safe in vege-table garden
methiocarb MESUROL TRUMP	yes—slugs	bait, dust, pellets wettable powder	contact and stomach	long residual action	not for use near vegetables; toxic to bees, birds, and fish
methoxychlor METHOXYCHLOR	no	aerosol, dust, emulsifiable con-centrate, wettable powder	contact and stomach	long residual action, up to 1 year	toxic to bees and fish, poor control of aphid and mite populations

Chemical	Selective?	Formulation	Action Mode	Residue	Comments
pyrethrin PYRETHRIN	no	dust, wettable powder	contact	nonresidual; breaks down on exposure to light, air, or moisture	a botanical product· little hazard to mammals and bees; toxic to fish
resmethrin RESMETHRIN	no	wettable powder	contact	short residual action, unstable in sunlight	toxic to bees and fish
rotenoe DERRIS	yes—aphids beetles, caterpillars, leaf hoppes, sawflies, thrips, weevils, white flies	dust, wettable powder	contact	short residual action, breaks down in air and sunlight	a botanical product; little hazard to mammals and bees very toxic to fish
trichlorfon DYLOX	yes—bugs, caterpillars, leaf hoppers, sawflies	dust, emulsifiable concentrate, granules, wettable powder	contact and stomach (used as a systemic	moderate residual action	not very effective against aphids or mites

Examples of trade names are in CAPITALS.

CHAPTER XVII

Plant Diseases

This chapter describes control measures for dealing with the majority of plant diseases found in the home garden. I have not attempted a discussion of all plant diseases (it would take up an entire book), but those included here are typical enough to help you with anything you are likely to encounter. A garden with a variety of different plants will never experience a devastating plague, and by following a few sound cultural practices, the occasional disease that does appear should not be a great calamity.

WHAT IS A PLANT DISEASE?

The term "plant disease" can apply to almost any plant health problem that is not obviously the feeding damage of insects and other pests. If you have a sick plant on your hands, first make sure that it isn't troubled by temporarily absent or almost invisible insects. Root-eating maggots, for example, might be the cause of stunting or collapse, and minute spider mites cause mottling of foliage.

If not the work of a pest, then what about growing conditions? Some of the more common causes of mystery diseases are winter injury of woody ornamentals, desiccation of conifers, nutrient deficiency, air pollution, soil salinity, and too much or too little water. Potted plants are particularly vulnerable to waterlogged or dried out soil—either of which can cause yellowing of the foliage.

House plants also suffer from dry air, drafts, poor light, too much heat, too much fertilizer, fluoridated water, heating gas leaks, and proximity to heat vents or cold windows. Sometimes the cause of plant distress will remain a mystery. (Did a party guest surreptitiously dump Christmas cheer into the nearest plant pot?)

Outdoor plants also have their share of troubles, and some of these may be termed "inflicted blight." The weapons used are sometimes crude, but more often quite subtle. Here are some common examples.

Lawn mowers and string trimmers—Though these tools are unquestionably useful, an overzealous operator may cause damage to the base of trees, which can reduce the flow of sap.

Stake ties and clothes-lines—Use stakes and ties only if absolutely necessary; constriction of woody plant stems by wires causes girdling. In windy regions, lean trees slightly into the prevailing wind. (Some natural swaying in the wind tends to promote better root systems.) To avoid girdling damage, clothes-lines and swings should never be tied around trees. Also, the use of metal spikes, nails, or bolts in trees should be avoided as the wounds afford free entry for various plant disease organisms.

Spades and rototillers—When a lawn is edged back into a circle around the trunk, or soil in the root zone is dug or rototilled, spades and rototillers may cut the feeder roots of young trees.

Plastic film—If plastic is used as a weed control mulch just beneath the soil surface, roots become starved for oxygen. They come close to the surface, resulting in a poor root system. There is now a fine-mesh poly "landscape cloth" for weed control; while this does allow water and air transfer, I find it is no barrier against determined perennial weeds. The material breaks down with age, and needs to be replaced every few seasons.

Salt—Winter application of salt to driveways and paths ends up in the soil, with detrimental results to the plants.

Fertilizers—Too much fertilizer may inhibit seed germination and root growth in the spring and induce soft, unhardened wood at the approach of winter.

Herbicides—Chemical drift can cause untold damage to cultivated plants for some distance from the point of application. Even more severe problems arise from the utilization of soil sterilants, which are not recommended for home garden use.

These hazards aside, there are minute organisms that are parasitic upon plants. Because there are literally thousands of such organisms with the potential for injuring plants and because symptoms may be similar to other forms of plant trees, precise diagnosis is not easy without special training and equipment. Fortunately for the home gardener, a very precise diagnosis is often not necessary, and there are a few basic steps that we can take to control any disease problem that we are likely to encounter.

DISEASE CONTROL

Most of these measures come under the heading of "prevention being the best cure," and many plant diseases can be avoided by observing good cultural practices.

The control of sap-sucking insects such as aphids, leaf hoppers, and plan bugs is part of the disease-control program, as these uninvited guests transmit infection from plant to plant. Many precautions taken to reduce the risk of disease are much the same as those taken to reduce insect pest infestations: rotate crops of vegetables and annual flowers (a four-year rotation is best); clear away garden litter in the fall; pull out diseased plants or prune away obviously infected plant parts before infection can spread.

Also maintain adequate light and air circulation above ground, as well as good drainage at the roots. It's a good policy to refrain from planting in cold, wet soil and to resist the temptation to overfertilize. Be aware that disease may be spread by splashing foliage when watering, or walking through infected crops after rain.

If a chemical control is needed, apply it before the damage becomes extensive. This sometimes means anticipating a problem that has occurred before; a soil treatment in seedling flats, for example, will prevent repeated outbreaks of damping off disease.

If you find that certain of your vegetable crops are frequently spoiled by disease, look for seed that has been certified disease free. You might also turn to the cultivars that have been bred and selected for their resistance to certain plant diseases.

Dig root crops when the soil is cool and relatively dry, and try not to bruise vegetables and fruit that are to be stored. Allow these to dry in a cool, dark place with some air circulation. The most important step in avoiding storage diseases is to provide the appropriate levels of humidity, temperature, and good air circulation, as described in chapter thirteen on vegetables. Storage rooms should be cleaned and disinfected each time before use.

The first step in disease control in woody plants is eradication—the removal of dying trees and known sources of infection on your property. Encourage your neighbors to do the same. During the dormant season, remove and burn and dispose of all cankered branches, cutting back into healthy wood about 12 inches. During the growing season, prune off and destroy any infected shoots, cutting 2 or 3 inches below the infection. Disinfect tools between cuts using household bleach (2 tablespoons to a quart of water). Rake up and dispose of fallen leaves from diseased trees and shrubs.

DIAGNOSING DISEASES

To play the role of a plant doctor with a reasonable chance of success, you will have to make your diagnosis based on all the evidence. Examine all parts of the troubled plant, including roots. As you study the injury, eliminate the possibilities that the sickness could be caused by something other than disease. If you still suspect a plant disease, consider the kind of plant and what diseases it is most subject to.

Examine the affected tissue closely. Are leaf spots circular or angular? What color are they and the surrounding rim? Are they dry or water soaked, with a velvety growth or with minute black spots? Does the center of the spot fall out leaving a shot-hole condition?

Are there growths on the stems, leaves, or roots? If there is leaf drop, what color are the leaves as they shed? In examining stem cankers, check the extent of the affected area. Is the dead tissue confined to the surface, or does it progress into the stem? Is the surface smooth, rough, or scaly? Are there small blisters or dots present?

When examining fruit rots, notice if the rot occurs on immature fruit or only on ripe and ripening fruit. Determine the size and the location of spots on the fruit. Is the rot sunken, dry, watery, spongy, or pithy?

Three kinds of minute organisms—fungi, bacteria, and viruses—are the cause of what we usually refer to as "plant disease."

Fungi—Most plant diseases are caused by fungi. Reproducing by minute spores, they are responsible for molds and mildews, cankers, smuts, and rusts, as well as some wilts and leaf spots.

Bacteria—Much smaller than fungi, bacteria are barely visible with an ordinary microscope. They enter plants through injured tissue or natural openings and cause a variety of plant ills. Most common are vascular wilts, blights, soft rots, scabs, and galls. Bacteria can remain dormant in the soil for years, becoming active only when a suitable host plant is present and environmental conditions are favorable.

Viruses—Viruses are so small that they live within plant cells, often penetrating cell after cell to invade the entire plant. Viruses produce symptoms known as mosaic, leaf spot, stunt, and ring spot. They are usually transmitted from plant to plant by sapsucking insects like aphids and leaf hoppers.

A similar group of organisms, once grouped with the viruses, is known as MLO (mycoplasma-like organism) and causes the disease called "yellows" that affect asters, carrots, and lettuce.

Diseases caused by fungi and bacteria can often be controlled by the application of a chemical, while most virus attacks can be controlled only by removing the infected plants as soon as the problem becomes evident.

Here are a few symptoms to watch for and the names of some diseases. Be aware that different organisms can produce similar symptoms, and that one organism often produces different symptoms on different plant species.

Growth on leaves

- White or grey growth indicates a mildew or botrytis.
- Black mold indicates the presence of honeydew from aphids on which a sooty mold is growing.

Leaf spots

- Sunken spots with dark rims and dry centers usually indicate anthracnose.
- Spots with yellow margins and centers not sunken and dry are simply known as leaf spot and may be caused by either bacteria or fungi.

Rot

- Soft rot of the plant stem may indicate a crown or stem rot.
- Soft rot of the root is known as root rot.
- Collapse of a seedling at the soil line is known as damping off.

If disease becomes more than just a passing phase and the general sanitary gardening measures already mentioned fail to keep it under control, you may need to consult your local extension agent to obtain the address of a plant pathology laboratory where samples may be sent for diagnosis. When sending samples to a lab for disease diagnosis, try to send portions of all parts of the plant, including typical damage. A diagnosis can rarely be made on the basis of a leaf or flower alone. The specimen should be neither dry nor very wet during transit. Lift the root system to keep it intact. Try to send several plants to show the various stages of trouble. Enclose the moist roots in a plastic bag with the top exposed. (The tops will rot if enclosed in plastic.) The bagged plant can then be placed in a box or mailing tube.

Spots can appear on a variety of plants and can be caused by either bacteria or fungi: fungal leaf spot on iris (left); bacterial leaf spot on begonia (right).

SELECTED DISEASE PROBLEMS IN GARDEN PLANTS

The major plant disorders are described briefly in the following pages, followed by a table that lists diseases of specific plants that may be controlled by a fungicide. You will notice that there is no "medicine" to cure many of the problems, only preventive action and prompt eradication.

Before purchasing or using a fungicide, read the manufacturer's directions for specific information on diseases controlled and on the rates of application. (By the way, never use a sprayer that has previously been used to apply herbicides for fungicides or insecticides. The herbicide residue is very persistent and may injure your plants.)

Anthracnose is caused by several different fungi and is particularly frequent on raspberries and strawberries. The spores are spread by wind and rain. All above-ground parts can show symptoms. Small circular purple spots appear on young raspberry canes, and these often enlarge to grey patches with purple edges. Spotted leaves may develop a "shothole" appearance. Unripe fruits dry up and fail to mature, while ripe fruits turn soft and brown. Prune out infected branches about 4 inches below the diseased sections. Discard badly infected plants and provide good air circulation at the growing site. Captan is a recommended fungicide.

Bacterial blight on bean foliage can spread rapidly throughout a crop and seriously reduce yield and quality. Sometimes the first sign of infection is the presence of small, translucent, water-soaked spots on the leaves. The leaves turn yellow, and in severe infections shrivel and fall off.

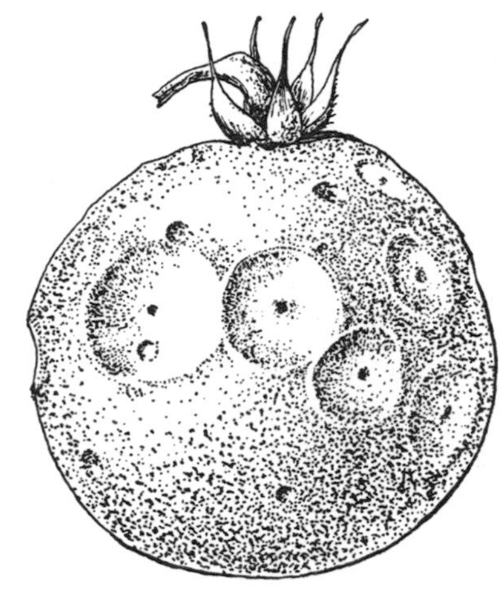

Anthracnose is the cause of the rot on this ripening tomato.

The bacteria overwinter in diseased bean plants and seeds. Infection can easily be spread by windblown rain, tools, and personal contact.

Control measures are to rotate at least three years between crops, to plant disease-free seed from a reputable supplier, and to use disease-resistant cultivars where available. Avoid overhead irrigation and walking through wet foliage. Dispose of diseased vines immediately after harvest. Apply basic copper sulfate if necessary.

Bacterial ring rot is one of several highly infectious diseases of potatoes. A first sign may be some of the leaves wilting and turning yellow soon after flowers appears. When an infected potato tuber is sliced, the vascular ring will be seen as a narrow yellow or light brown zone not far from the skin.

The bacteria overwinter in diseased potatoes and on tools and containers. Plant disease-free seed pieces, and if bacterial ring rot appears in your garden, be sure to sterilize tools and containers that might have been contaminated.

Black knot occurs on plums, cherries, and chokecherries. This fungal disease starts as soft green to light brown swellings on the current or previous year's twigs, sometimes reaching or exceeding the size of a dime. The following spring, the olive green swellings display a velvety texture and by autumn grow to encircle the twig, while turning hard and black. The knots continue to grow each season, eventually killing the branch. Prune out all knots as soon as they are noticed to avoid dispersal of spores to healthy branches by wind and rain. Disinfect pruning shears between cuts, using a solution (1 tablespoon to a pint of water) of household bleach.

Black scurf of potatoes occurs when the potato plants have been infected with rhizoctonia, a common soil-borne fungus. The fungus attacks the stems of potato plants below the ground, disrupting the flow of nutrients to the tubers. Potatoes are particularly susceptible to black scurf rhizoctonia if left in the ground for more than two weeks after the tops die.

The fungus is often harbored in old garden soil, so plant in a new area if black scurf has been a problem. Delay planting the potatoes until the soil warms up, and avoid planting them too deep. Hill them gradually as they grow. The seed pieces can be treated with captan to give them some protection against the disease.

Tell-tale signs of black spot on rose leaves.

Black spot is a disease of roses, especially prevalent on many of the more tender kinds. The disease is easily recognized by the characteristic ink spots, each surrounded by a yellow halo which expands to cover the whole leaf. The infected leaves soon fall off, and severely infected plants may lose most of their leaves. The disease overwinters in the dead leaves, so they should be raked up and disposed of by the end of the season. Fungicides will prevent the occurrence or spread of black spot but will not cure the condition once established. I find folpet a very effective preventive spray.

Blossom-end rot is an environmental rather than a parasitic disorder. Confined to the blossom end of tomatoes and garden peppers, it appears as a dry, sunken area that is dark in tomatoes and light-colored in peppers. The problem usually occurs after a period of drought or when excessive moisture is followed by dryer conditions. It is also associated with a nutrient imbalance, particularly excess nitrogen or calcium deficiency.

Avoid planting in poorly drained soils, apply mulch to conserve soil moisture, and avoid severe pruning and overcrowding. In soils deficient in lime, add calcium according to soil analysis recommendations.

Botrytis or grey mold is a serious disease striking beans, bedding plants, herbaceous perennials, and fruits. Symptoms vary, but young blossoms are very susceptible and may turn brown, dry up, and die. Fruit is very prone to infection. On annuals and perennials, young stalks suddenly wilt and collapse. A fluffy grey mold may appear on leaves and stems, surrounded by dead tissue. The disease overwinters at the base of infected stalks or in infected leaf debris.

Destroy diseased plant parts immediately, and remove herbaceous tops just below ground level in the fall if any symptoms have been evident. Avoid dense planting, overfertilizing, and overwatering. Use fungicide sprays as a preventive measure if botrytis has been a problem in previous years.

Characteristic browning and wilting of plants attacked by botrytis, on lily (left) and on peony (right).

Cankers are lesions that may appear on a wide variety of ornamental and fruit trees. The bacterial or fungal organism usually gains access through a wound and kills healthy bark. The resulting protective callus formed by the tree is also invaded, often increasing in thickness. Some of these cankers grow to a yard or more in length before the trunk is girdled and the tree dies.

Canker diseases can be minimized by avoiding wounding tree bark, by the prompt removal of infected tissue, and by pruning to remove small infected branches. (When cutting back into healthy bark, sterilize tools between cuts.)

Cankers are less likely to cause problems where trees are kept in good vigor by supplying adequate soil moisture and balanced soil nutrients. (See also frost cankers.)

Clubroot is a fungal disease of crucifers (including cabbage, cauliflower, broccoli, and rutabaga) resulting in club-shaped swellings of the roots. The plants become stunted and may fail completely. The fungus overwinters in the soil. If clubroot has been a problem in your garden, plant only resistant cultivars (as noted in seed catalogues) and avoid planting in infected soil. The application of lime to obtain an approximate pH 7 reading is helpful as the fungus requires a more acid soil.

Common scab is a bacteria-like organism commonly affecting potatoes. It is most severe in alkaline and freshly manured soils. The disease results in irregular, rough, and corky spots or patches on the tubers, but it does not affect eating quality. Warm, dry soils favor development of common scab, so try to maintain uniform soil moisture. Rotate crops to avoid planting in the same soil for four years or more. No potato cultivar is immune, but 'Russet Burbank' (also referred to as "Netted Gem") and 'Norgold Russet' show some resistance (See also scab.)

Damping off disease (seedling blight) is a common condition caused by any of a number of fungi. The disease destroys seedlings either before or soon after they emerge from the soil. Soft stems of the young seedlings may become brown or black at the soil line, the tissue shrinks (wirestem condition), and the plant frequently topples over at the soil line. There is no cure once seedlings are attacked.

To discourage damping off, use a well-drained seed bed, treat seed with a suitable fungicide like captan or thiram, avoid thick sowing of seed, and keep the fertilizer level low. A soil drench of oxine benzoate prior to seeding is a wise precaution. The best preventative is to use one of the "soilless" planting mediums developed by researchers to eliminate damping off.

Die back of twigs first noticed as trees and shrubs leaf out in spring is usually a case of winter-kill caused by extreme weather conditions. Damage may occur in the fall when active growth is subjected to sudden freezing. Hybrid tea roses are always damaged this way when the new stems fail to mature by the end of the season, and some poplars, willows, and elms are also commonly affected.

Little can be done to protect trees that are not well adapted to our short season, but the objective is to slow down growth in late summer. This hardening off process is encouraged by avoiding such stimulation as late summer and fall fertilizing and pruning.

Once the new shoots appear in spring, the dead twigs should be pruned back to vigorous new sprouts growing away from the center of the plant.

Dutch elm disease (often abbreviated DED) is an internationally notorious killer of elm trees. The disease is a fungus that blocks the sap flow, killing elms of all ages in one or two seasons. The fungus is introduced to healthy trees by elm bark beetles. The presence of these insects may be deduced from fine sawdust in the bark tissue at the lower part of the trunk. The appearance of elm bark beetles does not confirm the disease but does pose a real threat.

Early signs of Dutch elm disease appear in June or July with the leaves of one or two branches drooping and yellow, after which the branch dries up and the dead leaves hang on. As soon as you notice these symptoms, you should notify your local Department of Agriculture. Preventive inoculation is expensive and unreliable. Early detection and the prompt elimination of infected trees are the only sure controls. Never transport elm firewood from one area to another, as it may contain the fungus or the insect.

Fairy ring is a scourge of established lawns. Rings of dark green grass spread in a circumference that expands each year, leaving a ring of dead grass. Grass in the center recovers, but the exploding circle caused by the fungal disease disfigures large areas of lawn. The rings die out when they reach cultivated soil, paths, or walls and when they run into other fairy rings.

Deep aeration and heavy watering of the compacted soil rings was once a standard recommendation, but while this and regular fertilizing did help the grass to compete and recover, it rarely stopped the advance of the fungus. On the contrary, aeration by motorized equipment fails to attain an adequate depth to improve the situation, and the rented equipment is a common source of new infection.

Fairy rings may sometimes die out for no apparent reason, but aerating, watering, and the use of fungicides have all failed to give consistent control. There is word of a systemic fungicide that has been tried successfully in Europe against fairy rings, but nothing like this is available currently in North America.

The most practical approach is to dig out the damaged turf at the first sign, before it spreads, and to reseed or sod. Dig the entire ring to remove the compact soil, including 8 inches outside the green ring. The dry, infected soil may be safely added to cultivated flower and vegetable borders in exchange for well-cultivated soil, but take care not to spread the problem by spilling infected soil onto other parts of the lawn.

Because of the natural antagonism of one fairy ring to another, one satisfactory method is to excavate three or more different rings, mix the soil well with a rototiller, replace the soil, and reseed.

Fireblight is one of the most common afflictions of apple trees, a bacterial infection that also invades mountain-ash, hawthorn, and occasionally serviceberry and cotoneaster. Single branches appear scorched as if by fire, the brown leaves hanging on the tree and the top of the branch showing a characteristic shepherd-crook curve. The other branches of the tree remain healthy, but if the diseased branches are not cut out, fireblight can work rapidly down to main branches and the trunk, often killing the tree in one or two seasons. In time, cankers appear and discharge a bacterial ooze, spread by insects or wet blustery weather, that is a source of infection for other trees.

Preventive sprays such as streptomycin sulfate at blossom time have been used on a commercial basis but are not considered a practical solution for the home gardener. Prune out all affected parts, disinfecting tools between each cut. Burn and dispose of diseased parts. Plant cultivars that are not susceptible to the disease.

Frost cankers may become evident in spring, especially on the trunks of certain poplars and willows. This damage may be seen as lifting of the bark, vertical cracks, running sap, or swellings of the trunks and branches. There is little that we can do against this winter freezing and thawing injury except to avoid the more susceptible plants. Fill cracks with a commercial tree-wound compound to prevent infection by fungi and bacteria.

Fungal leaf spots—Attacking most plants, especially deciduous trees and vegetables, fungal leaf spots are caused by any of several species of fungi.

Fungal leaf spots may take many forms. Pictured here are the dark brown to black concentric rings of early blight on tomato leaves (left) and fungal leaf spots on strawberry foliage (right).

Symptoms vary from well-defined spots to patches of grey to white fuzz. Most overwinter on dead leaves and spread during wet weather. Although unsightly, these leaf spots do little damage to trees and shrubs other than to slow growth. Some vegetables and woody plants are more susceptible than others to leaf spots, and in wet shady areas where the problem recurs it pays to seek resistant cultivars. Rake up and dispose of infected leaves by the end of each season.

Powdery mildew—Infected leaves darken and curl up to expose the undersides covered with a powdery, whitish fungal growth. Powdery mildew attacks flowering plants, trees and shrubs, fruits, vegetables, and grasses. Warm weather and low soil moisture accentuate the symptoms. Grow mildew-resistant cultivars wherever possible. Avoid planting in shady locations and provide good air circulation. Apply a protective fungicide such a folpet or captan at the first sign of infection.

Powdery mildew on the underside of rose leaves.

Redleaf of rhubarb may be due to a bacteria or a virus. The bacteria causes rotting, and although spindly side shoots may grow, these are generally short lived. The leaves of infected plants are usually dull red. The virus is less obvious, but the rhubarb becomes stunted in growth and can survive for several years before the plant dies.

There is no cure for either of the redleaf diseases, and infected plants should be rogued out before the problem spreads. Plant healthy new stock in a new location.

Rots attack most plants (especially vegetables) and are caused by the same kinds of fungi and bacteria that cause leaf spots and blights. There are several precautions that you can take to reduce the likelihood of rot infections in your garden. Avoid seeding in cold, wet, and over-fertilized soils. Avoid wetting the plants unnecessarily with overhead irrigation. Promptly remove infected plants or plant parts. When using fungicides on edible crops be sure to note from the label how many days before harvest the last spray can be made. Use resistant cultivars where possible, and use seed treated to protect against disease. (See also shoestring root rot.)

Rust—The term covers a broad range of fungal diseases that are frequently seen on asparagus, onions, and chives. Powdery masses of spores cause brown, orange, or yellow spots on leaves or stems of infected plants. Rust-resistant cultivars of some plants, such as hollyhocks, are available.

A rust disease of certain woody plants is known as the apple-cedar rust or juniper rust. This fungus needs two different kinds of plant to complete its life cycle, and both kinds must be growing within a few hundred yards of each other for the disease to persist. Spores shed from horns developed on primary hosts—juniper or white-cedar—are blown to a secondary host—apple, mountain-ash, serviceberry, hawthorn, or cotoneaster. If you ensure that plants of the primary host are not planted anywhere near plants that serve as a secondary host, this rust is not likely to pose a problem.

Yet another rust, the western gall rust, is restricted to pines. It will debilitate the trees in time, but is currently not widespread in our region. Cut off all galls as they are noticed.

Scab may appear as roughened and crustlike areas of any part of a plant, but it becomes particularly evident on fruits and vegetables. Apple and cucumber are the two crops most affected. Scab may be caused by any of a number of fungi (and occasionally by bacteria). Remove and dispose of all infected plant parts, such as stems, branches, and rotten fruit. Where scab has recurred, plant or sow only resistant cultivars and treated vegetable seed. Early-season applications of captan or other fungicides will help prevent repeat outbreaks of the disease. (See also common scab.)

Shoestring root rot is a fungal disease that attacks the roots of many ornamental trees and shrubs. Mats of fungus develop between the bark and the wood. Symptoms range from a gradual dieback, to the sudden death of the plant. Honey-colored mushrooms around the base of the tree or shrub persist for months, and later remain shrivelled and black, as evidence of this serious condition. The fungal spores survive in the soil for many years, resuming growth each year to infect healthy roots. If discovered early enough, infected roots should be cut out. Provide good growing conditions, without excess nitrogen, which may result in soft, susceptible growth. Before replanting an infected area, consult your local horticultural extension agent concerning nonsusceptible plants and possible soil treatment. One recommendation is to use carbon disulphide as a soil disinfectant, to then leave the soil fallow for sixty days, and to dig thoroughly before replanting.

Silver-leaf is often overlooked until the damage has progressed too far for the tree or shrub to be saved. The disease affects plums and related plants, causing the leaves to develop a silvery green tint. Shoots die back from the tip and the infected parts, causing the leaves to develop a silvery green tint. Shoots die back from the tip, and the infected parts must be cut out to prevent the spread down into healthy wood. A fungus on dead branches is the source of new infection. This spreads by wind-borne spore to healthy trees, entering through wounds. As with fireblight, prune out all affected parts.

Snow mold shows up in the spring as grayish cobwebs on the lawn where the last of the winter's snow has been lying. If the mold penetrates to the grass roots, it will kill them and leave unsightly patches on the lawn.

Chemical control of snow mold is not recommended for home lawns. Grow resistant cultivars of Kentucky bluegrass such as 'Dormie,' 'Nugget,' and 'Sydsport.' If your lawn does show signs of snow mold, cut it fairly short and then sweep it with a stiff broom to speed up the drying process.

Sunscald is a condition caused by sunlight on tender bark. Usually it is the exposed lower trunk on the south and west sides that dries out from direct exposure to the sun or from the reflection of sun on snow. The bark lifts, and certain fungi gain access and decay the sap wood.

Apple trees, mountain-ash, mayday, and some poplars are quite susceptible to sunscald, and the condition is often mistaken for fireblight disease.

A white latex paint is often applied in orchards to protect the bark from this damage; burlap or sisal kraft paper are also used. A more acceptable procedure in the home garden is to provide shade by retaining some lower branches instead of pruning to a clear trunk.

Damaged bark should be cut back to a healthy tissue so the healing process can start. Once the bark lifts all around the trunk, the tree is girdled and will be dead above the damaged area. If the top is removed to leave a short stump, the tree will often sprout again from the base to form a clump specimen.

Wilt is a descriptive term for several bacterial, fungal, or viral diseases that can affect garden vegetables and other plants. In each case the sap flow is interrupted, and the leaves droop and die despite adequate soil moisture.

Tomato plants are often attacked by a verticillium wilt (lower leaves wilt first) or fusarium wilt (plants are affected more uniformly). Both diseases are soil borne and enter by the roots. Eradicate diseased plants promptly.

Where wilt has been a problem in the past, use sterilized soil for growing seedlings and disinfect all flats and pots. Use resistant cultivars where available.

MAJOR PLANT DISEASES CONTROLLED BY FUNGICIDES*

Plant	Disease	Chemical Control (Examples)
Apple	powdery mildew scab	benomyl, dinocap benomyl, captan, dichlone,
Asparagus	rust	zineb
Bean	Anthracnose bacterial blight botrytis (grey mold) rust stem rot	captan, maneb basic copper sulfate benomyl sulfur benomyl, chlorothalonil
Cabbage (and other related plants)	downy mildew botrytis (grey mold)	chlorothalonil, zineb chlorothalonil, zineb
Carrot	leaf blight	maneb, zineb
Celery	leaf blight early and late blights	anilazine, chlorothalonil anilazine, chlorothalonil
Clematis	leaf spot stem blight	captan, zineb captan, zineb
Cucumber	anthracnose damping off leaf spot scab	captan, maneb captan, thiram (seed treatment) benomyl, maneb, mancozeb, zineb benomyl, captan, chlorothalonil
Gladiolus (corms)	yellows and corm rot	benomyl (post harvest)
Hollyhock	rust	sulphur, zineb
Narcissus (bulbs)	basal rot	benomyl (post harvest)

Plant	Disease	Chemical Control (Examples)
Onion	smut	thiram
Pea	downy mildew seed rot	sulphur captan, thiram (seed treatment)
Pear	scab	captan, benomyl, dichlone
Peony	botrytis (grey mold)	benomyl, sulphur and zineb (preflower)
Pepper	verticillium wilt	thiram (seed treatment)
Plum	black knot	captan, sulphur
Potato	black scurf (rhizoctonia) early and late blights scab	captan (seed pieces) captan, basic copper sulfate, anjilazine, ferbam, maneb, mancozeb, chlorothalonil, zineb captan (seed pieces)
Raspberry	botrytis (grey mold) fruit rot powdery mildew	benomyl, captan benomyl, captan lime sulphur (dormant period) benomyl, dinocap (blossom on)
Rose	black spot powdery mildew rust	captan, ferbam, folpet, zineb also lime sulphur (dormant period) benomyl, folpet, sulphur ferbam, sulphur, zineb
Spinach	downy mildew	basic copper sulfate
Strawberry	fruit rot powdery mildew	benomyl, captan benomyl, captan, sulphur
Tomato	anthracnose early and late blights	captan, mancozeb, chlorothalonil, zineb mancozeb, chlorothalonil
Tulip	botrytis (grey mold)	benomyl, captan, ferbam
Tulip (bulbs)	basal rot	benomyl (post harvest)

*Note: Where a fungicide will be of little or no help, the disease is not listed and the problem must be treated by sanitation and eradication alone.

CHAPTER XVIII

Tools

There are no special tools for our gardening region, but a few suggestions may help the beginning gardener choose the more essential ones. Add garden gadgets and accessories later if you feel that you need them.

When selecting tools, look for the best quality that your budget allows. The investment will more than pay off in length of trouble-free service. Not only are cheap tools short lived, but also they are more difficult to use.

SPADES AND FORKS

Calling a spade a spade means knowing the difference between that excellent digging tool and a shovel used for moving soil and other material around. The long-handled, round-mouthed shovel is not for digging, although often people, including professionals, use them for that purpose. I prefer to see shovels adorning the tool shed wall, permanently.

All you need for digging and transplanting is a short-handled, square-mouthed spade. It should be kept keenly sharp with a file, and it follows that you should wear good solid footwear when using it and remember to keep your toes out of its way. The advantage of a sharp blade is that your digging chores will be lightened to an amazing degree. A square-mouthed spade is also ideal for transplanting because it will slice through roots; a round-mouthed shovel tends to slide around them. The spade also, with your help, does a neater job of digging, leaving each row straight and the sides of each chunk square.

The best quality spades have a solid shank—the wood of the handle even with the metal shaft of the blade—while cheaper spades have a wooden handle that is narrower than the metal shaft. This latter type soon works loose so the handle moves irritatingly in the shaft. Also, a blade made of good quality steel is often almost flat, while those made of cheaper metal are angled to afford more rigidity.

Digging forks are used mainly for loosening soil (and incorporating soil additives) with minimal root disturbance around established plants. If your soil is heavy, you probably don't need one. The only garden fork that I use often is a narrow-tined manure fork. It comes in handy for picking up piles of plant material and is almost essential for turning a compost heap.

HOES AND HOEING

A hoe of some kind is essential for cultivation and keeping the weeds down. Most gardeners tend to develop a liking for one type and use it in nearly all situations. There's nothing wrong with that

My own favorite is the common chop hoe. You will find slight variations of the chop hoe described variously as a swan-neck, draw, garden, farmers', nurseryman's, ladies', planter, weeding, beet, onion, or turnip hoe. There are other names, but I'll refer to it here as a chop hoe, a name descriptive enough to distinguish it from the other basic hoe design—the push hoe. (The latter is also called a Dutch, D, or scuffle hoe.)

Most people, I believe, find it easier to control the force and direction of a chop rather than a push hoe. The chop hoe is useful for making shallow furrows prior to seeding, for digging small planting holes, and for hilling potatoes. You can also sharpen the sides of a narrow-blade chop hoe to create a more versatile weapon against weeds, but be careful to avoid innocent bystanding plants until you gain some proficiency with the tool. Contrary to some well-publicized advice, it is easier (and therefore preferable) to walk forward over the soil just cultivated with the chop hoe. You can always rake off the weeds later to prevent them rerooting and to leave a nice finished appearance.

The stirrup or band hoe is a light form of chop hoe. Some like its lesser weight, but I still prefer a little more heft so gravity can help the work along. Furthermore, the stirrup lacks the handy sharp corners of the chop hoe blade.

The push hoe is best used between crop rows. Push the blade just beneath the soil surface to sever weed seedlings, and you can back down the row without treading on your work.

There are cultivators like a common chop hoe, but with tines instead of a blade. Their combing action aerates the soil, and they can be used to incorporate organic matter. Personally, I don't own one. They tend to expose moist soil, which hastens drying, and that's the last thing we need in our region of low precipitation. Unless you have an unusually wet soil, I would avoid using the hand cultivator altogether. Instead, you can achieve a shallow dust mulch to conserve soil moisture by wielding an ordinary hoe. Incorporate any organic materials later with the fall digging.

RAKES

Another indispensable tool to buy if you are getting started with a basic set of garden tools is the common steel-toothed rake. Most of the inexpensive ones are "level-headed" rakes, with the handle fitting directly onto the center

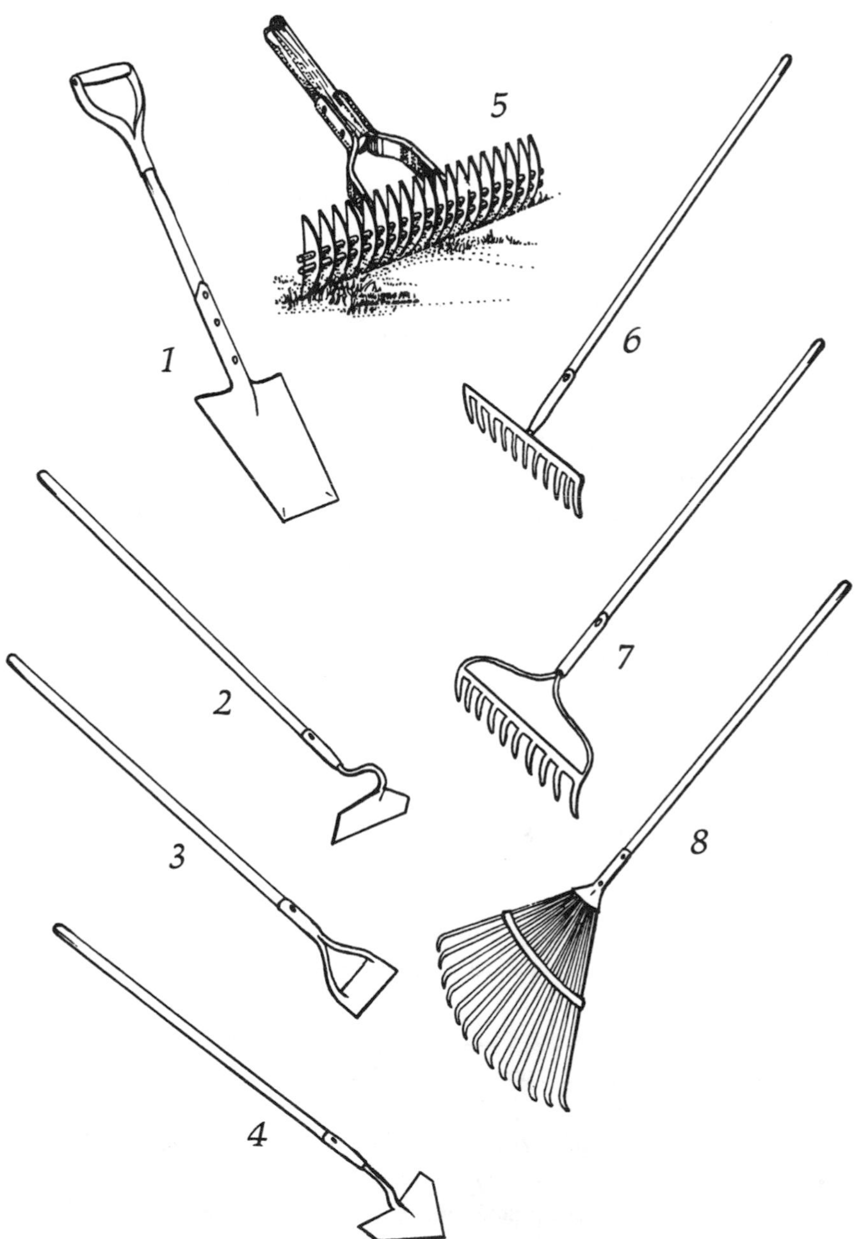

A selection of spades, hoes and rakes: 1. square-mouthed spade; 2. chop hoe (draw hoe); 3. push hoe (Dutch hoe); 4. push hoe; 5. thatching rake; 6. level-headed rake; 7. bow rake; 8. sweep rake.

of the rake head. The "bow rake," with the handle connected to each end of the head by a metal bow, is a preferred design that improves both balance and durability. The garden rake is ideal for putting the finishing touches to soil levelling and for pulverizing the surface to create a good seed bed.

Work backward when raking so you don't have to walk over raked soil. Pull the rake towards you, lift and place it ahead, and pull again. Never try to level soil with a push-pull action through the soil.

You may also want to add a fan-shaped sweep rake and a thatching rake to your collection. The fan-shaped sweep rake is the equivalent to a broom in the garden and can be put to use on lawns, paths, and shrub borders to leave a neat and finished appearance. They used to be made almost exclusively of bamboo, but the springy steel tines available today are very light-weight and last a lot longer if you get a good one. Avoid the adjustable ones; both the wide and the narrow spread positions are unsatisfactory. The thatching rake is designed for use in dragging dead grass thatch from the lawn. It is one rake that is pushed back and forth without lifting so the strong, curved tines self-clean.

These lawn rakes don't see as much action as they used to since the rotary mower with vacuum action became popular. This type of mower sucks leaves and grass into the bag unit just as fast as you can move it around. Those with a "roto-rake-bar" type of grass-scratcher attachment, which can be used temporarily in place of the regular rotary blade, do the work of loosening dead grass at the base of the old lawn with only a fraction of the effort needed for hand raking. More about power equipment later.

CUTTING TOOLS

Quality is especially important when selecting cutting tools. Inferior saws, pruners, and shears make hard work of simple jobs, and they often fail to last more than one season.

For general garden work I suggest a pruning saw with a 5 1/2-point blade, curved and designed to cut on the pull stroke. A good steel saw will hold its cutting edge well and reduce arm fatigue to a minimum.

A precision pair of scissor-action pruners, such as the Felco No. 2, is a good investment; thev last for many years with minimal attention. The main thing to remember when using hand prunes is not to push them beyond their capabilities. If a stem is too thick or hard to cut with a firm hand pressure, resist the temptation to use two hands or a wrist-twisting action. Anvil-type pruners will stand more abuse of this kind than the scissor type, but most experienced gardeners prefer the scissor type for their superior cut.

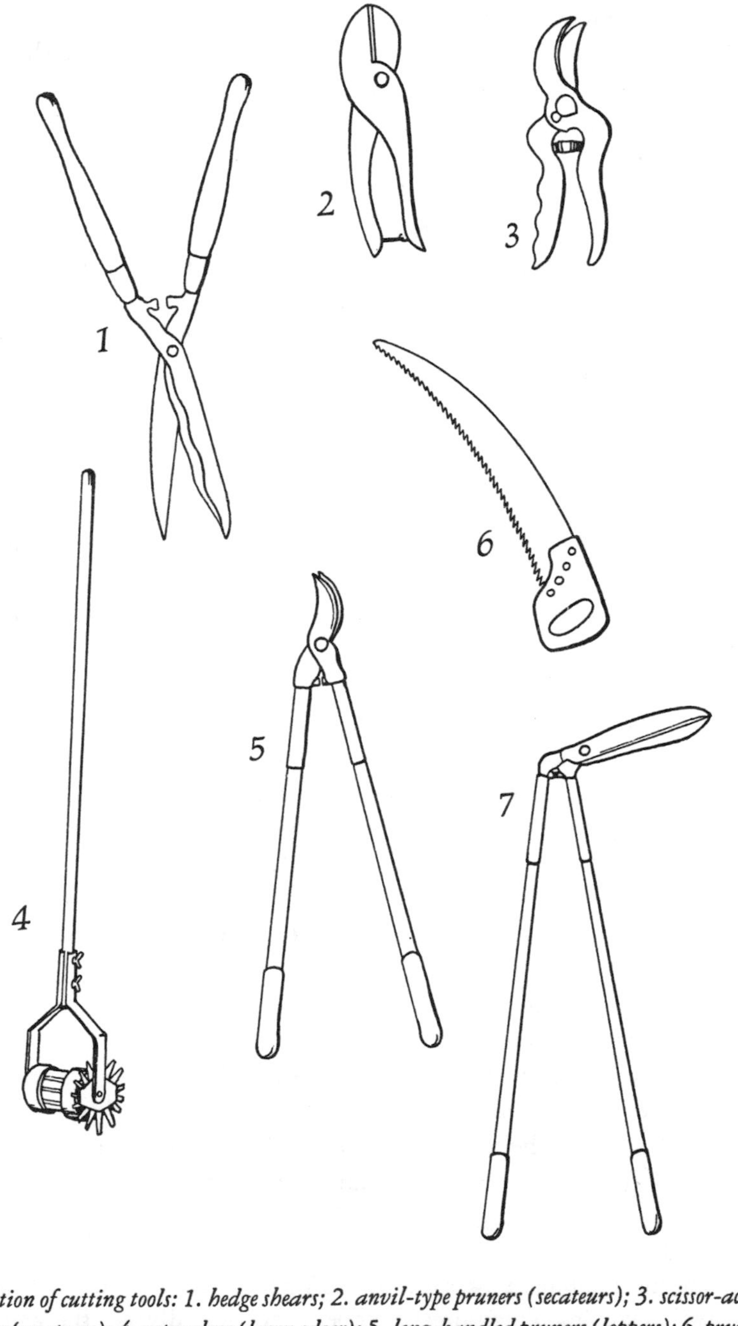

A selection of cutting tools: 1. hedge shears; 2. anvil-type pruners (secateurs); 3. scissor-action pruners (secateurs); 4. roto-edger (lawn edger); 5. long-handled pruners (loppers); 6. pruning saw; 7. long-handled grass shears.

For any branches that are too large for hand pruners, there is the long-handled version for strength and cutting leverage. For hard-to-reach branches of trees, there are pole pruners with sectional poles that can be extended. The cutter is operated by pulling a long cord. These are useful for medium-sized trees, and they are especially versatile when also equipped with a saw.

While pole pruners are handy to have, most home gardeners prefer to start with just the hand pruners and a good pruning saw, renting a pole pruner for an hour or so once a year if necessary. In fact, for very large trees your best tool is a professional tree surgeon with his own special equipment. Cutting down trees and removing large branches can be dangerous. Their great weight can cause them to fall in an unexpected direction, resulting in personal injury or damage to property.

For hedge trimming or cutting the tops off herbaceous perennials, you should have a pair of hedge shears. These are simply a very large pair of scissors operated by both hands. Again I warn you of inferior goods. If cheap ones work loose, the blades can cross and deal a painful experience to thumbs as the handles come together. I therefore recommend a pair of shock absorbers—two stops at the upper part of the handle that meet when the blades are closed. And, of course, keep the adjusting nut properly tightened. The better shears often have a wavy-edge blade that helps the cutting action, and I like the design with a notch at the base of the blade to serve as a convenient pruner for the occasional heavy stem.

Hand shears can be used for lawn edging, but it is well worth getting a pair with long handles so the job can be done standing up. Long-handled grass shears come with the blades set either flat to cut the lawn surface or on edge to trim around the edge of the lawn. There are a few that have blades that can be adjusted to do either job, but these versatile tools have the disadvantage of a single-hand squeeze action that is quite tiring. The most reliable and easy to use of the long-handled edging shears are those with a normal two-handled scissor action.

Better yet for lawn edging is the roto-edger. For this tool you must have your lawn level with and abutting a firm, flat surface such as a concrete sidewalk. By rolling the roto-edger wheel along the path, the cutter makes fast work of trimming off all overhanging grass blades.

MOWERS

The most popular power mower design today is the rotary, with one or two blades revolving like an aircraft propeller horizontally over the lawn. The wheels are usually adjustable, so you can select the height at which the blades

swipe the tops off the grass. The rotary mower has been widely accepted today because it can perform quite well with little maintenance (even when the blades are dull) and the machine is reasonably inexpensive and easy to maintain.

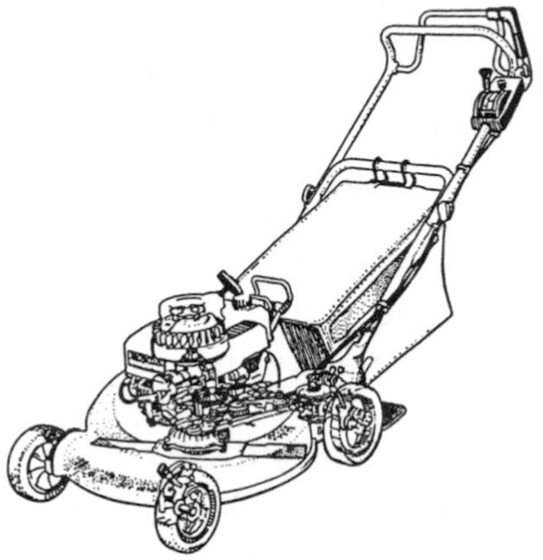

Rotary mowers are popular with home gardeners. This one is gas powered and has a rear bag attachment.

Another advantage of the rotary mower is that many are designed to work like a vacuum cleaner to suck clippings and leaves into a bag; the old side-bag units are now being challenged by rear-bag models that are easier to maneuver. The more sophisticated kinds are also self-propelled to take the push out of the work.

The only disadvantage of the ubiquitous rotary mower (gas or electric powered) is that the quality of the cut is not very good. Because the grass blades get slashed, the lawn may show a dead straw color at the ends of the blades. Keeping the blades sharp will overcome this problem to some extent.

You may come across a rotary mower designed without wheels. It works on the same principle as a hovercraft, with the blades creating enough downdraft so the mower floats just enough to clear the ground. This attribute is an advantage when working in tight corners or on steep grades where the mower may be lowered down slopes on the end of a rope. The hover mowers have no provision for bagging the grass clippings or for adjusting the cutting height.

The reel-type mower has the deserved reputation of giving an excellent scissor cut and can be purchased as a manual or as an engine-driven model. You will fully appreciate the lack of popularity of the manual model if you have ever pushed one with dull blades through tall, wet grass.

When your forward push not only propels the mower forward but also turns the blades and slices the grass, the blades must be sharp and perfectly aligned against the bed plate or the exercise is just too exhausting. And if the grass ever grows too long—as it inevitably will from time to time—then you will be faced with the forbidding prospect of cutting it down in stages.

The power-driven reel-type mowers also need a little extra attention to keep them operating properly. They generally cost more than the rotary mower because of their precision design, and they demand a higher level of maintenance to keep them running well. If you are willing to spend a little more time, cash, and effort to try for that perfect lawn, the consider the reel-type mower; but for the average yard a rotary mower is still the best choice.

For acreages and estates where the job of mowing grass with a walk-around mower simply takes too long, consider the alternative of a ride-around model. When selecting such a machine, I suggest that you stick with one designed to do no more than mow and bag grass. Resist the temptation to buy a mini-tractor that can be adapted to half a dozen different functions.

IRRIGATION SPRINKLERS

Irrigation sprinklers vary in complexity from a simple plastic tube with holes to a complex system of pop-up sprinklers with a control box for timing their operation.

Soaker hoses (the ones that dribble slowly) are best used between vegetable rows. Hose sprinklers—tubes that produce a fine fountain along their entire length—are good for newly seeded lawns. However, they are seldom used exclusively for mature lawns because the spray is so fine that a breeze tends to blow the spray pattern off to one side.

Reciprocating (putt-putt) sprinklers put down water quickly, but like the simple revolving sprinkler, their circular pattern is something of a disadvantage in most gardens. Unless the spray pattern overlaps properly (a waste of water), there will be corners and patches missed. They are, however, by far the most fun to set, as they seem to possess a foxy cunning in their determination to get you wet.

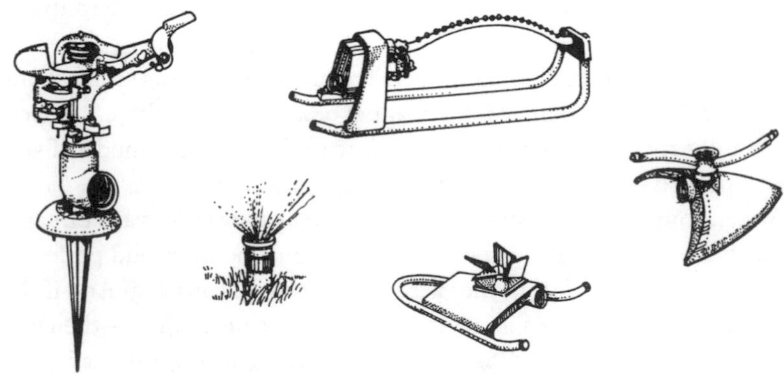

Irrigation sprinklers come in a variety of types. Clockwise from the left: reciprocating sprinkler, oscillating sprinkler, revolving sprinklers, and pop-up sprinkler.

The most popular of water sprinklers is the oscillating type that slowly sweeps from side to side automatically with the water pressure running the clockwork. They put down a square or oblong spray pattern that coincides with most lawn shapes. If you choose this kind, you might want to select an adaptable one that can be set to a full or partial movement.

With today's marvels of available technology epitomized by the automatic garage door opener, an underground sprinkler system might be just what you need to match your lifestyle. However, before joining the pop-up sprinkler set, you should contact a specialist (preferably more than one) to be found in the telephone yellow pages under a heading such as "Sprinkler systems, lawn" or "Landscaping." Because of the many variables involved, it would be wise to start by considering some of the features of your property, as well as some aspects of the proposed system:

- The slope and drainage characteristics of your property
- Wind patterns as they may relate to water placement
- Sprinkler nozzle design, size, and spacing based on the above
- System materials and specifications for efficiency and durability
- Automatic on/off timers and manual operation options of the system
- Availability of maintenance service, including the blowing out of lines at the end of the season.

The best time to install underground lawn irrigation systems is prior to seeding or sodding. Systems may also be added to established lawns by trenching or with vibrating ploughs that pull the pipe underground. You will find that some sprinkler irrigation companies do everything from planning to installation and maintenance, some will draw up plans for your particular lot, and some will provide the advice and materials for a do-it-yourself project.

Whether or not you install a pop-up sprinkler system, a length of garden hose is still useful for spot irrigation where supplemental water is needed. Rubber hose that remains pliable in cold weather is best.

MISCELLANEOUS GARDEN EQUIPMENT

It is in the line of the miscellaneous that you can clutter your tool shed to overflowing. Limit your initial purchases in this category until you know what you really use. You can always rent larger pieces of equipment such as rototillers, and who knows what exciting gadgets you may be able to borrow from neighbors.

Sprayers

Unless you intend to try a pest control system entirely without the benefit of chemicals, you should probably own a sprayer of some kind. For occasional use, a hose-end sprayer is handy and has the advantage of delivering enough pressure from your water supply to reach well up into trees that would otherwise be inaccessible without expensive, pump-driven equipment.

Compressed air sprayers with a hand pump are convenient for most situations. I prefer a 2 gallon unit made of high-density polyethylene with a "pump-through-the-cap" action. It is simple, inexpensive, durable, and not subject to the same corrosion as galvanized metal. There are mini-carts available for wheeling the heavier 5-gallon units around.

Very small versions that hold a pint or two and are operated by a finger pump are useful only in the smallest gardens or for spot treatment here and there.

At the other extreme are the power sprayers, but unless you have an orchard or a mini-arboretum, you are not likely to need these large units. They generally come with a three-horsepower gasoline engine to provide spray pressure and are incorporated into a wheel-around model with a capacity of up to 60 gallons.

Power operated or not, there are two important things to bear in mind with your spray equipment. First, wash and rinse the sprayer carefully after

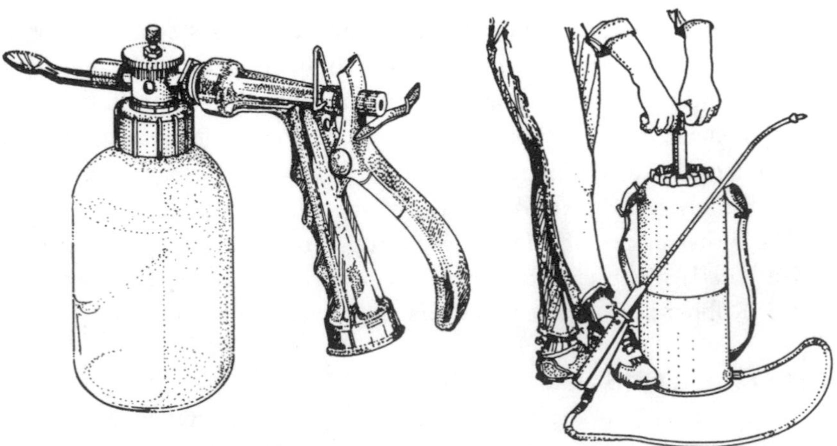

A hose-end sprayer (left) can spray a great distance and is not limited by the capacity of the carrying tank. Portable compressed air sprayers (right) lack the pressure of hose-end sprayers but can be adjusted to produce a fine spray.

each use and let it dry with the nozzle open to drain. Many chemicals are highly corrosive, and residues shorten the life of the equipment. Second, have a separate sprayer for herbicides. However carefully you may clean them after use, there is a chance of herbicide residues upsetting your plants when you next spray them for insects or mites.

Dusters

There are special mechanical applicators for insecticidal and fungicidal dusts. The best ones for the home garden have a handle that you turn to rotate an internal fan and a nozzle that can be directed at different angles. The ordinary hand-pump types are satisfactory too. If you buy only the occasional insecticidal or fungicidal dust, you could choose a product that comes in a container with perforations for direct application and save buying the duster altogether.

Rototillers

Mechanical cultivators are useful only if you have a large vegetable garden or extensive annual flower beds. Even then, considering that the job normally takes no more than an hour or two each year, renting is usually the best approach to avoid depreciation, maintenance, and storage. Some rentals come complete with the operator, or you might be able to come to some arrangement with a neighbor who already has a rototiller. My own reluctance

Note the difference in action between these two types of rototillers. The larger model (pictured at the top) is easier on the operator because of the rear position of the spinning blades; the smaller model is more maneuverable in confined spaces.

to own such a machine stems not only from a strong tendency to thrift but also from a firm suspicion that churning the land like a cake mix in a blender is, in the long run, detrimental to the soil.

If you really need to till the soil by machine, I suggest that you use a machine large enough to do the job with care. A small tiller does get the job done faster than a spade, but the back and arm muscles complain more than if the job had been done by hand in small stages.

The real "torture tillers" are generally the ones propelled forward by blades revolving in front of the engine. To gain any sort of digging depth, you pull up on the handles to get the blades to bite deeper. Far easier to use is the type with several forward gears, reverse, and the blades revolving behind the engine. These are longer machines and not for confined spaces, although they can be turned in their own length by lifting the handles high and spinning the machine around while balanced on its wheels.

Electric hedge trimmers

A rule of thumb is that if you have more than 50 feet of hedge, you probably deserve a power-operated hedge trimmer. The advantages of speed and accuracy associated with power trimmers are offset to some extent by the expense of the equipment and the time needed for repairs and maintenance. They are also designed to cut shoots no more than 1/4 inch in diameter; thicker branches need to be cut with appropriate hand pruners.

Power trimmers come with either an electric motor or a small, two-cycle engine. The engine types are heavier to wield but can be taken anywhere. The electric models are restricted by the length of power cord; the longer the cord, the less power reaches the motor. You must also develop a cutting style that keeps the cord well away from the blade. For either kind, a suitable blade length is 16 to 20 inches.

Take time after use to inhibit rust by wiping an oily rag over the blades, and check periodically for loose screws and bolts. As the blades become dull or worn, they will need replacing, as they are not designed to be sharpened.

String trimmers

Relatively safe power tools, string trimmers are gaining popularity for speeding up the job of edging grass and cutting in places where the lawn mower cannot reach. The better models have a "touch-and-go" feature, well worth the extra outlay, that delivers extra nylon line without you stopping your work.

String trimmers are especially useful along fence bottoms and around pots, but be aware that they can injure trees. Just beneath the bark is a tender

layer of cells vital to the woody plant's survival. So despite the claims of some manufacturers, remember that even established trees can be injured when lashed repeatedly around the base.

Spreaders

A spreader for granular fertilizers and grass seed is a useful addition to your collection. The drop-spreader type that runs on two wheels and trickles the application in bands is satisfactory if you can keep track of where you have, and have not, been. If you overlap or miss strips, then the evidence will appear to haunt you later. I favor a simple broadcast spreader, a cloth bag hung around the neck with the spreading action achieved by turning a handle. Just like the drop-spreaders, the aperture can be adjusted to the product being spread and to the required rate of application. Even application can be achieved with a broadcast spreader, but a disadvantage is that it doesn't recognize straight edges; there is usually a trade-off somewhere.

Wheelbarrows

Buying a wheelbarrow? Unless you are engaged in commercial work, get a small one. They are half the price of large wheelbarrows, are more easily maneuvered, and take up less room in storage, where they spend most of their time. The extra few trips with smaller loads won't even be noticed.

Even on large estates and acreages, a wheelbarrow remains a minor accessory. Any large quantities of soil or other garden material are best handled by the front-end loader of a small tractor. For once-only landscape

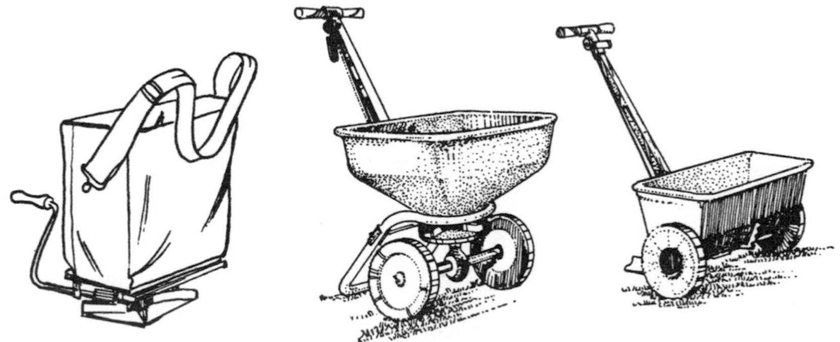

Spreaders with spinning rotors (left and center) broadcast seed and granular fertilizers; drop-spreaders (right) distribute fertilizers and seed in bands.

projects, first compare the price of landscape contractor with the cost and depreciation of expensive equipment.

ONE LAST WORD ON TOOLS

"If they're meant to cut, keep 'em sharp. If they're meant to run, keep 'em oiled." This was the advice of the ancient Cornish head gardener where I worked as a boy. While this may have been an oversimplification, his message was that a little time spent in cleaning and adjusting garden tools after use was time well spent. I am not Cornish, nor am I yet ancient, but I now tend to agree with his philosophy more than I did at the time.

CHAPTER XIX

Month by Month

Although a gardener must work with the natural cycle of the seasons, weather patterns vary from one year to the next and from place to place, so even in the same garden no two seasons are timed exactly alike. Perhaps this is why gardening remains an interesting challenge to so many people.

Despite the impossibility of putting immutable dates to specific garden activities, it may help the beginning gardener to have a list of common gardening activities arranged chronologically. For convenience, I have abided by convention and arranged the following job reminders by month, but you will notice that I have added a few subheadings referring to significant events in the gardener's year—such as the thawing of soil in spring and the first frost of autumn. A good gardener tries to keep in step with weather and soil conditions rather than to march strictly to the day of the month.

JANUARY

- Start a garden notebook for planting and seeding dates.
- Take note of local trees and shrubs attractive in the winter landscape.
- Plan on paper any garden changes you wish to implement next season.
- Mail catalog orders away.
- Inspect bulbs, corms, and tubers in storage.
- Clean house plant foliage and check for insects.

Every three or four weeks check on any plants in storage (such as glads, begonias, and dahlias). Any undetected rot can soon spread throughout the entire collection, so discard bad bulbs and corms. Cut off any new soft parts of dahlia tubers and treat the exposed surfaces with a sulphur dust or commercial preparation from a garden center. If tubers are starting to shrivel, moisten the vermiculite packing material a little.

Those of us with house plants have to be especially considerate during the winter months. Keep them away from hot furnace air and chilly windows.

Avoid feeding and overwatering as they slow down through the season of short daylight, and sponge the leaves occasionally if this is practical. Forget the cosmetics of leaf-gloss preparations. Every week or so dip ferns in a tub of water (with the chill off) to freshen them up. Maintain humidity through a furnace or portable humidifier, or set evaporating trays beneath the plants. Plant pots should have good drainage from the bottom and should never be left in saucers or cache pots with retained water.

One of the nicest things you can do for your plants is talk to them. The experiments of Cleve Backster about 1968 encouraged the belief that plants have feelings, and this was publicized in *The Secret Life of Plants* (1973) by Peter Tompkins and Christopher Bird. I doubt that our words or thoughts work any wonders, but at least a regularly talked-to plant comes under close scrutiny. Any change in the condition of the plant, such as over- or underwatering or the onset of insect or disease troubles, can be detected or corrected at once. Please do talk to your plants, even if you feel you have to first glance over your shoulder and then mutter under your breath.

FEBRUARY

- Greenhouse owners (and optimists with a cool, bright room) sow earliest seeds.
- Revive garden geraniums.
- Cut twigs of flowering shrubs for indoor forcing.
- Check plants in storage.

This is another quiet month unless you have a heated greenhouse. In that case, you will be preparing for spring with the sowing of the earliest seeds. Sow celery and annuals such as pansy, salvia, snapdragon, double-flowered petunia, lobelia, dwarf French marigold, China aster, and sweet William.

Starting your own seedlings in the greenhouse instead of waiting a couple of months and buying bedding plants can be fun and an interesting challenge. But start only if you have time to handle emergencies like damping off disease, and be prepared to acclimatize the young plants gradually to outdoor conditions in April and May.

Last year's geraniums in storage will never regain that old exuberance, so you might decide to bring them out of exile at the end of the month and introduce them to motherhood. If you have a bright room, pot the survivors in fertile soil, water well, and treat them to good light. In a few weeks there should be some good sprouts ready for rooting.

One of the more passive forms of gardening is to coax a few dormant twigs into early bloom. On a mild day select a few small branches—about 20 inches long—from your forsythia, double-flowering plum, flowering crabapple, lilac, or mayday tree. Wild pincherries, chokecherries, and serviceberries can also be cut for indoor forcing. You may notice two kinds of buds: the thinner ones produce leaves and stems; the fatter ones are flower buds. Split the stems a little and plunge them into a tub of lukewarm water for about twenty minutes to soften the buds. Then place the twigs in containers of clean water and keep them in a cool place such as a basement. Some people like to mist the buds daily to keep them soft. Change the water regularly enough to keep it fresh, at the same time slicing a little off the cut ends to induce the uptake of water.

It may take five or six weeks for the buds to start to open, ready for arrangement as room decoration. The later in the season, the easier it is to force them into flower. The exception is the forsythia, which will normally bloom in about ten days.

MARCH

- Purchase or repair garden tools and equipment.
- Prune most trees and shrubs.
- Greenhouse operators, continue indoor seeding and planting.
- Revive tuberous begonias and dahlias.
- Repot house plants as needed.
- Increase watering of house plants slightly and provide light feeding.

Warm, sunny days will tempt us outdoors to putter around the yard and poke at whatever the winter has left behind. But March in the North brings a phony spring, and we gain nothing by trying to hurry the garden season before it is ready. Better to stay off clay soils until the surface dries, or you will just compact it.

If the weather cooperates, you might be able to take care of tree and shrub pruning while branches are still dormant. Just leave the maple and birch trees as they will "bleed" from fresh cuts as the spring sap rises; summer or fall pruning is best for these.

It's a good time to check garden tools, repairing the handles of broken ones, and sharpening and overhauling the lawn mower—all the little jobs that could have been taken care of last fall but were put off because spring was a long way off. Your garden center should have its stock of tools and seeds by now and be ready for the spring rush. Human nature being what it is, the stampede won't materialize until the day the seeds should be put into the ground, so you can beat the crowd by doing your garden shopping now and taking advantage of the best selection and personal advice.

Indoors, the house plants are already feeling the surge of spring, and with the longer days, they could use a little more water and a touch of fertilizer. (Use a fertilizer that dissolves readily in water, and as a general rule use half the concentration recommended on the package.) Repot plants that have outgrown their containers, and make sure that the new pot has adequate drainage so the root zone does not become stagnant.

Owners of heated greenhouses can revive dahlia tubers early in March. If a heated greenhouse is not available, they are best left for outdoor planting in May. Tuberous begonias that have survived the long dormant season should be started into growth again at the end of the month. Plant them depression-side up in a tray of sand-peat potting medium.

If you are starting your own seedlings indoors for transplanting later into the garden, the first half of the month is about right for starting leeks, tall French marigolds, floss flowers, gloriosa daisies, portulaca, and violas. Cabbage, cauliflowers, parsley, peppers, and tomatoes should be seeded indoors in the middle of the month. The last half of the month is time to sow eggplants and the last of the annuals—godetias, single petunias, butterfly flowers, stock, and sweet alyssum. If you don't have cool, bright conditions indoors or a greenhouse, wait a couple of months and buy the young plants in packs ready for planting out.

APRIL

- Check the yard and make plans to renew, paint, or repair as necessary.
- Remove leaves from gutters.
- Complete pruning (except maple and birch left for summer or fall).
- Shear ragged hedges before growth starts.
- Continue seeding indoors.
- Pay attention to greenhouse ventilation during sunny weather.

As soil thaws and the surface dries a little

- Rake lawn free of leaves, twigs, and loose dead grass.
- Plant deciduous and coniferous trees and shrubs.
- Cut tops from herbaceous perennials before new growth appears.
- Cultivate shrub and perennial borders.
- Dig or rototill the vegetable garden.
- Fertilize the garden.
- Seed hardy vegetables outdoors.
- Harvest overwinter parsnips before new growth.
- As plants begin to grow, keep an eye out for insect pests.
- Root cutting of geraniums from mother plants indoors.

"Oh, to be in England, now that April's there." Robert Browning enjoyed the many manifestations of spring in April, but for us the month is one of preparation and anticipation.

The calendar doesn't tell us when to get out and get busy in the garden, but the state of the soil does. Once it is dry enough to walk on without causing any compaction, it's time to rake through the shrub border, stopping to dig out any perennial weeds. Try not to disturb the roots of woody plants growing close to the soil surface.

Perennial beds should be treated the same way. The tops may now be cut off the herbaceous perennials, but any winter mulch should be left in place until early next month. Otherwise, the warming of the soil may entice tender young shoots into action, only to be bitten by late spring frosts.

With the drying of the soil a little, it is time to rake the lawn free of leaves and twigs so air and sunlight can work their magic. And don't forget to check the eavestroughs for the same sort of rubbish before it gets stuck in the downpipe.

April is also a good month to take a close look at fences, gates, paths, retaining walls—and renew, paint, or repair as necessary before a jungle of new vegetation interferes.

If your hedge looks ragged, now is the time to shear it so the new spring growth will hide the cut ends. This is also the month to complete tree and shrub pruning (except birch and maple) if you didn't get it done last fall.

Most important, as soon as the soil can be worked, it is time to plant and transplant trees and shrubs of all kinds. Get the bare-root specimens planted before they break bud; the ones growing in containers can be planted anytime in the growing season, but they will appreciate getting into the ground before hot weather. Conifers should be planted now to give them plenty of time to develop their root systems before the onslaught of winter.

Broccoli seedlings can be started indoors in the middle of the month. Hardy vegetables and annual flowers should be sown outdoors as soon as the soil can be worked. (Don't forget to keep a note of seeding and planing dates and the complete plant names for future reference.) Seeding into a glass- or plastic-covered cold frame will get the plants off to a fast start by warming the soil.

Start looking for insect pests as soon as new growth appears, and if overwintering scale insects have been a problem on trees, use a dormant oil spray just before bud break.

Now is the time to start rooting your geranium cuttings. I push three or four cuttings (3 or 4 to a pot) around the edge of a plant pot in moist perlite. Dipping the bottom of each cutting in a rooting hormone powder may stimulate faster rooting but is not essential. In a greenhouse or near a bright window, they should have some root growth in two or three weeks. They are then repotted into small, individual pots (using a regular house plant potting soil) to grow more roots before being planted outdoors towards the end of May.

MAY

- Continue indoor planting.
- Complete the clean-up of lawns, fertilize, and start mowing.
- Complete the planting of bare-root trees and shrubs before bud break.
- Container-grown plants in leaf may be planted with little root disturbance.
- Gradually remove any winter mulch and protective mounds and screens.
- Plant glads and dahlias.
- Seed second batch of vegetables outdoors.
- Seed annuals outdoors.
- Lift and divide herbaceous perennials.
- Harden off indoor-started plants before planting out.
- Shade greenhouses as necessary.

As risk of frost diminishes

- Plant out young hardy vegetable seedlings and annual bedding plants.
- Thin vegetable seedlings before crowding occurs.
- As buds break, apply dimethoate soil drench against birch leaf miners if they have been a problem in the past.

- Start watering lawns and garden if necessary.
- Continue to control insect pests from now until first fall frost.
- Use herbicide to control broadleaf weeds in lawns.
- Clip hedges after first rapid spring growth.
- Prune elongated candles of compact conifers.
- Watch for perennial weeds and dig out the roots before they spread.
- Harvest rhubarb and asparagus from well-established plants.
- Check trees and shrubs for sucker sprouts.

Early in May start seedlings of tender vegetables such as cucumber and pumpkin indoors. This month is famous for the big annual rush to buy vegetable seedlings and bedding plants. Optimists plant them out early in the month and wager that there won't be a late frost, while pessimists hedge their bets until early June. Wise nurserymen have plants ready for both optimists and pessimists. Whichever approach you choose, it's a good plan to harden off your newly acquired seedlings for several days before planting them out. This involves gradually getting the plants accustomed to outdoor conditions. Cover them or bring them inside at night if temperatures are likely to drop near freezing.

Perennials that are spreading out of bounds or drying out in the center may now be lifted, divided, and replanted—discarding the old inner parts of the clump. Plant new perennials.

Remove the mulch from overwintered perennials, and gradually reduce the winter mounds from tender roses. Newly planted roses should be covered by a mound of peat moss or pegged-down burlap for ten days to allow roots to take before the tops are exposed to drying winds and sun. Be slow to remove all the soil cover over the root zone; by keeping the soil cool, you may be able to slow down those impatient first sprouts that tend to get blackened by late frosts. If they still sprout too soon, protect them with plant covers whenever frost is in the air.

May is the last chance to plant bare-root trees and shrubs before they break dormancy. Pinch back the candles of mugho pines to keep them neat.

Gladioli and dahlias should be planted about two weeks before the last anticipated date of frost. By the time they come up, frost danger should be past.

During the latter half of May, seed outdoors your second batch of vegetables and thin seedlings as necessary. This is also the time to sow any annuals you are going to grow from seed.

Continue with the lawn clean-up if not already done and start to mow as necessary—aim for a fairly low cut.

If broadleaf weeds are a problem in the lawn, choose a warm, still day to apply 2,4-D (see chapter fifteen on weeds).

Check trees and shrubs for sucker sprouts, and dig down to remove them as close to the root as possible. The only final cure for sprouting is to plant nonsuckering-type plants.

JUNE

As danger of late frost is reduced and soil warms

- Broadcast second application of lawn fertilizer.
- Seed outdoors tender vegetables that do not transplant well.
- Plant out prestarted warm-season crops.
- Plant out tuberous begonias.
- Store spare seeds in a cool place in an airtight container.
- Continue thinning vegetable seedlings.
- Start to hill potatoes as the tops grow and repeat until late summer.
- Prune elongated candles of compact conifers if you haven't done so already.
- Shear white-cedars if a formal effect is required.
- Slice annual weeds at ground level with a sharp hoe while they are still young.
- Take note of any trees and shrubs that you would like to grow.
- Compare notes with other gardeners; visit your botanic garden—notebook in hand.
- Prune early-flowering shrubs when blossoms fade.
- Leave foliage on bulbs that have finished flowering.
- Stake or string climbers.
- Move tough house plants outdoors into a shady spot for summer (reduces indoor watering).
- Remove any fireblight-infected branches—often seen on apple and mountain-ash.
- Continue insect and disease control.

During hot and windy weather

- Raise cutting height of lawn mower.
- Pay extra attention to watering.
- Apply mulch where needed to conserve soil moisture.

By mid-June the rush of spring work in the garden is over, and the last important job for the vegetable grower is to seed sweet corn and plant cucumbers, squash, and tomatoes—softies that have to wait for the chill to leave the night air and the soil temperature to rise.

In hot, dry weather a soil mulch can make all the difference to garden productivity. Although we can't do much to change some of the microclimatic conditions in the garden, one thing we can do is regulate the moisture level and temperature of the soil. Once the risk of late spring frost is minimal, we should remove all straw, peat, manure, or compost mulches away from the plant to encourage the warming of the soil in the root zone. Before we see the middle of June, chances are that the soil will become baked dry. When this happens, you can water the root zone and put a mulch in place to reduce evaporation and keep the soil cool.

Take care to put down only enough thickness of mulch to do the job: too much and you tempt the roots to stay close to the surface. A heavy mulch layer can prevent the penetration of moisture to the roots during rains, so the art of mulching is to keep it to a minimum and draw it away from the plants when soil warming rather than cool moisture retention is needed. In late summer and fall, roots should be free of mulch to encourage hardening and maturation of growth before winter.

JULY

- Harvest vegetables while still young and tender.
- Support staking tomato plants and remove axil shoots as they appear.
- Note your garden successes (and failures) for future reference.
- Make note of any changes needed in the positioning of plants for next year.
- Order spring-flowering bulbs and peonies now if using mail-order service.
- Remove spent flowers; this often encourages repeat bloom.
- Keep shrub and flower borders weed free with a sharp hoe.
- Thin out old wood from shrubs that have finished blooming.
- Continue to watch for and control insect pests and diseases.
- Apply nitrogen fertilizer to lawns and water in.

During hot dry weather

- Soak lawns, trees, shrubs, and flowering plants whenever surface soil dries.

- Apply mulch where practical.

During wet weather

- Pull mulches away from plants.
- Thin out plants to improve air circulation.

Enjoy the harvest and flavor of early vegetables fresh from the garden. Pinch the tops off broad bean plants to speed the development of the pods forming lower down. If using tunnel gardens to grow cucumbers or squash, you will need to remove the plastic as soon as the plants start to outgrow their space.

Downy or powdery mildews may quickly cover leaves and young stems, especially in wet weather. Some control over this problem may be achieved by clearing excess vegetation to allow more light penetration and air circulation. Remove and dispose of badly infected parts, and spray with a fungicide to control further spread.

Enjoy your garden in July and keep outdoor chores to a minimum.

AUGUST

- Continue vegetable harvest and remove spent crops.
- Visit horticultural shows for inspiration.
- Save tops of disease-free vegetables for composting.
- Thin out overcrowded perennials.
- Prune raspberry patch when harvest is completed.
- Divide and transplant oriental poppies and bearded iris.
- Fertilize lawns.
- Remove excess vegetation from the greenhouse to prepare for the fall season.
- Harvest tree fruits as they ripen, leaving spurs intact.

Towards the end of the month

- Transplant conifers with a good soil ball.
- Seed new lawns.
- Remove any whitewash on greenhouses.

With increasing risk of frost

- Move holidaying house plants back indoors.
- Pick all remaining tomatoes from outdoor plants for indoor ripening.

- Be ready to protect dahlias and tender annuals from the first frost.
- Check greenhouse heating system.

At this time of year garden produce is in such abundance that you may well be trying to pass some of the surplus over the garden fence. Usually it's the latter part of August when most of the fruits, flowers, and vegetables are at their best and the horticultural shows are staged. Entering exhibits into a show may not appeal to you unless you are already a keen hobby gardener, but a visit to your local annual show when it's open to the public provides a clear demonstration of what can be grown in your area. Be sure to talk to those in attendance, especially the exhibitors packing up after the show—I have always found these people to be helpful and more than willing to pass on advice and encouragement to those interested. They also welcome new members. Some clubs are able to provide practical advice and demonstration sessions, while others are committee groups geared almost exclusively to the staging of the annual show. A visit or two is all you will need before deciding whether or not a club membership is for you.

SEPTEMBER

Before hard frost

- Harvest root crops as needed, leaving some until just before the ground freezes.
- Harvest warm-season vegetables.
- Lift and store tuberous begonias.
- Transplant deciduous trees and shrubs as soon as leaves start to show dormancy.
- Lower the lawn mower blades a little and continue to mow when necessary.
- Plant spring-flowering bulbs as soon as they are available.
- Move garden chemicals to indoor storage for the winter.
- Put some soil indoors for use in the winter months (or keep a container for bringing inside when needed).
- Pot a flowering annual (for example, dwarf impatiens) for a sunny windowsill indoors.
- Dig a couple of garden geraniums for overwintering indoors.

After hard frost

- Cut all foliage from disease-prone perennials like peonies and lilies.

- Transplant peonies and lilies if they have to be moved.
- Lift and store dahlias (gladioli may be left until October).
- Clean all spray and fertilizer equipment and store in a dry place.
- Store fertilizers in a dry place for the winter.
- After curing, move squash and onions into cool storage.
- Check the ripening of tomatoes in storage.
- Check the greenhouse structure and repair where necessary.
- Repair fences, walks, and other elements of the hard landscape.
- Enjoy harvest time, fall foliage, and cooler weather.

These month-by-month reminders didn't keep you very busy through the middle of the gardening season, but with the cooler days of September there is a longer list of activities. This is the main harvest month for vegetables and fruit, bulbs need planting if we are to have the flowering next spring, and we should make a start on winter preparation.

If you have a policy of low maintenance in your garden, then you will be able to avoid some of the jobs mentioned. Storage of plants over winter in the average home is an uncertain venture, and you may prefer to forego such tender perennials as tuberous begonias, gladioli, and dahlias for that reason—or discard them in the fall and buy fresh specimens each spring.

To keep garden geraniums over winter, cut them back hard and pack them close together in a deep box, the roots covered with light soil. Store in the basement cool room at 40 to 43°F. Water the soil well as they are placed in storage, and then water occasionally throughout winter to prevent them from shrivelling.

Winter squash and onions keep best if they are given a couple of weeks of warm, dry conditions before being moved to a cool, well-ventilated storage place. The skin of the squash should become tough before storing and the neck of the onion should be shrivelled rather than plump and green.

If you cover your bedding plants on nights when the occasional frost threatens, you may be able to extend the flowering season for several weeks.

Plant your spring-flowering bulbs as early as you can so they have time to send down a few roots before the ground freezes hard.

When harvesting vegetables, you may wish to save the waste leaves and return them to the garden late in the form of compost. This, in principle, is a good idea, but it helps only if the material (cabbage leaves and what have you) is free of disease. If there is any risk of overwintering disease organisms, I strongly recommend that you garbage the stuff and stay with clean grass mowings combined with fallen tree leaves.

OCTOBER

Before the ground freezes down

- Complete the harvesting of vegetables such as cabbage and sprouts.
- Dig remaining root crops.
- Dig gladioli and cure corms in a warm, dry place.
- Complete planting of tulip bulbs for spring bloom.
- Continue to water woody plants if soil becomes dry.
- Mound up tender roses before heavy snowfall.
- Rake up leaves from lawn areas and save them for compost.
- Clean out gutters.
- Dig the vegetable garden, turning under decomposing organic matter.
- Pot up special tulips, daffodils, and hyacinths for winter forcing.
- Seed Swiss chard, head lettuce, onions, and parsnips for germination next spring.
- Drain all irrigation pipes.

After the ground freezes down

- Prune trees and shrubs.
- Complete the mounding of tender roses and place straw covering over strawberries.
- Protect woody plants against wild animals if they pose a problem.
- Service the lawn mower and other mechanical equipment.
- Store cold frames, wheelbarrow, and other garden equipment under cover.
- Clean and store hand tools under cover.
- Reduce watering of house plants but maintain humidity.

October is such an uncertain month. Although winter can come to stay at any time, we often enjoy an Indian summer through the entire month. If a heavy snowfall seems likely, rush to complete outdoor work—with emphasis on harvesting and winter protection. After mounding tender roses, cut the tops back to half their height; then if you have the time and patience, defoliate the remaining canes.

Before snow and after natural defoliation is a good time to prune all deciduous trees and shrubs. Consider the fall seeding of Swiss chard, head lettuce, Spanish onions, and parsnips.

Flower bulbs for winter forcing indoors are specially selected kinds pretreated to provide midwinter bloom. After potting and watering, they are kept in a cool, dark place to grow roots. When the roots are well developed, they will be ready to associate with the rest of the family and perform as they were intended.

NOVEMBER

- Complete the fall seeding of vegetables just before the ground freezes.
- If snow cover is uncertain, mulch perennials.
- On a fine day, complete pruning.
- On a not-so-fine day, send for government pamphlets on gardening in your area.
- Send for seed and plant catalogs.

Herbaceous perennials do best in our area when sheltered from prevailing winds and where winter snow cover is reliable. Where winter temperatures rise well above freezing for several weeks at a time, the plants may break dormancy too early and suffer damage when the mercury plunges again. In such a situation it helps to cover the crowns of perennials with wood chips or flax straw when the ground is thoroughly frozen. The insulation keeps the temperature more constant and reduces the risk of rotting through dormant plants sitting in wet soil.

DECEMBER

- Check pots of bulbs for winter blooming.
- Check plants in storage.
- Start an indoor light garden.
- Renew garden club memberships and plant magazine subscriptions.
- Drop hints about things you would like to see in your Christmas stocking—a potted plant, a special gardening book, hedging shears. A riding mower?

If you have a number of bulbs potted up for winter bloom, bring them out into warmth and light once the roots are well developed. (Move them from darkness to moderate light first for a few days before bringing them into full daylight.) Bring out only one or two pots at a time to provide some continuity of bloom. The tulip 'Christmas Marvel' could become a tradition with your family. Another favorite is the paper-white narcissus. But if you missed the planting time for winter blooming bulbs this year, make a note to get some started next September or October.

Winter's getting you down already? Try a few African violets under 4-foot long fluorescent tubes. Use one cool white and one warm white side by side in a two-tube fixture, and place the plants within 6 inches of the tubes to make the most of light intensity. Use the light as efficiently as you can by providing flat white reflecting surfaces at the back and sides, and include an automatic timer switch.

And one more thing. Have a happy holiday season.

GLOSSARY

AAS—All-America Selections. A nonprofit organization committed to evaluating new annual flowers and vegetable cultivars. AAS promotes superior plants tested in widespread North American trails.

Accent plant—Plants of distinctive appearance used occasionally in the landscape to provide interest and diversity.

Acclimatization—Similar to hardening off, but of longer duration and involving outplanted material. Sometimes refers to outdoor plants transplanted from a very different climatic zone that may take several weeks to "get up step" with the seasons. May also refer to indoor plants moved from optimum conditions and gradually acclimatized to a new site that is less than ideal.

Acid soil—A soil with a reading below 6.8 on the pH scale.

Activator—Any number of commercial substances, including microorganism cultures, claimed to activate and inoculate a compost heap to speed decomposition. Nitrogen, however, is the only addition that speeds compost production.

Aeration—The loosening or turning of soil to permit air penetration. May also refer to spiking or a compacted lawn.

Alkaline soil—A soil with a reading above 7.2 on the pH scale.

Ammonium nitrate—A chemical fertilizer with an analysis of approximately 34-0-0.

Ammonium phosphate—A chemical fertilizer with an analysis of approximately 11-48-0.

Ammonium sulfate—A chemical fertilizer with an analysis of approximately 21-0-0 (also spelled ammonium sulphate.)

Analysis—1. A procedure that reveals the chemical and physical make-up of soil. 2. Also a synonym for fertilizer grade.

Annual—Strictly speaking, a plant that germinates, flowers, fruits, and dies within one season; but more commonly applied to any flowering plant that is grown from scratch each year.

Antidesiccant—Also known as antitranspirants. Any of several liquid formulations that, when applied to foliage, reduce plant moisture loss.

Antistatic—In reference to some acrylic materials used in place of greenhouse glass, antistatic properties indicate a reduction in the inherent electrostatic charge that attracts dust.

Arboretum—A botanically labelled collection of trees or shrubs maintained for one or several purposes, including education, plant introduction, conservation, and research.

Atrium—An indoor courtyard of plants. An indoor landscape.

Bacillus thuringiensis—A bacterial organism parasitic upon caterpillars and sawfly larvae applied by gardeners as a nonchemical control. Often abbreviated to Bt.

Ball and burlap—A method of retaining the soil ball around a root system when transplanting, using burlap and twine. Used almost exclusively for transplanting conifers until the recent advent of container-grown stock. Often abbreviated as B & B.

Bare root—A plant lifted for transplanting without soil.

Base dressing—Fertilizer incorporated into the soil immediately before sowing or planting.

Bedding plants—Annuals planted for display as a seasonal ground cover.

Biennial—A plant that germinates one season, overwinters, and completes its life cycle the second year.

Biennial bearing—Plants that tend to bear only in alternate years. Often referring to fruit (such as apple trees) that alternate years of heavy cropping with little or no fruit.

Biological control—The control of pest organisms by manipulating natural methods to reduce the pest population.

Bleeding—Refers to running tree sap in the spring following earlier wounding or pruning. The condition is usually not serious if soil moisture is maintained.

Blight—An all-encompassing term for a number of plant diseases.

Bolting—A premature development of flowers and seed, often observed in vegetables as a consequence of hot weather.

Bone-meal—A rather expensive organic source of slowly released phosphorus. It increases soil alkalinity.

Bonsai—An artificially dwarfed and shaped plant (usually a tree) grown in a pot; originally an oriental art form.

Borderline hardy—A plant that, once established, will survive winter conditions in a given area but will suffer severe die back or death under unusually severe climatic conditions.

Botanical name—The international scientific name of a plant. Used by professional horticulturists (and frequently by laymen) to avoid the confusion caused by the ambiguity of common names.

Botrytis—A common mold fungal infection frequently seen in such herbaceous perennials as peonies and lilies.

Bottom heat—Heat applied underneath a propagating bench or container to raise the soil temperature above that of the air temperature.

Break—The development of a lateral shoot as a result of pruning back to an axillary bud.

Broadcast—The scattering of seeds, fertilizer, and so on evenly over the surface instead of in rows.

Bud blast—The abortion of a flower in bud before it is fully open.

Budding—An economical method of grafting using a single bud instead of a stem with several buds.

Bulbil—A small bulb which forms in the leaf axil of a stem or inflorescence.

Burn—1. A discolored spot on foliage caused by the concentration of sunlight through a drop of water. 2. A general term for the discoloration of foliage such as that caused by desiccation, chemical contact, or soil toxicity.

Candles—The elongated new shoots of conifers before the needles spread to their normal position.

Canker—A collective term for various fungal and bacterial diseases seen on the bark and wood of trees.

Capillary—The force that raises the surface of a liquid that is in contact with a solid. Evident when water rises in a plant pot after being applied to the saucer beneath.

Cellar gardening—The use of a cellar or basement to start, force, or mature certain plants—particularly during the winter months. Seedlings may be started with the aid of supplemental lighting. Flower bulbs and certain roots such as rhubarb and asparagus may be forced. Also, the plants of such long-season crops as Brussels sprouts may be dug at the end of a short season and moved to a cellar to mature the crop.

Chitting—The sprouting of seed prior to sowing.

Chlorosis—The yellowing of leaves caused by physiological or pest problems. A loss of the green pigment, chlorophyll.

Clone—A genetically uniform group of plants derived vegetatively from an individual plant.

Cold frame—An unheated, outdoor box-type shelter for plants with a removable glass or plastic cover. Used most often in the spring to start or harden off seedlings.

Companion planting—The growing of plants adjacent to each other in the belief that it is for their mutual benefit in promoting growth or repelling pests.

Complete fertilizer—A fertilizer containing all three of the major elements—nitrogen, phosphorus, and potash.

Compost—Well-decomposed organic matter, used mainly to improve the texture of soil.

Conifer—A plant bearing its seed in cones and having needle-type leaves. Most are evergreen.

Contact insecticide—An insecticide that must come in contact with the insect to be effective.

Container plant—1. A plant grown in a temporary container as a convenient means of handling until being planted. 2. A plant suitable for long-term growth in a decorative container.

Corm—A bulblike swollen stembase that acts as a storage organ.

Cross—A cross is the result of cross-pollination, the transfer (by natural or artificial means) of pollen between flowers of different kinds to produce hybrid offspring.

Crown—1. The main branch system of a tree. 2. The basal core of a herbaceous perennial.

Cultivar—A cultivated variety that has been named, for example, 'Cuthbert Grant' is a rose cultivar.

Cultural practices—Methods of growing plants under cultivation.

Cutting—A shoot, leaf, or piece of root cut for the purpose of propagation.

Damping off—A common fungal disease of seedlings.

Deadhead—To remove spent flowers from a plant. Deadheading is usually performed to prevent seed set or to induce repeat flowering.

Deciduous—Leaflosing woody trees and shrubs.

Determinate (Synonym self-determinate)—A term used for plants in which the terminal growth of shoots is topped by the production of flowers and fruit. Most frequently referring to tomatoes of the nonstaking kind.

Dethatching—The removal of dead grass from a lawn by raking.

Die back—The death of twigs or branches of woody plants, often because of winter cold or desiccation.

Disbudding—The removal of lesser flower buds to allow full development of those remaining.

Dormant spray (Synonym dormant oil)—An oil suspended in an emulsion which controls pests through suffocation. A control for scale and other sucking insects on orchard trees. Also referred to as miscible oil.

Double digging—A system of hand digging the garden to loosen or bring to the surface soil from beneath the top spit. Now infrequently practiced, except in a modified form for raised-bed gardening.

Double flower—A flower with many more petals or showy petals than normal for the species. Double-flowered plants are often selected as cultivars.

Double leader—Two top shoots of a tree vying for dominance. The weaker shoot is usually pruned away to ensure a good tree form.

Drawn—Referring to plants which become elongated and sickly as they reach towards the light. Frequently occurs when indoor plants receive inadequate light and when seedlings remain crowded.

Dressing—Material, such as organic matter, new soil, or fertilizer, incorporated into the soil. See also base dressing, side dressing, and top dressing.

Drift—The movement of chemical spray or dust in the air. Usually referring to unwanted dispersal that endangers nontarget plants.

Drill—A shallow furrow in which seeds are sown.

Drip-line—A term used to indicate the location of feeder roots directly beneath the outer reach of a tree canopy.

Drop-spreader—A wheeled hopper designed to spread seed or chemicals evenly over an area such as a lawn.

Emulsifiable concentrate—Usually a concentrated liquid that must be diluted with water according to directions before use. Abbreviated EC.

Epsom salt—Magnesium sulfate.

Espalier—A woody plant trained and pruned to spread flat along a fencelike support.

Everlastings—Plants (usually herbaceous) with flowers, stems, or pods, which retain most of their fresh form or color naturally when air dried. Used for winter bouquet arrangements.

Extension horticulturist—One who provides horticultural information to the public.

F 1 hybrid—A plant that results from the cross-fertilization of species or varieties. F 1 hybrids may display the desirable traits of both parents, but they do not breed true and may be self-sterile.

Fallowing—Allowing land to remain uncropped and free of vegetation. Once a commonly practised technique to "rest" the soil but now largely superseded by green manuring.

Fertilization—1. Pollen (the male element) applied to a flower's pistil (the female element) for the purpose of setting viable seed. 2. Occasionally, the application of fertilizer.

Fertilizer—Material that provides plant nutrients from decayed plants, animal matter, or inorganic sources.

Fertilizer grade—The chemical analysis of fertilizers, recorded on the container in the order nitrogen, phosphorus, and potash.

Flat—A shallow box or tray used for starting seedlings.

Foliar feed—A liquid fertilizer sprayed onto, and partially absorbed by, the leaves of a plant.

Forcing—Speeding up of plant growth by providing warmth and/or excluding light.

Formal landscaping—Geometrically structured garden designs, plants, and flowers; including the arrangement of plants, the pruning and training of plants, and often the plants themselves.

Foundation plant—Originally a term for plants used to hide the unsightly foundation of a building. Now commonly applied to low-growing woody ornamentals used in the vicinity of the home.

Friable—The condition of a soil without hard or wet lumps that crumbles easily when moist.

Frost lifting—The heaving of the ground during the winter months, resulting in the partial displacement of plants from the soil or the frost shifting of hard landscape features such as paths and posts.

Frost line—The anticipated depth of frost penetration into the ground.

Frost pocket—A low piece of land lacking good air drainage and therefore subject to late spring and early fall ground frosts.

Fumigation—1. The use of poisonous smoke preparations to combat greenhouse insects and diseases. 2. A method of soil pasteurization using chemicals that vaporize in the soil to become effective. This system is not recommended except for certain commercial applications.

Fungicide—A substance used to control diseases caused by fungi and certain bacteria.

Genus (Plural genera)—The major division within a plant family. Example: All larch are of the genus *Larix* within the larger pine family. The genus is the first part of the binomial, thus: *Larix* (genus) *laricinia* (species).

Girdling—1. The removal of bark around a woody stem, cutting off the normal flow of sap just beneath the bark. 2. The choking of a trunk or branch as it expands within the stricture of a rope or wire perhaps used as a label or support.

Glauber salt—Sodium sulfate

Grafting—The method of propagating desired plants by attaching the scion onto a root stock so the resulting plant gives the desired characteristics of scion or stock. Grafting may be performed for economic purposes or to modify scion growth.

Green manure—A grass or other crop grown to be tilled into the soil, adding nutrients and improving soil structure.

Ground cover—A plant, usually low growing, that is used to cover the ground as an ornamental, for soil stabilization, or for weed control.

Guarantee—1. Written plant guarantees are usually limited by the vendor to the plant being correctly named, or to becoming established the first season, or (occasionally) to being hardy enough to survive the first winter. 2. On the label of a garden pesticide product the word guarantee precedes the active ingredient(s) of the product.

Habit—The "form" of a plant (upright, spreading, weeping, compact, open).

Half hardy—Usually referring to an annual or biennial plant that will survive "normal" winters but not exceptionally harsh ones. See also borderline hardy.

Hard landscape—Elements of the landscape other than plants and general topography. Includes such items as paths, patios, and fences. See also soft landscape.

Harden off—The process of acclimatizing plants from an environment of optimum growth to full outdoor exposure. Over a period of a week or more, the plants are exposed to increasing intervals of time outdoors, so when planted out they make the transition with the minimum of shock.

Hardiness—The ability of the plant to succeed in a particular climate. In our region the degree to which it will survive winter.

Hardiness zones—Numbered zones on a given map that indicate the probable hardiness of plants, with the plants allocated corresponding numbers. Several such systems are in current use in North America.

Hardpan—A hard layer of clay or slit beneath the soil surface which acts as a barrier to root growth and water drainage.

Hardwood cutting—A cutting taken from a dormant woody plant. See also softwood cutting.

Heading back—Pruning branches back to a bud or side branch to promote more compact growth.

Heavy soil—A soil with a high clay content.

Heeling in—The practice of covering roots and stems of bare-root plants to prevent them from desiccating before they can be outplanted. They are usually set at an acute angle and thoroughly watered.

Herbaceous—A term to describe nonwoody plants, nearly always referring to herbaceous perennials. Often abbreviated HP.

Herbicide—A weed killer or, more accurately, a plant killer.

Hill up (synonym hilling)—To mound soil, peat moss, or other material around the stem base of a plant.

Honeydew—A secretion of sap-sucking insects such as aphids. The sweet substance attracts other insects, serves as a medium for sooty mold fungus, and may damage paint onto which it drips.

Hoof and horn meal—A rather expensive organic source of slowly released nitrogen.

Hormone—See rooting compound.

Hot bed—A heated cold frame.

Hot cap—Any small, easily moved structure used to cover plants and provide a miniature greenhouse effect

Humus—Organic matter in the final stages of decomposition; dark in color, friable, and without noticeable odor, it can be produced by composting.

Hybrid—A plant produced by the cross-fertilization of two different species or variants of species. Hybridization may be natural or controlled. It is more common within a single genus, but it may occasionally occur between different genera.

Hydroponics—The system of growing plants without soil. While some short-term crops may be successfully raised in nutrient solution, long-term growth poses problems in supplying necessary trace elements.

Inorganic fertilizer—Plant nutrients as chemicals without organic material.

Integrated Pest Management—The concept of using both chemical and cultural means to control plant pests and diseases. Central to this system is the timing of chemical controls for optimum effect with the least damage to natural controls. Often abbreviated IPM.

Intensive gardening—A method of growing plants, especially vegetable crops, at close spacing to maximize productivity in small spaces. Slightly raised beds are often used for increased soil depth.

Interplanting—Also known as intercropping. Growing more than one crop simultaneously on a piece of land. A concept particularly favored by advocates of companion planting and intensive gardening.

Lath house—Also known as a shade frame. A structure designed to house plants that require shade from full sunlight. Formerly almost always constructed of wooden lath, but modern shade frames may consist of a metal framework covered by synthetic cloth.

Latin name—See botanical name

Layering—Propagation by inducing shoots to produce roots while still attached to the parent plant.

Leaching—The loss of soluble materials by water passing through. In this way valuable nutrients, especially nitrogen, are carried to depths where they cannot be reached by roots. Leaching is also a method used to reduce salt accumulations in alkaline soils and to clear a buildup of toxic chemicals in plant containers.

Leader—The main stem or trunk of a plant. See also double leader.

Leggy—A term used to describe a plant with a long stem out of proportion to its foliage. For example, a seedling in poor light drawn to a brighter light source or an overmature shrub producing most of its flowers and foliage at the top of bare branches.

Limestone—Calcium carbonate used to increase soil pH to less acidic levels.

Line out—To plant young seedlings, cuttings, and so on, in a temporary nursery location.

Loam—A fertile soil consisting of sand, silt, clay, and humus.

Medium—A substance in which plants are grown. Usually referring to a mixture of soil and additives prepared for use in containers.

Microclimate—In general, the climatic conditions of a location that differ from the general climatic conditions of the area at large. The term is variously applied to large and small microclimates. For example, an area with the protection of buildings will differ from the surrounding countryside. Also, within a small garden there are several microclimates influenced by degrees of exposure to sun, wind, and moisture.

Micro-nutrients—See trace elements.

Miscible oil—See dormant spray.

Mosaic—A mottled or patchy appearance of normally green leaves that may indicate the presence of a viral disease.

Mulch—A covering of organic or inorganic material applied to the soil around a plant for the purpose of controlling weeds, avoiding mud-splash, conserving moisture, and reducing soil temperature fluctuations.

Muriate of potash—A chemical fertilizer with an analysis of approximately 0-0-60.

Naturalized plants—1. Cultivated plants included in an informal garden to simulate a natural plant population; for example, flowering bulbs planted in drifts in an unmowed lawn. 2. Plants that have become established and compete successfully with native plant populations.

Necrosis—The death of plant tissue, usually associated with plant disease.

Neutral soil—Soil with a pH of 6.8 to 7.2, indicating that it is neither acid nor alkaline.

Nodules—Irregular-shaped lumps that grow on the roots of certain legumes (such as peas and beans). The nodules contain colonies of nitrogen-fixing bacteria beneficial to the plant and ultimately to other plants.

Nonselective herbicide—Any herbicide that destroys plants indiscriminately. Most soil sterilants are nonselective.

Nose—The top or growing point of a bulb. The term is frequently used for grading daffodil bulbs.

Nymph—The active but immature stage of certain insects and mites.

Offsets—1. Small bulbs produced at the base of the parent bulb. 2. Young plants sprouting at or beneath the ground from the parent plant (sucker).

Organic gardening—1. The use of animal and plant products instead of chemical fertilizers. 2. A philosophy of natural gardening without using synthetic chemicals for plant nutrients or pest control.

Ornamental—A plant grown for its attractive appearance rather than for utilitarian purposes.

Outplanting—The moving of plants from temporary sites, such as nursery plots, to permanent locations.

Pasteurization—Soil pasteurization (often referred to as sterilization) is a means of temporarily controlling disease inducing organisms, insects, and weed seeds in soil by the judicious use of heat. Not all commercially packaged potting soils are as sterile as they are claimed to be. Small amounts of slightly moist soil mix may be pasteurized in an oven at approximately 160° to 180°F (71° to 82°C) for two hours, using a cooking bag to contain moisture and odor. See also fumigation.

Pathogen—A living organism that causes a disease.

Pelleted seed—Seeds coated to make them easier to handle when sowing and spacing.

Pergola—The word comes from the Latin *pergula*, a projecting roof. In garden terms it is a corridor of vertical columns joined with an openwork roof with climbing plants trained over it.

Perlite—A mineral expanded by heat to form very lightweight, porous white granules. The sterile substance is used as a rooting medium and as an ingredient of prepared soil mixes for retaining moisture and air. It lasts longer than vermiculite in use.

pH—A 14-point scale denoting acidity or alkalinity, with pH 6.8 to 7.2 indicating a neutral condition; the lower numbers are increasingly acid. The pH of soil may be a factor when selecting plants, but normally garden soils fall somewhere between pH 6 and 7.5 and most plants are very tolerant to variations within this range.

Pheromone—Insect sex attractant used to lure and trap or destroy specific insect pests.

Phytotoxic—Toxic or injurious to plants.

Pinching back (Synonym stopping)—The removal of a young stem (usually with a thumbnail) to induce side branching.

Planting mark—The slight change in color on the stem of a bare-root plant that indicates the depth at which it was originally growing.

Plunge—To bury a container-grown plant up to the rim. House plants kept outdoors for the summer are usually plunged into soil, sand, or peat to reduce the drying and heating of the root system. Hardy plants in containers are often plunged (especially over winter) to reduce severe temperature fluctuations at the root zone.

Pollination—The process by which pollen from the male part of the flower is transferred to the female part for the purpose of setting fruit or seed. Pollination is usually accomplished by natural means—self-pollination, wind, water, insects, and so on. See also cross-pollination.

Post-emergence—Referring to chemical herbicides that are applied and active on the emerged or growing plant. See also pre-emergence.

Pot-bound (Synonym root-bound)—The condition of a container plant when the root system is too large for the container. Some plants tolerate or even perform best with constricted roots. On the other hand, pot-bound plants transplanted from the container without proper disturbance of the matted root system will grow poorly or not at all.

Potting on—The transplanting of a potted plant to a large pot to allow more room for root development.

Pre-emergence—Referring to chemical herbicides that are placed on or in the soil to control weeds at the time of germination or emergence.

Presser board—A small board with a handle used to level and firm soils in flats prior to seeding or pricking out.

Primary elements—Nitrogen, phosphorus, and potash. The three mineral elements needed in largest quantity for plant growth. Packages of fertilizer have the percentage of each (in that same order) printed on the bag or carton. See also fertilizer grade.

Reaction—Usually referring to soil, the degree of acidity or alkalinity as measured on the pH scale.

Recurrent (Synonym remontant)—A plant that flowers more than once each season. In certain plants, recurrent bloom may be induced by cutting back and feeding immediately after flowering.

Renewal pruning—The pruning of woody plants to maintain a constant supply of new shoots.

Residual action—Usually referring to the degree of persistence of chemicals applied to soil or plants. Pesticides may have a short-, medium-, or long-term residual action.

Rogue—1. To weed out inferior individual plants, retaining only those with desirable qualities. 2. An undesired plant.

Root hardy—Woody plants that die back to the ground every year but survive because the root remains alive.

Root pruning—The root cutting of woody plants by forcing a sharp spade into the soil close to the stem or trenching around larger trees. The practice initiates additional fibrous feeder roots in preparation for transplanting, slows top growth, or simply curtails the spread of roots where they create a problem.

Rooting compound—A substance that, under certain conditions, improves the speed and success rate of rooting cuttings. Commercial preparations are commonly formulated as a powder and marketed in degrees of strength for soft- or hard-wood cuttings.

Rose end—In reference to potatoes, the end where the buds (or eyes) of the potato are spaced closest together.

Rotation—The practice of dividing the vegetable or flower garden into several sections and growing a given crop in a different section each year until it rotates back to the original location. By continuously rotating all crops, insect and disease problems are reduced and soil is not rapidly depleted by the more demanding crops.

Salinity—An excess of soluble salts in the soil. Under hot, dry conditions (and where the water table is high), saline soils develop a surface salt crust.

Scion—A separated shoot used as the upper portion of a grafted plant. See also grafting.

Selective herbicide—Any herbicide that, when used as directed, is effective against certain plants, while leaving other kinds relatively unharmed. For example, 2,4-D is selective against broadleaf weeds growing in lawn grasses.

Self-fertile—A plant able to pollinate itself and produce seed or spores without benefit of another plant of a similar kind close by.

Self-seeding—Plants that are self-reproducing by seeds, that is, plants that produce volunteer seedlings.

Self-sterile—Sterility due to a non-function of pollen or ovules, or because

these mature at different times.

Sets—Bulbs or tubers planted in place of seeds for faster maturity and uniformity.

Shelterbelt—A windbreak of trees and/or shrubs.

Side dressing—A narrow band of fertilizer buried deep enough on either side of a row of seed that it does not come into direct contact with the seed. May also refer to surface applications of fertilizer lightly incorporated into the soil on either side of a row of seeds or seedling plants.

Single flower—A flower with the normal number of petals or sepals for the species.

Slip—A shoot that is pulled or "slipped" off the main stem without cutting for the purpose of propagation.

Sod—Grass turf (with part of the root mat) cut into strips or tiles for the purpose of transplanting.

Soft landscape—The general topography and plants of a garden. See also hard landscape.

Softwood cutting (synonym slip)—A cutting taken from a leafy growing shoot of the current season for the purpose of propagation. Most likely to root when taken at the stage of growth when they snap off cleanly.

Species (Plural species)—A group of plants more similar to one another than to any other group and belonging to a single genus. In the example *Caragana pygmaea, "pygmaea"* is the species of *Cargana.* Often abbreviated sp. See also genus.

Specimen plant—An ornamental plant (usually a tree or shrub) featured alone in the landscape design rather than as part of a group.

Sphagnum—A moss which is able to absorb great quantities of moisture. The partially decayed and sterile material is a form of peat moss.

Spit—The depth of a normal spade blade (about 11 inches). Old gardening books often called for digging "two spits deep."

Spot treat—To control a pest by promptly treating a limited area (or plant) rather than undertaking a more widespread treatment.

Spreader—1. A garden tool for spreading seed and fertilizer. 2. A soaplike product added to a spray application to improve its even distribution on the target. Sometimes sold as "sticker-spreader." Spreaders are not recommended for all sprays; check the product label before using.

Spur—1. A woody stub or short branch that produces clusters of flowers and fruit. 2. A tubular projection of certain flowers such as columbines.

Standard—A shrub or small tree trained or grafted to a single short trunk and topped by a cluster of branches. For example, weeping caragana is normally grown as a standard, grafted atop a 3- to 5-foot trunk of common caragana.

Sterile—Referring to the inability of a plant to set viable seed after pollination.

Sterilization—See pasteurization.

Stock—1. The part of a grafted or budded plant that receives the scion. 2. A nurseryman's term for plants from which propagation material is obtained.

Stool—The base of a plant which gives rise to canes or other vegetative offshoots useful in propagation.

Strain—Usually referring to an improved or horticulturally distinct selection of a cultivar.

Structure—The aggregation of soil particles which determine the tilth of a soil.

Subspecies—A group of naturally occurring plants of the same species that differ from the accepted species description in some small but distinctive way. Often abbreviated ssp.

Succession planting—A frequently recommended method of planting a second crop soon after or just before the first is harvested. In the Great Plains region (because of our hot summers and short, frost-free period) succession planting is generally limited to one or two repeat sowings of short-season vegetables like lettuce, radishes, and string beans early in the season.

Sucker growth—A fast-growing shoot arising from the root or underground stem of a woody plant. Unwanted sucker sprouts should be cut off as close to the base as possible to discourage regrowth. See also water sprout.

Sunscald—A drying condition of the bark and sap beneath caused by direct sunlight on sensitive tissue. Mountain-ash and apple trees are among those susceptible. Allowing low branches to remain is perhaps the most aesthetically acceptable method of shading the trunk, although whitewash and burlap are alternatives. Scald of tomato and pepper plant foliage is also caused by intense sunlight.

Superphosphate—A chemical fertilizer with an analysis of 0-18-0.

Systemic—A chemical that is taken up by the plant and permeates the sap stream. Insects that cannot be reached by contact sprays may often be controlled by a systemic pesticide. Also, many herbicides are systemic in action.

Taxon—An all-encompassing term that includes such classifications as genus, species, subspecies, variety, and cultivar (plural, taxa).

Terrarium—A miniature garden in a transparent container with an adjustable cover. Used for growing certain ferns and other house plants and for starting cuttings.

Texture—The composition of soil based on the percentages of sand, silt, clay, air, water, and organic matter present.

Thatch—On a lawn, a layer of dead grass and other debris that builds on the soil surface. A little thatch is advantageous as a natural mulch. Excess thatch reduces water penetration to the roots and serves as a breeding zone for grass pests and disease.

Thinning—The technique of progressively removing excess seedlings (usually in the vegetable garden) to allow the full development of the remainder.

Tilth—The physical condition of soil. A soil in good tilth is easily cultivated, friable, well aerated, and easily penetrated by roots and emerging seedlings.

Tissue culture—The asceptic growth of plant cells or tissue in an artificial (usually liquid) medium. A recently developed technique most commonly used for the vegetative propagation of difficult subjects.

Tolerant—A plant that will grow and produce under adverse chemical and environmental conditions that frequently prove phytotoxic.

Top dressing—Material, such as organic matter, new soil, or fertilizer, applied to the soil surface without being incorporated in the soil.

Trace elements—Chemicals necessary in very small amounts to ensure proper plant growth. All are normally present in soil and organic matter but not in chemical fertilizers. Most trace elements (also called micro-nutrients) are toxic to plants when present in more than minute quantities.

Tree spade—A large, vehicle-mounted mechanical device for digging and transporting large trees with a root ball retained intact.

Tunnel gardening—The temporary use of plastic stretched over wire loops to form a tunnel. Used to create a favorable microclimate for row crops.

Type—Referring to a plant that is typical of its kind—species, cultivar, and so on, and therefore conforming to the official description of the taxon.

Union—The graft joint where a scion is joined to the stock. See also grafting.

UV treated—Some polyethylene films used to cover greenhouses are ultraviolet-light treated and do not deteriorate in sunlight as fast as untreated materials.

Variety—A naturally occurring variant population of wild plant species.

Often incorrectly applied to a cultivar (cultivated variety).

Vegetative propagation—Plant propagation by cuttings, grafting, or any means other than from seed or spores. Vegetative propagation ensures that all offspring are identical to the parent. See also clone.

Vermiculite—A light brown sterile medium containing expanding mica. Vermiculite is used mainly for improving the moisture- and air-holding capacity of soil mixes and for striking cuttings and starting seedlings. See also perlite.

Viable—Referring to seeds capable of germinating and growing.

Volunteer—A garden plant growing spontaneously (usually from seed).

Water sprout (Synonym water shoot)—A fast-growing vertical stem arising from an adventitious bud on a trunk or branch. See also sucker growth.

Water table—The groundwater level beneath which the soil is saturated.

Wet feet—A condition of container plants suffering from excessive watering and poor drainage. Symptoms include the yellowing and dropping of leaves.

Wettable powder—A pesticide in the form of a powder that may be suspended in water to facilitate application. Abbreviated WP

Wilt—1. Loss of turgidity with resulting leaf flagging caused by a lack of water in the plant system. 2. A common term for a number of plant diseases usually caused by various fungi or bacteria.

BIBLIOGRAPHY

There is an enormous amount of literature available on the many different aspects of gardening. Unfortunately, most of it is written for climates milder than our own. I have listed here a few titles and sources of information that are especially relevant to gardening on the plains.

You may also find it useful to contact the plant science or horticulture department of your nearest university for information on any gardening literature which might be available. Another likely source of publications on gardening topics is the horticulture branch of your state agriculture department or Cooperative Extension Service. From either of these services you could well discover helpful brochures, some of them free of charge, and all geared to local conditions. University plant science departments, Cooperative Extension Service offices and state departments of agriculture (horticulture branches) are also useful contacts for the current addresses of state horticultural associations. The state horticultural associations, in turn, are your introduction to local horticultural societies and neighborhood garden clubs. Another good source of information is the U.S. Department of Agriculture, which has offices in each state.

Austin, Richard. *Wild Gardening.* New York: Simon & Schuster, 1986.

Barton, Barbara J. *Gardening by Mail: A Source Book,* 3rd ed. New York: Houghton-Mifflin, 1990.

Bennett, Jennifer, ed. *The Harrowsmith Landscaping Handbook.* Camden East, Ontario: Camden House, 1985.

Bennett, Jennifer. *The Harrowsmith Northern Gardener.* Camden East, Ontario: Camden House, 1982.

Brickett, Christopher, ed. *The American Horticultural Society Encyclopedia of Garden Plants.* New York: Macmillan, 1989.

Buckley, A. R. *Canadian Garden Perennials.* Sanichton, British Columbia: Hancock House, 1977.

Buckley, A. R. *Trees and Shrubs of the Dominion Arboretum.* Research branch, Agriculture Canada, publication No. 1697, 1980.

Carr, Anna. *Rodale's Color Handbook of Garden Insects.* Emmaus, PA: Rodale Press, 1983.

Cole, T. J. *Annual Flowers for Canada.* Minister of Supply and Services Canada, publication No. 1608, 1978.

Coombes, Allen J. *Dictionary of Plant Names.* Portland, OR: Timber Press, 1985.

Crockett, James U. *Crockett's Victory Garden.* New York: Little Brown and Company, 1977.

Damrosch, Barbara. *The Garden Primer.* New York: Workman Publishing, 1988.

Department of Horticulture Science, University of Saskatchewan. *Hort Hints; Practical Tips for Prairie Gardeners.* Saskatoon: The Division of Extension and Community Relations, University of Saskatchewan, publication No. 541, 1985.

Esmonde-White, Anstace. *Vegetable Gardening in Canada.* Toronto: McGraw-Hill Ryerson, 1981.

Everett, Thomas. *The Illustrated Encyclopedia of Horticulture.* New York: Garland, 1982.

Fell, Derek, et al. *The Complete Garden Planning Manual.* Los Angeles, CA: Price Stern Sloan, Inc., 1989.

Garden Club of America. *Directory of Regional Gardening Resources.* New York: Garden Club of America, 1987.

Harp, H. F. *The Prairie Gardener.* Edmonton: Hurtig Publishers, 1970.

Hill, Lewis. *Cold-Climate Gardening: How to Extend Your Growing Season by at Least 30 Days.* Pownal, VT.: Storey/Garden Way Publishing, 1987.

Johnston, Marlis. *The Whole Garden Catalog.* DeKalb, IL: Media Marketing Group, Inc., 1980.

Kelway, Christine. *Gardening in Sandy Soil in North Temperate Areas.* Magnolia, MA: Peter Smith Publisher, Inc.

Knowles, R. H. *Woody Ornamentals for the Prairie Provinces.* Edmonton: University of Alberta bulletin No. 58, 1975.

Lawson, Joanne, and Carter, Louise. *The Nineteen Ninety Gardener's Guide: Northwest & Midwest, Zones 4, 5 & 6.* New York: Starwood Press, 1990.

Lloyd, Gordon B. *Don't Call It "Dirt"! Improving Your Garden Soil.* New York: Bookworm Publications, 1976.

Marson, Chuck. *In Your Own Back Yard: A Guide for Great Plains Gardening.* Baranski Publishing Co., 1983.

McKeown, Denny. *Denny McKeown's Complete Guide to Midwest Gardening.* Dallas, TX: Taylor Publishing Co., 1985.

Saskatoon Horticultural Society. *Clippings* (magazine). Saskatoon: Saskatoon Horticultural Society, P. O. Box 161.

Snyder, Leon. *Gardening in the Upper Midwest,* 2nd ed. Minneapolis: University of Minnesota Press, 1985.

Snyder, Leon. *Trees and Shrubs for Northern Gardens*. Minneapolis: University of Minnesota Press, 1980.

Staw, Jane, and Swander, Mary. *Parsnips in the Snow: Talks with Midwest Gardeners.* Ames, IA: University of Iowa Press, 1990.

Taylor, Norman. *Taylor's Guide to Water-Saving Gardening.* New York: Houghton-Mifflin, 1990.

Winnipeg Horticultural Society. *The Prairie Garden* (annual magazine). Winnipeg: Winnipeg Horticultural Society, P.O. Box 517.

SOURCES

Contact your local Cooperative Extension Service office or agent for specific information. Check telephone directory for location and telephone number.

SUPPLIES AND SERVICES

ATTRA (Appropriate Technology Transfer for Rural Areas), sponsored by USDA, 800/346-9140.

Alsto's Handy Helpers, P.O. Box 1267, Route 150 East, Galesburg, IL 61401 , 309/343-6181 (supplies, tools, furniture and ornaments).

Alternative Garden Supply, Inc., 297 N. Barrington Road, Streamwood, Il 60107, 800/444-2837 (supplies and tools).

The American Botanist, 1103 West Truitt Avenue, Chillicothe, Il 61523, 309/274-5254 (books and services).

Aquacide Company, P.O. Box 10748, White Bear Lake, MN 55110, 800/ 328-9350 (supplies).

Ardisam, Inc., Route 4, Box 666, Cumberland, WI 54829 (supplies).

Broadview Station, Route 2, Box 50A, Luverne, MD 58056, 701/769-2273 (supplies).

Capability's Books, P.O. Box 144, Highway 46, Deer Park, WI 54007, 800/ 247-8154 (books).

Clarel Laboratories, Inc. 513 Grove Street, Deerfield, Il 60015, 312/945-4013 (supplies)

Clothcrafters, Inc., P.O. Box 176, 90 Rhine Street, Elkhart Lake, WI 53020 (clothing for the gardener).

Dave's Aquariums and Greenhouse, RR 1, Box 97, Kelley, IA 50134, 515/ 769-2446 (supplies, tools, and books).

John Deere Catalog, 1400 Third Avenue, Moline, IL 61265, 800/544-2122 (supplies, tools, books and ornaments).

The Dramm Company, P.O. Box 1960, Manitowoc, WI 54221, 414/684-0227 (supplies and tools).

EnP, Inc., 2001 Main Street, Box 218, Mendota, IL 61342, 815/539-7471 (supplies).

The Floral Mailbox, P.O. Box 235, Lombard, Il 60148-0235 (flower arranging supplies).

Holland's Organic Garden, 8515 Stearns, Overland Park, KS 66214, 913/888-6817 (supplies, tools and books).

Hosta Resources, 7180 N. 62nd Plaza, Omaha, NE 68122 (plant finding service).

InterNet, Inc., 2730 Nevada Avenue North, Minneapolis, MN 55427, 8900/328-8456 (bird netting supplies).

North Star Evergreens, P.O. Box 253, Eastwood Plaza Building, Park Rapids, MN 56470, 800/732-5819, (tools and supplies and equipment).

Northern Greenhouse Sales, P.O. Box 42, Neche, ND 58265 (204/327-5540 (supplies).

Ringer Corporation, 9959 Valley View Road, Eden Prairie, MN 55344-3585, 612/941-4180 (organic gardening products).

Wikco Indutries, Inc., Route 2, Box 154, Broken Bow, NE 68822, 308/872-5327 (tools and furniture).

Wood Violet Books, 3814 Sunhill Drive, Madison, WI 53704-6283, 608/837-7207 (books).

ASSOCIATIONS

National Council of State Garden Clubs, Inc., 401 Magnolia Avenue, St. Louis, MO 63110.

Botanical Club of Wisconsin, Rudy G. Koch, Dept. of Biology, University of Wisconsin, La Crosse, La Crosse, WI 54601.

Kansas Wildlife Society, Mulvane Art Center, Washburn University, Topeka, KS 66611, 913/296-6324.

Minnesota Native Plant Society, Robin Fox, University of Minnesota, 1445 Cortner Avenue, 220 BioScie Center—MNPS, St. Paul, MN 55108.

Minnesota State Horticultural Society, 161 Alderman Hall, University of Minnesota, 1970 Folwell Avenue, St. Paul, MN 55108, 612/324-0430.

Seed Savers Exchange, Kent Whealy, Rural Route 3, Box 239, Decorah, IA 52101.

Southern Illinois Native Plant Society, Dr. Robert Mohlenbrook, Botany Dept., Southern Illinois University, Carbonadale, IL 52901.

INDEX

AAS. *See* All-America Selections
Abies 104
Abies balsamea 104
Abies balsamea 'Hudsonia' (dwarf balsam fir) 29, 106
Abies concolor (silver fir) 67, 104
Accent plant 321
Acclimatization 321
Acer ginnala (Amur maple) 28, 29, 67, 68, 69, 85
Acer negundo (Manitoba maple) 29, 66, 68, 69
Acer saccharum (sugar maple) 67, 69
Achillea millefolium (yarrow) 138, 145
Achillea ptarmica (sneezewort) 145
Aconitum x bicolor (monk's-hood) 145
Acroclinium 165, 173
Activator 321
Aegopodium podagraria variegata (variegated goutweed) 142, 146
Aeration 321
Ageratum houstonium (floss flower) 161, 167
Agrostis alba 46
Alcea rosea (annual hollyhock) 162, 167
Alder 68, 70
All-America Selections 321
Allium moly 127
Almond, Russian 80
Alnus (alder) 68, 70
Alyssum, perennial 141, 146
Alyssum saxatile (madwort or perennial alyssum) 141, 146
Alyssum, sweet 162, 165, 176
Amaranth, globe 165, 173
Amaranthus caudatus (love-lies-bleeding) 162, 167
Amelanchier alnifolia (saskatoon, service berry) 27, 68, 69, 74
American Crateagus douglasii (Douglas hawthorn) 76
American Rose Society 93
Ammonium nitrate 321
Ammonium phosphate 12, 321
Ammonium sulfate (sulphate) 12, 321
Anchusa azurea (Italian bugloss) 146
Anemone pulsatilla or *Pulsatilla vulgaris* 141, 146, 184
Anemone sylvestris (snowdrop anemone) 146
Annuals 18, 58, 161–83, 321
Antennaria parviflora (pussy toes) 185
Anthemis tinctoria (golden Marguerite) 146
Anthracnose 277, 278
Antidesiccants 98, 102, 321
Antirrhinum majus (snapdragon) 161, 167
Antistatic 321
Aphids 246
Apple-cedar rust. *See* Rust
Apple-crabapple 115, 117
Apples 107, 114, 115, 118, 119, 283, 286–7
Apricot, Manchurian 121
Apricots 121
Aquilegia alpina (alpine columbine) 184
Aquilegia hybrids (columbine) 146
Arboretum 321
Arborvitae 66
Aristolochia durio 89
Armeria maritima (thrift or sea pink) 147
Artemisia schmidtiana (silver mound) 141, 147
Aruncus dioicus or *Aruncus sylvester* (goat's beard) 147
Ash 28, 29, 70
  black 69, 70
  green 68, 70
  Manchurian 71
Asparagus 189, 204, 286

Aspen 72
Aster, China 161, 168
Aster hybrids (aster) *138, 147*
Atrium 322
Aurelian 128
Auricula 138, 157

Baby-blue-eyes 176
Baby's breath 138, 151
  annual 165, 173, 184
  creeping 141, 152
Bachelor's button 163, 165, 169, 184
Bacillus thuringiensis 322
Bacteria 12, 276, 277, 279
Bacterial blight 279
Ball and burlap 322
Balsam, garden 174
Bare root 322
Base dressing 322
Basil, ornamental 166, 177
Basswood 74
  American 74
Beans 281
  broad 189
  green bush type 189
  runner 163, 178, 189
  yellow bush type 189
Beard-tongue 156
Bedding plants 281, 322
Bee balm 155
Beets 189
Begonia rex 133
Begonia semperflorens 133
Begonia x semperflorens (wax begonia) 161, 163, 167
Begonias 133, 167
  tuberous 161
  wax 161, 163, 167
Bellflower
  Carpathian 141, 147, 184
  clustered 147
  peach-leaved 147
Bergamot 155
Bergenia cordifolia (giant rockfoil) 138, 147
Bergenia, heartleaf 138, 147
Betula (birch) 28, 68
Betula papyrifera (paper birch) 29, 66, 70
Betula pendula (weeping birch) 66, 70
Betula pendula 'Gracilis' (cut-leaf weeping birch) 28, 29
Bicarbonate 6
Biennial bearing 322
Biological control 322
Birch 28, 68, 70
  paper 29, 66, 70
  silver 70
  weeping 28, 29, 66
Birch leaf miner sawflies 247
Birds 62, 208, 209
Bird's-foot trefoil 184
Bittersweet 89
  American 89
Black knot 279
Black scurf 280
Black spot 280
Blanket flower 151
Blazing star, spike 154
Bleeding 322
Bleeding heart 150
Blight 322
Blister beetles 247
Blossom-end rot 280
Blue bonnets 158
Blue lettuce (*Lactuca pulchella*) 231
Bluebell
  California 178, 184
Blueweed (*Echium vulgare*) 231
Bolting 322
Bonemeal 18, 322
Bonsai 322
Borderline hardy 322
Botanical name 55, 322
Botrytis 277, 281, 322
Bottom heat 323
Bouncing bet 138, 158
Box elder 69
Brachycome iberidifolia (Swan River daisy) 168
Broadcast 323
Broad-leaved plantain (*Plantago major*) 234
Broccoli 189, 281
Bromegrass (*Bromus*) 233
Bronze birch borers 248

Broom 27, 76
Browallia (bush violet) 168
Browallia americana 168
Browallia speciosa 168
Brussels sprouts 189
Bud blast 323
Budding 323
Buffalo-berry, silver 28, 68, 82
Bugs. *See* Insect Pests
Bulbil 323
Bulbocodium vernum 127
Bulbs 123–36
  care 126
  digging 126
  tips 126
Burn 323
Burning bush 28, 77, 163, 166, 174
  dwarf winged 77
  winged 67, 77
Buttercup bush 79
Butterfly flower 179
Butternut 78

Cabbage 281
  Chinese 190
  early 190
  keeping 190
Calendula officinalis (pot marigold) 161, 168
Calliopsis 161, 163, 171
Callistephus chinensis (China aster) 161, 168
Campanula carpatica (Carpathian bellflower) 141, 147, 184
Campanula glomerata (clustered bellflower) 147
Campanula persicifolia (peach-leaved bellflower) 147
Campanula rotundifolia (harebell) 184
Candles 323
Candytuft 184
  globe 163, 174
  rocket 162, 173
Canker 281, 323
Capillary 323
Caragana
  fern-leaf 75
  globe 29, 75
Caragana (continued)
  pygmy 75, 85, 86
  Sutherland 28
  Walker 28
  weeping 28, 75
Caragana (caragana) 27, 66, 68, 75, 85
Caragana arborescens (common caragana) 66, 75, 85
Caragana arborescens 'Lorbergii' 75
Caragana arborescens 'Pendula' (weeping caragana) 28, 75
Caragana arborescens 'Sutherland' (Sutherland caragana) 28, 75
Caragana arborescens 'Walker' (Walker caragana) 28, 75
Caragana frutex 'Globosa' (globe caragana) 29, 75
Caragana pygmaea (pygmy caragana) 75, 85, 86
Carrots 190
Caterpillars 249
  forest tent 255
  sod webworm 261
Catmint 155
Cauliflower 190, 281
Celastrus scandens 89
Celery 190
Celosia cristata (cockscomb) 165, 168
Celosia cristata 'Apricot Brandy' 169
Celosia cristata plumosa (feathered celosia) 165, 169
Celosia, feathered 165, 169
Centaurea cineraria (dusty miller) 161, 163, 166, 169
Centaurea cyanus (bachelor's button or cornflower) 163, 165, 169, 184
Centaurea gymnocarpa (dusty miller) 166, 169
Centaurea montana (mountain bluet) 138, 148
Centipedes 250
Cerastium tomentosum (snow-in-summer) 141, 142, 148, 185
Chard, Swiss 190
Cheddar pink 149
Chemicals
  elements 12
  fertilizers 13

Ehemicals (continued)
  nutrients 6
  residues 5
  treatment 8
Cherries 72, 279
  Amur 27, 28, 66, 72
  bush 111, 113
  flower 27, 28
  Mongolian 113
  Nanking 27, 86, 113
Cherry-plum hybrids 111, 113
Chickweed (*Stellaria media*) 232
Chicory (*Cichorium intybus*) 231
China pink 164, 171
Chinodoxa luciliae 127
Chinooks 58
Chitting 323
Chives 286
Chlorosis 323
Chokecherry, Shubert 27, 28, 29, 72
Chrysanthemum carinatum (painted daisy) 169
Chrysanthemum coccineum (pyrethrum) 148
Chrysanthemum, daisy 148
Chrysanthemum maximum (shasta daisy) 148
Chrysanthemum morifolium (outdoor mums) 148
Chrysanthemum parthenium (feverfew or matricaria) 169
Chrysanthemum segetum (corn marigold) 169
Cinquefoil 79
  herbaceous 157
  shrubby 27, 79, 86
Clarkia 170
Clarkia amoena (godetia or satin flower) 169, 184
Clarkia unguiculata (clarkia) 170
Clay 2, 3
Clematis 55, 89
  golden 90
  Jackman 89, 90
  western white 90
Clematis 'Jackmanii' 90
Clematis ligusticifolia 90
Clematis tangutica 90
Cleome 164, 170
Cleome hasslerana (cleome or spider flower) 162, 164, 170
Climate 13, 58, 69
Climbers. *See* Vines
Clone 323
Clothes-lines 274
Clubroot 281
Cobaea scandens (cup-and-saucer vine) 162, 170
Cockscomb 165, 168
Cold frame 323
Coleus hybrids (coleus or flame nettle) 161, 163, 166, 170
Colorado potato beetles 251
Columbine 146
  alpine 184
Common names 55
Companion planting 323
Compost 3, 4, 5, 12, 324
Coneflower 158
  annual 165, 178
  orange 158
Conifer woolly aphids 251
Conifers 60, 95–106
Consolida ambigua or *delphinium ajacis* (annual or rocket larkspur) 161, 162, 165, 171
Container-grown plants 63, 64, 97, 98, 324
Convallaria majalis (lily-of-the-valley) 138, 142, 148
Coral bells 141, 152
Coreopsis
  dwarf lanceleaf 184
  dwarf plains 184
  threadleaf 148
Coreopsis lanceolata (dwarf lanceleaf) 184
Coreopsis tinctoria (calliopsis) 161, 163, 171, 184
Coreopsis verticillata (threadleaf coreopsis) 148
Corm 324
Corn borer 252
Corn spurry (*Spergula arvensis*) 231
Corn, sweet 190
Cornflower 163, 165, 169
Cornus (dogwood selections) 27, 28, 69
Cornus alba 'Argenteo Marginata' 76
Cornus alba 'Gouchaultii' 76
Cornus alba sibirica 76
Cornus sericea (red osier dogwood) 68, 75, 85

Cornus sericea 'Flaviramea' 75
Cosmos 162, 171
Cosmos bipinnatus (cosmos) 162, 171
Cotoneaster 76, 284, 286
European 76
hedge 28
Peking 76, 86
rock 76
Cotoneaster horizontalis 76
Cotoneaster integerrimus 76
Cotoneaster lucidus (Peking or hedge cotoneaster) 28, 76, 86, 87
Crabapples 27, 115, 116
flowering 27, 71
lowering 62
pyramid 28
Siberian 66, 71
Cranberries 27, 28, 69, 84
bush, dwarf 84, 86
European 84
highbush 84
Crane's bill 151
Crataegus (hawthorn) 27, 70, 76, 85
Crataegus chlorosarca (Manchurian black hawthorn) 76
Crateagus rotundifolia (the fireberry) 76
Crataegus sanguinea (Siberian Hawthorn) 76
Crataegus x mordenensis 'Snowbird' 70
Creeping Charlie, variegated 142, 151
Creeping Jenny 142, 155
Cress, heart-podded hoary (*Cardaria draba*) 231
Crocus 128
prairie 184
Crocus chrysanthus 'E. A. Bowles,' 128
Crocus vernus 128
Crocus vernus 'Purpureus Grandiflorus' 128
Cross 324
Crown 324
Crown rot 277
Crucifers 281
Cucumber 286
pickling 190
Cultivar 56, 57, 96, 324
Cup-and-saucer vine 162, 170
Currants 28, 107, 111
Currants (continued)
alpine 27, 69, 80, 86
black 111
flowering 80
fruit flies 252
Missouri or golden flowering 80
red and white 112
white 111
Cushion spurge 151
Cutting 324
Cutworms 208–9, 253
Cypress spurge 151
Cypress, summer 163, 166, 174
Cytisus (broom) 27, 76

Daffodils 123, 127
Dahlia (dahlia) 134, 161, 162, 171
Daisy
African 161, 163, 172
gloriosa 165, 178
Livingstone 162, 163, 172
painted 169
shasta 148
Swan River 168
Dame's rocket 183
Damping off disease (seedling blight) 277, 282, 324
Dandelion (*Taraxacum officinale*) 233
Daphne cneorum (rose daphne) 27, 77
Daylily 152
Dead twigs 282
Deadhead 324
Deciduous plants 4, 61, 62, 69, 284, 324
Decomposition 3, 5
DED. *See* Dutch elm disease
Delphinium ajacis (annual or rocket larkspur) 149, 161, 165, 171
Delphinium hybrids (delphinium) 149
Determinate (Synonym, self-determinate) 324
Dethatching 324
Dianthus 164, 171
Dianthus barbatus (sweet William) 161, 164, 171
Dianthus chinensis (China pink or dianthus) 164, 171

Dianthus deltoides (maiden pink) 141, 142, 149, 184
Dianthus gratianopolitanus (cheddar pink) 149
Dicentra spectabilis (bleeding heart) 150
Die back 282, 324
Dimorphotheca sinuata (African daisy or Cape marigold) 161, 163, 172
Disbudding 324
Disease control 274, 275, 277, 278
Dogwood 27, 28, 69, 75
  red osier 68, 75, 85
  Siberian 76
  silver variegated 76
  yellow-twig 76
Dormant season 57
Dormant spray (Synonym, dormant oil) 324
Doronicum cordatum or *Doronicum caucasicum* 150
Dorotheanus bellidiformis (Livingstone daisy) 162, 172
Double digging 324
Double flower 325
Double leader 325
Douglas-fir 96
Drainage 2, 7
Drawn 325
Dressing 325
Dried blood 18
Drift 325
Drill 325
Drip-line 325
Drop-spreader 325
Dusters 301
Dusty miller 161, 163, 166, 169, 179
Dutch elm disease 282
Dutchman's pipe (*Aristolochia durior*) 89
Dyer's greenweed 27, 77

Earthworms 253
Echinocystis lobata (wild cucumber) 89, 162, 172
Echinops ritro (globe thistle) 150
Edging lobelia 162, 176
Edible crops 12
Eggplant 190
Elaeagnus augustifolia (Russian olive) 27, 67, 68, 70
Elaeagnus commutata 70
Elders 82
  golden plum 82
  redberried 66, 82
  Sutherland golden 28
Elm bark beetles 283
Elms 74, 282
  American 66, 74
  Japanese 74
  Manchurian 29, 68, 74
  Siberian 74
Emulsifiable concentrate 325
Engelmann ivy 88. *See also* Virginia creeper
Environmental disorder 280
Epsom salt 7, 325
Erigeron hybrids (fleabane) 150
Eriogonum umbellatum subalpinum (umbrella plant) 142, 150
Eryngium planum (sea holly) 150
Erysimum capitatum (coast wallflower) 184
Eschscholzia californica (California poppy) 162, 163, 172, 184
Espalier 325
Euonymus (burning bush) 28, 77
Euonymus alata (winged burning bush) 67, 77
Euonymus alata 'Compacta' 77
Euonymus nana 'Turkestanica' 77
Euphorbia cyparissias (cypress spurge) 151
Euphorbia epithymoides (cushion spurge) 151
Eurasian Viburnum opulus 84
Evaporation 7
Evergreen. *See* Conifers
Everlastings 165, 325

F 1 hybrid 325
Fairy rings 283
Fall cankerworms 254
Fallowing 325
Ferment 5
Fertilizer 7, 9, 11–20, 43, 98, 101, 274, 325
  applications 15, 16, 17, 54
  crystalline 14
  grade 326
  inorganic 18, 328
  lawn 15
  nitrogen 13

Fertilizer (continued)
- organic 19
- phosphorus 16
- specialty 18
- vegetables and soft fruits 16

Festuca ovina (sheep fescue) 185
Festuca rubra 45
Feverfew 169
Fir 95, 96, 104
- balsam 104
- dwarf balsam 29, 106
- silver 67, 104

Fireberry 76
Fireblight 62, 114, 283
Flame nettle 161, 163, 166, 170
Flat 326
Flax 154
- blue 184
- flowering 175
- scarlet 175

Flea beetles 208, 209, 254
Fleabane 150
Fleshy roots 123, 130
Flixweed (*Descurainia sophia*) 232
Floss flower 161, 167
Flower tobacco 162, 165, 177
Flowering plants 285
Foliar feed 326
Forcing 326
Forks 291
Forsythia (forsythia) 27, 77
Forsythia 'Northern Gold' 77
Forsythia ovata 77
Foundation plant 326
Fraxinus (ash) 28, 29
Fraxinus mandshurica 71
Fraxinus nigra (black ash) 69, 70
Fraxinus pennsylvanicaa subintegerrima (green ash) 68, 70
Friable 326
Frost cankers 284
Frosts 12
- lifting 326
- line 326
- pocket 326

Fruit trees 114–22, 281
Fruit trees (continued)
- bush 111
- soft 16

Fruits 107–22, 281, 285, 286
- woody 58

Fumigation 326
Fungal leaf spots 284
Fungi 276, 277
Fungicide 278, 326
Fungus gnats 255, 263
Fusarium wilt. *See* Wilt

Gaillardia, annual 163, 172, 184
Gaillardia pulchella (annual gaillardia) 163, 172, 184
Gaillardia x grandiflora (blanket flower) 151
Gall insects 256
Gardening 187
- cellar 323
- cottage 183
- intensive 328
- rock 140
- tunnel 335

Garlic, golden 127
Genista 76
Genista tinctoria (dyer's greenweed) 27, 77
Genus (Plural, genera) 326
Geranium 162, 163, 177
Geranium ibericum (crane's bill) 151
Geranium, Lancaster 141, 151
Geranium sanguineum lancastriense (Lancaster geranium) 151
Geranium sanguineum prostratum (Lancaster geranium) 141, 151
German catchfly 155
Girdling 326
Gladiolus 131–33
Glauber salt 7, 326
Glechoma hederacea variegata 142, 151
Globeflower 160
Glory of the snow 127
Glossary 321–36
Goat's beard 147
Godetia 169, 184
Goldenrod 138, 159
Gomphrena globosa (globe amaranth) 165, 173

Gooseberries 111, 113
Goutweed, variegated 142, 146
Grafting 326
Grapes 91
  riverbank or wild 91
Grass 285
  clippings 4
  seed 45, 47
Greenhouse 213
  construction 219
  cooling and humidity 227
  covering materials 222
  drainage 214
  emergency heating 226
  flooring 225
  foundation 219
  frame 221
  heating 225
  interior 224
  lean-to design 216
  location 213
  orientation 21.
  planning 215
  planting benches 225
  self-standing design 216
  shading and lighting 228
  shelter 214
  site selection 213, 214
  solar 218
  supply and cost 219
  utilities 214
  ventilation 226
  water 228
Grey mold 281
Ground cover 141, 142, 143, 144, 324
Groundsel, golden 154
Growing season 13
Gypsophila elegans (annual baby's breath) 165, 173, 184
Gyposphila paniculata (baby's breath) 138, 151
Gypsophila repens (creeping baby's breath) 141, 152

Habit 327
Half hardy 327
Harden off 327
Hardiness 55, 57, 61, 66, 327
  index 67
  zone maps 58
  zones 327
Hardpan 327
Hardwood cutting 327
Harebell 184
Harison yellow 81
Hawkweed, orange (*Hieracium aurantiacum*) 231
Hawthorn 27, 70, 76, 85, 283, 286
  Douglas 76
  Manchurian black 76
  Siberian 76
Heading back 327
Hedges 85, 86, 88
  planting 87
Heeling in 327
Helianthus annus (common sunflower) 162, 173, 183
Helianthus debilis (dwarf sunflower) 173
Helichrysum bracteatum (strawflower) 165, 173
Heliopsis scabra (orange sunflower) 152
Helipterum roseum (acroclinium) 165, 173
Hemerocallis hybrids (daylily) 152
Hen-and-chicks 141, 142, 159
Herbaceous ornamentals 18
Herbaceous perennials 18, 56, 58, 137–60, 281, 328
Herbicides 5, 234, 235, 274, 278, 328
  nonselective 330
  post-emergence 235, 236
  pre-emergence 235, 236
  selective 332
Hesperis matronalis (Dame's rocket) 183
Heuchera hybrids (coral bells) 141, 152
Hill up (Synonym, hilling) 328
Hippophae rhamnoides (common sea-buckthorn) 27, 66, 68, 77
Hoes 292
Holly, sea 150
Hollyhocks 162
  annual 162, 167
Honeydew 277, 328
Honeysuckle 27, 78, 90

Honeysuckle (continued)
- Clavey's dwarf 78, 86
- sweetberry 78
- Tartarian 66, 69, 78, 85

Hoof and horn meal 18, 328
Hop plant 89
Hormones 328
Hoses 298
Hosta (plantain lily) 142, 153
Hosta fortunei 153
Hosta sieboldiana 153
Hosta undulata 153
Hot bed 328
Hot cap 328
House plants 273
Humulus lupulus 89
Humus 2, 3, 7, 328
Hyacinths 127
- grape 127

Hybrids 328
Hydrangea 78
Hydrangea 'Annabelle' (Annabelle hydrangea) 27
Hydrangea paniculata grandiflora (pee gee hydrangea) 67, 78
Hydrangea, pee gee 67, 78
Hydroponics 328

Iberis amara (rocket candytuft) 162, 173
Iberis umbellata (globe candytuft) 163, 174, 184
Ice plant 162, 163, 172
Immortelle 165, 180
Impatiens 162, 163, 174
Impatiens balsamina (garden balsam) 174
Impatiens glandulifera (policeman's helmet) 174
Impatiens wallerana (impatiens or patience plant) 162, 163, 174
Inflicted blight 273
Ingredients 11
Insect Pests 241–72
- tips 268

Insecticides 278
Integrated Pest Management 328
Interplanting 328
Iris 153
- bearded 153
- dwarf 141, 153
- Siberian 153

Iris pumila (dwarf iris) 141, 153
Iris sibirica (Siberian iris) 153
Iris x germanica (bearded iris hybrids) 153
Irrigation systems 43
- sprinklers 298
- underground system 43, 49

Italian bugloss 146

Johnny-jump-up 184
Juglans cinerea 78
Juniper rust. *See* Rust
Junipers 27, 68, 96, 101, 104, 105, 286
- Andorra 104
- Chinese 67, 104
- creeping 104
- Rocky Mountain 105
- savin 66, 104
- tamarix 104
- Waukegan 104

Juniperus (juniper selections) 27, 68
Juniperus chinensis (Chinese juniper) 67, 104
Juniperus communis 105
Juniperus horizontalis 104
Juniperus horizontalis 'Douglasii' 104
Juniperus horizontalis 'Plumosa' 104
Juniperus sabina (savin juniper) 66, 104
Juniperus sabina tamariscifolia 104
Juniperus scopulorum 105
Juniperus squamata 105
Juniperus virginiana 105

Kale 190
Kentucky bluegrass (*Poa pratensis*) 45–46
Knotweed 157
- prostrate (*Polygonum aviculare*) 234

Kochia scoparia (summer cypress or burning bush) 163, 166, 174
Kohlrabi 190

Lamb's-quarters, *(Chenopodium album)* 231, 232
Landscape 21–40, 41, 61

Landscape (continued)
cloth 274
design 23, 42
formal 326
hard 21, 39, 327
plan 22, 29, 32
private area 30, 31, 34, 36
public area 29, 30, 32
service area 31, 36
soft 21, 333
Larch 71, 96, 104
European 71
Siberian 71
Larix (larch and tamarack) 104
Larix decidua 71
Larix laricina (tamarack) 69, 71
Larix sibirica 71
Larkspur
annual 162
rocket 161, 162, 165, 171
Lath house 328
Lathyrus odoratus (sweet pea) 162, 175
Lavatera trimestris (annual mallow or tree mallow) 163, 175
Lavender, sea 154
Lawns 14, 41–54, 141, 283, 287
maintenance 54
Layering 329
Layia platyglossa (tidytips) 184
Laythrus odoratus (sweet pea) 164
Leaching 329
Leader 329
Leaf hoppers 256
Leaf spot 277
Leafy spurge (*Euphorbia esula*) 233
Lecanium scale 260
Leek 190
Leggy 329
Leopard's bane 150
Lettuce
head type 190
loose leaf 190
Liatris spicata (spike blazing star) 154
Ligularia clivorum (golden groundsel or ragwort) 154
Ligularia dentata or *Ligularia clivorum* (golden groundsel) 154
Ligularia przewalskii 154
Ligularia vietchiana 154
Ligularia wilsoniana 154
Lilac 23, 74, 83, 87
Chinese 84
"French" 66, 83
Hungarian 84, 86
Japanese tree 74
preston 84
Lilies 128, 129, 130
plantain 142, 153
Lily-of-the-valley 138, 142, 148
Lime 6, 7
Limestone 329
Limonium latifolium (common sea lavender) 154
Limonium sinuatum (statice) 165, 175
Linaria maroccana (spurred snapdragon) 184
Linden 69, 74
little leaf 29, 66, 74
Line out 329
Linum grandiflorum (flowering flax or scarlet flax) 175
Linum lewisii (blue flax) 184
Linum perenne (flax) 154
Loam 329
Lobelia erinus (edging lobelia) 162, 176
Lobularia maritima (sweet alyssum) 162, 165, 176
Lonicera (honeysuckle) 27
Lonicera caerulea edulis 78
Lonicera tatarica (Tartarian honeysuckle) 66, 69, 78, 85
Lonicera x 'Dropmore Scarlet Trumpet' 90
Lonicera xylosteoides (Clavey's dwarf honeysuckle) 78, 86
Loosestrife, purple 155
Lotus corniculatus (bird's-foot trefoil) 184
Love-lies-bleeding 162, 167
Lungwort 138, 157
Lupin 154
Lupinus polyphyllus hybrids (lupin) 154
Lychnis chalcedonica (Maltese cross) 154

Lychnis viscaria (German catchfly) 155
Lychnis x arkwrightii 155
Lysimachia nummularia (creeping Jenny or moneywort) 142, 155
Lythrum hybrids (purple loosestrife) 155

Madwort 141, 146
Magnesium sulfate 325. *See* Epsom salt
Maiden pink 141, 142, 149, 184
Malcomia maritima (Virginia stock) 165, 176
Mallow, annual 163, 175
Maltese cross 154
Malus (crabapples, purple-leaf selections) 27, 115
Malus baccata (Siberian crabapple) 66, 71
Malus baccata 'Columnaris' (pyramid crabapple) 28
Malux x adstringens 71
Manure 3, 12, 19
    green 327
Maples 69
    Amur 28, 29, 67, 68, 69, 85
    Manitoba 29, 66, 68
    silver 69
    sugar 67, 69
Marguerite, golden 146
Marigold 162, 163, 164, 179
    Cape 161, 163, 172
    corn 169
    "French" 162, 163, 164, 179
    pot 161, 168
Martagon 128
Matricaria 169
Matteuccia struthiopteris (ostrich fern) 155
Matthiola bicornis (night-scented stock) 165, 176
Matthiola incana (ten-week stock) 176
Matthiola longipetala or *Matthiola bicornis* (night-scented stock) 165, 176
Mayday 27, 72, 287
Meadow gardening 183–85
    maintenance 185
    making 185
    plants 184
Meadow rue 159
Mealy-bugs 257
Medium 329
Mesembryanthemum 172
Microclimate 58, 329
Micro-nutrients 329
Microorganisms 3
Mildew 277
Millipedes 250
Mineral particles 2
Miscible oil 329
Mockorange 27, 79
Moisture 3, 58
Mold, sooty 277
Monarda fistulosa 155
Monarda hybrids (bee balm or bergamot) 155
Moneywort 142, 155
Monk's-hood 145
Mosaic 329
Moss pink 141, 142, 157
Moss rose 162, 178
Mother-of-thyme 142, 159
Mountain bluet 138, 148
Mountain-ash 27, 28, 62, 71, 73, 283, 286, 287
    American 73
    European 28, 73
    Russian 73
Mowers 14, 54, 273, 296
Mugho or Swiss mountain pine 29, 66, 101, 104, 106
Mulch 48, 329
Mums, outdoor 148
Muriate of potash 329
Muscari 127
Muskmelon (cantaloupe) 190
Mycoplasma-like organism 277

Nannyberry 84
Nasturtium 162, 163, 165, 179
Naturalized plants 329
Necrosis 330
Nemesia 162, 176
Nemesia strumosa (nemesia) 162, 176
Nemophila menziesii (baby-blue-eyes) 176

Nepeta (including catmint) 155
Nepeta cataria 156
Nepeta faassenii 156
Nepeta mussinii 156
Nettle 8
Nicotiana alata (flower tobacco) 162, 165, 177
Nicotiana x sanderae or *Nicotiana alata* (flower tobacco) 162, 165, 177
Night-scented stock 165, 176
Ninebark 79, 85
 dwarf 79
 golden 27, 79
Nitrogen 5, 11, 12, 16, 17, 18, 43
 deficiency 12
Nodules 330
Nutrients 6, 11, 13
 deficiency 61
 levels 14
Nutritional value 12
Nymph 330

Oak 73
 bur 29
Ocimum basilicum 'Dark Opal' (ornamental basil) 166, 177
Offsets 330
Onions 286
 bunching 190
 cooking 190
 pickling 190
Organic gardening 330
Organic materials 2, 4, 5, 9, 11, 18
Orotheanus bellidiformis (Livingstone daisy) 163
Ostrich fern 155
Outdoor plants 273
Outplanting 330
Oystershell scale 257

Pachistima 69, 78
Paeonia (peony) 156
Paeonia tenuifolia 156
Pansy 162, 163, 180
 tufted 162, 163, 180
Papaver nudicaule (Iceland poppy) 184
Papaver orientale (oriental poppy) 156
Papaver rhoeas (Shirley poppy or corn poppy) 177, 184
Parsley, leaf 190
Parsnip 190
Parthenocissus quinquefolia (Virginia creeper) 28, 91
Pasqueflower 141, 146
Pasteurization 330
Pathogen 330
Patience plant 162, 163, 174
Paxistima canbyi (pachistima) 69, 78
Pear slugs 258
Pears 114, 121
Peas 190
Peashrubs 75
Peat moss 3, 48
Pelargonium x hortorum (geranium) 162, 163, 177
Penstemon (beard-tongue) 156
Peony 156
 fernleaf 156
Peppergrass, common (*Lepidium densiflorum*) 232
Peppers
 garden 280
 hot 190
 sweet 190
Perennials 56–8
 dwarf 141
 early-flowering 138
 late-flowering 138
Pergola 330
Periwinkle 142, 160
Perlite 330
Persian yellow 81
Pest Management 241
 aerosol formulations 244
 baits 243
 chemicals 243
 cultural controls 242, 324
 dormant oils 243
 dust formulations 244
 emulsifiable concentrates 244
 granule formulations 244
 microbials 244
 wettable powders 245

Petunia 162, 163, 165, 177

Petunia hybrids (petunia) 162, 163, 165, 177

pH 6, 18, 331

Phacelia campanularia (California bluebell) 178, 184

Phaseolus coccineus (scarlet runner bean) 163, 178

Pheromone 331

Philadelphus (mockorange) 27, 79

Phlox
- annual 162, 178
- creeping 141, 142, 157
- garden or summer 156

Phlox drummondii (annual phlox) 162, 178

Phlox paniculata (garden or summer phlox) 156

Phlox subulata (creeping phlox or moss pink) 141, 142, 157

Phosphorus 11, 12, 13, 14, 17, 18, 98
- deficiency 12

Physocarpus opulifolius (common ninebark) 79, 85

Physocarpus opulifolius 'Luteus' (golden ninebark) 27, 79

Physocarpus opulifolius 'Nanus' 79

Phytotoxic 331

Pica abies 103

Picea abies 'Nidiformis' (nest spruce) 29, 106

Picea amorika 103

Picea glauca 'Conica' (also known as Picea "Albert") 103, 106

Picea glauca 'Echiniformis' (hedgehog spruce) 29, 106

Picea pungens (Colorado spruce) 66, 103

Picea pungens glauca (Colorado blue spruce) 27, 103

Picea pungens 'Globosa' (dwarf blue spruce) 29, 106

Pigweed, redroot (*Amaranthus retroflexus*) 231, 232

Pinching back (Synonym, stopping) 331

Pincushion flower 165, 179

Pine needle scale 260

Pines 95, 102, 103
- lodgepole 103
- ponderosa 103
- red 103
- Scotch 28, 103

Pines (continued)
- Swiss mountain. *See* Mugho pines
- Swiss stone 67, 103

Pinus cembra (Swiss stone pine) 67, 103

Pinus contorta latifolia 103

Pinus mugo mugo (mugho pine) 29, 66, 106

Pinus mugo rostrata 104

Pinus ponderosa 103

Pinus resinosa 103

Pinus sylvestris (Scotch pine) 28, 103

Pinus uncinata 104

Planning 305–20

Plants
- availability 59
- disease 273–90
  - control measures 273
  - diagnosing 276
  - growth on leaves 277
  - leaf spots 277
- food mixtures 14
- lice. *See* Aphids
- mark 331
- nutrition 11
- pathology 277
- selection 55, 60
- succession 334

Plastic film 274

Plums 119, 120, 279, 287
- Asiatic 120, 128
- double flowering 27, 80
- flower 27, 28, 80
- Manchurian 119, 120
- purple-leaf 67, 80

Plunge 331

Poa pratensis 45

Poa trivialis 46

Policeman's helmet 174

Pollination 331

Polygonum (knotweed) 157

Polygonum bistorta 'Superbum' 157

Poplars 29, 69, 72, 284, 287
- Berlin 72
- boleana 28, 72
- lombardy 67

Northwest 72
Russian 72
Poplars (continued)
Swedish columnar 28, 72
white poplar 27, 67
Poppy
California 162, 163, 172, 184
corn 177, 184
Iceland 184
oriental 156
Shirley 177
Populus (poplars) 29, 69
Populus alba 'Pyramidalis' (boleana poplar) 28, 72
Populus alba (white poplar selections) 27, 67
Populus nigra 'Italica' (lombardy poplar) 67
Populus 'Northwest' 72
Populus tremula 'Erecta' (Swedish columnar poplar) 28, 72
Populus tremuloides 72
Populus x berolinensis 72
Populus x petrowskyana 72
Portulaca 162, 163, 178
Portulaca grandiflora (portulaca or moss rose) 162, 163, 178
Potash 11, 12, 17, 18
deficiency 12
Potassium 11
Potassium carbonate 11
Potato flea beetle 258
Potatoes 190, 279, 280, 282
Pot-bound (Synonym, root-bound) 331
Potentilla fruticosa (shrubby cinquefoil) 27, 79, 86, 87
Potentilla hybrids (herbaceous cinquefoil) 157
Potting on 331
Povertyweed (*Iva axillaris*) 231
Powdery mildew 285
Precipitation 6
Presser board 331
Primula auricula (auricula) 138, 157
Pruners 294
Prunes 65, 88
Pruning 115
renewal 332
root 332
Prunus (flower plums and cherries) 27, 28, 119
Prunus armeniaca mandshurica 121
Prunus besseyi (western sandcherry) 68, 113
Prunus cistena (purple-leaf plum) 67, 80
Prunus fruticosa 113
Prunus maackii (Amur cherry) 27, 28, 66, 72
Prunus nigra 119
Prunus padus 'Commutata' (mayday) 27, 72
Prunus salicina 119, 120
Prunus tenella 80
Prunus tomentosa (Nanking cherry) 27, 86, 113
Prunus triloba 'Multiplex' (double-flowering plum) 27, 80
Prunus virginiana 'Shubert' (Shubert chokecherry) 27, 28, 29, 72
Pulmonaria saccharata (lungwort or Bethlehem sage) 138, 157
Pulsatilla vulgaris (pasqueflower) 141
Pumpkin, bush 190
Purslane (*Portulaca oleracea*) 232
Puschkinia scilliodes 127
Pussy toes 185
Pyrethrum 148
Pyrus 121

Quack grass (*Agropyron repens*) 8, 233
Quercus macrocarpa (bur oak) 29, 73

Radish 190
Ragwort 154
Rakes 44, 292
Raspberries 107, 109, 110, 278
Recurrent (Synonym, remontant) 331
Red fescue, creeping (*Festuca rubra*) 45, 46
Red samphire (*Salicornia rubra*) 231
Red-cedar, eastern 105
Redleaf 285
Redtop (*Agrostis alba*) 46
Rhubarb 190, 204, 205, 285
Ribes (currants) 28
Ribes 'Albol' 111
Ribes alpinum (alpine currant) 27, 69, 80, 86
Ribes aureum 80
Ribes 'Boskoop Giant' 112

Ribes 'Buddenborg' 112
Ribes 'Consort' 112
Ribes 'Magnus' 111
Ribes 'Pankiw' 113
Ribes 'Pembina Pride' 113
Ribes 'Perfection' 112
Ribes 'Pixwell' 113
Ribes 'Red Lake' 112
Ribes 'Stephens' 112
Ribes 'Thoreson' 113
Ribes 'White Imperial' 112
Ribes 'Willoughby' 111
Ring rot 279
Rock foil 141, 158
giant 138, 147
Rogue 332
Root and onion maggots 7, 258
Rooting compound 332
Roots
hardy 332
rot 277
system 63, 65
zone 7, 12
Rosa (roses) 27, 56
Rosa 'Blanc Double de Coubert' (shrub rose cultivators) 67
Rosa foetida 'Persiana' 81
Rosa hybrids (hardy shrub roses) 85
Rosa hybrids (roses) 28
Rosa rubrifolia 81
Rosa rugosa 56
Rosa rugosa alba 56, 81
Rosa spinosissima 'Altaica' 81
Rosa x harisonii 81
Rose daphne 27, 77
Rose end 332
Rose moss 163
Rose weevils 259
Roses 27, 28, 80, 89, 90, 91, 93, 280
Altai 81
redleaf 81
shrub 67, 80, 85, 91
tender 93
Rotation 332
Rototillers 9, 274, 301
Rots 277, 285
Roughstalk bluegrass (*Poa trivialis*) 46
Rudbeckia (coneflower) 158
Rudbeckia fulgida 158
Rudbeckia hirta pulcherrima (gloriosa daisy) 165, 178
Rudbeckia laciniata 'Golden Glow' 158
Russian olive 27, 67, 68, 70
Rust 286
Rutabaga 190, 281

Sage
Bethlehem 138, 157
scarlet 162, 165, 179
Salix (willow) 69
Salix alba 73
Salix alba 'Britzensis' (redstem willow) 28, 81
Salix alba 'Tristis' (white weeping willow) 28, 67
Salix alba 'Vitellina' (golden willow) 28
Salix babylonica 73
Salix brachycarpa 'Blue Fox' 82
Salix pentandra (laurel-leaf willow) 29, 86
Salix purpurea 'Gracilis' (arctic willow) 81, 86
Salpiglossis 163, 178
Salpiglossis sinuata (salpiglossis or velvet flower) 163, 178
Salsify 190
Salt 7, 274
soluble 7
Salvia splendens (scarlet sage) 162, 165, 179
Sambucus racemosa (redberried elder) 66, 82
Sambucus 'Sutherland Golden' (Sutherland golden elder) 28, 82
Sandcherry, western 68, 113
Sanvitalia 162, 164, 179
Sanvitalia procumbens (sanvitalia or creeping zinnia) 162, 164, 179
Saponaria ocymoides (rock soapwort) 138, 141, 142, 158
Saponaria officinalis (bouncing bet) 138, 158
Saponaria officinalis (soapwort) 183
Saskatoon 27, 68, 69, 111
Satin flower 169
Sawdust 48

Sawflies 259
Saws 294
Saxifraga paniculata (saxifrage or rock foil) 141, 158
Saxifrage 141, 158
Scab 282, 286
Scabiosa atropurpurea (sweet scabious) 165, 179
Scabiosa caucasica (blue bonnets) 158
Scale insects 260
Schizanthus pinnatus (butterfly flower) 179
Scilla sibirica 127
Scion 332
Sea pink 147
Sea-buckthorn 27, 66, 68, 77
Seasons 305
Sedum (stonecrop) 141, 142, 158, 185
Sedum acre 158
Sedum kamtschaticum 158
Sedum spectabile 158
Seed, pelleted 330
Seedling blight 282
Self-fertile 332
Self-seeding 333
Self-sterile 333
Selix pentandra 73
Senecio cineraria (dusty miler) 166, 179
Sepervivum (hen-and-chicks) 141, 142, 159
Sepervivum tectorum 159
Serviceberry 69, 74, 283, 286
Shears 88, 294
Sheep fescue 185
Shelterbelt 333
Shepherdia argentea (silver buffalo-berry) 28, 68, 82
Shepherd's purse (*Capsella bursa-pastoris*) 232
Shoestring root rot 286
Side dressing 333
Silt 2
Silver mound 141, 147
Silver-leaf 114, 287
Single flower 333
Slip 333
Slugs 260
Snapdragon 161, 167
    spurred 184
Sneezewort 145
Snow mold 287
Snowball 84
Snowdrop anemone 146
Snow-in-summer 141, 142, 148, 185
Soapwort 183
    rock 138, 141, 142, 158
Sod 50, 51, 52, 333
Sodium sulfate 326. *See also* Glauber salt
Softwood cutting (Synonym, slip) 333
Soil 1–10, 13, 43, 45, 53, 58, 68, 69
    acid soil 6, 321
    acid-alkaline balance 6
    acidity 13
    alkaline soil 6, 12, 321
    analysis 13, 321
    heavy 327
    improvement 4
    maintenance 1
    neutral 330
    organic matter 2–5
    plastic 2
    quality 1
    reaction tester 6
    salinity 7, 332
    sandy 2, 3, 9
    sterilants 235
    subgrade 42
    subsoil 41, 42
    texture 1, 2, 335
    topsoil 1, 2, 6, 8, 41, 42
Solidago (goldenrod) 138, 159
Sorbaria sorbifolia (Ural false spirea) 69, 82
Sorbus (mountain-ash) 27, 28, 71
Sorbus americana 73
Sorbus aucuparia 73
Sorbus aucuparia 'Fastigiata' (European mountain-ash) 28
Sow-bug 261
Spades 274, 291
Sparrowgrass. *See* asparagus
Species (Plural, species) 333
Specimen plant 333
Speedwell 160
    creeping 160
    dwarf 141

spike 160
Sphagnum 333
Spider flower 162, 164, 170
Spider mites 262
Spinach 190
Spiny shrubs 85
Spiraea bumalda 'Goldflame' (Goldflame spirea) 28
Spiraea trichocarpa 83
Spiraea trilobata 82
Spiraea x arguta 82
Spiraea x billiardii 83
Spiraea x bumalda 'Froebelii' 83
Spiraea x bumalda 'Goldflame' 83
Spiraea x pikoviensis 82
Spiraea x vanhouttei (Vanhouttei spirea) 67, 82
Spireas 82
billiard 83
false 82
garland 82
goldflame 28
Korean 83
oriental 82
three-lobed 82
Vanhouttei 67
Spit 333
Spot treat 333
Sprayers 300
Spreader 15, 303, 333
Springtails 263
Sprinklers 298
Spruce 95, 96, 102, 103
Black Hills 103
Colorado 66, 103
Colorado blue 27, 95, 103, 104, 106
dwarf blue 29
dwarf Norway 106
dwarf white 106
hedgehog 29
nest 29
Norway 103
Serbian 103
white 103
Spruce budworm 263
Spur 334
Squash
summer 190
Squash (continued)
winter 190
Squill
Siberian 127
striped 127
Stake ties 274
Statice 165, 175
Stem rot 277
Sterilization 334
Stinging nettle (*Urtica dioica*) 233
Stinkweed (*Thlaspi arvense*) 232
Stock 334
Stonecrop 141, 142, 158, 185
Stool 334
Strain 334
Strawberries 107, 109, 278
Strawflower 165, 173
String trimmers 273, 302
Subspecies 334
Sucker growth 334
Suffron, spring 127
Sulphur treatment 7
Sunflower 162, 173, 183
dwarf 173
orange 152
Sunscald 287, 334
Superphosphate 334
Sweet pea 162, 164, 175
Sweet scabious 165, 179
Sweet William 161, 164, 171
Symphylans 263
Syringa (lilacs) 27
Syringa josikaea (Hungarian lilac) 84, 86
Syringa meyeri 'Palibin' 84
Syringa reticulata 74
Syringa villosa 84
Syringa vulgaria (common or French lilac) 66, 83
Syringa x hyacinthiflora 84
Syringa x prestoniae 84

Tagetes (marigold or French marigold) 162, 163, 164, 179
Tamarack 69, 71, 96, 104

Tamarisk 67, 84
Tamarix ramosissima (tamarisk) 67, 84
Tanecetum vulgare (tansy) 183
Tansy 183
Taxon 335
Taxus cuspidata 'Nana' 106
Terrarium 335
Thalictrum (meadow rue) 159
Thalictrum aquilegifolium 159
Thalictrum dipterocarpum 'Hewitt's Double 159
Thalictrum flavum 'Glaucum' 159
Thatch 335
Thinning 335
Thistle
    Canada 8
    globe 150
    perennial sow (*Sonchus arvensis*) 231
Thrift 147
Thrips 264
Thuja occidentalis (columnar white-cedar selection) 28
Thuja occidentalis (white-cedar or arborvitae) 66, 69, 86, 105
Thuja occidentalis 'Little Gem' (green globe white-cedar) 29
Thuja occidentalis 'Woodwardii' (Woodward globe white-cedar) 29
Thymus serpyllum (mother-of-thyme) 142, 159
Tidytips 184
Tilia (linden) 69
Tilia americana 74
Tilia cordata (little-leaf linden) 29, 66, 74
Tilth 335
Tissue culture 335
Tolerant 335
Tomatoes 280
    bush-determinate 190
    plants 288
    staking-indeterminate 190
Tools 291–304
    tips 304
Top dressing 335
Trace elements 13, 335
Tree, feeding 17
Tree mallow 175
Tree spade 335
Tree-orchid 174
Trees and shrubs 27, 28, 42, 58, 60, 61–94, 285, 286
    ornamental 281
    planting options 62
Trimmers, hedge 302
Trollius (globeflower) 160
Tropaeolum majus (nasturtium) 162, 163, 165, 179
Tulipa kolpakowskiana 127
Tulipa tarda 127
Tulips 123, 127
Turkestan burning bush 77, 127
Turnip, summer 190

Ulmus americana (American elm) 66, 74
Ulmus japonica 74
Ulmus pumila (Manchurian elm) 29, 68, 74
Umbrella plant 142, 150
Union 335. *See also* Grafting
Ural false spirea 69, 82
UV treated 336

Valerian, 160
Valeriana officinalis (valerian) 160
Variety 336
Vegetable marrow 190
Vegetable waste 3
Vegetables 16, 57, 187–211, 284, 285, 286, 287
    greenhouse 202
    growing 187
    harvesting 210
    perennial 204
    pests and disease 207
    planning 191
    planting 200
    propagation 336
    seeds 195
    selection 197
    site selection 194
    sowing 196
    thinning and maintenance 209
    transplanting 198

home transplants 201
nursery transplant 199
Velvet flower 178
Verbena, garden 165, 180
Verbena hybrids (garden verbena) 165, 180
Vermiculite 336
Veronica (speedwell) 160
Veronica latifolia 160
Veronica longiflora 160
Veronica repens (creeping speedwell) 160
Veronica repens (dwarf speedwell) 141
Veronica spicata (spike speedwell), 160
Veronica teucrium 160
Verticillium wilt. *See* Wilt
Viburnum (cranberries) 27, 28, 69
Viburnum lantana (wayfaring tree) 67, 69, 85–86
Viburnum lentago 84
Viburnum opulus 'Nanum' (dwarf cranberry bush) 84, 86
Viburnum opulus 'Roseum' 84
Viburnum trilobum 84
Viburnum trilobum 'Compactum' 84
Vigor 12
Vinca minor (periwinkle) 142, 160
Vinegar 6
Vines, or climbers 88
Viola, bedding 162, 163, 180
Viola cornuta (bedding viola or tufted pansy) 162, 163, 180
Viola tricolor (Johnny-jump-up) 184
Viola tricolor hortensis (pansy) 162, 163, 180
Viola x wittrockiana (pansy) 162, 163, 180
Violet, bush 168
Virginia creeper 28, 88, 91
Virginia stock 165, 176
Viruses 276
Vitis vulpina (also referred to as *Vitis riparia*) 91
Volunteer 336

Wallflower, coast 184
Water sprout (Synonym, water shoot) 336
Water table 336
Watermelon 190
Wayfaring tree 67, 69, 85, 86
Weather patterns 305
Weeds 8, 231–40
perennial 232
Weevil pests 264
Western ash bark beetle 265
Western gall rust. *See* Rust
Wet feet 336
Wheelbarrows 303
White clover (*Trifolium repens*) 234
White flies 266
White grubs 265
White-cedar 28, 66, 69, 86, 95, 96, 101, 104, 105, 286
green globe 29
Siberian 105
Woodward globe 29
Wild barley (*Hordeum jubatum*) 231
Wild bergamot 155
Wild cucumber 89, 162, 172
Willow 69, 73, 81, 284
arctic 81, 86
big weeping 73
golden 28
laurel-leaf 29, 73, 86
redstem 28, 81
shrubby 82
Siberian 73
white weeping 28, 67
Wilt 287, 336
Wirestem condition 282
Wireworms 267
Woody plants 286
Woody vines 89

Xeranthemum annuum (immortelle) 165, 180

Yarrow 138, 145
Yew 96, 101
dwarf Japanese 106

Zinnia hybrids (zinnia) 162, 163, 181
creeping 162, 164, 179

ABOUT THE AUTHOR

Born in England in 1934, Roger Vick obtained his junior royal Horticulture Diploma at the age of fifteen. In the early fifties, he enlisted in the Royal Air Force and served in Gibraltar. He then began a period of travel around the world, ending up in Canada in the Northwest Territories, where he began experimenting with growing garden vegetables in the short northern summer. After graduating *cum laude* in 1965 from Olds College with an Alberta diploma in Horticulture, he joined the staff of the University of Alberta Botanic Garden and Field Laboratory. The facility has since changed its name to the Devonian Botanic Garden, and Roger Vick has been its curator since 1971.

Past president of both the Alberta Horticultural Association and the Western Canadian Society for Horticulture, Roger Vick has published more than 250 articles since 1971. From 1980 to 1983 he served as the Alberta gardening editor for the popular magazine *Western Living*. In 1985 he was awarded the Alberta Horticultural Association Gold Medal for exceptional contributions to horticulture in Alberta. He lives in Edmonton with his wife, Lydia. They have three married sons.